THROUGH THE YEAR WITH
JOHN STOTT

Dedicated to Frances Whitehead,
who on 9th April 2006 completed fifty years
as my omnicompetent and faithful secretary.

THROUGH THE YEAR WITH
John Stott

*Daily Reflections from Genesis to
Revelation*

MONARCH
BOOKS

Published by
Lion Hudson Limited
Wilkinson House, Jordan Hill Business Park, Banbury Road, Oxford OX2 8DR, England

www.lionhudson.com

Hardback ISBN 978 0 8572 1964 0
Paperback ISBN 978 0 8572 1962 6
e-ISBN 978 0 8572 1963 3

First edition published in 2006 as *Through the Bible Through the Year*

Acknowledgments

Unless otherwise indicated, Scripture is taken from the Holy Bible, New International Version® (Anglicised) NIV®. Copyright © 1973, 1978, 1984, 2011 by Biblica, Inc.™ Used by permission of Zondervan. All rights reserved worldwide. www.zondervan.com

Scripture marked JB is taken from THE JERUSALEM BIBLE, copyright © 1966 by Darton, Longman & Todd, Ltd. and Doubleday, a division of Random House, Inc. Reprinted by permission.

Scripture marked KJV is taken from the King James Version of the Bible.

Scripture marked NAB is taken from the *New American Bible with Revised New Testament* © 1986, 1970 Confraternity of Christian Doctrine, Washington, D.C. and are used by permission of the copyright owner. All Rights Reserved. No part of the *New American Bible* may be reproduced in any form without permission in writing from the copyright owner.

Scripture marked NASB is taken from the New American Standard Bible®, Copyright © 1960, 1962, 1963, 1968, 1971, 1972, 1973, 1975, 1977, 1995 by The Lockman Foundation. Used by permission.

Scripture marked NJB is taken from THE NEW JERUSALEM BIBLE, copyright © 1985 by Darton, Longman & Todd, Ltd. and Doubleday, a division of Random House, Inc. Reprinted by permission.

Scripture marked NRSV is taken from the New Revised Standard Version of the Bible, copyright 1989, Division of Christian Education of the National Council of the Churches of Christ in the United States of America. Used by permission. All rights reserved.

Scripture marked REB is taken from the Revised English Bible © 1989 Oxford University Press and Cambridge University Press.

Scripture marked RSV is taken from the Revised Standard Version of the Bible, copyright 1952 [2nd edition, 1971] by the Division of Christian Education of the National Council of the Churches of Christ in the United States of America. Used by permission. All rights reserved.

A catalogue record for this book is available from the British Library

Printed and bound in the UK, November 2019, LH29

CONTENTS

Foreword   7
Following the Christian Calendar: An Explanation   10
Acknowledgments   11

**Part I: From Creation to Christ: An Overview of the Old Testament
(The Life of Israel)** *September to December*

**Part II: From Christmas to Pentecost: An Overview of the Gospels
(The Life of Christ)** *January to April*

Part III: From Pentecost to the Parousia: An Overview of the Acts,
the Letters, and the Revelation (Life in the Spirit) *May to August*

Foreword

By Chris Wright, international ministries director, Langham Partnership

Abrahamic and Apostolic

John Stott often spoke of his longing for "balanced biblical Christianity" ("BBC", as he called it), so I will balance the Old and New Testament in this brief assessment of his legacy. I suggest that in the global context of his ministry, the scale and scope of John Stott's stature was both Abrahamic and apostolic.

Stott was "Abrahamic" in two ways, the first being the most obvious. God called Abraham to be the vehicle of God's blessing to the nations. Paul says that "the gospel" announced in advance to Abraham was that all nations would be blessed through him (Gal. 3:8; Gen. 12:1–3). And, of course, that promise will ultimately be fulfilled through Christ and the mission of God's people in Christ: believing Jews and Gentiles. Stott, however, was Abrahamic in a more limited but significant way, in that right from the earlier stages of his ministry he reached out to the world. He had made fifteen international trips even before the 1966 Berlin Congress on World Evangelization, and in the years after the Lausanne Congress with Billy Graham in 1974 his influence within global evangelicalism spread even more extensively.

But Stott was no "evangelical tourist". He was passionate about bringing a truly global dimension to Christian mission and theology. Of course, he became well known in North America and Australia, for example, but his heart warmed to the sisters and brothers of the "majority world" of the global South, and their hearts warmed to him. He listened, he learned, he adapted, and he articulated a mission theology that was contextually sensitive and holistically integrated, while sustaining and deepening the lifelong roots of his biblical and evangelical convictions.

This Abrahamic dimension can be measured by the towering role he played in many different global affiliations and ministries; sometimes as an entrepreneurial initiator, and sometimes as a passionate advocate and ambassador. We could name the Lausanne Movement, the World Evangelical Fellowship, the International Fellowship of Evangelical Students, Scripture Union, The Evangelical Fellowship in the Anglican Communion, Tearfund, and, of course, his own Langham Partnership.

The second way in which Stott was Abrahamic was not just in the scope of his ministry, but also in the substance of his personal life, which manifested all that Paul must have meant by his phrase "the obedience of faith." We read that, "By faith Abraham… obeyed" (Heb. 11:8). God's promise to Abraham came with the demand that he should walk in the way of the Lord, and teach his own household and descendants after him to do the same in righteousness and justice (Gen. 18:19). God's people were to be a blessing by living among the nations in a way that was clearly and ethically distinctive: a holy people in order to be a priestly people. Or, as Jesus put it (in one of Stott's favourite texts), we are called to be salt in a corrupt world and light in a dark world. That is, we are to be distinct from, but deeply engaged with, the world around us.

Stott was passionate about the engagement and penetration of society with the gospel by Christians in their everyday lives and locations, including the workplace. This was as important to him as the truth of the gospel itself. Indeed, he would argue that the truth of the gospel has not truly been grasped until the demands, as well as the promises of, the gospel were understood and being lived out in the world by what he called "integrated" Christians: Christians whose lives were consistent with their faith. The gospel must penetrate *every* area of life, including the professions, culture, politics, family, and sexual ethics. Bearing witness to this dimension of Stott's thought and influence are the title of his book on the Sermon on the Mount, *Christian Counter-Culture*, his exploration of *Issues Facing Christians Today*, and his founding of the London Institute for Contemporary Christianity.

Stott was also "apostolic" in two senses: in evangelism and in teaching. The commission of the New Testament apostles was, first of all, to bear witness to Christ by proclaiming the good news that Jesus of Nazareth was Lord, King and Saviour; that in him the one true God of Israel had inaugurated his reign, had acted to save the world through the death and resurrection of his Son, and was calling people to receive the salvation God offers through repentance, faith, baptism, and obedience. Stott was an evangelist at heart, from his conversion as a teenager at Rugby School until his last days in the care home at St Barnabas. As a student he was involved in leading evangelistic camps for schoolboys. He conducted some fifty university missions in five continents between 1952 and 1977. As rector of All Souls Church, Langham Place in London, he established a model of what the sustained evangelistic life of a parish church can be. And shortly before his death he told me, with obvious joy, how he had been able to share the way of salvation with one of his carers while she was attending to him in his wheelchair after lunch. And, of course, his bestselling book, *Basic Christianity*, has been instrumental in leading many thousands of people, in multiple languages, to faith and salvation.

Secondly, however, the New Testament apostles were not only evangelists, but also *teachers* of the church, being obedient to what Jesus had told them in the Great Commission: "teaching them to obey everything I have commanded you" (Matt. 28:20). Paul not only spent considerable time himself teaching the churches he planted when he could (Acts 20:20; 27), but made sure that others, such as Timothy, Titus, and Apollos, were motivated and trained to do the same.

John Stott was as passionate and committed to the work of apostolic teaching as to apostolic evangelism. Like Paul, he longed to see churches worldwide growing up to maturity in Christ and into the likeness of Christ. He lamented the shallowness, immaturity, and ineffectiveness he saw in so many places. He particularly disapproved of the anti-intellectualism that easily infected the more fundamentalist sections of the broad evangelical world. His early small book, *Your Mind Matters,* inspired generations of students to become *thoughtful* Christians who could argue graciously and persuasively for their faith in the secular or multi-religious arena, just as Paul did.

Probably the two most apostolic dimensions of John Stott's legacy, in this area of fostering the maturity of the church through solid biblical teaching, are his lifetime of writing and the ministries of the Langham Partnership.

Over a fifty-five-year span, Stott wrote or co-authored some seventy books, forty of which are still in print with translations in more than sixty languages. He edited many other volumes, including the New Testament titles within the benchmark *Bible Speaks Today* series of commentaries. His books have a universal appeal and relevance, notwithstanding their very British author, because they are constantly rooted either in direct biblical exposition or in the application of biblical principles to theological and contemporary issues. And his style of writing has a simplicity and clarity, even on the most profound texts and topics, that lends itself to straightforward translation and cultural adaptation.

Stott bequeathed to Langham Partnership what he called "the Langham Logic," consisting, he would say, of three biblical convictions and one inescapable conclusion:

- God wants his church to grow in maturity, not just to grow larger in numbers.
- The church grows through God's Word.
- The Word of God comes to the people of God mainly through preaching.
- The logical question to ask, then, is "What can we do to raise the standards of biblical preaching?"

So, to raise a new generation of faithful, clear, and relevant biblical preachers and teachers, Stott invested in scholarships that would enable majority-world seminaries to enhance evangelical theological education with doctoral level teachers; recycled his own royalties into a ministry that not only distributes books to pastors and seminary libraries but also develops indigenous authors and publishers; and initiated a movement that is now training biblical preachers in more than seventy countries.

John Stott was Abrahamic in his missional vision for all nations and in his passion for the obedience of faith that demands whole-life discipleship in every area in which Christians engage with the world. And apostolic in his commitment to proclaiming the biblical gospel, and in his investment in the teaching ministry of the church through his own disciplined writing and his support for evangelical theological education and faithful biblical preaching.

Enjoy your year in his company!

Following the Christian Calendar

An Explanation

In 1963 a "Joint Liturgical Group" was formed in Britain, representing eight churches. Its unofficial report was entitled *The Calendar and Lectionary: A Reconsideration*. It proposed a calendar in which the Advent period (December) would focus on preparation for the first coming of Christ, without the awkwardness of trying to celebrate both his comings simultaneously. It would also extend backward toward the Sundays after Pentecost. In this way the cycle of the church's year would be more or less complete.

Since then several further attempts have been made to provide the church with an agreed calendar and lectionary, particularly for public worship on Sundays.

My concern, however, is rather to offer a resource for daily private devotion. It should enable us, whether we belong to a so-called liturgical church or not, to recapitulate every year the whole biblical story from the creation in Genesis to the consummation in Revelation 22. Moreover, when the church's year is conceived in this way, it divides itself naturally into three equal periods of four months each.

The first period runs from the beginning of September (when the Eastern Orthodox church year begins and when European churches hold their harvest festival) until Christmas. It enables us to relive the Old Testament story from the creation until the coming of Christ.

The second period runs from the beginning of January to the end of April, culminating in Whitsun, or Pentecost. It enables us to relive the story of Jesus in the Gospels, from his birth, through his ministry, to his death, resurrection, ascension, and gift of the Spirit.

The third period runs from the beginning of May to the end of August and consists of the weeks that follow Pentecost. It enables us to relive the story of the Acts and to recall that the Holy Spirit is both God's power for living now and his pledge of our final inheritance when Christ returns. During this period we reflect on the Christian life and the Christian hope as set forth in the letters and the revelation.

Thus the church calendar unfolds in three periods, the Bible divides itself into three sections, and Almighty God is seen to have revealed himself in three persons, the Father, the Son, and the Holy Spirit.

Moreover, these three threes may be superimposed on one another in a healthy trinitarian structure. It covers the whole biblical story. In period one (September to December), we reflect on the work of God the Father and on his preparation of his people through the Old Testament for the coming of the Messiah. In period two (January to April), we reflect on the work of God the Son and on his saving ministry as described in the Gospels. In period three (May to August), we reflect on the work of God the Holy Spirit and on his activity as documented in the Acts, the letters, and the book of Revelation.

To recall, relive, and celebrate annually this divine story should lead us into a wholesome and balanced trinitarian faith, should increase our familiarity with the framework and content of the Bible, and should establish our confidence in the God of history who has been and still is working out his purpose before, during, and after the incarnate life of our Lord Jesus Christ until he comes in power and glory.

A Note to the Reader

This book is organized in such a way that the user can start reading at any of its three parts.

For example, it is natural to begin with "Creation" at week 1 (in September) and follow the biblical story from its beginning to its end.

But some readers will prefer to wait until December/January so as to begin with "The Nativity" at week 17.

A third option is to begin with Easter in March/April. Since the date of Easter is movable (within the five weeks between March 22 and April 25), it is not possible to fix it, or to fix the other great Christian festivals which find their place in relation to Easter Day.

The best way to keep in step with the Christian calendar is to pinpoint the date of Easter in the year in which you are using this book. Then during the two weeks before it (Passion Week and Holy Week) we can read the meditations set for Week 31 ("The Seven Words from the Cross") and Week 32 ("The Meaning of the Cross"). On Easter Day itself, and during the remaining days of Easter Week, we can then read the meditations for Week 33 ("The Resurrection Appearances"), and during the following week the meditations set for Week 34 ("The Significance of the Resurrection").

This will ensure that during the vital weeks before and after Easter Week we will be reading appropriate texts and reflections. It will also be possible for us to fit dislodged and leftover weeks into the remaining gaps, and to observe Ascension Day (forty days after Easter) and Pentecost Sunday (ten days later still). Trinity Sunday is the climax; it is always the Sunday after Pentecost.

ACKNOWLEDGMENTS

I thank Matthew Smith, my study assistant from 2002 to 2005, for carefully reading the whole typescript and for making numerous suggestions for clarification and improvement.

Above all I am indebted to Frances Whitehead, who not only typed one more manuscript but in April 2006 completed fifty marvellous years as my omnicompetent secretary.

John Stott - September 2005

PART I

FROM CREATION TO CHRIST

AN OVERVIEW OF THE OLD TESTAMENT
(THE LIFE OF ISRAEL)

September to December

There is an inherent problem in the fact that the secular year begins on January 1, whereas the Christian year begins with Advent (in late November or early December).

Moreover, in this calendar I am pushing Advent back a further three months, partly in order to give us a much longer period of preparation for Christmas and partly in order to divide the year into three equal periods of four months each. Then it is marvellous to have four months in which to cover the whole Old Testament, stretching from creation to Christ.

We naturally focus during week 1 on Genesis 1, the creation. If, however, the reader prefers to begin the New Year with the birth of Christ it is easily possible to do so.

Week 1: Creation

"Nothing is more beautiful than Genesis," wrote Luther, "nothing more useful." I think we should agree with his evaluation, for there is great beauty and great practical usefulness in this book. Here, especially in its early chapters, the great doctrines of the Bible are established – the sovereignty of God as Creator, the power of his word, the original nobility of human beings, male and female, made in his image and given stewardship of the earth, the equality and complementarity of the sexes, the goodness of creation, the dignity of work and the rhythm of rest. These central truths are all laid down at the beginning of Genesis like massive foundation stones on which the biblical superstructure is built.

Sunday: The Creator's Initiative

Monday: From Chaos to Cosmos

Tuesday: Light Out of Darkness

Wednesday: The Sobriety of the Genesis Narrative

Thursday: The Image of God

Friday: Human Sexuality

Saturday: The Sabbath Rest

Sunday

The Creator's Initiative

IN THE BEGINNING GOD CREATED THE HEAVENS AND THE EARTH.

Genesis 1:1

The first four words of the Bible ("In the beginning God") are an indispensable introduction to the whole. They tell us that we can never anticipate God or take him by surprise. For he is always there "in the beginning." The initiative in every action lies with him.

This is especially true of creation. Christians believe that when God began his creative work, nothing existed except him. Only he was there in the beginning. Only he is eternal. The God-centredness of Genesis 1 stands out prominently in the narrative. God is the subject of nearly every verb. "God said" occurs ten times and "God saw that it was [very] good" seven times.

We do not have to choose between Genesis 1 and contemporary cosmology or astrophysics. For the Bible was never intended by God to be a scientific textbook. Indeed, it should be evident to readers that Genesis 1 is a highly stylized and beautiful poem. Both accounts of creation (scientific and poetic) are true, but they are given from different perspectives and are complementary to one another.

When the Apostles' Creed affirms our belief in "God the Father Almighty," it is referring not so much to his omnipotence as to his control over what he has made. What he created he sustains. He is immanent in his world, continuously upholding, animating, and ordering all things. The breath of living creatures is in his hand. He causes the sun to shine and the rain to fall. He feeds the birds and clothes the flowers. Again, it is poetry, but it is true.

Hence the wisdom of churches that hold an annual Service of Harvest Thanksgiving and of Christians who say grace before meals. It is both right and helpful thus regularly to acknowledge our dependence for life and all things on our faithful Creator and Sustainer.

For further reading: Matthew 5:43–45; 6:25–34

Monday

From Chaos to Cosmos

NOW THE EARTH WAS FORMLESS AND EMPTY, DARKNESS WAS OVER
THE SURFACE OF THE DEEP, AND THE SPIRIT OF GOD WAS HOVERING
OVER THE WATERS.

Genesis 1:2

Although Isaiah assures us that God "did not create it to be empty, but formed it to be inhabited" (Isa. 45:18), the earth was at first empty, formless, dark, and uninhabitable. So stage by stage in Genesis 1 we watch God reducing disorder to order, chaos to cosmos. The author of Genesis evidently understood that the creation was a process, although of unspecified length.

This process is vividly portrayed in verse 2. Some translators understand it as referring to an impersonal phenomenon such as a storm at sea. The New Jerusalem Bible, for instance, renders it that there was "a divine wind sweeping over the waters." But I agree with other commentators that in the context the reference is not to the wind but to the personal Holy Spirit himself whose creative activity is likened to a bird hovering over its young (REB).

Further, to the work of the Spirit of God in creation the author adds an allusion to the Word of God: "And God said." "For he spoke, and it came to be" (Ps. 33:9). It does not seem to me fanciful to detect here a reference to God the Father, to his Word, and to his Spirit. In other words, to the Trinity.

In these days of frequent overemphasis on one or other of the persons of the Godhead, it is healthy to keep returning to the three persons. Indeed, it is important to note that from the very earliest verses, the Bible affirms its witness to the Trinity. At the beginning of our studies we rejoice to acknowledge that we are trinitarian Christians.

For further reading: Psalm 104:29–31

Light Out of Darkness

AND GOD SAID, "LET THERE BE LIGHT," AND THERE WAS LIGHT.

Genesis 1:3

The little territory of Israel was sandwiched between the mighty empires of Babylon to their north and Egypt to their south, and in both countries some form of the worship of sun, moon, and stars was popular. In Egypt the centre of sun worship was On, whose Greek name was Heliopolis, "the city of the sun," a few miles outside Cairo. In Babylon astronomers had already developed elaborate calculations of the movements of the five planets they knew and had begun to map the heavens.

It is not altogether surprising, therefore, that many Israelite leaders became contaminated with the astral cults that surrounded them. Ezekiel was horrified to see twenty-five men "with their backs towards the temple of the LORD and their faces towards the east… bowing down to the sun in the east" (Ezek. 8:16).

Jeremiah also condemned the leaders of the nation for loving and serving "the sun and the moon and all the stars of the heavens" (Jer. 8:2).

It is against this background of idolatry that Genesis 1 needs to be read and understood. The Egyptians and the Babylonians were worshipping the sun, the moon, and the stars; the author of Genesis insists that they are not gods to be worshipped but the creation of the one true God.

God promised Abraham descendants "as numerous as the stars in the sky and as the sand on the seashore" (Gen. 22:17). The extraordinary thing is that, with our knowledge of about one hundred billion stars in our galaxy, and of billions more galaxies billions of light-years away, the equivalence of sand and stars may well be fairly accurate.

The apostle Paul took God's majestic fiat "Let there be light" as a model of what happens in the new creation. He likens the unregenerate human heart to the dark primeval chaos and the new birth to God's creative command, "Let there be light." This had certainly been his own experience. "For God, who said, 'Let light shine out of darkness,' made his light shine in our hearts to give us the light of the knowledge of God's glory displayed in the face of Christ" (2 Cor. 4:6).

For further reading: 2 Corinthians 4:3–6

Wednesday

The Sobriety of the Genesis Narrative

AND GOD SAID, "LET THERE BE...' AND IT WAS SO...
AND GOD SAW THAT IT WAS GOOD.
Genesis 1:6, 9–10

It is often claimed that there are striking parallels between the creation myths of the ancient Near East (especially the Babylonian epic known as "Enuma Elish") and the biblical account of creation in Genesis 1. But what is remarkable about the Babylonian and the biblical stories is not their similarity but their dissimilarity. So far from copying the Babylonian account, Genesis 1 critiques and challenges its basic theology. In the Babylonian myths the gods, amoral and capricious, squabble and fight with one another. Marduk, the loftiest of gods, attacks and kills Tiamat, the mother-goddess. He then proceeds to split her body in two, half of it becoming the sky and the other half the earth. From this crude polytheism it is a relief to turn to the ethical monotheism of Genesis 1, in which the whole creation is attributed to the command of the one true and holy God.

According to the book of Revelation, the eternal worship of heaven focuses on the Creator:

> *You are worthy, our Lord and God, to receive glory and honour and power,*
> *for you created all things, and by your will they were created*
> *and have their being.*
> **Revelation 4:11**

Scientists will continue to investigate the origins, nature, and development of the universe. But, theologically speaking, it is enough for us to know that God created all things by his will as expressed in his simple and majestic Word. For this is the repeated refrain of Genesis 1: "And God said..." Moreover, as God contemplated what he had made, he "saw that it was good." We need, therefore, to rejoice in all God's created works – whether food and drink; or marriage and family; or art and music; or birds, beasts, and butterflies; and many other things besides.

> *For everything God created is good, and nothing is to be rejected if it is*
> *received with thanksgiving...*
> **1 Timothy 4:4**

For further reading: Jeremiah 10:12–16

Thursday

The Image of God

SO GOD CREATED MANKIND IN HIS OWN IMAGE,
IN THE IMAGE OF GOD HE CREATED THEM...

Genesis 1:27

The climax of God's creative activity was the appearance of human beings, and the way in which Genesis expresses this high point is to describe them as having been created "in the image of God." But scholars are not altogether agreed on what the divine image in human beings means.

Some think it means that human beings are God's representatives, exercising dominion over the rest of creation in his place. Others conclude that God's image alludes to the special relationship that he has established between himself and us. But if we see the expression both in its immediate context in Genesis and in the broader perspective of Scripture, it seems to refer to all those human qualities or capacities that render us unlike the animals and like God. What are these?

Firstly, we human beings are rational and self-conscious. Secondly, we are moral, having a conscience that urges us to do what we perceive to be right. Thirdly, we are creative like our Creator, able to appreciate what is beautiful to the ear and the eye. Fourthly, we are social, able to establish with one another authentic relationships of love. For God is love, and by making us in his own image, he has given us the capacity to love him and others. Fifthly, we have a spiritual faculty that makes us hunger after God. Thus we are uniquely able to think and to choose, to create, to love, and to worship.

Unfortunately, however, we have to add that the image of God in us has been defaced, so that every part of our humanness has been tainted with self-centredness. Yet God's image has not been destroyed. On the contrary, both the Old Testament and the New Testament affirm that human beings still bear God's image and that this is the reason why we must respect them. The sanctity of human life arises from the value of God's image bearers (Gen. 9:6). Human beings are Godlike beings. They deserve to be loved and served.

For further reading: James 3:7–12

FRIDAY

Human Sexuality

MALE AND FEMALE HE CREATED THEM.

Genesis 1:27

It is a beautiful truth, clearly affirmed from the first chapter of the Bible onward, that heterosexuality is God's purpose in creation and that men and women are equal in dignity and worth before God their Creator. Both were created in his image (v. 27), and both were blessed and told to be fruitful, to subdue the earth, and to care for its creatures (v. 28). Thus men and women are equal bearers of the divine image and equal sharers in the earthly stewardship. And nothing that may be said later (e.g., in Gen. 2) must be allowed to undermine, let alone contradict, this fundamental equality of the sexes. What creation has established no culture is able to destroy. True, equality does not mean identity. Although the sexes are equal, they are different; equality is fully compatible with complementarity.

And something more needs to be said. Although our human disobedience and fall upset our human sexual relationships, God's intention is to restore and even deepen them through the gospel. Thus Paul could write to the Galatian Christians, "There is neither Jew nor Greek, neither slave nor free, nor is there male and female, for you are all one in Christ Jesus" (Gal. 3:28). This does not mean that ethnic, social, and sexual differences are eradicated by Christ. No, men are still men, and women are still women. But in Christ, when we are personally related to him, our sexual distinctives constitute no barrier to fellowship with God or with each other. For we are still equal before him, equally justified by faith, and equally indwelt by his Spirit.

Men and women in the Christian community should honour and value one another more than they do in non-Christian society. For we recognize our status. We are equal by creation, and even more equal (if there can be degrees in equality!) by redemption.

For further reading: Genesis 2:18–25

Saturday

The Sabbath Rest

GOD... RESTED FROM ALL THE WORK OF CREATING THAT HE HAD DONE.
Genesis 2:3

What was the crown of God's creation? It was not the creation of humans but the provision of the Sabbath, not the commissioning of humans to take up tools and work for six days but his commission to lay them down and worship on the seventh day. God's plan was not only to create *homo faber* (man the worker) but to create *homo adorans* (man the worshipper). For human beings are seen at their noblest when they are worshipping God.

This divine purpose was later enshrined in the Decalogue, whose fourth commandment said, "Remember the Sabbath day by keeping it holy," that is, by setting it apart from other days for both rest and worship (Exod. 20:8). God knew what he was doing when he made provision for our rest of mind and body. Several attempts have been made to change the divine rhythm of one day in seven. The French revolutionaries introduced a republican calendar with a ten-day week, but Napoleon in 1805 restored the seven-day week. Then the Russian revolutionaries turned Sunday into a working day, but it did not last long. Stalin restored Sunday as a day of rest. God knows best.

Then, secondly, one day in seven was intended for worship. Although some Christians insist on observing the seventh day as the Sabbath, it seems that the early believers worshipped on the first day, to celebrate the resurrection of Jesus Christ (John 20:19, 26; Acts 20:7), and that the important consideration is not which day is observed but that the one-day-in-seven rhythm is maintained.

Jesus himself observed the Sabbath and taught his disciples to do the same. But he also laid down an important principle: "The Sabbath was made for man, not man for the Sabbath" (Mark 2:27). Sunday observance is meant not to be dreary and restrictive but rather to be a joyful weekly celebration in which we make time for rest, worship, and (we should add) the family.

For further reading: Deuteronomy 5:12–15

Week 2: The Institution of Work and Marriage

It is in God's good providence that we have been given two accounts of creation, which complement one another. Both focus on the creation of human beings. Yet there is a significant difference between them. In Genesis 1 the Creator, who is named "God," upholds the whole cosmos, while in Genesis 2 he is given his covenant name, "the Lord God," who enjoys intimate fellowship with his human creatures. In particular, two foundation stones for human life on earth are laid in Genesis 2, namely work and marriage. Both are seen as the loving provision of Yahweh.

Sunday: Keeping Sunday Special

Monday: Collabourating with God

Tuesday: Caring for Creation

Wednesday: True Freedom

Thursday: Male and Female

Friday: The Creation of Eve

Saturday: The Biblical Definition of Marriage

SUNDAY

Keeping Sunday Special

GOD BLESSED THE SEVENTH DAY AND MADE IT HOLY...

Genesis 2:3

What does it mean that God "blessed" the seventh day and sanctified it or "made it holy?" Clearly the day itself has not experienced any inherent change; only its use has changed. For God has set it apart from the other six days of the week for special purposes.

In 1985 in the United Kingdom a campaign was launched called "Keep Sunday Special." It stressed the need to protect the workforce from being obliged to work on Sundays in any but essential jobs. At the same time it sought to safeguard Sunday for rest and recreation, worship and family. It nearly succeeded. It has now been refocused to ensure that everybody has "a regular shared day off."

This campaign has nothing in common with repressive sabbatarianism. The rabbis in Jesus' day calculated that the law of Sabbath observance contained more than fifteen hundred regulations. But Jesus had no sympathy with such casuistry. Claiming to be "Lord even of the Sabbath" (Mark 2:28), he meant that he had the authority to give a true interpretation of the fourth commandment. It was always right to "do good" on the Sabbath day (Mark 3:4), he said. He would have been in full agreement with the divine sentiments expressed in Isaiah 58:13–14:

> *If you keep your feet from breaking the Sabbath*
> *and from doing as you please on my holy day,*
> *if you call the Sabbath a delight*
> *and the LORD's holy day honourable,...*
> *then you will find your joy in the LORD,*
> *and I will cause you to ride... on the heights of the land*
> *and to feast on the inheritance of your father Jacob.*

For further reading: Mark 2:23–28

MONDAY

Collaborating with God

THE LORD GOD TOOK THE MAN AND PUT HIM IN THE GARDEN OF EDEN
TO WORK IT AND TAKE CARE OF IT.

Genesis 2:15

"I've got the Monday morning blues," we sometimes say in a melancholy tone of voice. It is a common human experience. But after enjoying the refreshment that the rest and worship of Sunday brings, we should be eager for the beginning of the working week. We should exclaim in the words of Mark Greene's well-known book, *Thank God It's Monday!*

What we need is an authentic Christian philosophy of work. Too many Christians see their work as no more than a painful necessity, since we have to earn our living somehow. By contrast, I think we should imagine Adam (evidently a neolithic farmer) going to work each day in the Garden of Eden with energy and enthusiasm. For God put the man he had made into the garden he had planted, in order "to work it and take care of it" (v. 15). Thus God deliberately humbled himself to need Adam's cooperation. Of course, he could have done all the work himself. After all, he had planted the garden. So presumably he could have managed it too! But he chose not to.

I like the story of the Cockney gardener who was showing a clergyman around his magnificent herbaceous borders, which were in full bloom. The clergyman broke into the praise of God, until the gardener was fed up that he was receiving no credit. "You should 'ave seen this 'ere garden," he complained, "when Gawd 'ad it to 'isself!" His theology was entirely correct. Without the human worker, the garden would have been a wilderness.

We need, then, to make an important distinction between nature and culture. Nature is what God gives us; culture is what we make of it (agriculture, horticulture, etc.). Nature is raw materials; culture is commodities prepared for the market. Nature is divine creation; culture is human cultivation. God invites us to share in his work. Indeed, our work becomes a privilege when we see it as collaboration with God.

For further reading: Genesis 2:7–9, 15

TUESDAY

Caring for Creation

THEN GOD SAID, "LET US MAKE MANKIND IN OUR IMAGE... SO THAT THEY
MAY RULE ["HAVE DOMINION" (REB)] OVER... ALL..." GOD BLESSED THEM
AND SAID TO THEM, "BE FRUITFUL AND INCREASE IN NUMBER;
FILL THE EARTH AND SUBDUE IT."

Genesis 1:26, 28

In March 2005 the results of the Millennium Ecosystem Assessment were published. It was a scientifically rigorous analysis of the conditions for human well-being on planet Earth. "We are living beyond our means," it declared, rapidly consuming, depleting, polluting, and destroying the "natural capital" on which our own livelihood depends.

Christians should be in the vanguard of the conservation movement, because we believe that God has called us to care for his creation. To be sure, some people blame us not only for not solving the ecological crisis but for actually causing it. In particular, one critic has seized on what he has called "three horrifying lines" in Genesis 1 and "this ghastly, calamitous text."[1] He was referring to the statements that God had given humankind the commission to "rule" and "subdue" the earth.

It is quite true that the first of these two verbs in Hebrew can mean to "trample on" and that the second was used for bringing people into subjection. Was Ian McHarg right, then, in his accusation? No, he was not. It is an elementary principle of biblical interpretation that the context must be allowed to determine the meaning of the text. We must note, therefore, that the "dominion" God has given us is a delegated and responsible stewardship. It would be ludicrous to suppose that, having first created the earth, God then handed it over to us to destroy it. It is the care of creation, not its exploitation, to which we have been called.

For further reading: Genesis 1:26–31

---

1   Ian McHarg, Dunning Trust Lectures, quoted in the *Ontario Naturalist*, March 1973..

WEDNESDAY

True Freedom

AND THE LORD GOD COMMANDED THE MAN, "YOU ARE FREE TO EAT
FROM ANY TREE IN THE GARDEN; BUT YOU MUST NOT EAT FROM THE TREE
OF THE KNOWLEDGE OF GOOD AND EVIL,
FOR WHEN YOU EAT FROM IT YOU WILL CERTAINLY DIE."

Genesis 2:16–17

God gave Adam two simple and straightforward instructions – one positive and the other negative. The first was a liberal permission (he might eat from any and every tree in the garden). The second was a single prohibition (he must not eat from the tree of the knowledge of good and evil, which was in the middle of the garden).

The liberal permission gave an almost completely unfettered access to the rich variety of trees in the garden. They were both "pleasing to the eye" and "good for food" (v. 9), thus offering Adam and Eve aesthetic and material satisfaction. God's generous provision also included access to "the tree of life," symbolic of continuous fellowship with God, which is eternal life (see John 17:3) and is glimpsed in the later statement that the Lord God himself walked with them in the garden (Gen. 3:8).

The tree of the knowledge of good and evil referred to in the solitary prohibition is so called not because it had magical properties but because it stood for the probation on which Adam and Eve had been placed. Created in God's image, they already had a degree of moral discernment, but if they disobeyed God, they would have a disastrous experience of evil as well as good.

A Finnish student at the University of Helsinki once said to me, "I'm longing for freedom, and I'm getting more free since I gave up God." But true freedom is found not in discarding Christ's yoke but in submitting to it, that is, through refraining from what he has forbidden us. Obedience means life, and disobedience death.

For further reading: Matthew 11:28–30

THURSDAY

Male and Female

THE LORD GOD SAID, "IT IS NOT GOOD FOR THE MAN TO BE ALONE. I WILL
MAKE A HELPER SUITABLE FOR HIM" [OR "AS HIS PARTNER" (NRSV)]

Genesis 2:18

Attentive readers are likely to be rudely awakened by Genesis 2:18. Six times in the creation narrative of Genesis 1 we come across the refrain "and God saw that it was good." Then follows the conclusion that "God saw all that he had made, and it was very good" (v. 31).

But now suddenly we read of something that is "not good." How can there be anything that is "not good" in God's good creation? Answer: it is not good for man to be alone, for man without woman is incomplete.

Mind you, we must not press this into an absolute statement, for some people are called to singleness, as the apostle Paul made plain (1 Cor. 7:7). Besides, Jesus our Lord, although the perfection of humanness, was himself single, which indicates that it is possible to be human and single at the same time! (See Matt. 19:11–12.)

Nevertheless, returning to Genesis 2, we read that God determined to give Adam a partner corresponding to him. Although the two Hebrew words used here have been variously translated, they combine the concepts of partnership and suitability. They supply no basis for either of the two extremes of male supremacy (men ruling over women) or radical feminism (women dispensing with men). Nor do they make room for gay or lesbian partnerships.

It would be a mistake, however, to restrict the application of Genesis 2:18 to marriage. Calvin was one of many commentators who have seen its wider reference. "Solitude is not good," he wrote. It is not good for any human beings to be alone. God has made us social beings. Friendship is a precious gift of God.

For further reading: Genesis 2:18–25

FRIDAY

The Creation of Eve

SO THE LORD GOD CAUSED THE MAN TO FALL INTO A DEEP SLEEP;
AND WHILE HE WAS SLEEPING, HE TOOK ONE OF THE MAN'S RIBS AND
THEN CLOSED UP THE PLACE WITH FLESH. THEN THE LORD GOD MADE
A WOMAN FROM THE RIB HE HAD TAKEN OUT OF THE MAN, AND HE
BROUGHT HER TO THE MAN.

Genesis 2:21–22

How literally we are intended to understand the divine surgery under a divine anaesthetic is not clear. But something profound and mysterious took place, which prompted Adam at the sight of Eve to break out into history's first love poem:

This is now ["at last" (REB)] bone of my bones
and flesh of my flesh;
she shall be called "woman,"
for she was taken out of man.

verse 23

That she was taken out of his side has been seen by commentators to have symbolic significance. Peter Lombard, who became bishop of Paris in 1159, for example, wrote a year or two earlier in his famous summary of Christian doctrine entitled *The Book of Sentences*, "Eve was not taken from the feet of Adam to be his slave, nor from his head to be his lord, but from his side to be his partner." And Matthew Henry, who began his biblical commentary in 1704, may have been elabourating Peter Lombard when he wrote that Eve was "not made out of his head to top him, not out of his feet to be trampled upon by him, but out of his side to be equal with him, under his arm to be protected, and near his heart to be beloved."

It is right, therefore, that in virtually all societies, marriage is a recognized and regulated institution. But it is not a human invention. Christian teaching on marriage begins with the joyful affirmation that it is God's idea, not ours. As the Preface to the 1662 Marriage Service says, it was "instituted by God himself in the time of man's innocency."

For further reading: Song of Songs 2:14–17

SATURDAY

The Biblical Definition of Marriage

THAT IS WHY A MAN LEAVES HIS FATHER AND MOTHER AND IS UNITED
WITH HIS WIFE, AND THEY BECOME ONE FLESH

Genesis 2:24

Marriage is under such threat in the Western world today that it is good to be reminded of its biblical basis. Genesis 2:24 is the Bible's own definition of marriage; it is even more important because it was endorsed by the Lord Jesus Christ (Mark 10:7). It is a relationship with five facets.

Firstly, *Heterosexual.* It unites a man and his wife. A homosexual partnership can never be a legitimate alternative.

Secondly, *Monogamous.* "A man" and "his wife" are both in the singular. Polygamy may have been tolerated for a while in Old Testament days, but monogamy was God's purpose from the beginning.

Thirdly, *Committed.* When a man leaves his parents to marry, he must "cleave" to his wife, sticking to her like glue (as the New Testament equivalent implies). Divorce may be permitted in one or two defined situations. "But it was not this way from the beginning," Jesus insisted (Matt. 19:8). Also, what is missing in cohabitation is precisely the element of commitment, which is foundational to marriage.

Fourthly, *Public.* Before the "cleaving" of marriage there should be the "leaving" of parents, and the "leaving" in mind is a public social occasion. Family, friends, and society have a right to know what is happening.

Fifthly *Physical.* "They become one flesh." On the one hand, heterosexual marriage is the only God-given context for sexual union and the procreation of children, and on the other, sexual union is so much a constitutive element of marriage that wilful nonconsummation is in many societies a ground for its annulment. Certainly Adam and Eve experienced no embarrassment regarding sex. "Adam and his wife were both naked, and they felt no shame" (Gen. 2:25).

Thus marriage, according to God's purpose in its institution, is a heterosexual and monogamous union that involves the loving, lifelong commitment of each to the other, should be entered upon by a public leaving of parents, and should be consummated in sexual union.

For further reading: Ephesians 5:21–33

The love, joy, and peace of paradise were shattered by human disobedience, or "the fall."

But is not the story of Adam and Eve a myth, a tale that is true theologically but not historically? Many say so, but I am among the dissenters. Certainly the talking snake and the named trees of the garden appear to be mythical, for they reappear later in Scripture in obviously symbolic form. For "the tree of life" see Revelation 2:7; 22:2, 14, and for "that ancient snake... the devil" see Revelation 12:7; 20:2.

But the apostle Paul plainly affirms the historicity of Adam. He draws a careful parallel between Adam and Christ. He argues that as sin and death entered the world through the disobedience of the one man Adam, so salvation and life have become available through the obedience of the one man Jesus Christ (Rom. 5:12–21). His argument would lack cogency if Adam's disobedience were not as historical as Christ's obedience.

Sunday: Denying God's Truthfulness

Monday: Denying God's Goodness

Tuesday: Denying God's "Otherness"

Wednesday: Shame and Blame

Thursday: The Disruption of Relationships

Friday: Glimpses of Grace

Saturday: Special Grace and Common Grace

SUNDAY

Denying God's Truthfulness

NOW THE SNAKE WAS MORE CRAFTY THAN ANY OF THE WILD ANIMALS
THE LORD GOD HAD MADE. HE SAID TO THE WOMAN, "DID GOD REALLY
SAY, 'YOU MUST NOT EAT FROM ANY TREE IN THE GARDEN'?"

Genesis 3:1

We remind ourselves that God had given Adam and Eve three instructions – a permission to eat freely of every tree in the garden, a prohibition to eat of one tree, and a penalty for disobedience. So they knew precisely what they might do, what they might not do, and what would happen if they disobeyed. Now we need to consider how the snake, being craftier than all God's other creatures, twisted these things into temptations. The subtlety of Satan still employs the same tactics.

Today we will consider that the devil denied the truthfulness of God. God had said that "when you eat from it you will certainly die" (2:17), but the devil said, "You will not certainly die" (3:4). So Eve was faced with a contradiction. They could not both be right; one of them must be lying. Which? Alas! She believed the devil's lie and doubted the truthfulness of God.

But God was telling the truth. On the one hand, Adam and Eve died spiritually. Until they sinned they ate freely from the tree of life, but now they forfeited this privileged access, and the way to the tree of life was strictly guarded (3. 22–24). On the other hand, their bodies became mortal. God said to Adam, "dust you are and to dust you will return" (v. 19). The fossil record clearly indicates that death had existed in the vegetable and animal kingdoms from the beginning. But it seems that God intended human beings made in his image to experience a nobler end than the disintegration we call death, perhaps a "translation" like Enoch and Elijah without tasting death.

The devil still denies God's warnings of his judgment and of the awful reality of hell for those who refuse to repent. We continue to hear the devil's whisper, "You will not die." But it is false prophets who say, "Peace," when there is no peace (e.g., Ezek. 13:10). And, as Jesus said, the devil is "a liar and the father of lies" (John 8:44).

For further reading: John 8:42–44

Denying God's Goodness

THE SNAKE... SAID TO THE WOMAN, "DID GOD REALLY SAY, 'YOU MUST
NOT EAT FROM ANY TREE IN THE GARDEN'?"
THE WOMAN SAID TO THE SNAKE, "WE MAY EAT FRUIT FROM THE TREES
IN THE GARDEN, BUT GOD DID SAY, 'YOU MUST NOT EAT FRUIT FROM THE
TREE THAT IS IN THE MIDDLE OF THE GARDEN,
AND YOU MUST NOT TOUCH IT, OR YOU WILL DIE.'"
"YOU WILL NOT CERTAINLY DIE," THE SNAKE SAID TO THE WOMAN. "FOR
GOD KNOWS THAT WHEN YOU EAT FROM IT YOUR EYES WILL BE OPENED..."

Genesis 3:1–5

The second element in the subtlety of Satan was that he denied the goodness of God. Not only would disobedience bring no penalty ("you will not certainly die"), but it would bring a positive blessing ("your eyes will be opened"). Further, God knows this, and (the devil insinuates) that is why he forbade you to eat the fruit. He is deliberately withholding from you the knowledge you would get if you ate. He is seeking not your welfare but your impoverishment.

In his original instructions about the fruit of the garden, God had been absolutely straightforward. He had clearly distinguished between the "may" of their freedom and the "must not" that limited it. In this the devil conveniently ignored God's ample provision of fruit that Adam and Eve might eat freely. In consequence they lacked nothing. But Satan twisted this. He made the permitted things seem unsatisfying and the forbidden things seem desirable.

Still today one of the devil's favourite occupations is to make God's permitted things tame and his prohibited things attractive. He portrays God as an ogre who is denying us what is good.

We need the discernment to "test" everything and then to "hold on to what is good" and "reject every kind of evil" (1 Thess. 5:21–22). We also need the assurance that "as for God, his way is perfect" (Ps. 18:30).

For further reading: 1 John 2:15–17

TUESDAY

Denying God's "Otherness"

THE SNAKE SAID TO THE WOMAN, "... GOD KNOWS THAT WHEN YOU
EAT FROM IT YOUR EYES WILL BE OPENED, AND YOU WILL BE LIKE GOD,
KNOWING GOOD AND EVIL." WHEN THE WOMAN SAW THAT THE FRUIT OF
THE TREE WAS GOOD FOR FOOD AND PLEASING TO THE EYE, AND ALSO
DESIRABLE FOR GAINING WISDOM, SHE TOOK SOME AND ATE IT.

Genesis 3:4–6

The devil's third tactic was to deny the "otherness" of God. He had said to the woman, "God knows that when you eat from it your eyes will be opened, and you will be like God, knowing good and evil" (v. 5).

He tempted Eve with the possibility of becoming like God. In this diabolical suggestion the very essence of sin is laid bare. For Adam and Eve had been created in the likeness of God and were already "like God" in every way in which God intended them to be Godlike – in those rational, moral, social, and spiritual capacities that he had given them.

The fundamental way in which Adam and Eve were unlike God and like the animals was in their creaturely dependence on him. God is self-dependent. He depends for himself on himself. All other beings depend on him as their Creator and Sustainer, including human beings. It is against this that Adam and Eve rebelled. Why should they continue in their humiliating position of dependence and subordination? Why should they not make a bid for independence and become equal with God? They would not die; they would become Godlike.

Many echoes of this spirit of proud independence are heard in our day. We are told that humans have now "come of age." We no longer need God. We can learn to live without God. Indeed, we can become like God.

But this is the fundamental nature of sin. Sin is an unwillingness to let God be God, a refusal to acknowledge his "otherness" and our continuing dependence on him. Sin is a revolt against God's unique authority; it is an attempt at self-deification.

For further reading: Isaiah 14:3, 11–15

WEDNESDAY

Shame and Blame

THEN THE EYES OF BOTH OF THEM WERE OPENED, AND THEY REALISED
THAT THEY WERE NAKED; SO THEY SEWED FIG LEAVES TOGETHER AND
MADE COVERINGS FOR THEMSELVES.

Genesis 3:7

Shame and blame were two of the immediate consequences of the fall of Adam and Eve. Firstly, shame. As a result of their disobedience in eating the forbidden fruit, "the eyes of both of them were opened." It was not, of course, their bodies' eyes but the eyes of their conscience. They now saw with unclouded clarity the folly and wickedness of their rebellion against God. Moreover, their physical nakedness, of which they had previously "felt no shame" (2:25), now filled them with embarrassment, which was symbolic of their sense of guilt before God. But, although they confessed their sin, there is little evidence that they realized its magnitude if they thought they could overcome their shame by pathetic aprons of fig leaves (3:7)!

The second device to which both Adam and Eve resorted was to shift the blame from their own shoulders. Adam blamed Eve for giving him some of the fruit to eat and then went further to blame God for giving her to be with him in the garden (v. 12). Then, when God challenged Eve as to what she had done, she blamed the snake for having deceived her (v. 13).

This shaming and blaming is right up to date. We can become very ingenious in our superficial attempts both to lessen our sense of shame and to shift the blame onto others. "It's my genes," we say, "or my parental upbringing, or a congenital weakness that is not my fault." But it is an essential feature of our Godlike humanness that we accept responsibility for the choices we make.

For further reading: John 16:8–11

THURSDAY

The Disruption of Relationships

> TO THE WOMAN [GOD] SAID, "I WILL MAKE YOUR PAINS IN CHILDBEARING
> VERY SEVERE... YOUR DESIRE WILL BE FOR YOUR HUSBAND, AND HE WILL
> RULE OVER YOU." TO ADAM HE SAID, "... CURSED IS THE GROUND BECAUSE
> OF YOU; THROUGH PAINFUL TOIL YOU WILL EAT FROM IT ALL THE DAYS OF
> YOUR LIFE."
>
> **Genesis 3:16–17**

The first two chapters of Genesis have affirmed that God made man male and female in his own image and that the divine image was to be seen above all in our human relationships – to God himself (who engaged Adam and Eve in conversation), to one another (reflecting the fellowship between the persons of the Godhead), and to the good earth (over which they were given responsible dominion).

But the disobedience of our first parents led to the disruption of these three major relationships.

Firstly, Adam and Eve went into hiding, and the greatest of all tragedies began, namely that human beings made by God like God and for God should now try to live their lives without God. All our sense of disorientation stems ultimately from this alienation from God. "Your iniquities have separated you from your God; your sins have hidden his face from you" (Isa. 59:2).

Secondly, Adam and Eve not only blamed each other but found that their sexual relationship had become skewed. Their promised fruitfulness (Gen. 1:28) would now be accompanied by pain as well as pleasure, and in place of the intended partnership between the sexes there would be discord, for Adam would "rule" over his wife (3:16).

Thirdly, although Adam and Eve had been given dominion over the earth and the responsibility to till and take care of the garden, the ground was now cursed, and the cultivation of the soil would be an uphill struggle (vv. 17–19).

Only through Christ and his gospel of reconciliation would this threefold disruption of relationships be remedied.

For further reading: Colossians 1:15–20

Glimpses of Grace

THEN THE MAN AND HIS WIFE HEARD THE SOUND OF THE LORD GOD AS
HE WAS WALKING IN THE GARDEN IN THE COOL OF THE DAY, AND THEY
HID FROM THE LORD GOD AMONG THE TREES OF THE GARDEN. BUT THE
LORD GOD CALLED TO THE MAN, "WHERE ARE YOU?"... THE LORD GOD
MADE GARMENTS OF SKIN FOR ADAM AND HIS WIFE AND CLOTHED THEM.

Genesis 3:8–9, 21

The situation is now dire, and the prospect bleak. Adam and Eve have rebelled against God's authority; they can expect only to reap the harvest of their own wrongdoing. But against this background of sin, guilt, and judgment, glimpses of grace begin to appear.

Firstly, the Lord God "was walking in the garden in the cool of the day." The day's work was over. The Lord was taking his customary evening stroll. Normally, we may assume, Adam and Eve accompanied him. But now they were nowhere to be seen, for they had gone into hiding. Yet he continued his walk seeking, searching for the missing couple.

Next, "The LORD God called to the man, 'Where are you?'" Nowadays the roles tend to be reversed, and we talk about humankind's search for God. But the reality is that God is searching for us. While Adam and Eve were hiding among the trees, the Lord God missed them, sought them, and called out after them.

Thirdly, although the self-conscious nakedness of Adam and Eve was their fault, being due to their disobedience, the Lord God felt for them in their shame and wanted to do something to alleviate it. So he "made garments of skin for Adam and his wife and clothed them" (v. 21). Now, skin would be available only after the killing of an animal. Is it then hinted at here, as it is plainly taught elsewhere, that the covering of human guilt in forgiveness is possible only through the shedding of blood in sacrifice, thus foreshadowing salvation through the blood of Christ? Maybe. But what is explicit is that God determined to give Adam and Eve a covering far better than they could give themselves, providing them with his own personally tailored skin garments in place of their aprons of flimsy fig leaves. In each case God took the initiative, and the proper name for an unmerited divine initiative is *grace*.

For further reading: Psalm 32:1–7

SATURDAY

Special Grace and Common Grace

THE LORD GOD SAID TO THE SNAKE, "... I WILL PUT ENMITY BETWEEN
YOU AND THE WOMAN, AND BETWEEN YOUR OFFSPRING AND HERS; HE
WILL CRUSH YOUR HEAD, AND YOU WILL STRIKE HIS HEEL."

Genesis 3:14–15

Yesterday we looked at three glimpses of grace. But I have reserved for today what is often called the "protevangelium," or the first proclamation of the gospel of grace, namely Genesis 3:15. It occurs in God's judgment on the snake and is in two parts.

Firstly, God announces that he will put enmity between the snake and the woman, which will continue into the future as a hostility between the snake's family (see John 8:44) and Eve's posterity (evidently meaning her spiritual seed).

Secondly, God foretells that this age-long conflict will culminate in suffering, though more for Satan than for Eve's descendant, for a single champion is now in mind. God says, "He will crush your head," dealing a lethal blow to the serpent, while "you will strike his heel." That is, he will not escape injury himself.

This decisive though painful victory over the devil was won at the cross, when Jesus Christ disarmed and dethroned the principalities and powers and triumphed over them (Col. 2:15). It sets us free from Satanic bondage and is the most splendid act of God's special grace.

Meanwhile, God's common grace is extended to everybody. For example, Eve became pregnant, gave birth to Cain, and said, "With the help of the LORD I have brought forth a man" (Gen. 4:1). "With the help of the LORD"? But she and her husband had just been banished from him (3:22–24)! How could she claim his help in childbirth? The answer is that, although God's special grace brings salvation to believers, his common grace is extended to all humankind in the provision of life and health and all things necessary for survival.

For further reading: Revelation 12:1–9

Week 4: Social Deterioration

If Genesis 3 records the first act of disobedience, Genesis 4 records the first act of murder. For sin is social as well as individual, and the God who asked Adam, "Where are you?" (3:9) now asks Cain, "Where is your brother Abel?" (4:9). Indeed, throughout the story of Genesis 4 to 11, the social situation steadily deteriorates. We see outbreaks of anger, jealousy, arrogance, violence, resentment, revenge, fear, and self-pity, culminating in God's judgments in the flood and the tower of Babel.

But the beauty of these chapters as a whole is that alongside the horrors of human sin, human culture began to flourish – farming, building, technology, and music.

Sunday: Cain the First Murderer

Monday: The Beginnings of Culture

Tuesday: The Spread of Corruption

Wednesday: Noah and the Flood

Thursday: God's Eternal Covenant of Mercy

Friday: The Origin of the Nations

Saturday: The Tower of Babel

Cain the First Murderer

Now Cain said to his brother Abel, "Let's go out to the field."
While they were in the field, Cain attacked his brother Abel
and killed him.

Genesis 4:8

Eve gave birth to two boys, first Cain and then Abel. Abel became a shepherd and "kept flocks," while Cain became a farmer and "worked the soil" (v. 2). Both brothers brought an offering to the Lord, each according to his occupation – Cain "some of the fruits of the soil" and Abel "fat portions" from newborn lambs (vv. 3–4). And the Lord looked with favour on Abel's offering but with disfavour on Cain's. Cain was very angry at this, and in his jealous rage he murdered his brother Abel.

Many readers sympathize with Cain. After all, he brought an offering appropriate to his vocation. So God's rejection of it seems unfair. We may be sure, however, that there was nothing arbitrary about God's reaction. He asked Cain, "Why are you angry?... If you do what is right, will you not be accepted?" (vv. 6–7). In what way, then, was Abel's offering right and Cain's not right? Some commentators draw attention to the fact that Cain was self-righteous in bringing the work of his own hands, whereas Abel brought a sacrificial lamb.

If we consult the New Testament, however, we read three times that Abel acted "by faith" (Heb. 11:4). Moreover, Hebrews 11 defines *faith* as an obedient response to God's word of revelation. Applied to Abel, it implies that somehow God had revealed to the brothers the kind of sacrifice he desired and that only Abel had responded in the obedience of faith.

The apostle John takes up the story, contrasting Cain and Christ. Whereas Cain hated and murdered his brother, we are called like Christ to love others and lay down our lives for them (1 John 3:11–17).

For further reading: Hebrews 11:1–4

The Beginnings of Culture

JABAL... WAS THE FATHER OF THOSE WHO LIVE IN TENTS AND RAISE
LIVESTOCK. HIS BROTHER'S NAME WAS JUBAL; HE WAS THE FATHER OF ALL
WHO PLAY STRINGED INSTRUMENTS AND PIPES... TUBAL-CAIN... FORGED
ALL KINDS OF TOOLS OUT OF BRONZE AND IRON.

Genesis 4:20–22

The second half of Genesis 4 (vv. 17–26) introduces us to a paradoxical man called Lamech, one of Cain's descendants. On the one hand, he committed bigamy (v. 19) and bragged to his two wives that he had killed a young man for injuring him and that in the future he would even outdo Cain in his brutality. For if Cain avenged himself seven times, Lamech boasted that he would do so seventy-seven times. Much better is the requirement of Jesus that we should forgive an offending brother seventy-seven times.

On the other hand, Lamech's two wives gave birth to some very talented children, whose descendants inherited the same skills. Through their leadership, civilization began to develop. Cain, in spite of being himself a fugitive from God, had started building a city (perhaps only a village) for his extended family, which he named after his son Enoch (v. 17). As for Lamech's sons, Jabal was a nomad, living in tents and raising livestock, while his brother Jubal's family were musicians, specializing in wind and stringed instruments. As for their half brother, Tubal-Cain, he and his people had left the Stone Age behind them, for they "forged all kinds of tools out of bronze and iron." Thus construction, farming, music, science, and technology were being developed. At the same time, some people engaged in the rudiments of ordered worship: "People began to call on the name of the LORD" (v. 26).

Human ambiguity was now very evident. Created in the image of God, human beings never lost their dignity or their cultural ingenuity. But being fallen, they also manifested an ugly depravity that sometimes broke out in terrible arrogance and violence. Lamech was an outstanding example of this human paradox.

For further reading: Genesis 4:19–24, 26

TUESDAY

The Spread of Corruption

THE LORD SAW HOW GREAT THE WICKEDNESS OF THE HUMAN RACE
HAD BECOME ON THE EARTH, AND THAT EVERY INCLINATION OF THE
THOUGHTS OF THE HUMAN HEART WAS ONLY EVIL ALL THE TIME.

Genesis 6:5

Just as God created Adam in his own likeness, so now Adam had a son (Seth) in his likeness (5:1–3). Does this mean that Adam's likeness to God and Seth's likeness to Adam were the same likeness, or different? Surely both – for the divine likeness in which Adam and Eve were created and which was transmitted to their descendants, and has been transmitted to us, is both authentic (9:6) and distorted by the fall.

The genealogy in Genesis 5 traces Seth's line from Adam to Noah. Each generation is described in identical terms, with one main exception, namely Enoch. Instead of declaring that he lived so many years and then died, it is written that he "walked faithfully with God" and then "was no more, because God took him away" (v. 24). Thus in the case of this godly man, both life and death were transformed. As Delitzsch wrote, "On a sudden he was gone, without sickness, without dying, without burial."[1]

But the general moral situation, which was soon to provoke God's judgment of the flood, was one of extreme decadence. The author singles out the strange story of the "sons of God" being attracted by "the daughters of humans" and marrying them (6:2). Most ancient church fathers thought this was angels marrying humans, but (as Calvin wrote) this theory "is abundantly refuted by its own absurdity."[2] For Jesus taught that angels are sexless creatures. The Reformers, following Chrysostom and Augustine, thought it was Sethites marrying Cainites, the godly marrying the ungodly. In either case, these mixed marriages were unnatural and polygamous, an arrogant rejection of God's original ordinance of marriage.

The narrative concludes that the earth was "full of violence" (v. 11) and that the Lord's heart was filled with grief and pain (v. 6). The scene is set for the flood.

For further reading: Genesis 6:1–12

---

1 Franz Delitzsch, *A New Commentary on Genesis*, trans. Sophia Taylor (Edinburgh: T & T Clark, 1888), 218.

2 John Calvin, *A Commentary on Genesis* (Edinburgh: Banner of Truth, 1965), 238.

Noah and the Flood

I AM GOING TO BRING FLOODWATERS ON THE EARTH TO DESTROY ALL LIFE
UNDER THE HEAVENS...

Genesis 6:17

Noah stood out of the general depravity like a fragrant flower on a manure heap. He had "found favour in the eyes of the LORD" (v. 8). He also "walked faithfully with God" like Enoch (v. 9), practising the presence of God in the midst of prevailing godlessness.

When God warned Noah of the coming deluge and told him to build an ark, he believed and obeyed God, following his instructions regarding materials, measurements, and construction. His contemporaries must have thought it a huge joke that Noah should have spent many months assembling such an enormous ocean-going barge inland under a clear blue sky. "By faith Noah, when warned about things not yet seen, in holy fear built an ark to save his family" (Heb. 11:7).

But was the flood historical and universal? Historical, yes, for Jesus himself spoke of it, and moreover, flood stories feature among the sagas of many ancient peoples. But universal? Some Christians argue that the whole earth of both hemispheres was inundated. Not only is this inherently improbable, but the biblical narrative does not require us to believe it. True, the narrator says that "all the high mountains under the entire heavens were covered" (Gen. 7:19). But Scripture often uses universal language (e.g., "all" and "every") not in an absolute sense but relative to the horizons and perspective of the writers. Thus we read that "all the world came to Egypt to buy grain from Joseph, because the famine was severe everywhere" (41:57). But "all the world" clearly means the countries around Egypt. Thus the flood was surely universal from the viewpoint of the writer and covered much of the Middle East, though not the whole world.

More important than the extent of the deluge, however, is the lesson that Jesus bids us learn from it: namely, "As it was in the days of Noah, so it will be at the coming of the Son of Man" (Matt. 24:37). His judgment will find the world largely unprepared.

For further reading: Matthew 24:37–39

Thursday

God's Eternal Covenant of Mercy

WHENEVER THE RAINBOW APPEARS IN THE CLOUDS, I WILL SEE IT AND
REMEMBER THE EVERLASTING COVENANT BETWEEN GOD AND ALL LIVING
CREATURES...

Genesis 9:16

In due course the flood waters receded, and all the passengers in the ark – human and animal – emerged. Next, Noah built an altar and sacrificed burnt offerings on it, symbolizing the dedication of his new life to God. Even before the flood, looking to the future beyond it, God had said to Noah, "I will establish my covenant with you" (6:18). Now after the flood he confirmed it (9:8–11).

Covenant is a key biblical word. It denotes a solemn promise of God in which he takes an initiative in undeserved mercy. So what was God's covenant promise following the flood? It had both a negative and a positive aspect. Negatively, five times in succession, God said to himself, "Never again" (8:21; 9:11, 15).

To this negative promise God now added a positive blessing, in which he repeated his fourfold original command to be fruitful, to multiply, to fill the earth, and to subdue it (9:1, 7). He thus renewed his commitment to his creation. In addition, he promised that, as long as the earth lasted, the yearly cycle of the seasons (seedtime and harvest, cold and heat, summer and winter) and the daily sequence of day and night would never cease. All life depends to some extent on the regularity of these rhythms, and did so long before it was known that they were caused by the earth's revolutions on its own axis and around the sun. The Royal Navy had sufficient confidence in this that it once posted the following directive: "The Fleet will sail at sunrise, and the sun will rise at 5.52 a.m."

God has remained faithful to his covenant, which he signed and sealed by the rainbow (vv. 12, 17). Against the dark background of a threatening sky, the light and beauty of this phenomenon appears, uniting heaven and earth. Similarly, the apostle John saw God's throne encircled with a rainbow, for he rules the world in mercy (Rev. 4:3).

For further reading: Genesis 8:20–22; 9:1, 7–17

Friday

The Origin of the Nations

**FROM THESE THE NATIONS SPREAD OUT OVER THE EARTH
AFTER THE FLOOD.**

Genesis 10:32

God did not promise after the flood a return to the Garden of Eden, for human hearts were still evil (8:21). Even righteous Noah got drunk and became involved with one of his sons (Ham) and grandsons (Canaan) in an act of indecency. Already inebriation and immorality were linked. The rather sordid story is told in Genesis 9:18–27.

Nevertheless, from Noah's three sons – Shem, Ham, and Japheth – the nations arose and spread out over the earth. Genesis 10 documents this dispersal, first disposing of the collateral lines of Ham and Japheth, and finally focusing on the descendants of Shem (Semites), with whom, because of Abraham, Genesis is mainly concerned. From the region of Ararat, Japheth's descendants moved west to what is now Asia Minor and Europe; Ham's southwest to Canaan, Egypt, and North Africa; and Shem's southeast to Mesopotamia and what we call the Persian Gulf.

As we reflect on these migrations, it is evident that God is concerned with all people. Seventy nations or tribes are listed, a symbol of completeness, and it may well be that Jesus had them in mind when he sent out seventy disciples two by two (Luke 10:1).

We must always bear in mind this universal extent of God's concern and not interpret the curse on Canaan (Gen. 9:25) as limiting it or as justifying either the slave trade in West Africa or apartheid in South Africa, as some Christians did in the nineteenth and twentieth centuries respectively.

Jesus Christ has broken down such divisive barriers, and now "there is no Gentile or Jew... barbarian, Scythian, slave or free, but Christ is all, and is in all" (Col. 3:11; see Eph. 2:11–22).

For further reading: Genesis 9:18–27

The Tower of Babel

SO THE LORD SCATTERED THEM... OVER ALL THE EARTH, AND THEY
STOPPED BUILDING THE CITY.

Genesis 11:8

It seems that the tower of Babel was a ziggurat, a huge Babylonian terraced pyramid. Several have been excavated, and the earliest is said to date from the third millennium BC.

What was it about the tower of Babel that aroused the displeasure of God? After all, human technological prowess is due to the inventive genius of human beings made in God's image. What was wrong, then? It was the builders' self-centred motivation.

Firstly, they were guilty of an act of disobedience. God's original command to human beings, repeated after the flood, had been to "fill the earth and subdue it" (1:28; see 9:1). The descendants of Noah began to do it, but when they reached the alluvial Mesopotamian plain, they "settled there" (11:2). Instead of pressing on to explore the earth and develop its potential, they settled down in comfortable security. The world is still suffering from their disobedience. For we have not yet solved the energy problem. Nor have we invented a cheap way to desalinate seawater so as to irrigate the deserts and feed the hungry.

Secondly, building the tower was an act of presumption. "Let us make a name for ourselves," they said, "by constructing a tower that reaches to the heavens." Unwilling to remain within earthly limits, they aspired to heaven, the dwelling place of God. So throughout Scripture Babylon represents that proud insolence that the Greeks called *hubris*. It is the very essence of sin.

No wonder God's judgment fell upon them. Firstly, he scattered them over all the earth, obliging them to do what they had failed to do voluntarily. Secondly, as the means to their scattering, he confused their languages. For language is a living, changing thing; it can increase the isolation of communities from each other, just as isolation can cause further language change.

The story of Babel looks forward to its reversal on the great day of Pentecost, when people heard in their own languages the wonders of God.

For further reading: Genesis 11:1–9

After the terrible judgments of the flood and the tower of Babel, God planned a new beginning. Babel spelled a scattering of the people, but Abraham spelled their gathering under the promise of God. It was in his outstanding condescension that he called himself the God of Abraham, Isaac, and Jacob (Exod. 3:6; Mark 12:26). For all three patriarchs, together with Joseph of the next generation, were swayed by strong human emotions, a sorry mixture of good and evil, greatness and pettiness. Yet through them God was working out his purpose; they occupy a unique position in salvation history, that is, in God's plan for the redemption of the world.

Sunday: The Call of Abraham

Monday: The Birth of Isaac

Tuesday: The Testing of Abraham's Faith

Wednesday: God's Covenant with Abraham

Thursday: Isaac and the Faithfulness of God

Friday: Jacob and the Persevering Love of God

Saturday: Joseph and the Providence of God

The Call of Abraham

THE LORD HAD SAID TO ABRAM, "... ALL PEOPLES ON EARTH WILL BE
BLESSED THROUGH YOU."

Genesis 12:1, 3

It is no exaggeration to say that the first three verses of Genesis 12 summarize God's plan of salvation, namely to bless the world through Christ, who is the seed of Abraham. This promise was accompanied by a double divine call. On the one hand, Abram was to leave his own country and go to a land that God would show him. On the other hand, he was to leave his household, and God would make him into a great nation. In general God would both bless him and make him a blessing to others – in fact, to all the peoples of the earth.

These promises of a seed and a land kept being repeated and elaborated to Abraham at different stages of his life. On one occasion, for example, God told Abraham to look north, south, east, and west, because everything he saw would be given to him and his descendants (13:14–15). On another occasion, God told Abraham to look up at the night sky and count the stars, because his descendants would be as numerous as they (15:5).

The successive fulfilments of God's promise of a seed are wonderful. Firstly, it was fulfilled in the multiplication of the people of Israel (Deut. 1:10–11). Secondly, it is being fulfilled through the mission of the church, so that all those who belong to Christ are Abraham's seed (Gal. 3:29), since he is the father of all believers (Rom. 4:16–17). Thirdly, it will be fulfilled in the great company of the redeemed in heaven, international and innumerable (Rev. 7:9–17). Only then will Abraham's descendants be as numerous as the stars in the sky and the sand on the seashores of the world.

For further reading: Genesis 11:27–12:5

MONDAY

The Birth of Isaac

THE LORD DID FOR SARAH WHAT HE HAD PROMISED. SARAH BECAME
PREGNANT AND BORE A SON TO ABRAHAM IN HIS OLD AGE...

Genesis 21:1–2

At the time when the promise of descendants was made to Abraham, he and his wife Sarah were childless, apparently infertile. So God's promise strained their credulity to the limit. How could they have a stream of descendants if they did not have even one?

Once Abraham complained that, since he remained childless, the heir to his estate would be his servant Eliezer of Damascus. But the Lord assured him that his heir would be his own son coming from his own body (15:1–4). And Abraham believed God.

Next, Sarah had the bright idea that she would give her Egyptian maidservant Hagar to Abraham as his concubine. "Perhaps I can build a family through her," she said. Abraham agreed, Hagar conceived, and Ishmael was born. But Sarah became jealous, and it was obvious that Ishmael was not the promised child (16:1–6).

Meanwhile, far from withdrawing his promises, God confirmed them, even changing the chief actors' names, calling Abram "a father of many nations" and Sarah "the mother of nations" (17:5, 15–16). As if to reinforce this, three men (who collectively are identified as "the LORD") visited Abraham in his tent. The Lord promised him that in about a year's time Sarah would have a son. Eavesdropping near the tent's entrance, Sarah laughed, incredulous that she and Abraham could possibly have a child at their advanced age. No wonder the Lord asked Sarah, "Is anything too hard for the LORD?" (18:14). Rebuked, Sarah told a lie, affirming that she had not laughed, although she had.

In due course the Lord was gracious to Sarah, as he had said. She became pregnant and bore Abraham a son. Abraham gave the child the name Isaac ("Laughter"), for the laughter of incredulity had now been replaced by the laughter of celebration and joy (21:1–3, 6).

For further reading: Genesis 18:1–15

TUESDAY

The Testing of Abraham's Faith

SOME TIME LATER GOD TESTED ABRAHAM.
Genesis 22:1

A welcome mark of the realism of the Bible is that it does not conceal the faults and failings of the great. Abraham is an example. In an amazing act of faith, he had left his home and family "even though he did not know where he was going" (Heb. 11:8). But then, driven by famine to take refuge in Egypt, he asked Sarah (because she was a very beautiful woman) to tell people that she was his sister, not his wife. It was a despicable action, risking her safety to secure his. The root of it was unbelief (Gen. 12:10–20).

After noting this glaring contrast between faith and doubt, we naturally ask ourselves how Abraham will respond to the extreme test of his faith, namely God's instruction to him to sacrifice Isaac as a burnt offering. We may be sure that the first purpose of this terrible command was to tell Abraham that Yahweh did not require human sacrifice, for it was one of the chief abominations committed by the people of Canaan on account of which God commanded their destruction (see the discussion on Sunday of week 8).

But the story also had a deeper meaning. Three times Isaac is most touchingly described as "your son, your only son, whom you love" (22:2). This identifies him not only as a precious only boy but as the unique one of whom God had said that "it is through Isaac that your offspring will be reckoned" (21:12). Abraham and Sarah had waited for years for the birth of this child of promise; were they now to secure his death?

Abraham clung to God's assurance that his promises would be fulfilled in Isaac's line. He even "reasoned that God could even raise the dead, and so in a manner of speaking he did receive Isaac back from death" (Heb. 11:19). It was a superlative act of faith and obedience.

For further reading: Hebrews 11:8–19

God's Covenant with Abraham

I WILL MAKE MY COVENANT BETWEEN ME AND YOU.

Genesis 17:2

It was in the aftermath of the flood that we first encountered the biblical theme of "covenant." We saw that a covenant in Scripture is an agreement between God and human beings that is initiated by his grace, founded on his promise, and sealed with a sign.

God's first covenant was with Noah; his second is now with Abraham. His promise to Noah was that he would maintain the rhythms of nature, while his promise to Abraham was to multiply his descendants and give them the land. The covenant signs were the rainbow on the one hand and circumcision on the other. The covenant with Noah was universal, whereas the covenant with Abraham was particular. It involved the covenant formula, repeated endlessly throughout the Old Testament, namely "I will be your God and you shall be my people" (see vv. 7–8).

Mention of covenant promises naturally raises the question of their fulfilment. Take as an example the promise of the land. Abraham never occupied it. He only passed through it, living in a tent. But when Sarah died, Abraham needed somewhere to bury her. So he said to some Hittites, with whom he was staying, "I am a foreigner and a stranger among you. Sell me some property for a burial site" (23:4). There followed a typical Near-Eastern bargaining procedure, which ended with Abraham paying four hundred shekels of silver for a field with its cave and trees near Mamre (Hebron), in which in due course all the patriarchs were buried.

They all received the promise but "did not receive the things promised" (Heb. 11:13, 39). Promised a land, they received only a field; they were longing for a better country, "a heavenly one" (Heb. 11:16). For God's promises are not inherited through faith only, but "through faith and patience" (Heb. 6:12).

For further reading: Genesis 17:1–14

THURSDAY

Isaac and the Faithfulness of God

ISAAC PRAYED TO THE LORD ON BEHALF OF HIS WIFE, BECAUSE SHE WAS
CHILDLESS. THE LORD ANSWERED HIS PRAYER...

Genesis 25:21

Isaac began well. His parents must have told him the circumstances of his birth, why he was called Isaac ("Laughter"), and the meaning of his circumcision. Then stamped forever on his memory was his traumatic adolescent experience on Mount Moriah – the horror when he realized that he was to be sacrificed and the ecstasy when he was released. Twice he owed his life to God's faithfulness – his supernatural birth and his providential rebirth.

Then came Abraham's resolve that Isaac should marry not a Canaanite woman but one of his own relatives. It was not an ethnic but a religious decision, to ensure that the line of the covenant would be preserved. The whole of Genesis 24 is devoted to the story of how, in answer to prayer and common sense, Rebekah became Isaac's wife. As her brother Laban said, "This is from the LORD" (v. 50). Yet for twenty years Rebekah failed to conceive. But when Isaac prayed for her, she became pregnant with twins. It was one more clear example of the faithfulness of God to his covenant.

But with her pregnancy things changed. Aware that she was carrying twins, she consulted the Lord about their future, and he told her that two peoples were within her and that the older would serve the younger. It was an unequivocal revelation of God's will. His promise to Abraham and Isaac was to be fulfilled not through the firstborn, Esau, but through the younger twin, Jacob. But Isaac resisted God's will and determined to give the blessing of the firstborn to Esau.

It is wonderful that, in spite of Isaac's mixed-up behaviour, God is still willing to style himself the God of Abraham, Isaac, and Jacob.

For further reading: Genesis 24:59–67

Jacob and the Persevering Love of God

JACOB REPLIED, "I WILL NOT LET YOU GO UNLESS YOU BLESS ME."

Genesis 32:26

Jacob is a particularly important patriarch because he was the father of the chosen people, who came to be known as "the children of Jacob" or "the children of Israel." He is introduced in the Old Testament narrative, however, as a man who knew God's promises but could not trust him to keep them, so that he took things into his own hands to engineer their fulfilment. First he tricked Esau in Canaan. Then in Paddan Aram (Mesopotamia) he and his brother-in-law Laban spent their time deceiving one another. Jacob was more a schemer than a believer.

Now, on his return from Paddan Aram, we read that "Jacob was left alone" (v. 24). Yet God refused to leave him alone. He came to him in his aloneness. That night Jacob met God in a decisive and transforming encounter. It was in two stages.

First God wrestled with Jacob. We know that it was God (a theophany) because Jacob later called the place Peniel, meaning "the face of God." God wrestled with him in order by love to conquer him and continued the struggle until daybreak without success. Then when he "saw that he could not overpower him" (v. 25), God touched and dislocated his thigh. A single touch of the divine finger was enough; Jacob surrendered. With us too God begins gently and perseveres in love. But if we still resist, he resorts to more drastic measures until he touches and breaks us.

In the second stage the wrestlers changed places, and Jacob wrestled with God. "Let me go," God said, but Jacob responded, "I will not let you go unless you bless me" (v. 26). It is as if Jacob said to God, "You promised to bless Abraham, my father Isaac, and me. Now fulfil your promise and bless me!" So "he blessed him there" (v. 29). God wrestles with us in order to break down our stubbornness; we wrestle with God in order to inherit his promises.

For further reading: Genesis 32:22–32

Joseph and the Providence of God

Joseph said... "You intended to harm me, but God intended it for good..."

Genesis 50:19–20

The Old Testament sometimes teaches several lessons from the same events. The story of Joseph is a notable case in point. Firstly, a lesson in history. Through the clash of empires (secular history), God has been working out the story of his own people ("salvation history"). The God of Abraham, Isaac, and Jacob reconfirmed his covenant in each generation. But now in Jacob's old age God's purpose was threatened by famine. So Jacob sent his sons to buy grain in Egypt. As Joseph was to say to them later, "God sent me ahead of you to preserve for you a remnant on earth and to save your lives by a great deliverance" (45:7).

Secondly, a lesson in providence. Joseph was the victim of a series of injustices. He was successively captured, sold, enslaved, falsely accused, imprisoned without trial, and forgotten by his fellow prisoners, who had promised to speak up for him. Yet even through these evils God was at work for good. As Joseph said to his brothers, "You intended to harm me, but God intended it for good... the saving of many lives" (50:20).

Thirdly, a lesson in forgiveness. Joseph could have reacted to his brothers either in revenge or in cheap forgiveness. Instead, he put their apparent repentance to the test. He took his younger brother Benjamin as a hostage. It was a dramatic moment. The brothers had sacrificed Joseph; would they now sacrifice Benjamin? No! Judah came forward and pleaded for the boy's release, even offering himself for slavery as a substitute. What a transformation had come over Joseph's brothers! Their repentance was evidently real. Joseph was satisfied. So he made himself known to them and demonstrated his forgiveness by embracing them.

For further reading: Genesis 50:15–21

Week 6: Moses and the Exodus

The book of Genesis ends with two deaths in Egyptian exile. First Jacob died and was taken back to Canaan to be buried in the cave of Machpelah, near Hebron, which Abraham had bought as a burial place for his relatives. Later Joseph died, also in Egypt, although with a double assurance, namely that in due course God would bring his people into the land of promise, and meanwhile that they would bring his bones to the family burial ground.

Now we move on and will spend this week following the career of Moses, Israel's greatest leader after Abraham. It was Moses who secured the release of the Israelites from their oppression in Egypt, who led them across the Red Sea (or "the Sea of Reeds") into safety, and who took them to Mount Sinai. Moses continued to lead the people during their forty years of wilderness wanderings. It was he who assembled them in the desert east of the Jordan, ready to cross over into the Promised Land, and who reminded them of their history, pleading with them to be faithful to the covenant. This story of Moses dominates four books of the Pentateuch – Exodus, Leviticus, Numbers, and Deuteronomy. Finally, he died, having seen the Promised Land from Mount Nebo, though he was not permitted to enter it.

Sunday: A Cruel Oppression

Monday: The Call of Moses

Tuesday: The Challenge to Pharaoh

Wednesday: The Passover

Thursday: The Exodus from Egypt

Friday: The Blessings of Mount Sinai

Saturday: Wilderness Wanderings

A Cruel Oppression

THE ISRAELITES GROANED IN THEIR SLAVERY... GOD HEARD THEIR
GROANING AND HE REMEMBERED HIS COVENANT...

Exodus 2:23–24

The book of Exodus opens with a vivid description of the oppression of the Israelites by a new pharaoh (probably Rameses II), who did not know about Joseph. The Egyptians "made their lives bitter with harsh labour in brick and mortar and with all kinds of work in the fields" (1:14). Their oppression lasted 430 years. But they cried to God for deliverance, and he remembered his covenant with Abraham, Isaac, and Jacob. Indeed, he was already preparing their deliverer.

As a child Moses narrowly escaped being drowned in the River Nile. Then he was brought up first by his own mother and then by Pharaoh's daughter. We can only guess the conflict he experienced between the Egyptian and Hebrew cultures. But he never lost either his sense of Hebrew identity or his hot indignation over his people's sufferings. At some point he made a costly and courageous decision: "By faith Moses, when he had grown up, refused to be known as the son of Pharaoh's daughter. He chose to be ill-treated along with the people of God rather than to enjoy the fleeting pleasures of sin" (Heb. 11:24–25).

But although his love for his people and his resolve to identify with them were admirable, he was reckless enough to take the law into his own hands. He killed an Egyptian who was beating a Hebrew, and the following day he tried to arbitrate between two fighting Hebrews. His intervention was not appreciated. What he had done had become known, and he had to flee to the land of Midian (the Sinai peninsula) to cool his heels for forty years. He had to learn that God's will must be done only in God's way.

For further reading: Exodus 2:11–15, 23–25

MONDAY

The Call of Moses

THE LORD SAID [TO MOSES]... "SO NOW, GO. I AM SENDING YOU TO
PHARAOH TO BRING MY PEOPLE THE ISRAELITES OUT OF EGYPT."

Exodus 3:7, 10

Being a fugitive from Pharaoh, Moses must have been apprehensive that his hiding place would be discovered. But at some point Pharaoh died (2:23). Hoping that a change of regime might mean a change of policy, the Israelite slaves increased their cries for help.

So the scene seemed to be set for a fresh commissioning of Moses. It happened near Mount Horeb (i.e., Mount Sinai). Here God spoke to him from within a burning bush. He had seen his people's misery, he said. He had heard their groaning, he was concerned about their suffering, and so now he had come down to rescue them from Egypt, to bring them into the Promised Land and to do it through Moses.

How did Moses respond to the divine call? He had evidently learned his lesson during those forty years of humbling in the desert. Indeed, he had now swung too far in the opposite direction. He advanced five excuses. Did he feel unfit for the task? God would be with him. Would the Israelites question the identity of his God? He must announce him as the God of his fathers, Yahweh, the living and eternal God. What if the people did not listen or believe? Moses must use his staff to perform miracles and so authenticate his ministry. Fourthly, Moses insisted, he was slow of speech and lacked eloquence. But God responded that he was the creator of the mouth and would tell Moses what to say. When finally Moses blurted out, "Please send somebody else," God was angry but also gave him his brother Aaron to be his mouthpiece.

It is always best to respond to God's call neither with extreme self-confidence nor with complete self-doubt, but with humble trust in the living God who equips those he calls.

For further reading: Exodus 3:1–11

TUESDAY

The Challenge to Pharaoh

AND THE EGYPTIANS WILL KNOW THAT I AM THE LORD WHEN I STRETCH
OUT MY HAND AGAINST EGYPT AND BRING THE ISRAELITES OUT OF IT.

Exodus 7:5

Moses and Aaron went boldly to Pharaoh, and in the name of Yahweh demanded the release of the Israelite slaves. But they had been warned that Pharaoh would refuse to humble himself. The narrative sometimes attributes his stubbornness to God (e.g., "I will harden Pharaoh's heart" [v. 3]) and sometimes to Pharaoh himself (e.g., "He hardened his heart and would not listen" [8:15]). We do not have to choose, for God hardens those who harden themselves.

Moses had brought his staff with him, and whenever he stretched it out, a fresh judgment fell on the Egyptian population. There were successively ten so-called plagues. The waters of the Nile were turned into blood, and frogs overran the land. Next came the plagues of gnats and of flies, followed by a killing disease afflicting livestock and boils afflicting man and beast. A hailstorm destroyed crops and stripped trees, and a huge swarm of locusts consumed whatever the hail had left. A strange darkness crept over the land, and as a terrible climax, the firstborn of all human beings and animals died.

Consider the nature and purpose of these plagues. They were not all supernatural. For example, the plague of locusts was a common natural phenomenon. The miraculous element lay in the timing, that they were blown in by an east wind at the exact moment when Moses lifted his staff.

What was their purpose? Partly to bring judgment on the recalcitrant Egyptians and partly to persuade Pharaoh to release the Israelites, but supremely, God said that "you may know that there is no one like me in all the earth" (9:14). Throughout these chapters the simple refrain keeps ringing out – "that you may know that I am the LORD." We could have no higher ambition than this.

For further reading: Exodus 7:1–7

The Passover

WHEN THE LORD GOES THROUGH THE LAND TO STRIKE DOWN THE
EGYPTIANS, HE WILL SEE THE BLOOD ON THE TOP AND SIDES OF THE
DOOR-FRAME AND WILL PASS OVER THAT DOORWAY...

Exodus 12:23

God gave clear instructions about the tenth and final plague. At about midnight he would pass through Egypt in judgment, and all the firstborn of all social classes would die.

But the Israelites would be spared if they killed an unblemished year-old lamb, one per household, and smeared some of its blood on the top and sides of their front doors. They must not go outside, for that night God would pass through Egypt, and when he saw the blood, he would pass over the house to protect it. This Passover festival was to be the beginning of the Israelites' calendar year and was to be celebrated annually.

For Christians, Jesus Christ is "the Lamb of God" concerning whom we proclaim, "Christ, our Passover lamb, has been sacrificed. Therefore let us keep the Festival" (1 Cor. 5:7–8). We can learn several truths from the Passover story. Firstly, the Judge and the Saviour are the same person. God who passed through Egypt to judge the firstborn also passed over Israelite homes to shelter them. We must never characterize the Father as Judge and the Son as Saviour. It is one and the same God who through Jesus Christ saves us from his own judgment.

Secondly, salvation was (and is) by substitution. The only firstborn males who were spared were those in whose household a firstborn lamb had died instead. Thirdly, the lamb's blood had to be sprinkled after it had been shed. There had to be an individual appropriation of the divine provision. God had to see the blood before he could save the family.

Fourthly, each family rescued by God was thereby purchased for God. Their whole life now belonged to him. So does ours. And consecration leads to celebration. The life of God's redeemed people is a continuous feast, ritually expressed in the Eucharist, which is our Christian festival of thanksgiving.

For further reading: Revelation 5:6–14

The Exodus from Egypt

WHEN THE ISRAELITES SAW THE MIGHTY HAND OF THE LORD DISPLAYED
AGAINST THE EGYPTIANS, THE PEOPLE FEARED THE LORD AND PUT THEIR
TRUST IN HIM...

Exodus 14:31

After the Israelites had made their escape, Pharaoh and his officials changed their minds. "What have we done?" they asked themselves, realizing that they had lost the valuable slave labour of the Israelites. So Pharaoh marshalled his army, and they went in hot pursuit of the fugitives. Hemmed in by desert, water, and mountain, the Israelites saw the approaching Egyptians and were terrified. "Was it because there were no graves in Egypt that you brought us to the desert to die?" they cried to Moses (v. 11). But Moses, with sublime confidence in God, replied, "The LORD will fight for you; you need only to be still" (v. 14).

Israel's actual deliverance from the pursuing Egyptian army is described in graphic detail. Twice, at the command of God, Moses lifted his rod and stretched out his hand over the sea. On the first occasion it was night, the sea was driven back by a strong east wind, and the Israelites went through, but the Egyptians were thrown into confusion. The second time it was daybreak, the water resumed its place, and the Egyptians were drowned, but the Israelites went through to safety.

Israel never forgot the exodus. It was a signal display of Yahweh's power and mercy in saving them from their enemies and in establishing them as his special people. Moses sang of it. So did his sister Miriam, with tambourines and dancing. Indeed, it became a major theme of Israel's public worship:

> I will sing to the LORD,
> for he is highly exalted.
> The horse and driver
> he has hurled into the sea.
> The LORD is my strength and my song;
> he has become my salvation.

Exodus 15:1–2

We find it easy to translate this into Christian language, for we celebrate an even greater victory (Jesus Christ's) and an even greater redemption (from sin and death).

For further reading: Psalms 106:7–12; 114

FRIDAY

The Blessings of Mount Sinai

ALTHOUGH THE WHOLE EARTH IS MINE, YOU WILL BE FOR ME A KINGDOM
OF PRIESTS AND A HOLY NATION.

Exodus 19:5–6

It took the Israelites about three months to reach Mount Sinai for the rendezvous with Yahweh that he had proposed to Moses. Once encamped at the foot of the mountain, they stayed about a year. And here God gave his redeemed people three precious gifts – a renewed covenant, a moral law, and atoning sacrifices.

The renewal of the covenant came first. Again and again during the story of the patriarchs, God had announced himself as the God who had made a covenant with Abraham and renewed it with Isaac and Jacob. And the exodus took place because he had remembered his covenant. But now that the exile was over and the prospect of the Promised Land was before them, it was time to confirm or renew the covenant. So God told Moses to say to Israel, "You yourselves have seen what I did to Egypt, and how I carried you on eagles' wings and brought you to myself. Now if you obey me fully and keep my covenant, then out of all nations you will be my treasured possession" (vv. 4–5).

Secondly, God gave Israel a moral law, obedience to which would be Israel's side of the covenant. Its essence was the Ten Commandments, elaborated and supplemented by other statutes. These we will be considering next week. Thirdly, God made generous provision for remedying any breaches of his law. This involved the building of the tabernacle, the institution of a sacrificial system, and the appointment of a priesthood to administer it.

The essential significance of these arrangements was a profound paradox. On the one hand, God said, "I will dwell among them" (25:8). But on the other hand, nobody was permitted to penetrate through the veil into the inner sanctuary of the tabernacle except the high priest on the Day of Atonement, taking sacrificial blood with him. So the veil stood for the inaccessibility of God to sinners. This paradoxical combination of access and inaccessibility was done away by Christ, when the veil of the temple was torn down from top to bottom. Now all of us are invited to draw near to God through Christ.

For further reading: Hebrews 10:19–25

Saturday

Wilderness Wanderings

WE ARE SETTING OUT FOR THE PLACE ABOUT WHICH THE LORD SAID,
"I WILL GIVE IT TO YOU."

Numbers 10:29

It must have been a moment of great excitement when the people of Israel set out for the Promised Land. At long last, some seven centuries after God had first made his promise to Abraham, it was about to be fulfilled. But their expectation was short-lived. Moses' plan to send twelve scouts (one for each tribe) to reconnoitre the land ended in disaster. For although they returned with ripe fruit to prove that Canaan was indeed a land flowing with milk and honey, ten of them also declared that its inhabitants were invincible. This majority view prevailed. So none of that generation would enter the Promised Land, only the faithful Caleb and Joshua.

Forty years were now to elapse between the exodus from Egypt and the entry into Canaan – years in which they wandered from oasis to oasis and in which they experienced a variety of adventures, which are recorded in the book of Numbers. At last, however, the forty years were ended, and the whole adult generation had died out. Israel was now encamped on the plains of Moab, a little north and east of where the River Jordan flows into the Dead Sea.

Here Moses addressed the people for the last time, and his speeches are recorded in the book of Deuteronomy. He rehearsed their recent history and its lessons, and he sought to prepare them for taking possession of the Promised Land. But his main emphasis was on the covenant of love that bound Yahweh and his people together. Yahweh had set his love on them and chosen them, Moses said, not because of any merit in them but solely because he loved them (Deut. 7:7–8). So now they must love him in return with all their being and express their love in their obedience (Deut. 6:4–9; 10:12–13).

It is extraordinary that our Lord Jesus took these words to himself, saying, "Whoever has my commands and keeps them is the one who loves me" (John 14:21). The test of love is obedience.

For further reading: Deuteronomy 6:1–12

Week 7: The Ten Commandments

As during this week we consider the Ten Commandments and their implications for us today, we need to remember three truths about them.

Firstly, the Ten Commandments were laid down by the covenant God of Israel as his will for his people. They were introduced by the statement, "I am the LORD your God, who brought you out of Egypt" (Exod. 20:2). Obedience to the commandments was Israel's side of the covenant.

Secondly, the Ten Commandments were summarized by Jesus, who brought together the separate injunctions to love God with our whole being and to love our neighbour as ourselves (Deut. 6:5; Lev. 19:18; Matt. 22:37–39): "All the Law and the Prophets hang on these two commandments," Jesus said (Matt. 22:40).

Thirdly, the Ten Commandments can be obeyed only by the power of the indwelling Holy Spirit. As Paul put it, God sent his Son "in order that the righteous requirement of the law might be fully met in us, who… live… according to the Spirit" (Rom. 8:4). Without the Spirit's inner working, the radical heart obedience Jesus demanded in the Sermon on the Mount would be impossible.

Sunday: Commandments 1 and 2

Monday: Commandments 3 and 4

Tuesday: Commandment 5

Wednesday: Commandment 6

Thursday: Commandment 7

Friday: Commandment 9

Saturday: Commandments 8 and 10

Sunday

Commandments 1 and 2

YOU SHALL HAVE NO OTHER GODS BEFORE ME. YOU SHALL NOT MAKE FOR
YOURSELF AN IMAGE... YOU SHALL NOT BOW DOWN TO THEM OR WORSHIP
THEM.

Exodus 20:3–5

To forbid the worship of other gods "before" or "beside" Yahweh implies that there are no other gods. "I am the LORD, and there is no other" (Isa. 45:6).

We do not need to worship the sun, the moon, and the stars to break this first commandment. We break it whenever we give first place in our lives to anybody or anything other than God. Instead, we are to love him with all our powers, making his will our delight and his glory our goal.

If the first commandment demands our exclusive worship, the second requires that our worship is spiritual and sincere. For, as Jesus said, "God is spirit, and his worshippers must worship in the spirit and in truth" (John 4:24). The prohibition of idols should not be interpreted as forbidding us to make any visual representations but rather as forbidding us to worship one. It also surely forbids external forms that have no inward reality, drawing near to God with our lips when our hearts are far from him (Isa. 29:13; Mark 7:6).

Two problems confront us in the second commandment. First, it is here that God describes himself as "a jealous God" (Exod. 20:5). There is no need to be offended by this, however. Jealousy is the resentment of rivals, and God is jealous in this sense. He refuses to share his glory with another because there is no other with whom to share it.

The second problem is that God is said to punish children for the sins of their fathers. This may appear unfair. But it is certainly true that children suffer the consequences of their parents' sins. These may be transmitted physically (by inherited disease), socially (in the poverty caused by excessive gambling or drinking), psychologically (by the tensions and conflicts of an unhappy home), and morally (in behaviour learned from a bad example).

For further reading: John 4:19–24

Commandments 3 and 4

YOU SHALL NOT MISUSE THE NAME OF THE LORD YOUR GOD...
REMEMBER THE SABBATH DAY BY KEEPING IT HOLY.

Exodus 20:7–8

By bracketing these two commandments, we see that both the Lord's name and the Lord's Day are to be treated with great respect. What kind of misuse of God's name is envisaged? The commandment certainly forbids blasphemy and profanity. It will also include false swearing, that is, taking an oath and breaking it. It is better, Jesus taught, not to swear at all. Honest people do not need to make promises by oath; a simple yes or no should be enough (Matt. 5:33–37). Then there is a yet more serious misuse of God's name. It arises from the fact that a name is more than a word; it is a person and that person's character. We then misuse God's name whenever our behaviour is incompatible with his character. To call God "Father" and mistrust him or to call Jesus "Lord" and disobey him: this is to misuse his name.

Moving on from the third to the fourth commandment, and so from the Lord's name to the Lord's Day, we notice that it begins, "Remember the Sabbath day." This indicates that it was already being observed. Indeed, as we have seen, it goes back to the beginning of Genesis. So, being a creation ordinance, it is God's provision for everybody and not only for his covenant people. It was also extended to your manservant and maidservant, the reason being that the Israelites themselves had been slaves in Egypt until the Lord delivered them (Deut. 5:15).

Luke tells us that it was Jesus' custom to attend the synagogue on the Sabbath day (Luke 4:16). But he was entirely free from the traditional rules and regulations that had encrusted the law of Sabbath observance (a grand total of 1,521 according to Rabbi Johanan and Rabbi Simeon ben Lakish). In contrast, Jesus insisted on the principle that "the Sabbath was made for man, not man for the Sabbath" (Mark 2:27).

For further reading: Matthew 5:33–37

Commandment 5

HONOUR YOUR FATHER AND YOUR MOTHER, SO THAT YOU MAY LIVE LONG
IN THE LAND THE LORD YOUR GOD IS GIVING YOU.

Exodus 20:12

Since the first four commandments clearly relate to our duty to God (his being, worship, name, and day), some think that the fifth commandment introduces our duty to our neighbour, since it concerns the honouring of our parents. It seems more appropriate to other students, however, to regard the fifth commandment as still belonging to our duty to God. This is partly because five commandments are then attributed to each duty and partly because our parents (at least during our minority) stand in the place of God and mediate his authority to us.

The apostle Paul understood this honouring of our parents to require obedience and called this both right and pleasing to Christ (Eph. 6:1; Col. 3:20). Disobedience to parents is seen in the New Testament as a symptom of social disintegration (see Rom. 1:30; 2 Tim. 3:2).

At the same time, parental authority is not absolute. It is restricted to those who, according to their particular culture, are regarded as minors. Moreover, if children have a duty to their parents, parents also have a duty to their children. They must neither "exasperate" nor "embitter" them but rather "bring them up in the training and instruction of the Lord" (Eph. 6:4; Col. 3:21). The reciprocal nature of their duties should place a firm check on both.

As life expectancy rises in the Western world, and the average age of the population rises proportionately, an increasing number of old and infirm people are neglected and even forgotten by their own children. It is a shocking phenomenon largely confined to the West. In Africa and Asia the extended family always finds room for the elderly. So does the traditional Chinese culture. I think we should give Paul the last word on this matter: "Anyone who does not provide for their relatives, and especially for their own household, has denied the faith and is worse than an unbeliever" (1 Tim. 5:8).

For further reading: Ephesians 6:1–4

WEDNESDAY

Commandment 6

YOU SHALL NOT MURDER.
Exodus 20:13

The more familiar translation "you shall not kill" is misleading. The sixth commandment cannot be interpreted as an absolute ban on all killing, including the killing of animals, since the same Mosaic law contained the sacrificial system, capital punishment for extreme offences, and even "holy war" against the Canaanites. It is certainly possible to argue in favour of being a vegetarian, an abolitionist, or a pacifist on other grounds, but not on this ground. What the sixth commandment prohibits is the unauthorized shedding of innocent blood, that is, murder. For Scripture insists on the sanctity not so much of life in general (which is a Buddhist doctrine) as of human life in particular, because it is the life of human beings made in God's image. It is this that makes murder such a heinous offence and indeed a capital offence (Gen. 9:6; Rom. 13:4), even if, since God himself protected the first murderer, the sentence should be commuted if there are any mitigating circumstances.

The same principle of the sanctity of human life is at stake when the human embryo is threatened. The embryo is at the very least a human being in the making and should therefore be inviolable. Consequently, most Christian opinion is pro-life rather than pro-choice. It rejects the destruction of the embryo by abortion as a form of murder, except for a very few carefully defined exceptions, and believes that experimentation on human embryos should be banned by law.

War is another issue that involves the taking of human life. Throughout the centuries Christian opinion has been divided. Pacifists argue that Jesus' teaching and example prohibit all retaliation. But defenders of the "just war" theory believe that war may be permissible as the lesser of two evils if several conditions are fulfilled. They justify war as a last resort only and reject the use of all weapons of mass destruction because in the nature of the case these are both uncontrolled and indiscriminate. Our final comment on the sixth commandment is to note that Jesus in the Sermon on the Mount went beyond the deed of murder to murderous thoughts and insulting words (Matt. 5:21–22). The apostle John was quite outspoken, writing, "Anyone who hates a brother or sister is a murderer" (1 John 3:15).

For further reading: 1 John 3:11–15

Thursday

Commandment 7

You shall not commit adultery.
Exodus 20:14

Christians believe that sex, marriage, and family are all good gifts of a good Creator, in spite of the reputation we seem to have acquired to the contrary. We believe that from the beginning of human history God made us male and female, that our distinctive sexuality (masculinity and femininity) is therefore his creation, and that he instituted marriage (for it is his idea, not ours) for the mutual fulfilment of both partners as well as for the procreation of children. Then Paul added the beautiful truth that husband and wife in their love for one another are intended to reflect the relationship between Christ and his church.

It is when these great positives have been established that the biblical prohibitions make sense. It is precisely because God has instituted marriage as his own intended context for sexual enjoyment that he forbids it in all other contexts. True, only adultery is explicitly condemned, because it is a direct assault on marriage. But other forms of sexual immorality are implicitly included, because they too undermine marriage. Cohabitation, for example, involving sex before marriage, even sex without marriage, is an attempt to experience love without commitment. It can also become cruel by arousing in one partner desires for a long-term relationship that the other is not prepared to fulfil. Then it should also be clear that a same-sex partnership is not a legitimate alternative to heterosexual marriage but is rather incompatible with God's created and natural order. The only "one flesh" experience God has authorized is within heterosexual monogamy. As George Carey, former Archbishop of Canterbury, said in April 2002, "Any sexual relationship beyond the confines of a heterosexual marriage is a deviation from Scripture."

Finally, as with murder, Jesus extended the prohibition of adultery to include our thoughts as well as our deeds. "Anyone who looks at a woman lustfully has already committed adultery with her in his heart" (Matt. 5:28). In consequence, Jesus continued, if our eye causes us to sin, we must "gouge it out" (Matt. 5:29). That is, if temptation comes to us through our eyes (whether of flesh or of fantasy), the only way to resist is by a radical rejection and not even to look.

For further reading: Proverbs 5:15–23

FRIDAY

Commandment 9

YOU SHALL NOT GIVE FALSE TESTIMONY AGAINST YOUR NEIGHBOUR.

Exodus 20:16

Because commandment 8 ("You shall not steal") and commandment 10 ("You shall not covet") obviously belong to each other, we will take them together tomorrow and consider commandment 9 ("You shall not give false testimony") today.

The second half of the Decalogue expresses that respect for other people's rights that is implicit in true love. For "love does no harm to a neighbour" (Rom. 13:10), whereas the sins prohibited here would rob others of some of their most precious possessions. These commandments are therefore designed to protect people – their life against the murderer; their marriage, home, and family against the adulterer; their property against the thief; and now their reputation against the false witness. Certainly a good name is a most treasured possession; indeed, it is "more desirable than great riches... better than silver or gold" (Prov. 22:1).

The main context to which this commandment belongs is of course the law court. As judge and jury listen to the case for the prosecution and the defence, the accused person's fate is largely in the hands of the witnesses who are called to testify on oath and who then submit to questioning and cross-questioning. Perjury (the wilful giving of false witness) is an extremely serious offence. Yet it is not unknown. Jesus is by no means the only prisoner who has suffered at the hands of false witnesses.

False witness can also be borne in other contexts, for example, in the home, the neighbourhood, and the workplace. Then it takes the form of slander. It will include deliberate exaggerations and distortions of the truth. The prohibition of false witness carries with it the complementary responsibility to be a true witness. Even if, in extreme circumstances, a so-called white lie may be justified as the lesser of two evils, it is still an evil. Our word should be known to be trustworthy, and above all we should bear a bold witness to our Lord Jesus Christ.

For further reading: James 3:1–12

SATURDAY

Commandments 8 and 10

YOU SHALL NOT STEAL... YOU SHALL NOT COVET...
Exodus 20:15, 17

You shall not steal. The prohibition of theft presupposes that citizens have a right to hold private property and that a distinction needs to be drawn between what is mine and what is yours. Otherwise an ordered, just, and stable society would be impossible. Moreover, what is prohibited is more than the straightforward stealing of money or property; it includes all forms of dishonesty and cheating, tax evasion and customs dodging, working short hours, overcharging, and underpaying.

You shall not covet. The tenth commandment is particularly important because it transforms the Decalogue from a civil code into a moral law. We cannot be prosecuted in court for covetousness, since covetousness is not an action but an attitude of the heart. In fact, covetousness is to theft what anger is to murder and lust is to adultery.

The prohibition of covetousness speaks loudly to the consumerism that has engulfed the Western world today. Yet Jesus told us to beware of covetousness, and Paul pointed us instead to a life of contentment, simplicity, and generosity. For like the Israelites in the wilderness, we are pilgrims travelling to the Promised Land, and we will be wise to travel light.

The Ten Commandments are an exposition of what it means to love God and our neighbour, and they expose and condemn our sin. As Paul confesses, he would never have known what sin was if the law had not said, "You shall not covet" (Rom. 7:7). Similarly, Luther called the law a mighty "hammer" to crush our self-righteousness; it is in this sense that the law is our "schoolmaster" to bring us to Christ (Gal. 3:24 KJV). When C. H. Spurgeon, the famous nineteenth-century London preacher, was only a teenager, he had a profound sense of his sinfulness. It was not that he had been guilty of any particular sins, but he said, "I met Moses" carrying the law, and it condemned him and showed him his need of a Saviour.

For further reading: 1 Timothy 6:6–10

Deuteronomy ends with the death of Moses. But before he died he laid his hands on Joshua, appointing him as his successor. At last, under Joshua's leadership promise became possession as the Israelites entered into their inheritance in Canaan. Then as an old man Joshua challenged Israel to remain true to Yahweh's covenant. Following Joshua's death, throughout a period of nearly two hundred years, Israel was ruled by so-called judges, and the same monotonous cycle of backsliding, oppression, and deliverance kept repeating itself. Samuel was the last judge. He yielded to popular demand and appointed Saul king. Saul's reign, however, was largely a disaster on account of his repeated unfaithfulness.

Sunday: Taking Possession of the Land

Monday: Keeping the Covenant

Tuesday: Israelite Backsliding

Wednesday: Judging the Judges

Thursday: The Life and Ministry of Samuel

Friday: Saul's Early Promise

Saturday: Saul's Later Unfaithfulness

Sunday

Taking Possession of the Land

So the Lord gave Israel all the land he had sworn to give their ancestors, and they took possession of it and settled there.

Joshua 21:43

After crossing the River Jordan, Joshua first turned south and routed a confederate army led by five Amorite kings. Then he marched north where he defeated a coalition of armies. Thus he took the whole land and allotted its territory to the twelve tribes. We cannot read the story of Israel's conquest, however, without asking ourselves about the ethics of such a campaign, with its policy of total destruction. Can the holy God of Israel really have ordered this? Three points may be made.

Consider, firstly, *the promise made to the patriarchs*. Repeatedly God had promised the land to Abraham's descendants. But the possession of it would not have been possible without the dispossession of its former inhabitants. Secondly, there was *the wickedness of the Canaanites*. Abraham was told that his descendants would inherit the land only when "the sin of the Amorites… reached its full measure" (Gen. 15:16). It was not because of Israel's righteousness but on account of the Canaanites' wickedness that Yahweh would give the Israelites the land (Deut. 9:4–5). So disgusting, idolatrous, and immoral was the Canaanite fertility religion, including the abomination of child sacrifice, that their ejection by Israel was portrayed as the land vomiting her out. God even warned Israel that if she defiled the land, he would vomit her out as he had vomited out the nations (Lev. 18:24–30; 20:22–23; Deut. 12:31).

Thirdly, there was *the danger of corruption*. "Make no treaty with them," Moses told the Israelites (Deut. 7:2). They were to destroy all Canaan's idolatrous paraphernalia, for Israel was a people holy to the Lord (Deut. 7:6). They must not imitate Canaan's detestable practices (Deut. 18:9) or do anything to violate Yahweh's covenant with them (Judg. 2:1, 20; Ezra 9:1, 10–12). This "holy war" is the only one authorized by Yahweh. If Israel had obeyed God and had totally destroyed the Canaanites and their corrupt practices, future conflicts with surrounding tribes would not have been necessary. We too are called to radical surgery in relation to sin.

For further reading: Joshua 24:8–13

MONDAY

Keeping the Covenant

ON THAT DAY JOSHUA MADE A COVENANT FOR THE PEOPLE, AND THERE
AT SHECHEM HE REAFFIRMED FOR THEM DECREES AND LAWS.

Joshua 24:25

Yahweh is a covenant God who has bound himself to us in a solemn pledge saying, "I will be your God, and you shall be my people." It began with Abraham. It continued with Isaac, Jacob, and Joseph. Moses was clear that his ministry was in fulfilment of it. And now it was essential for Joshua to know that he stood in the same succession. So the beginning and end of the book of Joshua contain important references to the covenant. After the Israelites crossed the River Jordan, God told Joshua to make flint knives and circumcise the Israelites, since circumcision was the sign of the covenant and there had not been any circumcision during the forty years of wilderness wanderings. Now that they were circumcised, they were eligible to celebrate the Passover.

Then the book of Joshua concludes with a renewal of the covenant at Shechem. What is particularly fascinating is that, in presenting the covenant, Joshua deliberately followed the pattern of vassal-treaties (recently discovered in the ancient Near East) between a conquered nation and the great king or conqueror. After an introduction of the parties to the treaty, a historical sketch is given. Then follow the treaty conditions and a list of witnesses, and the document concludes with blessings if the treaty is kept and warnings if it is violated. All these aspects of a vassal-treaty can be found in Joshua 24.

The followers of Jesus Christ are heirs of God's covenant with Abraham. Baptism and the Lord's Supper are signs of what Jesus called "the new covenant," corresponding to circumcision and the Passover in the Old Testament. Vassal-treaties were renewed annually, but our covenant with God should be renewed daily, or at least every time we attend the Lord's Supper.

For further reading: Joshua 24:19–27

Israelite Backsliding

THEN THE ISRAELITES DID EVIL IN THE EYES OF THE LORD AND SERVED THE BAALS.

Judges 2:11

After the death of faithful Joshua, Israel lapsed for nearly two hundred years into a distressing cycle of disobedience, oppression, and deliverance. Firstly, they forsook Yahweh, the God of their fathers, who had brought them out of Egypt, and they worshipped the gods of the people around them, provoking Yahweh to anger.

Secondly, Yahweh handed them over to raiders who plundered them, defeated them in battle, and oppressed them.

Thirdly, in answer to his people's cry, the Lord raised up "judges" who delivered them from their oppressors. But they refused to listen to their deliverers, and so the dismal cycle of backsliding, defeat, and recovery was repeated again and again (vv. 11–17).

The so-called judges combined several functions. First and foremost, they were military leaders, whom Yahweh raised up to rescue Israel from their oppressors. Thus Ehud delivered Israel from the Moabites, Deborah from the Canaanites, Gideon from the Midianites, Jephthah from the Ammonites, and Samson from the Philistines. Next, they were spiritual leaders, persons of faith and of the Spirit, although exhibiting their devotion to Yahweh in different ways and degrees. Thirdly, they were judges, as their name indicates, hearing cases referred to them and administering justice in Israel.

Yet there appears to have been but little law and order in the land during this period. So twice we read the bald statement that "in those days Israel had no king" (18:1; 19:1), while twice the inevitable consequence of anarchy is added, once as a fitting conclusion to the book: "In those days Israel had no king; everyone did as they saw fit" (17:6; 21:25). It is wonderful that, in spite of Israel's seemingly inveterate backsliding, Yahweh remained faithful to his covenant.

For further reading: Judges 2:10–19

Judging the Judges

EVERYTHING THAT WAS WRITTEN IN THE PAST WAS WRITTEN
TO TEACH US...

Romans 15:4

Paul wrote about Old Testament characters: "These things happened to them as examples and were written down as warnings for us" (1 Cor. 10:11). By "these things" he meant God's judgments on the Israelites' idolatry, immorality, and unbelief. So if they are examples, they are mostly bad examples to be avoided, not good examples to be copied.

We should have no hesitation, therefore, in criticizing some of the judges' behaviour. True, Samson and Jephthah are celebrated among the heroes of faith in Hebrews 11:32, since they were loyal to Yahweh even when surrounded by Baal worshippers. But some of their conduct was deplorable. Samson behaved like an adolescent exhibitionist, and Jephthah should definitely not have sacrificed his daughter to his vow. We know this because child sacrifice was one of the main evils that Yahweh abominated in Canaanite culture.

Not all Israelite people and leaders, however, had been sucked into the vortex of prevailing evil. A beautiful exception was Ruth, whose story is told immediately after the book of Judges. A Bethlehemite couple, Elimelech and Naomi, with their two sons, were driven by famine into the land of Moab. Both sons married Moabite women, one of whom was Ruth. In the course of time, all three husbands died, and Naomi was left with her two daughters-in-law. One of them returned to her Moabite family, but Ruth refused to do so. "Your people will be my people," she said to Naomi, "and your God my God" (Ruth 1:16). She had evidently believed in Yahweh, "under whose wings" she had "come to take refuge" (Ruth 2:12). Then, by a remarkable series of divine providences, a relative of Naomi's named Boaz became Ruth's kinsman-redeemer and married her. Then in due course they became the great-grandparents of David.

The book of Ruth is a touching story of faithfulness in the midst of almost universal disloyalty, a shining light in the dark age of the judges.

For further reading: 1 Corinthians 10:1–11

The Life and Ministry of Samuel

THE LORD WAS WITH SAMUEL AS HE GREW UP, AND HE LET NONE OF
SAMUEL'S WORDS FALL TO THE GROUND.

1 Samuel 3:19

Samuel was the last, and undoubtedly the greatest, of the judges. Dedicated to the Lord by his parents even before his birth, he was brought up at Shiloh under the tutelage of the high priest Eli. While he was still a young man, we are told that "all Israel from Dan to Beersheba recognised that Samuel was attested as a prophet of the LORD" (v. 20). As a judge he went on an annual circuit to the towns around his home (7:15–17), and he sometimes acted as priest as well. Thus he combined within himself the ministries of prophet, priest, and judge.

When Samuel was old, however, and appointed his sons as judges, they did not walk in their father's ways but "accepted bribes and perverted justice" (8:3). So the elders of Israel demanded that Samuel should appoint a king to govern them, thus rejecting God as their king. For Israel had been a theocracy (a nation ruled by God) since its beginning some 250 years previously. Therefore Samuel remonstrated with the elders and warned them that their future kings would oppress them. But the people refused to listen to him and said, "No!... We want a king over us. Then we shall be like all the other nations" (8:19–20). Thus twice Israel demanded a king, and twice they gave the same reason: they wanted to be "like all the other nations." And the Lord told Samuel to acquiesce in their demand.

But it was a tragedy. For Israel had been chosen out of the other nations precisely in order to be a holy nation, a people for God's own possession, different from everybody else. The same dilemma faces the people of God today. Our calling is not to conformity to the world around us but to a radical nonconformity.

For further reading: 1 Samuel 12:1–4

FRIDAY

Saul's Early Promise

SAMUEL SAID TO ALL THE PEOPLE, "DO YOU SEE THE MAN THE LORD HAS
CHOSEN? THERE IS NO ONE LIKE HIM AMONG ALL THE PEOPLE."

1 Samuel 10:24

Israel's first king was Saul. He started well. To begin with, he had an impressive physique, being described as "a head taller" than all his contemporaries (9:2; 10:23). He was also young, handsome, brave, and popular.

In addition, Saul was a patriot. He was incensed by the incursions being made into Israelite territory by the surrounding nations. Near the beginning of his reign he heard that Jabesh Gilead, east of the River Jordan, was being besieged by Nahash, the Ammonite leader. His response was immediate. He mustered a large Israelite army, made a bold dash across the Jordan, and rescued the town's inhabitants. It was such a signal victory that the people reaffirmed Saul as their king with a great celebration.

Saul was not so successful, however, in overthrowing the Philistines, who maintained military garrisons on Israelite soil, from which they sent out raiding parties. It was a constant humiliation to Israel. Yet two Israelite exploits are singled out for mention. First Jonathan, Saul's son, performed a brilliant feat; he climbed up a steep cliff, using his hands and feet; overpowered the Philistine outpost; and secured the pass. The other exploit was, of course, young David's dramatic defeat of Goliath.

Instead of recognizing these and other exploits, however, and giving credit where credit was due, Saul was filled with an insane jealousy. At the beginning of his reign he seems to have had a genuine spiritual experience. For the Spirit of God came upon him in power and changed him into a different person (10:6). But this early promise did not last. He was unable to control his emotions. "An evil spirit from God came forcefully on Saul" (18:10), and anger, bitterness, and jealousy engulfed him.

For further reading: 1 Samuel 9:1–2, 15–17

SATURDAY

Saul's Later Unfaithfulness

SAUL DIED BECAUSE HE WAS UNFAITHFUL TO THE LORD...
1 Chronicles 10:13

Saul's unfaithfulness took the form of disobedience, and three distinct examples of it are given to us. Firstly, Saul usurped a priestly prerogative. He had been told to wait seven days in Gilgal until Samuel arrived in the role of priest to offer sacrifices. But when the specified week passed and Samuel had not come, Saul took the law into his own hands. He was full of excuses. He had "felt compelled" to act, he said. But Samuel said to him, "You have done a foolish thing... You have not kept the command the LORD your God gave you" (1 Sam. 13:12–13). His sin was a mixture of impatience, arrogance, sacrilege, and disobedience.

Secondly, Saul failed to destroy the Amalekites. He had been told that God intended to judge Amalek for attacking Israel soon after they escaped from Egypt when they were weary and unprepared. We considered last Sunday why these nations were to be "devoted to Yahweh," that is, totally destroyed, both people and livestock. But Saul spared Agag, their king, together with the best of the sheep and cattle. When Samuel accused Saul of disobedience, Saul blamed his soldiers and added that they had done it to sacrifice the animals to the Lord. Samuel responded with the memorable words, "To obey is better than sacrifice, and to heed is better than the fat of rams" (1 Sam. 15:22).

Thirdly, Saul consulted a medium. All forms of necromancy (trying to communicate with the dead) were forbidden by the law of Moses (Lev. 19:31; Deut. 18:9–14), and earlier in Saul's reign he "had expelled the mediums and spiritists from the land" (1 Sam. 28:3). So Saul broke both God's law and his own edict.

Saul is an object lesson in the dangers of disobedience. Because he had rejected the word of the Lord, the Lord had rejected him from being king over Israel (1 Sam. 15:26). No wonder the Lord sought in his place "a man after his own heart" (1 Sam. 13:14; see also Acts 13:22). We turn next week to David.

For further reading: 1 Samuel 28:11–20

Week 9: The Monarchy

This week we attempt an overview of nearly five hundred years from the death of Saul to the fall of Jerusalem. At first, under David and Solomon, the monarchy remained united. But with Rehoboam, Solomon's son and heir, it divided into two, the northern kingdom (Israel) and the southern (Judah), which were in constant conflict with one another. The story is told from different perspectives in the books of Samuel, Kings, and Chronicles.

The most striking feature of this period is the rise and increasing influence of the writing prophets. This noble succession began in the middle of the eighth century BC with Amos, the prophet of God's justice, and Hosea, the prophet of God's love. It continued toward the end of the eighth century with Isaiah, the prophet of God's sovereignty, while Jeremiah warned God's people of imminent, inevitable judgment at the hands of the Babylonians and Ezekiel accompanied them into exile and then looked beyond it to their restoration.

Sunday: King David

Monday: King Solomon

Tuesday: The Northern Kingdom

Wednesday: The Message of Amos

Thursday: The Message of Hosea

Friday: Church and State in Judah

Saturday: The Fall of Jerusalem

King David

DAVID SHEPHERDED THEM [GOD'S PEOPLE] WITH INTEGRITY OF HEART...
Psalm 78:72

Already before David ascended the throne, he appeared an attractive and promising character. As a youth, by faith in the living God, he had rid Israel of Goliath, the Philistine champion. He had made a covenant of friendship with Jonathan. Then, having been secretly anointed king by Samuel, the Spirit of the Lord had come upon him. And later, with an extraordinary magnanimity of spirit, he twice spared Saul's life. He also showed statesmanlike qualities, not least in establishing Jerusalem as his capital city.

It is all the more tragic, therefore, that David did not live up to these expectations. In his uncontrolled lust for the beautiful Bathsheba, he broke at least five of the Ten Commandments: he murdered, committed adultery, coveted, stole, and bore false witness. And in his insistence on the taking of a census of men capable of bearing arms, he manifested another kind of weakness, putting his confidence in the arm of the flesh instead of in the arm of the Lord.

In the light of these serious sins, how could he be described as a man "after God's own heart" (1 Sam. 13:14; see also Acts 13:22)? Certainly he had genuinely repented. But, above all, unlike Solomon his successor, his heart did not turn aside to other gods but was "fully devoted to the LORD" (1 Kings 11:4). It is not altogether incongruous, therefore, that the promised Messiah would be "the son of David." He could sing from his heart,

I love you, LORD, my strength.
The LORD is my rock, my fortress and my deliverer;
my God is my rock, in whom I take refuge...
Psalm 18:1–2

For further reading: Psalm 78:70–72

MONDAY

King Solomon

GOD GAVE SOLOMON WISDOM AND VERY GREAT INSIGHT... HE WAS WISER
THAN ANYONE ELSE...

1 Kings 4:29, 31

Soon after Solomon succeeded David on the throne, Yahweh appeared to him in a dream and told him to ask for whatever he wanted. Acknowledging his inexperience, Solomon asked for neither wealth nor fame, neither long life nor victory over his enemies, but for wisdom to govern his people with justice. In consequence, Solomon became something of an administrative genius. He divided the country into twelve regions under twelve royal commissioners. He built a standing army and founded Israel's merchant navy. Its ships, kept in the Gulf of Aqabah, went on adventurous voyages for trade.

Having built palaces for himself and his queen, together with other public edifices, Solomon went on to construct the great temple that his father had wanted to build. Solomon also became a patron of the arts and the composer of many songs and proverbs. His reputation for wisdom, splendour, and justice spread far and wide, and under his rule his people enjoyed peace and prosperity. No wonder Jesus spoke of "Solomon in all his glory" (Matt. 6:29 KJV). Israel had reached the zenith of its magnificence.

All was not well under the surface, however. Solomon did not love the Lord his God with all his heart. Nor did he love his neighbour as himself. On the one hand, he kept a harem of princesses, who "turned his heart after other gods" (1 Kings 11:4). On the other, he was able to maintain his grandiose lifestyle only by oppressive measures such as high taxation and forced labour.

We have now reviewed the three kings of the united monarchy – Saul, David, and Solomon. Each reigned for approximately forty years. Each, in differing degrees, was a mixture of good and evil. And each was a monument to the grace of God.

For further reading: 1 Kings 11:4–6

Tuesday

The Northern Kingdom

IF TODAY YOU WILL BE A SERVANT TO THESE PEOPLE AND SERVE THEM...
THEY WILL ALWAYS BE YOUR SERVANTS.

1 Kings 12:7

When Solomon died, the people assembled to make his son Rehoboam king. They appealed to him to lighten his father's yoke of oppression; then they would serve him. But Rehoboam rashly followed the advice of his young and inexperienced counsellors, who urged him to make his father's yoke even heavier. This folly provoked the ten northern tribes to proclaim their independence of the dynasty of David, and so the divided monarchy began. The northern kingdom was Israel, with Jeroboam its first king and its capital Shechem (later Samaria), while the southern kingdom was Judah, with Rehoboam its first king and its capital Jerusalem.

In order to wean the hearts of his subjects away from the house of David, Jeroboam was resolved to stop them going on pilgrimage to Jerusalem. So he established two alternative sanctuaries (Dan in the north and Bethel in the south) and installed a golden calf in each. Five rather nondescript kings followed him, and then the dynasty of Omri, whose son Ahab married the Phoenician princess Jezebel, began. Jezebel actively promoted the worship of Baal within the royal court and beyond.

This brazen apostasy provoked the prophet Elijah, who, although not a literary prophet like his successors, wins our admiration for his fearless witness. Firstly, he challenged the prophets of Baal to a public contest on Mount Carmel, in which Yahweh was decisively vindicated as the true and living God. Secondly, Elijah confronted the king for murdering Naboth and stealing his vineyard.

Only about thirty years after Jehu's dynasty ended, during which a succession of military rulers occupied the throne, Samaria fell (in 722 BC) to the Assyrians, and the country was colonized, resulting in the mixed population we know as the Samaritans. The judgment of God had fallen on two hundred years of religious unfaithfulness.

For further reading: 1 Kings 12:1–17

The Message of Amos

BUT LET JUSTICE ROLL ON LIKE A RIVER, RIGHTEOUSNESS LIKE
A NEVER-FAILING STREAM!

Amos 5:24

Amos was the first of the eighth-century writing prophets. His fierce denunciations were uttered when Jeroboam II was king of Israel. This second Jeroboam had succeeded in restoring Israel's frontiers almost to what they had been during the reigns of David and Solomon. Peace had brought prosperity, and prosperity luxury. There was also a religious boom, as the local sanctuaries were crowded with worshippers.

But alongside these externals the nation suffered from a profound social and moral decay. In every sphere of society Amos saw evils that needed to be exposed. In the law courts magistrates trampled on the face of the poor, for justice had to be bought with bribes (v. 12). In the marketplace merchants were guilty of "skimping the measure" and "boosting the price" (8:5). In upper-class mansions the wealthy were indulging in luxurious living, eating, and drinking, while ignoring the plight of the poor (4:1; 6:4–6). And in the sanctuaries worshippers were longing for the festivals to be over so that they could get back to their buying and selling (8:5).

One may perhaps single out in Amos's teaching one particular distinctive. Amos insisted that privilege brings responsibility, not immunity to the judgment of God. This is well illustrated in the opening two chapters of Amos's prophecy. He warned of God's judgment on the six surrounding nations – Syria, Philistia, Tyre, Edom, Ammon, and Moab. One can easily imagine the growing enthusiasm of the crowd. But suddenly Amos added God's coming judgment on Judah and Israel too. True, they were God's chosen and covenant people, but this would bring punishment, not immunity to it. It is a solemn warning to us too:

You only have I chosen
of all the families of the earth;
therefore I will punish you
for all your sins.

Amos 3:2

For further reading: Amos 5:18–24

The Message of Hosea

FOR I DESIRE MERCY, NOT SACRIFICE, AND ACKNOWLEDGMENT OF GOD
RATHER THAN BURNT OFFERINGS.

Hosea 6:6

If Amos was the prophet of God's justice, Hosea was the prophet of his love. Moreover, the means by which each received his message from God was different. To Amos God spoke directly, "Go, prophesy to my people Israel" (Amos 7:15), but he revealed his message to Hosea through the pain of his broken marriage.

Perhaps the key sentence in the prophecy of Hosea is the command, "Go, show your love to your wife again… Love her as the LORD loves the Israelites" (Hosea 3:1). This drawing of an analogy between Hosea's love for his wife Gomer and Yahweh's love for his bride Israel is crucial to our understanding. It is not entirely clear how Gomer had misbehaved, but it is evident that she had deserted Hosea, as Israel had Yahweh, and that now Hosea was to woo her back as Yahweh was seeking to bring Israel home again.

Israel's unfaithfulness is called their lack of *hesed*. Often translated "mercy" or "loving-kindness," *hesed* refers essentially to covenant faithfulness and so is well translated "steadfast love." This was Yahweh's will for his people: "I desire mercy [*hesed*]" (6:6). And this was his complaint: "There is no faithfulness [*hesed*], no love, no acknowledgment of God in the land" (4:1). What was there instead? "There is only cursing, lying and murder, stealing and adultery" (4:2). In other words, breaches of the covenant commandments. For "like an adulterous wife this land is guilty of unfaithfulness to the LORD" (1:2) and in turning aside to her "lovers," the fertility gods of the local shrines (2:13). So the call comes to them to repent and return to the Lord. For he is seeking Israel and promises, "I will betroth you to me for ever" (2:19).

The same complaint and call are addressed to us today. As the Lord Jesus said to the church in Ephesus, "I hold this against you: You have forsaken the love you had at first… Repent and do the things you did at first" (Rev. 2:4–5).

For further reading: Hosea 14:1–8

FRIDAY

Church and State in Judah

DO NOT BE AFRAID OF WHAT YOU HAVE HEARD – THOSE WORDS WITH
WHICH THE UNDERLINGS OF THE KING OF ASSYRIA
HAVE BLASPHEMED ME.

2 Kings 19:6

During the rise and fall of the northern kingdom, the southern kingdom lived its parallel existence, although its kings were not very well known. Then, after the fall of Samaria to the Assyrians in 722 BC, and the consequent demise of the northern kingdom, Judah lasted another 135 years (722–587 BC). This period was distinguished by two religious reforms in which kings and prophets cooperated. The first was led by King Hezekiah, with the encouragement of the prophets Micah and Isaiah. The second was led by King Josiah, with the encouragement of his distant cousin the prophet Zephaniah and of the young prophet Jeremiah. We will read more about these prophets in three and four weeks' time.

Hezekiah purged Judah of all the remaining vestiges of Assyrian idolatry, and Isaiah and Micah fulminated against the nation's religious hypocrisy and social injustice. Their witness was summed up in Micah's moving appeal:

> *He has showed you, O mortal, what is good.*
> *And what does the LORD require of you?*
> *To act justly and to love mercy*
> *and to walk humbly with your God.*
>
> **Micah 6:8**

A national crisis occurred in 701 BC when the Assyrian leader Sennacherib laid siege to Jerusalem, shutting Hezekiah up (in his own words) "like a bird in a cage." But Isaiah urged him to stand firm, and the siege was wonderfully lifted. Though Hezekiah's apostate son Manasseh reversed his father's religious policy, Hezekiah's great-grandson Josiah (639–609 BC), while still a young man, initiated another great reform, aided and abetted by the prophet Jeremiah.

These two examples of church–state cooperation should inspire us today. It was not that the king tried to prophesy or that the prophet entered politics. Each stuck to their own calling, but together they were effective.

For further reading: Micah 6:6–8

Saturday

The Fall of Jerusalem

How deserted lies the city, once so full of people! How like a
widow is she, who once was great among the nations!
Lamentations 1:1

In spite of the two religious reforms pioneered by King Hezekiah and King Josiah, their results were neither radical nor lasting. Jeremiah kept complaining that the people "followed the stubborn inclinations of their evil hearts" (Jer. 7:24). King Jehoiakim, in particular, though another of Josiah's sons, rapidly undid his father's good work. He used slave labour to build a luxurious palace for himself (Jer. 22:13–17), and when a scroll containing Jeremiah's words was read to him, he shredded and burned it (Jer. 36:21–23).

Meanwhile, the mighty empire of Assyria had come to an end, as its capital Nineveh fell to the Babylonians in 612 BC. Nebuchadnezzar of Babylon appointed Zedekiah to succeed his brother Jehoiakim. But the new king was weak and indecisive, and "did not humble himself before Jeremiah the prophet, who spoke the word of the Lord" (2 Chron. 36:12). Instead, he openly rebelled against Babylon, and the Babylonian army laid siege to Jerusalem. The famine conditions were appalling, and in 587–586 BC the city fell. Its walls were broken into rubble, Solomon's magnificent temple was burned to the ground, and the people were taken into captivity.

It is hard for us to understand the trauma that God's people felt at the loss of their holy city and temple, the focus of their national life. Had God abandoned his people? Only if we read the book of Lamentations can we begin to sense the hopelessness into which the people plunged. Yet the godly remnant did not despair but trusted in God's unchanging character and covenant:

Yet this I call to mind
and therefore I have hope:
Because of the Lord's great love we are not consumed,
for his compassions never fail.
They are new every morning;
great is your faithfulness.
Lamentations 3:21–23

For further reading: Lamentations 1:1, 6, 12

Week 10: The Wisdom Literature

The Christian mind acknowledges God as the supreme and ultimate reality behind all phenomena. The God-centredness of the Bible (its recognition of God as Creator, Sustainer, Lord, Saviour, Father, and Judge) is basic to the Christian mind. The Christian mind is a godly mind. The biblical view is that goodness is primarily godliness, since the first and great commandment is to love the Lord our God with all our being.

This explains the meaning of true wisdom. Wisdom is a prominent theme in the Bible. In the Old Testament, in addition to the Law and the Prophets, there are the five books of wisdom, namely Job, Psalms, Proverbs, Ecclesiastes, and the Song of Songs. These wisdom books are all concerned with what we call "meaning." What does it mean to be a human being? And how do suffering, evil, injustice, and love fit in with this meaning? This is our topic this week and next.

Sunday: The Book of Ecclesiastes

Monday: Job's Comforters

Tuesday: Job and God

Wednesday: Proverbs – the Fool

Thursday: Proverbs – the Mocker

Friday: Proverbs – the Sluggard

Saturday: The Song of Songs

The Book of Ecclesiastes

THE FEAR OF THE LORD IS THE BEGINNING OF WISDOM...

Proverbs 9:10

The book of Ecclesiastes is best known for its pessimistic refrain. In the familiar King James version it is translated, "Vanity of vanities..., all is vanity." But in the New International Version it is excellently rendered, "Meaningless! Meaningless!... Utterly meaningless!" (Eccles. 1:2).

This language of "meaning" and "meaninglessness" strikes a chord in many people today who are engaged in the quest for personal significance. Viktor Frankl, for example, who survived the Auschwitz concentration camp as a boy and later was appointed professor of psychiatry at the University of Vienna, became convinced that we human beings have a basic "will for meaning." "The striving to find a meaning in one's life," he wrote, "is the primary motivational force in man."[1]

The book of Ecclesiastes expresses many swings of mood and emotion, but it specially emphasizes the futility of a human life that is imprisoned in time and space and that ignores or denies the reality of God. If reality is restricted to time, to the brief human life span with all its injustice and pain, beginning with birth and ending like that of the animals, with death and dissolution, then everything is "meaningless! Meaningless!... Utterly meaningless!"

Or if reality is restricted to space, to human experience under the sun, with no ultimate reference point above and beyond the sun, then again it is all "meaningless! Meaningless!... Utterly meaningless!" Everything is futile, a chasing after wind.

Only God can give meaning to life, because only he can supply the missing dimensions. God adds eternity to time, and God adds transcendence to space. That is why "the fear of the Lord is the beginning of wisdom," for wisdom begins with a humble acknowledgment of the reality of God.

For further reading: Ecclesiastes 1:1–11

---

1   Viktor E. Frankl, *Man's Search for Meaning* (1959; repr., New York: Washington Square Press, 1963), 154.

Job's Comforters

The Lord... said to Eliphaz the Temanite, "I am angry with you and your two friends, because you have not spoken the truth about me, as my servant Job has."

Job 42:7

The Bible does not claim to solve the problem of suffering, but it does take it seriously, and it provides a perspective from which to face it. To this the book of Job makes an important contribution.

The book begins with a double glimpse – firstly, of Job's righteousness, family, and wealth, and secondly, of the heavenly council chamber in which God and Satan discuss Job. It is clear from this that Job's sufferings happened by God's permission. Only then is he overwhelmed with a series of disasters in which he is deprived of his livestock, servants, sons and daughters, and health.

Then his three so-called comforters arrive. At first they sit on the ground with him for a whole week and say nothing. One wishes that they had continued to keep their mouths shut! Instead, one after another they trot out their conventional orthodoxy, which they repeat ad nauseam, namely that Job is suffering for his sins. "All his days the wicked man suffers torment," says Eliphaz (15:20). "The lamp of the wicked is snuffed out," adds Bildad (18:5), while Zophar's contribution is that "the mirth of the wicked is brief" (20:5).

Although Job was certainly wrong to wallow in self-pity, he was not wrong to reject his friends' doctrine or to call them "worthless physicians" (13:4) and "miserable comforters" (16:2) who talk nothing but "nonsense" (21:34). And God later confirmed Job's verdict. He refers to their "folly" and twice insists that they have not spoken of him "what is right" (42:7–8).

The book of Job is also important for our understanding of Scripture. It tells us that we may not quote anything out of the comforters' speeches as Scripture, for their speeches are included in order to be contradicted, not affirmed.

For further reading: Job 42:1–9

TUESDAY

Job and God

> JOB ANSWERED THE LORD: "I AM UNWORTHY – HOW CAN I REPLY TO
> YOU?... I SPOKE ONCE, BUT I HAVE NO ANSWER – TWICE, BUT I WILL SAY
> NO MORE."
>
> Job 40:3–5

Several possible attitudes toward suffering are brought before us in the book of Job. Job's own combination of self-pity and self-assertion is clearly to be rejected. So is the comforters' recommendation of self-accusation. The attitude proposed by the young man Elihu could be called self-discipline, because he represents God as a teacher (36:22) who speaks to us in our affliction (36:15) in order to "turn them from wrongdoing and keep them from pride" (33:17). But even this explanation is only partial.

The right attitude that human beings should adopt toward God is that of self-surrender. God invites Job to look afresh at the creation and bombards him with questions. Where was he when God created the earth? Can he control the snow, the storm, and the stars? Does Job supervise the world of wild animals and birds? Above all, does he comprehend the mysteries and subdue the strength of behemoth the hippopotamus and of leviathan the crocodile?

If it was reasonable for Job to trust the God whose wisdom and power have been revealed in the creation, how much more reasonable is it for us to trust the God whose love and justice have been revealed in the cross? The reasonableness of trust lies in the known trustworthiness of its object. And no one is more trustworthy than the God of the cross. The cross does not solve the problem of suffering, but it gives us the right perspective from which to view it.

So we need to learn to climb the hill called Calvary and from that vantage point to survey all life's tragedies. Since God has demonstrated his holy love in a historical event (the cross), no other historical event (whether personal or global) can override or disprove it.

For further reading: Job 38:1–11

WEDNESDAY

Proverbs – the Fool

THE FEAR OF THE LORD IS THE BEGINNING OF KNOWLEDGE, BUT FOOLS
DESPISE WISDOM AND INSTRUCTION.

Proverbs 1:7

The book of Proverbs is evidently the product of prolonged reflection and careful composition. Each epigram has been chiseled by a skilful carver in words. Moreover, many of them appear to express common sense as much as the truth of God. Yet human and divine wisdom are not necessarily incompatible with each other. Through these ancient nuggets God still speaks his Word to us today.

One of the attractive features of the proverbs is that many of them are not just bare sentences but are clothed in tragicomic characters like the fool, the scoffer, and the sluggard.

It is obvious that the fool lacks wisdom. Indeed, "fools despise wisdom and instruction" (v. 7). This combination of wisdom and instruction or discipline is significant, for the fool's folly is more moral than intellectual. The fool is not unintelligent but rather lacking in restraint.

One particular area in which the fool lacks self-discipline is in the control of the tongue. It is natural to call them "a chattering fool" (10:8) whose mouth "gushes folly" (15:2). If they should ever succeed in keeping silent, then "even fools are thought wise" (17:28), but it would be uncharacteristic for them to do so. One hopes that "in the assembly at the gate," where the elders meet for discussion, they might have something to contribute, but in this situation "they must not open their mouths" (24:7). Normally, however, they "delight in airing their own opinions" (18:2). They even "answer before listening," which is "folly and shame" (v. 13).

So we are warned to avoid fools, for it is "better to meet a bear robbed of her cubs than a fool bent on folly" (17:12).

For further reading: Proverbs 9:13–18

Proverbs – the Mocker

THE PROUD AND ARROGANT PERSON – "MOCKER" IS HIS NAME...

Proverbs 21:24

A second character who emerges from the pages of the book of Proverbs is the one called in older versions the scoffer but is better named the mocker. For their dominant characteristic is that they decline to take life seriously. One might almost identify them as a cynic, because they hold virtue in contempt and use sarcasm to question human sincerity. They sneer at do-gooders.

According to one telling verse, "fools mock at sin" (14:9 NASB). Scholars are not agreed about this translation. But it seems to portray the mocker as denying the seriousness of sin, guilt, and judgment, and as treating too lightly the need for reconciliation and forgiveness.

One painful sphere in which the fool mocks is the home. Much of the book of Proverbs is parental instruction: "Listen, my son, to your father's instruction and do not forsake your mother's teaching" (1:8). One would have thought that even a cynic would listen respectfully to his parents. But no. "A wise son heeds his father's instruction, but a mocker does not respond to rebukes" (13:1). Such disdain for parental guidance is certainly not compatible with obedience to the fifth commandment to honour our father and mother.

The mocker behaves similarly in their wider relationships. They neither seek advice nor take it if it is offered, and "resent correction" (15:12). So "do not rebuke mockers or they will hate you" (9:8). A wise person, on the other hand, "listens to advice" (12:15). Indeed, it is characteristic of the wise that they listen both to rebuke and to counsel.

The conclusion is that the Lord "mocks proud mockers" (3:34), for how can he be expected to take seriously those who do not take him seriously?

For further reading: Proverbs 9:7–12

Friday

Proverbs – the Sluggard

AS A DOOR TURNS ON ITS HINGES, SO A SLUGGARD TURNS ON HIS BED.
Proverbs 26:14

Throughout the book of Proverbs the sluggard is a figure of fun. He (or she) is too drowsy to get up in the morning (6:9–11), and he gives the ludicrous excuse that there is a lion outside in the street (22:13; 26:13). He is so lazy that he allows his fields and vineyards to become completely overgrown with weeds (24:30–31), and when he buries his hand in the dish, he even lacks the energy to bring it back to his mouth (19:24; 26:15).

Because Scripture assures us that we are not animals but human beings made in God's image, it goes on to rebuke us whenever animals manage to do by instinct what we are supposed to do by choice. One of the best examples of this is the contrast between the ant and the sluggard: "Go to the ant, you sluggard; consider its ways and be wise!" (6:6).

The ant's energy and industry are phenomenal. Ants never seem to rest, and they carry loads bigger and heavier than themselves. Although they are social creatures whose community life is more highly organized than that of bees and wasps, and although they have "no commander, no overseer or ruler" (v. 7) – that is, nothing comparable to human leadership or forethought – instinct prompts them to gather and store their food in the summer (v. 8; 30:25). Our critics respond that ants are carnivores and do not store their food. But some ant species, notably harvester ants, which are common in Palestine, are seed eaters and store seeds in moist granaries where they germinate. So ants teach us forethought as well as industry. The apostle Paul went so far as to write that if we do not provide for our relatives, and especially for our immediate family, we have "denied the faith" (1 Tim. 5:8).

Thank God for the ants!

For further reading: Proverbs 24:30–34; 26:13–16

SATURDAY

The Song of Songs

MY BELOVED IS MINE AND I AM HIS...

Song of Songs 2:16

Many people have questioned the propriety of including the Song of Songs in the canon of the Old Testament. They find the intimate exchanges between the lover and his beloved embarrassing and inappropriate within the pages of Holy Scripture. Others can come to terms with the book only by allegorizing it as expressing the love between Yahweh and Israel or between Christ and his church. There has in fact been a long tradition – both Jewish and Christian – of this allegorical interpretation. The best-known is probably the *Sermon on the Canticle of Canticles* by Bernard of Clairvaux. During the last eighteen years of his life (1135–53), Bernard preached eighty-six sermons on the Song of Songs, but he does seem to have gone over the top in his fanciful allegorizations.

The place to begin is surely to affirm without any sense of shame a literal interpretation of the Song of Songs. Anybody reading the Song of Songs for the first time would understand it to be an uninhibited love poem. Erotic it could be called in the sense of expressing sexual love, but pornographic it is definitely not. It is important to emphasize this difference.

Christians have a very negative or puritanical reputation in the area of sex. But the Song of Songs gives the lie to this; it is a beautiful celebration of conjugal love.

Is it legitimate, then, to use the Song of Songs also as an allegory between Christ and his people? My answer is that it is legitimate to use allegory to illustrate, but not to substantiate, a truth. Thus Scripture teaches in many places that God and his people are committed to each other in a covenant of love. Therefore it is legitimate to use the Song of Songs, which expresses the love of bride and bridegroom for each other, in order to illustrate this truth.

For further reading: Ephesians 5:21–33

The largest section of the Old Testament wisdom literature is, of course, the Psalter. It is also the most varied, for it contains several different genres, or types, of literature, including public liturgy and private devotion, lament and penitence, praise and prayer, remembrance and prophecy.

Calvin was right to call the Psalter a "mirror," for it reflects all the moods of our human experience – joy and sorrow, excitement and depression, confidence and doubt, triumph and defeat. As another writer has put it, the Psalter "contains the whole music of the heart of man."

Although different psalms were written by different authors, many without doubt came from David, who called himself "the hero of Israel's songs" (2 Sam. 23:1) and whose harp playing brought relief to Saul's tormented soul (1 Sam. 16:14–23).

Sunday: Psalm 1 – the Righteous and the Wicked

Monday: Psalm 19 – God's Self-Revelation

Tuesday: Psalm 32 – the Forgiveness and Guidance of God

Wednesday: Psalms 42 and 43 – Spiritual Depression

Thursday: Psalm 104 – the Works of God in Nature

Friday: Psalm 130 – a Cry from the Depths

Saturday: Psalm 150 – the Final Doxology

SUNDAY

Psalm 1 – the Righteous and the Wicked

THE LORD WATCHES OVER THE WAY OF THE RIGHTEOUS, BUT THE WAY OF
THE WICKED LEADS TO DESTRUCTION.

Psalm 1:6

The wisdom literature makes a clear-cut distinction between "the righteous" and "the wicked" as also between their present fortunes and their future destinies. In doing so, the psalmist is only anticipating the teaching of Jesus that men and women are either on the broad road that leads to destruction or on the narrow way that leads to life (Matt. 7:13–14).

On the one hand, the righteous will prosper, although not always materially. They choose their company carefully and whose counsel they seek. They delight in God's law and make it their constant meditation. Indeed, God's people still experience the same thing. Daily meditation in the Bible is our unending pleasure. As a result, we are like a tree planted by streams of water, enjoying perpetual refreshment, nourishment, and fruitfulness.

The wicked, on the other hand, will perish. Instead of being like a well-rooted and fruitful tree, they are like dry chaff blown away by the wind. It was a familiar scene in Palestine. The threshing floor was usually a hard, flat surface on a hill exposed to the wind. The wheat was lifted by large winnowing fans or shovels and tossed into the air. Then the precious grain would fall and be harvested, while the light husks of chaff would be scattered to the four winds. As John the Baptist was later to say of the Messiah, "His winnowing fork is in his hand, and he will clear his threshing-floor, gathering his wheat into the barn and burning up the chaff with unquenchable fire" (Matt. 3:12).

Thus the wicked are like chaff in two senses. Firstly, they are desiccated and useless in themselves, and secondly, they are easily blown away or burned. So the tree is planted firmly, but the chaff is unstable. Stability should always be a characteristic of the people of God.

For further reading: Psalm 1:1–6

MONDAY

Psalm 19 – God's Self-Revelation

THE HEAVENS DECLARE THE GLORY OF GOD... THE LAW OF THE LORD IS
PERFECT, REFRESHING THE SOUL.
Psalm 19:1, 7

According to C. S. Lewis, Psalm 19 is "the greatest poem in the Psalter and one of the greatest lyrics in the world." From the Christian point of view, it contains the clearest summary of the doctrine of revelation to be found in the Old Testament, namely that God has made himself known to all humankind as Creator (vv. 1–6), to Israel as Law Giver (vv. 7–10), and to the individual as Redeemer (vv. 11–14).

Firstly, there is *general revelation* (vv. 1–6), so called because it is made to all people everywhere. This witness is given in nature, especially the heavens. It is continuous and universal. In dramatic imagery the psalmist likens the sunrise to the emergence of a bridegroom, and the sun's daily course across the sky to the running of an athlete.

Secondly, there is *special revelation* (vv. 7–10). Abruptly the subject changes from God's general revelation through nature to his special and supernatural revelation through *torah*, the Old Testament. The excellencies of the law are set forth in perfect Hebrew parallelism. It revives the soul, makes wise the simple, gives joy to the heart, and gives light to the eyes. Indeed, the commandments of the Lord are "more precious than gold" and "sweeter than honey" (v. 10), because they reveal God to us.

Thirdly, there is *personal revelation* (vv. 11–14). The psalmist now mentions himself for the first time and expresses his personal spiritual aspirations as God's servant. He prays for forgiveness and for holiness. And he concludes with a prayer, which is frequently echoed by Christian preachers, that all his words, and even his thoughts, will be pleasing in the sight of God, whom he now declares to be both his Rock and his Redeemer.

For further reading: Psalm 19:1–14

TUESDAY

Psalm 32 – the Forgiveness and Guidance of God

BLESSED IS THE ONE WHOSE TRANSGRESSIONS ARE FORGIVEN, WHOSE SINS
ARE COVERED.

Psalm 32:1

There are two basic problems that confront all human beings everywhere. The first is our sense of guilt about the past, and the second is our anxiety about the future. Psalm 32 addresses both directly.

Firstly, *God promises his forgiveness*. The psalm begins with a beatitude: "Blessed is he whose transgressions are forgiven." But how can God refuse to count our sins against us and forgive them instead? The apostle Paul answered this question. He quoted the first two verses of this psalm as an Old Testament example of God's justification of sinners by his grace through faith, altogether apart from good works (Rom. 4:6–8).

We must confess our sins, however. God cannot cover our sins in forgiveness unless we uncover them in confession. So David goes on to describe the misery of those who refuse to own up. Long before the term *psychosomatic* had been invented, David tells how his tortured conscience resulted in alarming physical symptoms (Ps. 32:3–4).

Secondly, *God promises his guidance*. Four times in verse 8 God makes the same promise, "I will instruct you and teach you in the way you should go; I will counsel you and watch over you." We need to note, however, that the promise is immediately followed by a prohibition: "Do not be like the horse or the mule, which have no understanding" (v. 9).

So God promises that he will guide us, but we must not expect him to guide us as we guide horses and mules. Why not? Because they have no understanding, whereas we do. God's normal way of directing us is through our mental processes, not in spite of them.

For further reading: Psalm 32:1–11

WEDNESDAY

Psalms 42 and 43 – Spiritual Depression

WHY, MY SOUL, ARE YOU DOWNCAST?... PUT YOUR HOPE IN GOD.

Psalm 42:5

Depression seems to be a fairly common condition among Christian people. I am referring not to clinical depression, which may need expert psychotherapy, but to spiritual depression, which we should be able to handle ourselves.

The author of Psalms 42 and 43 (for they evidently belong together as one psalm) is clear about the causes of his depression. To begin with, he is thirsty for God (as thirsty as a deer for water), because he is estranged from him, enduring some kind of forced exile. He remembers the great festivals of the past when he used to "go and meet with God" (42:2), and he longs to be allowed to return "to the altar of God," to God his joy and delight (43:4).

His depression is due, however, not only to the absence of God but also to the presence of enemies. They keep taunting him, asking, "Where is your God?" (42:3, 10). It is partly that they are idolaters, serving gods they could see and touch, whereas "the living God" (42:2) is invisible and intangible, and partly that God appears unable to vindicate his people.

Each stanza concludes with the same refrain (42:5, 11; 43:5). In it the psalmist speaks to himself. Talking to oneself is popularly said to be the first sign of madness. But on the contrary, it is a sure sign of maturity – though depending on what we are talking to ourselves about! Here the psalmist refuses to acquiesce in his condition or give in to his moods. He takes himself in hand. Firstly, he questions himself: "Why are you downcast, O my soul?" His question includes an implied rebuke. Secondly, he exhorts himself: "Put your hope in God." For God is worthy of our trust. Thirdly, he assures himself: "For I will yet praise him, my Saviour and my God." His double use of the personal possessive "my Saviour and my God" is highly significant. He is reminding himself of his covenant relationship with God, which no fluctuating moods can ever destroy.

For further reading: Psalm 42:1–11

THURSDAY

Psalm 104 – the Works of God in Nature

HOW MANY ARE YOUR WORKS, LORD! IN WISDOM YOU MADE THEM ALL;
THE EARTH IS FULL OF YOUR CREATURES.

Psalm 104:24

Psalm 104 expresses what C. S. Lewis called the psalmist's "gusto for nature." He has in mind the creation narrative of Genesis 1, following approximately the same order, and describing with great poetic beauty how God made and sustains the heavens and the earth (vv. 1–9).

Then in the middle of the psalm the psalmist shows how God provides food, drink, and shelter for all the earth's birds and beasts (vv. 10–23). *Ecology* would be a term too grandiosely scientific to apply to this paragraph, yet this is what the author is depicting. He is fascinated by God's marvellous adaptation of the earth's resources to the needs of living creatures, and vice versa.

Food and life are the basic needs of every creature, and here their presence is attributed to the open hand and quickening breath of God, and their absence to his hidden face. To our modern ears it all sounds very naïve, and indeed it is figurative, whether in the use of poetic or of anthropomorphic imagery.

But the truth behind the figures stands. God the Creator is Lord of his creation. He has not abdicated his throne. He rules what he has made. No Christian can have a mechanistic view of nature. The universe is not a gigantic machine that operates by inflexible laws, nor has God made laws to which he is himself now a slave. The very term *natural law* is only a convenient expression for the observed consistency of God's working. He is living and active in his world, and we depend upon him for our "life and breath and everything else" (Acts 17:25). So it is right to thank him not only for our creation but for our preservation as well.

For further reading: Psalm 104:10–31

FRIDAY

Psalm 130 – a Cry from the Depths

OUT OF THE DEPTHS I CRY TO YOU, LORD; LORD, HEAR MY VOICE.

Psalm 130:1–2

The psalmist depicts himself as floundering in deep waters, and out of these depths he appeals to God to rescue him. Since he cries for mercy, it is evident that the deep waters are a picture of his sin, guilt, and remorse, together with his sense of God's judgment upon him – and also upon the nation with which he identifies himself. He knows well that if God were to keep a record of his sins, reckoning them up against him, neither he nor anyone else could stand. "But with you," he adds immediately, "there is forgiveness" (v. 4).

It was this offer of a free forgiveness, by grace and without works, that led Martin Luther to call this penitential song one of the "Pauline Psalms." Verse 4 was also one of the Scripture verses that brought comfort to John Bunyan, author of *Pilgrim's Progress*, when his conscience troubled him and he was convicted of sin. The verse contains a beautiful balance, because its first part brings assurance to the despairing ("with you there is forgiveness"), while its second part sounds a warning to the presumptuous ("therefore you are feared"). Far from encouraging sinners in their sins, God's forgiveness promotes that fear of the Lord, or reverent awe in his presence, that leads us to depart from iniquity (see Prov. 16:6).

Confident of the forgiving mercy of God to penitent sinners, the psalmist now does two things. Firstly, he affirms his own determination to trust God for forgiveness, relying on God's promise. So he waits for the Lord, as expectantly and patiently as "watchmen wait for the morning" (v. 6). For however long the night may seem, and however deep the darkness, watchmen know for certain that the dawn will come in the end. Secondly, he urges Israel to do the same, for he knows that Yahweh's "unfailing love" (v. 7) will "redeem Israel from all their sins" (v. 8).

Many times I too have needed to make this penitential psalm my own, and many times its promises have brought me the assurance of God's forgiveness.

For further reading: Psalm 130

SATURDAY

Psalm 150 – the Final Doxology

LET EVERYTHING THAT HAS BREATH PRAISE THE LORD.

Psalm 150:6

This doxology forms a magnificent conclusion to the Psalter. As a summons to worship, it is unsurpassed in grandeur. Every verse is an invitation to praise, instructing us where, why, how, and by whom the praise of God should be expressed.

Firstly, if we wonder *where* we should worship, the answer is both "in his sanctuary" (referring originally to the temple in Jerusalem) and "in his mighty heavens" (v. 1). So heaven and earth, angels and humans, unite in praising God.

Secondly, *why* should we worship? We are to praise him both "for his acts of power" and "for his surpassing greatness" (v. 2). Israel never tired of celebrating God's mighty acts of creation and redemption.

Thirdly, when we come to the *how* of worship, every conceivable instrument is to be played – wind, strings, and percussion. The "trumpet" (v. 3) was doubtless the ancient curved ram's horn, still in use in the synagogue, and the expert, writes one commentator, "can make a prodigious noise with it." The other instruments are more or less recognizable. So the orchestra is assembled. Worshippers are to blow the horn and pluck the harp, beat the drums, sweep the strings, play the flute, and clang the cymbals.

The fourth question concerns the *who* of worship. The psalmist calls on "everything that has breath" to praise the Lord (v. 6). He may include the animal creation in whom too is "the breath of life" (Gen. 6:17), but it seems more probable that he is referring to the whole human race. Sometimes in the course of public worship, when the choir is singing and the organ or a band is playing, we are transported beyond ourselves to join with angels, archangels, and all the company of heaven around the throne of God.

Our worship is not to be confined to church services, however. On the contrary, while we breathe, we praise.

For further reading: Psalm 150

Week 12: The Prophet Isaiah

We have already referred (in week 9) to the prophet Isaiah, and in particular to his ministry to the reforming King Hezekiah. Now we are to spend the whole of this week in his company, delving into a few of the main themes of his prophetic message. This is introduced in the first verse as "the vision… that Isaiah son of Amoz saw" (Isa. 1:1), which in verse 2 he boldly calls on heaven and earth to listen to. He is conscious that his God-given revelation has cosmic proportions, for in the book's final chapter his vision has expanded to "the new heavens and the new earth," which one day God will create (66:22). His message combines both judgment and comfort.

Sunday: The Song of the Vineyard

Monday: The Prophet's Commissioning

Tuesday: The Challenge to Faith

Wednesday: The Double Identity of God

Thursday: The Divine Burden Bearer

Friday: The Reasonableness of Revelation

Saturday: The New World

The Song of the Vineyard

Then he looked for a crop of good grapes, but it yielded only bad fruit.

Isaiah 5:2

Using the literary device of a love song, Isaiah audaciously refers to Yahweh as his beloved and to Yahweh's people Israel as his vineyard. Yahweh had planted his vineyard on a fertile hillside, had cleared it of stones, had built a protective watchtower in it, and had made a wine vat ready. In fact, he had done absolutely everything necessary to ensure a bumper vintage. But instead of good grapes, his vine yielded only wild grapes.

So now Yahweh pronounces judgment on his people. He will destroy his vineyard, he says.

> The vineyard of the LORD Almighty
> is the house of Israel,
> and the people of Judah
> are the vines he delighted in.
> And he looked for justice, but saw bloodshed;
> for righteousness, but heard cries of distress.
>
> **Isaiah 5:7**

The bad vintage is now interpreted by six "woes" – illegal acquisition of land (v. 8), excessive consumption of alcohol (vv. 11–12), a brazen defiance of God (vv. 18–19), a perverse transfer of moral categories (v. 20), conceit (v. 21), and corruption and the denial of human rights (vv. 22–23). These social sins characterized the second half of the eighth century BC when King Uzziah of Judah led the nation to its peak of prosperity and luxury. In these different ways the people "spurned the word of the Holy One of Israel" (v. 24). Therefore Yahweh's anger was kindled against them, and he warned them of a coming invasion from the north, doubtless by the Assyrian army (vv. 26–30).

I have often wondered whether the song of the vineyard was in Jesus' mind when he developed his allegory of the vine (John 15). Certainly both metaphors imply the same expectation of fruitfulness, even as Paul was to write later of the fruit of the Spirit.

For further reading: John 15:1–11

Monday

The Prophet's Commissioning

THEN I HEARD THE VOICE OF THE LORD SAYING, "WHOM SHALL I SEND?
AND WHO WILL GO FOR US?" AND I SAID, "HERE AM I. SEND ME!"

Isaiah 6:8

Isaiah chapter 6 is well known to many churches as a challenging text for a missionary sermon. But its original application was much more particular; it records the call of Isaiah to be a prophet. The vocabulary of "sending" ("Whom shall I send? Send me") makes this plain. For Yahweh sent the prophets, as later Jesus was to send the apostles, and commissioned them to teach in his name. Similarly Yahweh said of the false prophets, "I never sent you."

The essence of Isaiah's call was his vision of Yahweh, exalted and transcendent, seated on his heavenly throne, attended by seraphs crying, "Holy, holy, holy" (v. 3). It was a vision of the King ("my eyes have seen the King," v. 5) and was deliberately granted him in the year 740 BC when King Uzziah celebrated his golden jubilee and died. Inevitably Isaiah would compare and contrast the two kingdoms, and his whole future ministry would be coloured by his conviction that Yahweh is King, worthy to be trusted and obeyed.

Next came Isaiah's confession of sin, his cleansing, and his commissioning. He was also warned that the people would harden their hearts and reject God's word, so that God's judgment would fall upon them. Jesus himself quoted these words (Matt. 13:14–15) and so did the apostle Paul (Acts 28:25–29).

Yet there was a glimmer of hope. As when a tree is felled a stump is left, so will it be with Israel. "The holy seed will be the stump in the land" (Isa. 6:13). These words introduce us to one of the distinctives of Isaiah's message, namely that there would be a remnant of faithful disciples, gathered around the prophet himself (see 8:16–18).

For further reading: Isaiah 6

TUESDAY

The Challenge to Faith

IF YOU DO NOT STAND FIRM IN YOUR FAITH, YOU WILL NOT STAND AT ALL.

Isaiah 7:9

It was about 734 BC, during the reign of Ahaz king of Judah (Uzziah's grandson), that Rezin king of Aram (Syria) and Pekah king of Israel formed a foolhardy alliance. Their object was to oppose the growing threat of Tiglath-Pileser III, king of Assyria in the far north. They were determined to attack Jerusalem first in order to persuade King Ahaz of Judah to join forces with them. As they approached, the heart of Ahaz and his people "shook as the trees of the forest shake before the wind" (v. 2 RSV). But Yahweh sent Isaiah to meet Ahaz and to say to him, "Take heed, be quiet, do not fear, and do not let your heart be faint because of these two smoldering stumps of firebrands" (vv. 3–4 RSV).

This was the first crisis of faith for Ahaz, and the second followed soon afterward. Although the coalition were boasting of the success of their plan, the Lord God said to them, "It shall not stand, and it shall not come to pass" (v. 7 RSV). For the kings were only human leaders, whereas (it is implied) Ahaz was king in the divine line of David. So, "If you do not stand firm in your faith, you will not stand at all" (v. 9, where the NIV attempts to reproduce in English the pun in the Hebrew text).

But Ahaz had no intention of trusting God. It seems that he had already made up his mind. Instead, he sent messengers to King Tiglath-Pileser of Assyria, saying, "I am your servant and vassal. Come up and save me out of the hand of the king of Aram and the king of Israel, who are attacking me" (2 Kings 16:7–8). At the same time Ahaz paid Assyria a handsome tribute of silver and gold. In consequence, Syria was crushed in 732 BC, and Israel in 722.

Central to Isaiah's message was the challenge to faith. He pleaded with the nation's leaders not to turn to the mighty empires of Egypt and Assyria, but rather to trust in the living God. The same challenge is addressed to us today, as we take Isaiah's promises to ourselves. "He who believes will not be in haste" (Isa. 28:16 RSV). Again, "In returning and rest you shall be saved; in quietness and in trust shall be your strength" (30:15 RSV).

For further reading: Isaiah 7:1–9

WEDNESDAY

The Double Identity of God

THE LORD IS THE EVERLASTING GOD, THE CREATOR OF THE ENDS OF THE
EARTH.

Isaiah 40:28

Isaiah 40 focuses on verse 27, in which God confronts his people with awkward questions: "Why do you complain Jacob,… 'My way is hidden from the LORD; my cause is disregarded by my God'?" The God they think has forgotten them (during their Babylonian exile) has overheard their complaint, listened to their conversation, and read their thoughts. They are in a terrible plight, and God does nothing about it. Either he is blind and cannot see, or he is unjust and cannot bother, or he is impotent and cannot rescue them. Such a complaint is familiar to our modern ears.

God's response is to throw their question back to them. They are asking, "Why doesn't God do something?" He replies, "Why do you ask why?" Then he lifts their minds above their sufferings, to him and the kind of God he is. For nothing is more important when we are in trouble than a fresh vision of God. In particular, two complementary truths about him need to be emphasized. Firstly, "the LORD is the everlasting God." Yahweh, their own covenant God, is also "the Creator of the ends of the earth." It is absurd, therefore, to imagine that the Creator is lacking in knowledge, justice, or power (v. 28).

The second truth complements the first. It is that the Creator is also the LORD (Yahweh), the God of Israel, who has bound himself to them by a solemn covenant and will never go back on his steadfast love for them. This chapter is full of affirmations that he is our God forever.

The key question, then, that God himself asks twice is, "To whom, then, will you compare God?" (v. 18; see v. 25). The answer is that he is both the Creator God and the Covenant God. As God of the creation we cannot doubt his power; as God of the covenant we cannot doubt his love. Unless we hold fast to this, his double identity, then "our God is too small," as J. B. Phillips wrote.

For further reading: Isaiah 40:18–31

The Divine Burden Bearer

YOU WHOM I HAVE UPHELD SINCE YOUR BIRTH, AND HAVE CARRIED SINCE
YOU WERE BORN. EVEN TO YOUR OLD AGE... I AM HE...

Isaiah 46:3–4

Isaiah's satire about idolatry reaches its climax in chapter 46. We are introduced to Babylon's two chief deities – Bel (also named Marduk) and Nebo (Bel's son). Their manufacture by a goldsmith is described (vv. 6–7), after which their worshippers lift them onto their shoulders, carry them away, and hoist them into position, from which they cannot move or speak.

Suddenly Babylon is overthrown by Cyrus the Persian, whose soldiers begin at once to plunder the city's temples. "Bel bows down, Nebo stoops" (v. 1). That is, these deadweight idols are ignominiously snatched from their pedestals and carried headfirst like corpses into the street. Here they are loaded onto carts and carried away. How are the mighty fallen! The gods that had been proudly carried shoulder high in religious processions are now cartloads of useless rubbish, a burden to their worshippers.

The laughter in the prophet's voice subsides, and in the silence God speaks. In effect, he says, "I am not like Bel and Nebo. I do not need to be carried. I am the living and the lifting God. I have carried you from before your birth, and now even when you turn grey I will carry you" (vv. 3–4 paraphrase).

So the question before us today is, who is carrying whom? Is religion to us an uplift or a burden? Is God himself even a burden to us? Jesus Christ is depicted in the New Testament as the world's supreme burden bearer. He has borne our sins (see Is. 53). He also bears our sorrows. As Peter wrote, "Cast all your anxiety on him because he cares for you" (1 Pet. 5:7). It is a major tragedy if we reverse our God-given roles, for then we attempt to carry him when he is committed to carrying us!

For further reading: Isaiah 46:1–9

FRIDAY

The Reasonableness of Revelation

AS THE HEAVENS ARE HIGHER THAN THE EARTH, SO ARE MY WAYS HIGHER
THAN YOUR WAYS AND MY THOUGHTS THAN YOUR THOUGHTS.

Isaiah 55:9

Christianity is essentially a revealed religion. We would know nothing about God if he had not made himself known. This is especially true of God's gracious character. He offers a free drink to the thirsty, a free place in the covenant to the nations, and a free pardon to the wicked (vv. 1–7). Who could have invented such a gospel of grace? It is too good to be true! It could be known only by divine revelation. Consider its logic.

Firstly, Yahweh's thoughts are inaccessible to us. They are as much higher than our thoughts as the heavens are higher than the earth. Our little minds cannot climb up into the infinite mind of God (vv. 8–9).

Secondly, Yahweh's lofty thoughts must come down to us as the rain and the snow come down from heaven to earth (v. 10).

Thirdly, Yahweh's thoughts have in fact been brought within our reach because they have been put into words. Thus human speech is the model of divine revelation. It is by the words of our mouth that we communicate the thoughts of our minds. We cannot even read each other's minds unless we speak; how much less can we read God's mind unless he speaks? And God has spoken; his word has come down to us.

Fourthly, Yahweh's word is powerful; it always achieves its purpose (vv. 10–11).

The last two verses of the chapter (vv. 12–13) describe in vivid Hebrew poetic imagery the immense blessings enjoyed by the people of God who have received the word of God. They experience a new exodus (v. 12), and they inherit a new promised land (v. 13). No wonder we are filled with joy and gladness.

For further reading: 1 Corinthians 2:6–10

The New World

AS THE NEW HEAVENS AND THE NEW EARTH THAT I MAKE WILL ENDURE
BEFORE ME,... SO WILL YOUR NAME AND DESCENDANTS ENDURE.

Isaiah 66:22

Isaiah's prophetic eyes now peer into the future and focus on the universal mission of the church (vv. 18–21) and on the ultimate regeneration of the universe (vv. 22–24). As for the Christian mission, the prophet singles out three aspects of it. Firstly, its scope is all the nations. Four times in verses 18–20 he refers to the nations being gathered together. Secondly, its occasion (what triggers it) is the rejection of the gospel by Israel. Luke affirms this fact on four separate occasions in the Acts. This is the apostle Paul's vision of Jews and Gentiles united in Christ. Thirdly, the goal of the Christian mission is the glory of God (vv. 18–19) – proclaimed by the missionaries and seen and acknowledged by their converts.

Now with verse 22 the prophet makes a big jump to the end of history when God will create a new heaven and a new earth. He has already referred to it in the previous chapter (65:17), and later Jesus and his apostles will make the same prediction (Matt. 19:28; 2 Pet. 3:13; Rev. 21:1, 5). Two features of this expectation are noteworthy. Firstly, the new universe will be partly material, since it will include a new, transformed, and glorified earth. As Paul wrote later, the whole creation will be liberated from its present bondage (Rom. 8:18–25). As our resurrection bodies will enjoy both continuity with and discontinuity from our present bodies, so the new earth will also enjoy continuity and discontinuity. Secondly, the new heaven and earth will be as enduring as their inhabitants. Only those who have deliberately rebelled against God will be destroyed (like the rubbish consigned to the dump outside Jerusalem [Isa. 66:24]).

These two emphases (universal mission and ultimate regeneration) were linked in the teaching of Jesus. For he told us to take the gospel to the ends of the earth and added that only then the end of time would come. The two ends will coincide. Meanwhile, the gap between the first and second comings of Christ is to be filled with the worldwide mission of the church.

For further reading: 2 Peter 3:1–13

WEEK 13: THE PROPHET JEREMIAH

The opening sentences of Jeremiah's first chapter throw light on the Christian view of inspiration. They state both that these are "words of Jeremiah" (Jer. 1:1) and that "the word of the LORD came to him" (v. 2). So Scripture is neither the word of God only nor the words of men only, but the word of God through the words of men. This is the double authorship of Scripture, to which we need to hold fast.

From his call onward Jeremiah comes before us as the reluctant prophet. We watch his very human reactions to every situation. King and courtiers, priests and people are all against him. His own priestly family opposes him. He is put in the stocks and thrown into a cistern. God's word burns like fire in his bones; he cannot hold it in. But nobody listens to him. He is essentially a patriot but is thought to be a traitor. He witnesses the decline and death of his own nation. Even Yahweh seems at times to be against him. He is alone and in anguish. He weeps bitter tears (see 4:19 and 9:1).

Sunday: The Call of Jeremiah

Monday: A Backsliding People

Tuesday: Stubborn Hearts

Wednesday: The Plans of God

Thursday: Prophets – False and True

Friday: The New Covenant

Saturday: The Steadfast Love of the Lord

The Call of Jeremiah

BEFORE I FORMED YOU IN THE WOMB I KNEW YOU, BEFORE YOU WERE
BORN I SET YOU APART; I APPOINTED YOU AS A PROPHET TO THE NATIONS.

Jeremiah 1:5

It is instructive to compare the respective calls of Isaiah and Jeremiah. Both involved a "sending." To Isaiah Yahweh had asked, "Whom shall I send?" (Isa. 6:8). To Jeremiah he said, "You must go to everyone I send you to" (Jer. 1:7). But then there was a difference. In the case of Isaiah, at least after his lips had been cleansed, he readily volunteered his services: "Here am I. Send me!" (Isa. 6:8). In the case of Jeremiah, however, he was reluctant (as Moses had been) on account of his youth and inexperience. "Alas, Sovereign LORD," he protested, "I do not know how to speak; I am too young" (Jer. 1:6).

There is no contradiction here with the teaching of Jesus. For Jesus commended the humility of a child, whereas Yahweh rebuked Jeremiah for pleading the irresponsibility of a child.

Another similarity between the calls of Isaiah and Jeremiah is that in both cases a prominent feature concerned their sense of inadequacy in the lips (Isaiah) and the mouth (Jeremiah). Isaiah was conscious that his lips were unclean, and Jeremiah that he did not know what to say. So before they could assume the prophetic office, Isaiah's lips were cleansed by a burning coal, and Jeremiah's mouth was touched by the divine hand, symbolizing the fact that Yahweh had put his words in Jeremiah's mouth.

Finally, Jeremiah was told that his message would be both negative (destroying and overthrowing) and positive (building and planting). And this was elaborated in two visions. Firstly, Jeremiah saw "the branch of an almond tree" (v. 11). The Hebrew word for almond tree resembled *watching* and so signified Yahweh's promise, "I am watching to see that my word is fulfilled" (v. 12). Secondly, Jeremiah saw a boiling pot, tilting from the north (v. 13), in other words, an invading army, probably the Scythians.

For further reading: Jeremiah 1:1–19

MONDAY

A Backsliding People

WHY THEN HAVE THESE PEOPLE TURNED AWAY?
Jeremiah 8:5

Jeremiah begins his prophetic ministry with a sustained appeal for repentance. Though his message is directed primarily against Judah, he brackets "faithless Israel" (3:6) with "her unfaithful sister Judah" (v. 7). True, good King Josiah's reform met with some response, but it was largely superficial. So God complains, "Judah did not return to me with all her heart, but only in pretence" (v. 10). The people still persisted in their sins. They worshipped foreign deities on the high places. They broke the Ten Commandments. They failed to care for the widow, the orphan, and the alien. They even engaged in the horrors of child sacrifice. But although Jeremiah exposed these evils, they refused to repent.

Now the prophet adds metaphor to metaphor in an attempt to prick Judah's conscience. When people fall down, he asks, don't they get up again? If they go astray, don't they turn back to where they went wrong? Why then have God's people turned away in perpetual backsliding? They have refused to come back, like a horse plunging headlong into battle (8:4–6).

Most telling of all his metaphors is the behaviour of migratory birds: "Even the stork in the sky knows her appointed seasons, and the dove, the swift and the thrush observe the time of their migration. But my people do not know the requirements of the LORD" (v. 7).

Palestine is a corridor of bird migration. Jeremiah had evidently noticed that many birds fly south over the Middle East in order to winter in the warmer climate of Africa, but in the spring without fail they return. God's people, however, had gone away, but they had not returned. White storks are an excellent example. It is estimated that nearly half a million of them use this migratory flyway. Jeremiah's reference in the sixth century BC is perhaps the first reference to bird migration in the literature of the world.

Oh that we had as powerful an instinct to return to God as storks have to return to their breeding grounds in the spring!

For further reading: Jeremiah 8:4–7

TUESDAY

Stubborn Hearts

BUT THEY DID NOT LISTEN OR PAY ATTENTION; INSTEAD, THEY FOLLOWED
THE STUBBORN INCLINATIONS OF THEIR EVIL HEARTS.

Jeremiah 7:24

One of the distinctives of Jeremiah's teaching is that he diagnosed Israel's unwillingness to repent as a deep-seated condition of the heart. "But these people have stubborn and rebellious hearts," God says (5:23). Again, "They are all hardened rebels" (6:28). In fact, all their manifold misbehaviour is due, Jeremiah says at least seven times, to "the stubborn inclinations of their evil hearts" (7:24).

And since the heart is the source of the trouble, Jeremiah emphasizes that there is no human remedy. Even if the people of Judah were to scrub themselves with soda and use large quantities of soap, the stain of their guilt would not be removed (2:22). Only if Ethiopians can change their skin, and leopards their spots, will Judah be able to do good "who are accustomed to doing evil" (13:23). Again, since Judah's sin has been written with an iron pen and engraved with a diamond point, it cannot be erased (17:1). Further, the heart is deceitful above every other thing and desperately sick (17:9). All four images vividly illustrate the fact that human sin is beyond human cure. It is like a stain that cannot be eradicated, like skin pigmentation that cannot be changed, like an engraving that cannot be removed, and like a sickness that is incurable. Only God can change us.

True, Jeremiah cries out, "Jerusalem, wash the evil from your heart" (4:14), but he knows that they cannot do it. So he looks forward to the day when God will establish a new covenant with them that will include his promise to write his law on their hearts (31:31–34), indeed, to give them a new heart (32:39; see also. Ezek. 36:26). This promise is wonderfully fulfilled today whenever an individual experiences the new birth.

For further reading: John 3:1–15

The Plans of God

> "FOR I KNOW THE PLANS I HAVE FOR YOU," DECLARES THE LORD,
> "PLANS TO PROSPER YOU AND NOT TO HARM YOU,
> PLANS TO GIVE YOU HOPE AND A FUTURE."
>
> Jeremiah 29:11

While the false prophets confidently predicted that Judah would be delivered from the Babylonian threat, Jeremiah with equal confidence predicted that Jerusalem would fall to the besieging Babylonian army, and called on them to surrender. But Jeremiah was of course right. The city fell in 597 BC, and the leaders of the nation were taken into Babylonian exile.

Once the people had settled there, Jeremiah wrote a letter to all the exiles, telling them to build houses and live in them, to plant gardens and eat their produce, to develop their family life, and to seek the welfare of the city. They were not to listen to the dreams of the false prophets that they would soon return to Jerusalem; only after seventy years of exile would the Lord bring them back.

The promise that God then made to the Babylonian exiles has often been legitimately reapplied to Christians in distress and pain: "'I know the plans I have for you,' declares the LORD, 'plans to prosper you and not to harm you, plans to give you hope and a future'" (v. 11).

Firstly, *God has plans for his people*. Life may appear haphazard. History has been described as being like the tracks made on white paper by the feet of a drunken fly. But no, life is not random, meaningless, or absurd. God had plans for the exiles; he has plans for us as well.

Secondly, *God knows his plans*. He does not necessarily divulge them, but he has them and knows them. Parents begin to make plans for their children before they are born; so does our heavenly Father.

Thirdly, *God's plans are good plans*. The Babylonian exiles must have found this hard to believe, but God was determined to give them "hope and a future." Perhaps the New Testament equivalent is Romans 8:28, where we are assured that God works all things together for our good.

For further reading: Romans 8:28–39

THURSDAY

Prophets – False and True

LET THE PROPHET WHO HAS A DREAM TELL HIS DREAM, BUT LET THE ONE
WHO HAS MY WORD SPEAK IT FAITHFULLY.

Jeremiah 23:28

Jeremiah was deeply distressed by the ministry of false prophets, who opposed him. "My heart is broken within me," he cried, "all my bones tremble" (v. 9). The situation today is both different and the same. There are plenty of false prophets (as Jesus said there would be), but there is nobody resembling Jeremiah. Certainly some are gifted with prophetic insight into the meaning and application of the biblical text. But there is nobody with the inspiration or authority of the biblical prophets themselves like Jeremiah. Instead, we are blessed to have the written Word of God. So the contrast today is between true teachers who submit to Scripture and false teachers who reject or manipulate it.

Here are the five distinctive characteristics of false teachers, whom Jeremiah exposes.

1. They abuse their power. They are marked more by autocracy than by the gentleness of Christ. They "use their power unjustly" (v. 10).

2. They live a lie, a double life between their private and their public persona (vv. 13–14).

3. They strengthen the hands of evildoers instead of calling them to repentance (vv. 14, 22).

4. They fill people with false hopes, saying that no harm will come upon them (vv. 16–17).

5. "They speak visions from their own minds, not from the mouth of the LORD" (v. 16).

Only the Word of God is effective. Like a hammer it breaks the rock of stubborn human hearts. Like fire it burns and purifies. Like wheat it is nutritious, unlike straw (vv. 28–29).

It should not be difficult to choose the Word of God over human dreams, to choose revelation rather than speculation. Perhaps the church's most urgent need today is pastors who faithfully expound and apply the Word of God and who practise what they preach.

For further reading: Jeremiah 23:21–32

114   THROUGH THE YEAR WITH JOHN STOTT

FRIDAY

The New Covenant

"THE DAYS ARE COMING," DECLARES THE LORD, "WHEN I WILL MAKE A
NEW COVENANT WITH THE PEOPLE OF ISRAEL
AND WITH THE PEOPLE OF JUDAH."
Jeremiah 31:31

It is important to grasp that there is only one covenant of grace throughout the Bible, namely the promise God made to Abraham some four thousand years ago to bless him and his posterity and through them to bless the world. It is this covenant that Jesus ratified ("This cup is the new covenant in my blood" [1 Cor. 11:25]). It is new only in relation to Mount Sinai (see Jer. 31:32); it is not new in itself, for it is as old as Abraham. Consider now the terms of the new covenant.

Firstly, in the new covenant the law of God is *internal*: "I will put my law in their minds and write it on their hearts" (v. 33). As a result, we understand it, love it, and obey it. There is strange teaching around today that Christians are no longer under obligation to keep God's moral law. But, on the contrary, God writes his law in our hearts in order that we may obey it.

Secondly, in the new covenant the knowledge of God is *universal*: "'No longer will they teach their neighbour, or say to one another, "Know the LORD," because they will all know me, from the least of them to the greatest,' declares the LORD" (v. 34). This universality includes the Gentiles and the "priesthood of all believers." That is, in the covenant community of Jesus Christ, there is no hierarchy of privilege but rather an equal access of all to God through Christ.

Thirdly, in the new covenant the forgiveness of God is *eternal*: "For I will forgive their wickedness and will remember their sins no more" (v. 34). Of course, there was forgiveness in the Old Testament (see Ps. 32:1–2). Yet the sacrifices continued to be offered repeatedly and interminably. But the Lord Jesus Christ offered one sacrifice for sins forever, and on the ground of his finished work God remembers our sins no more.

So these are the priceless blessings of the new covenant – an internal law, a universal knowledge of God, and an eternal forgiveness.

For further reading: Hebrews 10:11–18

The Steadfast Love of the Lord

BUT THIS I CALL TO MIND, AND THEREFORE I HAVE HOPE: THE STEADFAST
LOVE OF THE LORD NEVER CEASES, HIS MERCIES NEVER
COME TO AN END...

Lamentations 3:21–22 NRSV

The book of Lamentations is an ancient poem called a dirge. It is anonymous, although both Jewish and Christian tradition have long attributed it to Jeremiah. It was obviously written in or after 587 BC, when Jerusalem was besieged and its temple destroyed. Lamentations belongs to the aftermath of that overwhelming calamity.

The description is graphic. The city walls have been broken down, and the buildings are in ruins. The streets are deserted. A tiny handful has survived and is resorting even to secret cannibalism. The city is like a widow, bereft of her husband and children. She is friendless, defenceless, comfortless, helpless, and hopeless. Worse still, "The Lord has rejected his altar and abandoned his sanctuary" (2:7). That is, sacrifices, festivals, and Sabbaths are no longer being observed. The fearful judgment of God has fallen on his people. The prophet describes his experience as "darkness rather than light" (3:2). Now listen to his account of what happened:

> My soul is bereft of peace; I have forgotten what happiness is… But this I call to mind, and therefore I have hope: The steadfast love of the LORD never ceases, his mercies never come to an end; they are new every morning; great is your faithfulness.

Lamentations 3:17, 21–23 NRSV

Jeremiah uses three words – steadfast love, mercy, and faithfulness; all three refer to God's covenant with Israel and express his fidelity to it. It is this that the prophet calls to mind and that gives him hope. Around him lies utter devastation. Within him are doubt, fear, and pain. Only the assurance of God's covenant faithfulness can give him security.

In verse 20 Jeremiah thinks of his afflictions, but in verse 21 he calls to mind God's covenant love. It is the same with us. To think about ourselves and our suffering brings despair; to think about God and his faithfulness brings hope: "For the Lord will not reject forever. Although he causes grief, he will have compassion according to the abundance of his steadfast love; for he does not willingly afflict or grieve anyone" (vv. 31–33 NRSV).

For further reading: Lamentations 3:17–33

Week 14: The Exilic Prophets

Ezekiel and Daniel are often referred to as the "exilic" prophets because they prophesied mainly during the sixty years of Israel's Babylonian exile, which elapsed between the first fall of Jerusalem (597 BC) and the edict of Cyrus permitting the exiles to return (538 BC).

There were, in fact, three deportations to Babylon. The first was in 605 BC and included Daniel and his three friends. The second took place in 597 BC, when Jerusalem fell for the first time, and many national leaders were taken into exile, including King Jehoiachin and Ezekiel. The third deportation happened ten years later, in 587 BC, when Jerusalem and the temple were destroyed. Ezekiel had his overwhelming vision of the glory of God in 593 BC.

Sunday: The Glory of God

Monday: The Call of Ezekiel

Tuesday: Sin and Judgment

Wednesday: God's Holy Name

Thursday: Cultural Conformity and Nonconformity

Friday: The Sovereignty of God

Saturday: The Humbling of the Proud

The Glory of God

THIS WAS THE APPEARANCE OF THE LIKENESS OF THE GLORY
OF THE LORD.

Ezekiel 1:28

Ezekiel's prophecy is clearly structured around three visions of the glory of God. In the first the glory arrives in Babylon (1:1–28). In the second it departs from Jerusalem (chaps. 8–11), and in the third it returns to Jerusalem (chap. 43).

Firstly, *the glory arrives in Babylon.* It seems to have been on Ezekiel's thirtieth birthday that he was granted his vision – transcendent and magnificent – of the glory of God. It began with a ferocious storm from the north and then focused on four living winged creatures, each with four faces (representing the creation) and each with its own wheel. It is hard to visualize the construction of wheels within wheels darting to and fro in all directions. Above the living creatures (later identified as cherubim) there was a shining dome; above it was something like a throne, rainbow-circled; and above that something like a human was seated in splendour. "This was the appearance of the likeness of the glory of the LORD" (1:28). The astonishing thing was that when Ezekiel received his vision, he was among the exiles in Babylonia. God had not abandoned his people.

Secondly, *the glory departs from Jerusalem.* Ezekiel was now transported in his vision to the temple, and "the glory of the God of Israel" was there (8:4). But the prophet was horrified by the rampant idolatry he saw, provoking God to anger. So Ezekiel saw the glory of the Lord rise up from the earth, then stop, then move out, then stop again stage by stage as if reluctant to go (10:4, 16–19), and finally leave the city and stop on the mountain to the east (11:23). It must have filled Ezekiel with anguish to watch God's glory gradually but steadily leave the temple to which it rightly belonged.

Thirdly, *the glory returns to Jerusalem.* Perhaps the most moving feature of Ezekiel's final vision occurs in chapter 43, verses 1–5, in which in his vision he is brought to the temple gate facing east. And there "the glory of the LORD entered the temple through the gate facing east… and the glory of the LORD filled the temple" (vv. 4–5). At last God had returned to his home among his worshipping and obedient people.

For further reading: Ezekiel 1:22–28

Monday

The Call of Ezekiel

YOU MUST SPEAK MY WORDS TO THEM, WHETHER THEY LISTEN OR FAIL
TO LISTEN, FOR THEY ARE REBELLIOUS.

Ezekiel 2:7

As we have seen, it is instructive to compare the calls of Isaiah and Jeremiah (see p. 110). We can now add the call of Ezekiel. Isaiah heard God's question: "Whom shall I send?" (Isa. 6:8). Jeremiah was told, "You must go to everyone I send you to" (Jer. 1:7), and Ezekiel was told, "I am sending you to the Israelites" (Ezek. 2:3). Each thus received the commission to be a prophet and to speak God's word in God's name.

Each call, therefore, included a reference to the prophet's mouth or lips. Isaiah's unclean lips needed to be cleansed. Yahweh touched Jeremiah's mouth and said, "I have put my words in your mouth" (Jer. 1:9). And Ezekiel was to speak Yahweh's very words to Israel (Ezek. 3:4).

Beyond these similarities, however, each prophetic call was distinctive. In Ezekiel's case it was Yahweh's dramatization in offering him a scroll to eat and in telling him to fill his stomach with it. He ate it and found it to taste like honey (3.1–3). What did this signify? Surely that he must assimilate Yahweh's Word himself before he could proclaim it to others. Also that he must obey God's Word and "not rebel like that rebellious people [Israel]" (2:8), for God's Word is sweet to the taste.

We have already had occasion to observe that there are no prophets today, no organs of direct revelation like Isaiah, Jeremiah, or Ezekiel. Instead, there are stewards of the revelation God has given us in Christ and in Scripture.

Those of us who have been called to the privileged task of Christian stewardship must above all be faithful, first digesting God's Word ourselves, and then obeying it, before we are in any position to make it known to others. As Donald Coggan, former Archbishop of Canterbury, wrote, "The Christian preacher is not at liberty to invent... his message; it has been committed to him, and it is for him to declare, expound and commend it to his hearers."

For further reading: Ezekiel 2:1–3:3

TUESDAY

Sin and Judgment

YOUR PEOPLE SAY, "THE WAY OF THE LORD IS NOT JUST."
BUT IT IS THEIR WAY THAT IS NOT JUST.

Ezekiel 33:17

If one reads straight through the middle chapters of Ezekiel (4–24), there is no doubt of their dominant thought. It is human sin and divine judgment – on the one hand, an exposure of Israel's sin and, on the other, a justification of God's judgment. Moreover, the sins that Ezekiel exposes are clearly breaches of both tablets of the Ten Commandments.

Firstly, God's people were not loving God with all their being. Instead, when Ezekiel paid his visionary visit to Jerusalem, he was horrified by the idolatrous images he found even in the temple itself. "Evil abominations" he called them (6:11 RSV). Men and women, priests and laypeople, were desecrating God's house. One group had turned their backs on the temple and their faces toward the east, prostrating themselves before the sun (8:16). Others were worshipping at the high places of Canaanite fertility religion. Some did not even stop short of the horrors of child sacrifice. Moreover, theirs was no superficial idolatry; they had "set up idols in their hearts" (14:3).

Secondly, God's people were not loving their neighbour. They had "fill[ed] the land with violence" (8:17). They had failed to care for the poor, feed the hungry, clothe the naked, and secure justice for the oppressed. Worse still, they had gained a reputation for Jerusalem as "the city of bloodshed" (22:2), which is what the prophet Nahum had called Nineveh (Nah. 3:1), because so much innocent blood was being shed in it.

Since the word *idols* is the acme of sin against God, and *blood* is the acme of sin against our neighbour, one could not sink lower than to combine the two, and this was Ezekiel's accusation: "You... look to your idols and shed blood" (33:25; see also 36:18). Such was the record of the rebellious house of Israel. No wonder they had driven Yahweh far from his sanctuary (8:6) and caused his glory to depart.

For further reading: Ezekiel 14:1–8

God's Holy Name

IT IS NOT FOR YOUR SAKE... THAT I AM GOING TO DO THESE THINGS, BUT
FOR THE SAKE OF MY HOLY NAME, WHICH YOU HAVE PROFANED AMONG
THE NATIONS WHERE YOU HAVE GONE.

Ezekiel 36:22

There is one particular and distinctive phrase that is repeated by Ezekiel some ninety times like a refrain. It is usually called the "recognition formula" spoken by Yahweh: "Then you [or they] will know that I am the LORD." It expresses God's ultimate and overriding desire that he will be recognized – indeed, acknowledged – for who and what he is. Moreover, there are three main situations in which Yahweh desires this, namely when he judges his people, when he saves his people, and when he reaches out beyond Israel to the nations.

Perhaps the most striking example of the first is chapter 6, in which Ezekiel is told to prophesy against the mountains of Israel. Yahweh is about to demolish their high places, to scatter the survivors into exile, to bring his three judgments (sword, famine, and pestilence) upon the idolaters, and to make their whole land desolate. And after each of these four solemn warnings, the same refrain occurs: "They [you (v. 7)] will know that I am the LORD" (vv. 7, 10, 13–14).

Secondly, the identical formula is used when Yahweh saves his people. Take the vision of dry bones. God promises Israel that he will put his Spirit within them and bring them back to their land, and adds, "Then you... will know that I am the LORD" (37:13). But Ezekiel's horizons are wider than Israel and embrace the world. So in chapters 25 to 32 Ezekiel addresses Israel's seven surrounding peoples, and the recognition formula is scattered some twenty times throughout these chapters, sometimes in judgment but also in foreseeing some kind of incorporation into the covenant people of God. Ezekiel has not forgotten God's promise to Abraham that through his posterity all the nations will be blessed.

Behind the recognition formula is Yahweh's concern for his holy name, which Israel had profaned in the sight of the nations (36:21). Yahweh acts for the sake of his name, so that it may receive the honour due to it. And we should share his concern. There is no greater motivation for mission.

For further reading: Ezekiel 36:22–32

THURSDAY

Cultural Conformity and Nonconformity

BUT DANIEL RESOLVED NOT TO DEFILE HIMSELF WITH
THE ROYAL FOOD AND WINE...

Daniel 1:8

The second exilic prophet was Daniel. His story began in 605 BC, that is, in the third year of the reign of Jehoiakim, king of Judah. It was also the year of the first deportation of Jewish captives from Jerusalem to Babylon, and in this first batch of exiles were some young men of both royal and noble birth. They were handsome, without any physical defect, intelligent, and knowledgeable. King Nebuchadnezzar ordered Ashpenaz, his chief chamberlain or palace master, to select a few of them to be educated in Babylonian culture so as to be fitted for the civil service. They were assigned a daily portion of the royal rations of food and wine, and at the end of three years they would be expected to serve in the king's court. Among them were four candidates – Daniel, Hananiah, Mishael, and Azariah, whose names the palace master changed to Belteshazzar, Shadrach, Meshach, and Abednego.

"But," as the narrative abruptly changes direction, "Daniel resolved not to defile himself with the royal food and wine" (v. 8). It is not clear to us which dietary prohibition Daniel was determined to observe, but it was evidently clear to him. He was willing to be taught "the language and literature of the Babylonians" (v. 4), to assume a new name, and no doubt to submit to cosmetic treatments, but there he drew the line. He emphatically would not break the law of his God.

This incident is a remarkable example of cultural discrimination. The fact is that every culture, being a human construct, is a mixture of good and evil, truth and error, beauty and ugliness. Daniel and his friends resolved to assimilate all that was good in Chaldean culture but were equally determined to reject everything that was incompatible with their revealed faith.

Moreover, as they began, so they continued. Their integrity soon involved them in serious civil disobedience, as they refused to bow down and worship Nebuchadnezzar's image (chap. 3) and as Daniel refused to stop praying to Yahweh (chap. 6). These faithful Jews paid a high price for their integrity – the fiery furnace in the first case and the lions' den in the second.

For further reading: Daniel 1

FRIDAY

The Sovereignty of God

THE MOST HIGH IS SOVEREIGN OVER ALL KINGDOMS ON EARTH AND
GIVES THEM TO ANYONE HE WISHES.

Daniel 4:32

It is difficult for us to imagine the instability that the exiles felt in Babylon. Jerusalem, the stable centre of their national life, was far away and in ruins. They themselves were defeated and humiliated aliens. "The Beautiful Land," as Daniel called it (11:41), which God had promised to give them, had been depopulated and was now occupied and farmed by foreigners. Throughout the six hundred or so years of their existence, the tiny kingdoms of Israel and Judah were sandwiched between the mighty empires of the north (Assyria and Babylon) and the south (Egypt). Again and again their sacred territory was invaded and overrun by foreign troops. The very foundations of their faith were undermined. Where was their God? The answer of the book of Daniel was that, in spite of all appearances to the contrary, the Most High God rules over all human kingdoms.

This was the message of Nebuchadnezzar's dream in chapter 2. The enormous statue that he saw had a golden head, silver chest and arms, a bronze torso, iron legs, and feet of iron and clay. These different parts symbolized successive empires, which Daniel did not specifically identify but which have been traditionally understood as referring to Babylon, Medo-Persia, Greece (which "will rule over the whole earth" [v. 39]), and Rome. Then, as we watch, a little rock came hurtling through the air, shattered the image, and then grew into a huge mountain that filled the earth. This was the kingdom of God, which "will never be destroyed" (v. 44). So the violent scenario of kingdoms in conflict continues throughout the book. It culminates in the he-goat, whom we recognize as Alexander the Great, charging from the west (8:5–8). He is succeeded by the kings of the north and of the south, namely the dynasties of the Seleucids and the Ptolemies of chapter 11.

We read in the Psalms that "the LORD reigns" (e.g., Pss. 97 and 99), and the book of Daniel is a vivid illustration of this cry of faith.

For further reading: Daniel 2:36–45

Saturday

The Humbling of the Proud

THOSE WHO WALK IN PRIDE HE [GOD] IS ABLE TO HUMBLE.

Daniel 4:37

The epigram of Lord Acton, William Gladstone's friend, is well known: "Power corrupts; absolute power corrupts absolutely." We certainly see the corruption of power in the megalomaniacs of Daniel's day. Nebuchadnezzar was a conspicuous example of it. In Nebuchadnezzar's dream of a colossus or obelisk, only the statue's head was made of gold (2:32), but when the king built a gigantic statue some ninety feet high, presumably representing himself, he made sure that the whole of it was made of gold (3:1).

A bit later, we are told, he was strutting like a peacock on the flat roof of his palace in Babylon, soliloquizing. The subject of his conversation with himself was his own imperial greatness: "Is not this the great Babylon I have built as the royal residence, by my mighty power and for the glory of my majesty?" (4:30). It was the exact antithesis of the doxology with which we are familiar and which attributes the kingdom, the power, and the glory to God, not to any human being. It is not surprising, therefore, that while the words were still on Nebuchadnezzar's lips, God's judgment fell upon him. He was deprived of his kingdom and driven from his palace. He lived with animals and ate like them. His hair grew long like eagles' feathers and his nails like the claws of a bird. In other words, he went mad.

Only when he humbled himself, acknowledged that the Most High God rules over all human kingdoms, and lifted his eyes to heaven in worship were his sanity and his kingdom simultaneously restored to him. For pride and madness go together, as do humility and reason.

This was the lesson Nebuchadnezzar learned. As he put it, "Those who walk in pride he [God] is able to humble" (v. 37). So it has always been. As Jesus expressed it, "For all those who exalt themselves will be humbled" (Luke 18:14). Those who put themselves up God puts down. We saw this principle fulfilled many times in the twentieth century – in Hitler, Mussolini, and Stalin; in Amin and Pol Pot; and (as we confidently anticipated) in Saddam Hussein and others.

For further reading: Daniel 4:28–37

The Babylonian Empire fell in 539 BC and was succeeded by the Persian Empire under the rule of Cyrus. We have already been introduced to him as Yahweh's anointed, a brilliant soldier who subdued nations before him (Isa. 41:2; 45:1). The Jewish exiles must have been watching his military exploits with increasing excitement until at last even Babylon capitulated to him.

Then in the first year of Cyrus's reign "the LORD moved the heart of Cyrus" (Ezra 1:1) to issue two edicts, firstly to repatriate the Jews whom the Babylonians had deported and secondly to rebuild their temple. This was fully in keeping with his known religious policy. Whereas the Assyrians and Babylonians had imposed the worship of their own gods on their conquered subjects, the Persians sought to conciliate them by respecting their gods and even worshipping them.

Sunday: The Rebuilding of the Temple

Monday: Opposition and Encouragement

Tuesday: Ezra the Scribe

Wednesday: Nehemiah's Vision

Thursday: Nehemiah's Plan

Friday: Nehemiah's Perseverance

Saturday: The Story of Esther

The Rebuilding of the Temple

THEY FINISHED BUILDING THE TEMPLE ACCORDING TO THE COMMAND OF
THE GOD OF ISRAEL AND THE DECREES OF CYRUS...

Ezra 6:14

Psalm 126 gives us a sense of the enormous relief and rejoicing felt by the Babylonian exiles when they were repatriated:

When the LORD brought back the captives to Zion,
we were like those who dreamed.
Our mouths were filled with laughter,
our tongues with songs of joy.

Psalm 126:1–2

Although scholars are still debating the exact order of events, I am following the traditional chronology, namely that the restoration of Judah took place in three stages under three leaders.

Firstly, in 538 BC Zerubbabel, grandson of King Jehoiachin, and Jeshua the high priest returned to Jerusalem and rebuilt the temple. Secondly, in 458 BC Ezra the priest and scribe arrived in Jerusalem. He has been described as a kind of secretary of state for Jewish affairs in Babylonia, and his task was to regulate and restore Israel's religious and moral responsibilities in accordance with the law. Thirdly, in 445 BC Nehemiah, cupbearer to the Persian King Artaxerxes, and later governor of Judah, was sent to restore the city of Jerusalem, and in particular to rebuild its walls.

So Zerubbabel was the first to arrive, with the main party of returning exiles. Cyrus's decree authorized their return, which was encouraged by his generous gesture in giving back to the Jewish leaders 5,400 articles of gold and silver from the temple, all carefully inventoried. No sooner had they returned than they built the altar of burnt offerings and resumed the regular sacrifices. In the seventh month they celebrated the Feast of Tabernacles. They also laid the foundation of the new temple. For years their worship had been silenced. "How can we sing the songs of the LORD," they had asked, "while in a foreign land?" (Ps. 137:4). But now their tongues were loosed, and they burst out singing the familiar covenant song: "He is good; his love towards Israel endures for ever" (Ezra 3:11). Some shouted. Others wept. It was a time of great emotion in worship.

For further reading: Haggai 1

MONDAY

Opposition and Encouragement

ZERUBBABEL... AND JOSHUA... SET TO WORK TO REBUILD THE HOUSE OF
GOD... AND THE PROPHETS OF GOD WERE WITH THEM,
SUPPORTING THEM.

Ezra 5:2

Whenever a work of God is prospering, we can expect opposition to arise. In Jerusalem it began with the Samaritans and continued later with others who were anxious to bring the rebuilding of the temple to a halt. They succeeded for a while, and during this period two encouragements took place.

Firstly, research into the royal archives revealed that the Jews had been fully authorized to rebuild the temple, and the message came to the governor of the Trans-Euphrates province in Jerusalem: "Do not interfere with the work on this temple of God" (6:7).

Secondly, two of Yahweh's special prophets, Haggai and Zechariah, strongly encouraged Zerubbabel to finish the work. Here is Haggai's exhortation: "'Who of you is left who saw this house in its former glory? How does it look to you now? Does it not seem to you like nothing? But now be strong... and work. For I am with you,' declares the LORD Almighty" (Hag. 2:3–4).

The word of God also came to Zechariah, saying, "The hands of Zerubbabel have laid the foundation of this temple; his hands will also complete it" (Zech. 4:9). So "Zerubbabel... and Joshua... set to work to rebuild the house of God in Jerusalem. And the prophets of God were with them, helping them" (Ezra 5:2). The reconstruction of the temple began again in 520 BC and finished in 515 BC, some seventy years after the destruction of its predecessor, as Jeremiah had predicted. After the dedication of the building with joy, priests and people celebrated the Passover, as if they were newly redeemed. Indeed, that is exactly what had happened. They began to detect the threefold pattern of their redemption, as Yahweh called Abraham out of Ur, Israel out of Egypt, and the exiles out of Babylon. All three foreshadow that greater redemption that God has accomplished through Jesus Christ.

For further reading: Revelation 5:9–10; 14:1–6

Ezra the Scribe

EZRA HAD SET HIS HEART TO STUDY THE LAW OF THE LORD, AND TO DO
IT, AND TO TEACH THE STATUTES AND ORDINANCES IN ISRAEL.

Ezra 7:10 NRSV

From the completion of the rebuilding of the temple in 515 BC, we jump nearly seventy-five years to the second stage in the reconstruction of Israel's national life following the exile. This was led by Ezra, who was a priest, a scribe, and a teacher. He was sent to Jerusalem by none other than the Persian King Artaxerxes I. His instructions were to regulate Israel's religious, social, and moral behaviour in accordance with the law of Moses.

What kind of a man was Ezra? We are not left to guess. A succinct description of him is given to us: "Ezra had set his heart to study the law of the Lord, and to do it, and to teach the statutes and ordinances in Israel" (v. 10 NRSV). This threefold characterization is very significant. Firstly, he was a diligent student of God's law. Not content with a superficial acquaintance, he sought out its meaning and its application. Secondly, he was resolved to be not a forgetful hearer but an obedient doer of God's Word. Thirdly, he went beyond a personal study and observance to a ministry of teaching others. Moreover, on all three tasks (to study, to do, and to teach) he had set his heart.

This humble submission to the Word of God was Ezra's primary characteristic. During a particular public assembly the Word of God was given its due honour. Standing on a high wooden platform built for the occasion, Ezra read the law out loud from daybreak until noon. When he opened the book, the people spontaneously rose to their feet. Then "they bowed down and worshipped the LORD with their faces to the ground" (Neh. 8:6). They did not worship the book. Nor, of course, should we. But we worship the Lord and honour the Bible because of him.

For further reading: Nehemiah 8:1–8

Nehemiah's Vision

COME, LET US REBUILD THE WALL OF JERUSALEM, AND WE WILL NO
LONGER BE IN DISGRACE.

Nehemiah 2:17

After the restoration of the temple under Zerubbabel and the restoration of the law under Ezra, came the restoration of the city walls under Nehemiah. Nehemiah had a unique role to play in salvation history, that is, in God's purpose to rehabilitate his people. Although nobody has a similar function today, nevertheless in a secondary sense God does want Christian leaders to develop the leadership qualities that Nehemiah displayed. At least six can be identified.

Firstly, *the Christian leader has a clear vision*. Vision is compounded of two complementary things, namely a deep dissatisfaction with what is and a clear grasp of what could be. It begins with indignation over the status quo and grows into the earnest quest for an alternative. For example, a journalist wrote of Bobby Kennedy after his assassination in 1968 that "his distinguishing quality was his capacity for… moral outrage. 'That is unacceptable,' he said of many conditions that most of us accepted as inevitable… Poverty, illiteracy, malnutrition, prejudice, crookedness, conniving – all such accepted evils were a personal affront to him." One might say that apathy is the acceptance of the unacceptable, whereas leadership begins with a decisive refusal to do so. How can we tolerate what God finds intolerable?

Secondly, *the Christian leader feels deeply about his vision*. When Nehemiah heard that the wall of Jerusalem was in ruins and that its gates had been burned down, the news overwhelmed him until God put into his heart what to do. "Come, let us rebuild," he said (v. 17). It is not enough to see the present situation as displeasing to God and to discern how it could be changed. We must also feel both indignation and compassion. Nehemiah's grief showed on his face, and the king noticed it.

For further reading: Nehemiah 1:1–4

Thursday

Nehemiah's Plan

THEN I PRAYED TO THE GOD OF HEAVEN, AND I ANSWERED THE KING...

Nehemiah 2:4–5

The third lesson we can learn from Nehemiah is that a *Christian leader seeks support from both God and human beings.* When the king asked Nehemiah what he wanted, he first "prayed to the God of heaven" and then asked the king for permission to go to Jerusalem to rebuild it. He was neither so super-spiritual that he cried only to God and considered human help superfluous nor so super-confident in human resources that he considered prayer to God unnecessary.

No. Prayer and action are not alternative options. Nor are they incompatible with each other. They belong together, and either without the other is dangerously unbalanced. It is evident from Nehemiah's first two chapters that he was a man of prayer. But this did not prevent him from asking the king for permission to go to Jerusalem, for letters to the governors of the province of Trans-Euphrates to grant him safe conduct, and for an additional letter to Asaph, keeper of the king's forest, asking for timber for the rebuilding operations.

Fourthly, *a Christian leader develops a realistic plan.* The world tends to be scornful of dreamers. "Here comes that dreamer!" Joseph's elder brothers had said. "Come now, let's kill him... Then we'll see what comes of his dreams. (Gen 37.19–20). The dreams of the night often evaporate in the cool light of the morning. So dreamers have to become thinkers, planners, and workers. People of vision need to become people of action. So Nehemiah, though inspired by his vision of the rebuilt city, had to make a plan. Soon after his arrival in Jerusalem he undertook a personal reconnaissance. By night he went out, examining the walls of Jerusalem. Thus in true leadership vision and action, a dream and a plan go together.

For further reading: Nehemiah 3

FRIDAY

Nehemiah's Perseverance

ALL THE SURROUNDING NATIONS... REALISED THAT THIS WORK HAD BEEN
DONE WITH THE HELP OF OUR GOD.

Nehemiah 6:16

The fifth lesson to be learned from Nehemiah is that *a Christian leader attracts a following*. Indeed, the very word *leader* implies this. The leader takes the initiative, but he persuades others to join him. Of course, some leaders in history have been strong individualists. The authentic leader, however, inspires people to follow their lead, for they see their task as a cooperative enterprise. Chapter 2 of Nehemiah's book seems to chart his conversion from individualism to collective action, from verse 5 ("Let him [the king] send me to the city... so that I can rebuild it") to verses 17–18 ("Then I said to them... 'Come, let us rebuild'").

Sixthly, *the Christian leader refuses to be discouraged*. Once a work of God begins, opposition can be expected. The forces of reaction muster, and hostility comes out into the open. Indeed, discouragement is the chief occupational hazard of a leader. In the case of Nehemiah, virulent antagonism was mounted by Sanballat the Horonite, Tobiah the Ammonite, and Geshem the Arab. First they mocked and ridiculed Nehemiah, and then they misrepresented him, suggesting that he was rebelling against the Persian régime. Derision and slander are poisonous weapons in the hands of an enemy. But the true leader refuses to give in. He or she perseveres.

These six qualities can apply to leadership of all kinds – not only to national or international top brass but to leadership in the professions, in business and industry, in the media and the church. Parents are leaders in the home, and so are teachers in school or college. Student leaders are also hugely influential in many parts of the world. Nehemiah's example can inspire us all.

For further reading: Nehemiah 6

SATURDAY

The Story of Esther

WHO KNOWS BUT THAT YOU HAVE COME TO YOUR ROYAL POSITION FOR
SUCH A TIME AS THIS?

Esther 4:14

The book of Esther contains no single mention of God, but it is full of events that can be understood either as human coincidences or as divine providences, or indeed as both. The scene is set in the palace of the Persian King Ahasuerus, or Xerxes (486–465 BC). Mordecai was a Jew whose cousin and ward, Esther, was selected by the king as his new queen and who had reported an assassination plot against the king but had never been rewarded for it.

Mordecai's rival was Haman, grand vizier to the king. Conscious of his importance, he required everybody to bow down before him. But Mordecai, conscious of the first commandment, refused to do so. Infuriated, Haman determined to take revenge on all Jews throughout Persia and secured the royal assent to his liquidation plan. As the feud between these two men grew, it seemed impossible for Mordecai to rescue his people. But it is now that God's providence came into operation.

It so happened (to use the language of coincidence) that Queen Esther was a Jewess, that she was willing to risk her life in begging the king for mercy, and that she made her petition at a private banquet at which the king and Haman were her only guests. Haman went home "happy and in high spirits" (5:9), boasting of his high honour – though it gave him no satisfaction as long as he saw Mordecai sitting at the king's gate.

It so happened also that the king was unable to sleep that night, that he ordered the royal chronicles to be read to him, that in them he heard the record of the assassination plot for which Mordecai had not been rewarded, and that Haman (intending to talk to the king about hanging Mordecai) arrived in the outer court at that very moment. The king asked Haman what should be done for the man the king delights to honour. Jumping to the conclusion that the king meant him, Haman replied that he should be paraded through the city in royal splendour. "'Go at once,' the king commanded Haman. '... do just as you have suggested for Mordecai the Jew" (6:10). Such is the irony of the providence of God. The roles of the two men were reversed. Haman was humiliated, Mordecai honoured.

For further reading: Esther 7

One of the salient features of the Old Testament is its growing expectation of the coming Messiah. It began immediately after the fall. No sooner had Adam and Eve sinned than God announced his intention to save sinners and to do so through a descendant of the very person by whom sin had entered the world. From then on God's promise of the Messiah became increasingly rich and varied. For example, he would be a prophet like Moses, a priest like Melchizedek, and a king like David – Calvin's familiar trio of Prophet, Priest, and King. So, as we conclude our survey of the Old Testament, it seems appropriate to consider the main messianic images.

Sunday: A Descendant of Eve

Monday: The Seed of Abraham

Tuesday: A Prophet like Moses

Wednesday: A King like David

Thursday: A Priest like Melchizedek

Friday: The Servant of the Lord

Saturday: The Son of Man

A Descendant of Eve

AND I WILL PUT ENMITY BETWEEN YOU AND THE WOMAN, AND BETWEEN
YOUR OFFSPRING AND HERS; HE WILL CRUSH YOUR HEAD, AND YOU WILL
STRIKE HIS HEEL.

Genesis 3:15

However confusing this combination of warning and promise, of hostility and victory, certain truths may be affirmed. Firstly, God has established between the human race (Eve's offspring) and the principalities and powers of evil (the snake's offspring) a reciprocal enmity. We must never come to terms with evil.

Secondly, although this continuous feud has been relentless, it will not be eternal. So it is not a case of "dualism," for it will culminate in a final contest between Christ and Antichrist.

Thirdly, although the enmity is reciprocal, its outcome is not. For the head of the enemy will be crushed, that is, destroyed by the man Christ Jesus. At the same time, the victor will not altogether escape injury; he will suffer bruising to the heel.

This promise to Eve that one of her descendants would ultimately crush the snake's head is often – and rightly – called the protevangelium, that is, the very first proclamation of the gospel. It was, of course, fulfilled on the cross, for it was there that the devil was disarmed and overthrown at the cost of the Messiah's suffering. Now all things have been put under his feet (Eph. 1:22), and we are confident (as Paul wrote) that "the God of peace will soon crush Satan under your feet" (Rom. 16:20). It may seem strange that in this context of conflict Paul should refer to "the God of peace," since enjoying peace and crushing Satan do not sound altogether compatible with each other. But God's peace allows no appeasement of the devil. Indeed, it is only through the destruction of evil that true peace can be attained.

For further reading: Ephesians 1:15–23

The Seed of Abraham

I WILL BLESS YOU... AND YOU WILL BE A BLESSING... AND ALL PEOPLES ON
EARTH WILL BE BLESSED THROUGH YOU.

Genesis 12:2-3

Abraham is a towering figure of the Old Testament, being the first of the three great patriarchs, or founding fathers, of Yahweh's covenant people. In addition to his promises to give Abraham a land and a seed, God promised in more general terms to bless him, to make him a blessing, and even through him (i.e., through his descendant, the Messiah) to bless all the families of the earth.

It is no exaggeration to claim that the rest of the Old Testament, and indeed the rest of human history, has been a fulfilment of these promises. Consider Paul's argument. Because God made his promises to Abraham and to his seed (in the singular), his use of this collective noun alluded to Christ and so to all who are united to Christ by faith. For if we belong to Christ, then we are Abraham's posterity (Gal. 3:16, 29).

The apostle goes on to contrast the words *curse* and *blessing*, or more particularly "the curse of the law" and "the blessing of Abraham." "Christ redeemed us," he writes, "from the curse of the law [that is, the judgment that the law pronounces on those who disobey it] by becoming a curse for us... in order that the blessing given to Abraham might come to the Gentiles through Christ Jesus" (Gal. 3:13-14). He bore the curse that we might inherit the blessing.

God's promise to bless the world through Abraham's seed lies at the foundation of the Christian missionary enterprise. We must continue to share the gospel with both Jews and Gentiles until the countless number of the redeemed is drawn from every nation and language and so is as numerous as the stars in the sky and the dust of the earth. Only then will God's promise to Abraham be fulfilled.

For further reading: Galatians 3:6-25

A Prophet like Moses

THE LORD YOUR GOD WILL RAISE UP FOR YOU A PROPHET LIKE ME FROM
AMONG... YOUR FELLOW ISRAELITES. YOU MUST LISTEN TO HIM.

Deuteronomy 18:15

One of humankind's most ardent desires is to discover the will of God. But how?
Broadly speaking, Israel was faced with two options. On the one hand, the Canaanites
practised witchcraft, sorcery, and divination of different kinds, but God forbade his
people to copy them. On the other hand, they could pay attention to the voice of God
as it came to them through the prophets. It was a question of listening. They must not
"listen to those who practise sorcery... But as for you... The LORD your God will raise
up for you a prophet like me... You must listen to him" (vv. 14–15).

This divine promise seems to have referred originally to the succession of prophets
God gave Israel. But when the voice of prophecy fell silent in the intertestamental
period, "the Prophet" became a recognizable messianic title. So when Jesus came, the
crowds said, "Surely this is the Prophet who is to come into the world" (John 6:14).
And in one of Peter's early sermons he plainly applied the promise to Jesus (Acts 3:22).
Although Jesus was not one more prophet in the long succession of the centuries,
but rather the fulfilment of all prophecy, in whom all God's promises find their "yes"
(2 Cor. 1:20), we still hail him as "the Prophet" who like Moses knows God "face to
face" (Deut. 34:10) and in whom God's revelation has reached its culmination.

It is moving that on the Mount of Transfiguration the voice of God the Father
quoted his own command in Deuteronomy 18:15 and applied it to Jesus. His command
to all of us is the same: "Listen to him!" (Mark 9:7).

For further reading: Deuteronomy 18:14–22

WEDNESDAY

A King like David

FOR TO US A CHILD IS BORN, TO US A SON IS GIVEN, AND THE
GOVERNMENT WILL BE ON HIS SHOULDERS. AND HE WILL BE CALLED
WONDERFUL COUNSELLOR, MIGHTY GOD, EVERLASTING FATHER, PRINCE
OF PEACE.

Isaiah 9:6

God's original purpose for his people was not a kingdom but a theocracy. That is, he would rule over them himself directly without a human intermediary. Thus when they demanded a king like the other nations, it was God, not Samuel, whom they were rejecting. Samuel proceeded to warn them of the oppressive régimes that their human kings would introduce. And so it came to pass. It is not surprising, therefore, that the prophets began to dream of a future ideal kingdom that would exhibit all those characteristics that the kings of Israel and Judah lamentably failed to exhibit, although David approximated to them.

Firstly, *God's kingdom would be righteous.* The Messiah would be righteous and would rule his people with justice. "The days are coming," Yahweh declared, "when I will raise up from David's line a righteous Branch, a King who will reign wisely and do what is just and right in the land" (Jer. 23:5).

Secondly, *God's kingdom would be peaceful.* David's reign had been marred by endless wars, and it was in deliberate contrast to this that his son and successor was named Solomon, *shalom*, peace (1 Chron. 22:6–10).

Thirdly, *God's kingdom would be stable.* The thrones of Israel and Judah were mostly unstable and comparatively brief, but the messianic kingdom would last forever.

Fourthly, *God's kingdom would be universal.* At its most extensive, Israel's territory stretched only "from Dan to Beersheba" (2 Sam. 3:10). But the messianic kingdom would "extend from sea to sea and from the River to the ends of the earth" (Zech. 9:10).

Thus righteousness and peace, eternity and universality are the main characteristics of the messianic kingdom that was ushered in by Jesus. It is not far-fetched to detect these qualities in the four names of the boy king (Isa. 9:6).

For further reading: Psalm 72

THURSDAY

A Priest like Melchizedek

YOU ARE A PRIEST FOR EVER, IN THE ORDER OF MELCHIZEDEK.

Psalm 110:4

Melchizedek is without doubt one of the most mysterious characters in the whole of Scripture. He is mentioned in only three passages, and in each of them he is identified as a priest. He appears first in the narrative of Genesis where he meets Abraham returning from his campaign to rescue Lot (Gen. 14:12, 18–20). Secondly, he is named in Psalm 110:4, where Yahweh addresses his king in these words: "You are a priest for ever, in the order of Melchizedek." Thirdly, the writer of Hebrews alludes to both these texts and draws out their implications in relation to Jesus.

Jesus the Messiah is a priest. Yet he is not a Levitical priest, since he was not descended from Levi. Indeed, Jesus' priesthood is not only different from that of the Levitical priests but also superior to it. It belongs to the priesthood of Melchizedek. This superiority is evident because Melchizedek both blessed Abraham (Levi's ancestor) and received from him a tenth of the spoils, and these were both superior roles.

In what way, then, is the priesthood of Jesus superior to that of Levi? Several reasons are given, but one is emphasized, namely that he is a priest "for ever." Because the Levitical priests were human beings and therefore mortal, "death prevented them from continuing in office" (Heb. 7:23) and they had to be continually replaced. Not Jesus, however. "Because Jesus lives for ever, he has a permanent priesthood" (Heb. 7:24). Not that his sacrifice can in any way be repeated or prolonged, but rather that it has eternal efficacy. For when Christ had made on the cross his one sacrifice for sins forever, he sat down at the Father's right hand, his atoning work having been accomplished (Heb. 10:11–14). Assurance of forgiveness comes from resting and rejoicing in the finished work of Christ on the cross.

For further reading: Hebrews 10:11–22

The Servant of the Lord

HERE IS MY SERVANT, WHOM I UPHOLD, MY CHOSEN ONE IN WHOM I
DELIGHT...

Isaiah 42:1

The second part of Isaiah contains four so-called Servant Songs, although there has been much debate about the servant's identity. Some see him as an individual like Isaiah himself or Jeremiah, while others understand him as a collective portrait of Israel or of the godly remnant within Israel. But the New Testament sees the Servant Songs as fulfilled in Jesus. In his early sermons, recorded in the Acts, Peter four times spoke of Jesus as "the servant"; Paul wrote that he took "the very nature of a servant" (Phil. 2:7); and there are many quotations of, and allusions to, Isaiah 42 to 53 in the teaching of Jesus himself.

What the four Servant Songs give us is a composite picture of the servant of the Lord. In the first song (Isa. 42:1–4) the servant is portrayed as a teacher, teaching in a spirit of gentleness, endued with the Spirit, and reaching out to the nations.

In the second song (Isa. 49:1–6) the servant is portrayed as an evangelist. The emphasis now is on the distant nations. It was too small a thing, God said, for his servant to restore backsliding Israel; the Lord would also make his servant "a light for the Gentiles" and would bring his salvation "to the ends of the earth" (v. 6). Paul used this verse to justify his bold decision to evangelize the Gentiles (Acts 13:46–47).

Thirdly, the servant is portrayed as a disciple (Isa. 50:4–9). For it is recognized that we cannot teach if we do not first listen and learn. Hence the need for Yahweh to waken his servant's ear "morning by morning" (v. 4). His ear must be opened first, before his tongue, even if what he learns and teaches is unpopular and provokes persecution.

In the fourth song the servant is portrayed as the suffering Saviour (Isa. 52:13–53:12), who (speaking prophetically) was wounded for our iniquities and who bore our sins. It is truly extraordinary that eight specific verses of Isaiah 53 are quoted by New Testament writers, in some cases several times. No wonder that Philip, when the Ethiopian asked to whom Isaiah 53:7–8 referred, "began with that very passage of Scripture and told him the good news about Jesus" (Acts 8:35).

For further reading: Isaiah 42:1–9

SATURDAY

The Son of Man

THE SON OF MAN MUST SUFFER MANY THINGS AND BE REJECTED... AND...
BE KILLED AND AFTER THREE DAYS RISE AGAIN.

Mark 8:31

We come today to the seventh and last image of the Messiah, the image that was the favourite of Jesus himself, namely "the Son of Man." It sounds, at first hearing, the most innocuous of titles. Jesus frequently used it in the third person so that when he said (for example), "the Son of Man will be ashamed," he meant, "I will be ashamed." Besides, "son of man" is a Hebrew idiom for "human being," and it is in this sense that God regularly addressed Ezekiel.

But it is also evident that Jesus used this title in direct reference to the prophecy of Daniel 7. Here in a vision Daniel saw "one like a son of man [i.e., looking like a human being] coming with the clouds of heaven" (Dan 7:13). He stood before the Ancient of Days (Eternal God) and was given authority, glory, and power so that all peoples of all languages worshipped him. And Daniel added, "His dominion is an everlasting dominion that will not pass away, and his kingdom is one that will never be destroyed" (Dan. 7:14).

Then several times Jesus applied this amazing vision to himself. For example, he said to the high priest, "You will see the Son of Man... coming on the clouds of heaven" (Mark 14:62). It was a claim to supreme authority and an everlasting kingdom. But what is truly extraordinary is that Jesus also used the same title in a totally different context. For example, echoing Isaiah 53, he said, "The Son of Man must suffer many things and be rejected... be killed and after three days rise again" (Mark 8:31). Thus Jesus did what nobody had done before him: he fused the glory of Daniel 7 with the suffering of Isaiah 53 in order to teach that it was only through suffering that he would enter into his glory. His words "the Son of Man must suffer" bring the two images together.

We have spent this week studying seven images of the Messiah. He is the seed of Eve, of Abraham, and of David. He is Prophet, Priest, and King. He is both suffering Saviour and majestic Ruler. Our place is on our faces before him.

For further reading: Mark 8:27–9:1

Week 17: The Nativity

We come now at last to the culmination of the Old Testament, the event to which the prophets have all in their different ways been leading, namely the Nativity, the birth of Jesus the Messiah, especially as the story is told by Matthew and Luke. We are immediately struck by a change of atmosphere. Not only are these early gospel narratives steeped in Old Testament language and culture, but they are also accompanied by the miraculous. There is no need for us to be embarrassed by this. It is surely fitting that a supernatural person should enter the world in a supernatural way. If we believe in the incarnation, it is logical to believe also in the virgin birth.

Sunday: The Annunciation

Monday: Mary's Song

Tuesday: The Virgin Birth

Wednesday: Mary's Submission

Thursday: Bethlehem

Friday: The Shepherds

Saturday: The Fullness of Time

SUNDAY

The Annunciation

GOD SENT THE ANGEL GABRIEL TO NAZARETH... TO A VIRGIN PLEDGED
TO BE MARRIED TO A MAN NAMED JOSEPH...

Luke 1:26–27

After some four hundred years of silent waiting, suddenly God broke the silence, though not through a prophet but through an angel. The message that Gabriel brought to Nazareth all but overwhelmed Mary – partly because she was to become a mother although she was still unmarried and a virgin, and partly because of the superlative threefold description she was given of her son to be born.

Firstly, he was to be named Jesus, indicating that he would be given a saving mission.

Secondly, he would be great, for he would be given a further and more elaborate name, the Son of the Most High. Mary would not have understood this as meaning what we mean when we call Jesus the Son of God but rather that he would be the Messiah, since Son of God was an acknowledged messianic title (see Ps. 2:7–8).

Thirdly, he would reign over Israel forever. Indeed, his kingdom would never end.

Saviour, Son, and King were the three titles that the angel told Mary to give him. No wonder Mary was "greatly troubled" (v. 29), even completely mystified by the angel's message, and asked him what it meant. Here is Gabriel's majestic reply: "The Holy Spirit will come on you, and the power of the Most High will overshadow you. So the holy one to be born will be called the Son of God... For no word from God will ever fail" (vv. 35–37). We will reflect on the fact and meaning of the virgin birth on Tuesday and Wednesday this week, but meanwhile, tomorrow we must listen to Mary's Song.

For further reading: Luke 1:26–32

Monday

Mary's Song

MY SOUL GLORIFIES THE LORD AND MY SPIRIT REJOICES IN GOD MY
SAVIOUR, FOR HE HAS BEEN MINDFUL OF THE HUMBLE STATE OF HIS
SERVANT.

Luke 1:46–48

Ever since at least the sixth century the church has cherished Mary's Song and has included it as the Magnificat in its liturgies. But this raises an important question. How can we sing her song? A Hebrew virgin chosen by God to give birth to the Messiah, the Son of God, gives inspired expression to her wonderment that she should have been thus honoured. How can we take her words on our lips? Is it not entirely inappropriate for us to do so?

But no. It has been recognized down the ages that Mary's experience, which in one way was absolutely unique, in another is typical of the experience of every Christian believer. The God who had done great things for her has also lavished his grace on us. Mary seems herself to have been aware of this, for her "me" and "my" of the beginning of her song moved later into the third person: "His mercy extends to those who fear him, from generation to generation" (v. 50). As in the song of Hannah after the birth of Samuel, so in Mary's Song, God turns human values upside down. There are two main examples.

Firstly, God dethrones the mighty and exalts the humble. He did it with Pharaoh and with Nebuchadnezzar, in both cases rescuing Israel from their exile. He still does it today in our experience of salvation. Only if we get on our knees beside the penitent publican will God exalt us with his accepting forgiveness.

Secondly, God dismisses the rich and feeds the hungry. Mary was hungry. She knew from the Old Testament that one day God's kingdom would come, and she was longing for that day to come. Hunger is still an indispensable condition of spiritual blessing, while complacent self-satisfaction is its greatest enemy.

If we want to inherit Mary's blessings, we must display Mary's qualities, especially humility and hunger.

For further reading: Luke 1:46–55

TUESDAY

The Virgin Birth

THE HOLY SPIRIT WILL COME ON YOU, AND THE POWER OF THE MOST
HIGH WILL OVERSHADOW YOU. SO THE HOLY ONE TO BE BORN WILL BE
CALLED THE SON OF GOD.

Luke 1:35

"Virgin birth" is a misleading expression, suggesting that there was something unusual about Jesus' birth, whereas his birth was entirely normal and natural. It was his conception that was abnormal, indeed supernatural, for he was conceived by the operation of the Holy Spirit, without the cooperation of a human father.

Matthew and Luke make an unambiguous affirmation that Jesus was born of the Virgin Mary. It is evident, moreover, that they were writing prose, not poetry, history, not myth. Why, then, did Mark and John not do the same thing? Answer: because they both chose to begin their narrative with John the Baptist. Their silence about the virgin birth no more means that they did not believe in it than their silence about his childhood means that they thought that he had none. The important point is that the only two evangelists who recorded his birth both declare that he was born of a virgin.

We move on now from the historicity of the virgin birth to its significance. Does it matter? It does. The angel's annunciation was in two stages.

The first (vv. 31–33) stressed the *continuity* that Mary's child would enjoy with the past, because she would bear him, and he would occupy the throne of his father David. That is, he would inherit from his mother both his humanity and his title to the messianic kingdom. The second section (v. 35) stressed the *discontinuity* between the child and the past, because the Holy Spirit would come upon Mary, and the creative power of God would overshadow her, so that her child would be unique, sinless ("the holy one"), and the Son of God.

In this way what was announced to the Virgin Mary was her son's humanity and messiahship, derived from her, while his sinlessness and deity would be derived from the Holy Spirit. As a result of the virgin birth, Jesus Christ was simultaneously Mary's son and God's Son, human and divine.

For further reading: Luke 1:33–35

WEDNESDAY

Mary's Submission

"I AM THE LORD'S SERVANT," MARY ANSWERED. "MAY YOUR WORD
TO ME BE FULFILLED."

Luke 1:38

"The first and most indisputable fact about the birth of Jesus," wrote Bishop John A. T. Robinson, "is that it occurred out of wedlock. The one option for which there is no evidence is that Jesus was the lawful son of Joseph and Mary. The only choice open to us is between a virgin birth and an illegitimate birth."

Rumours of Jesus' possible illegitimacy were being spread during his public ministry in an attempt to discredit him. For example, when he declared that certain unbelieving Jews had not Abraham but the devil as their father, they retorted, "We are not illegitimate children," which sounds like an innuendo that he was (John 8:41). These rumours persisted long after his death. In the Jewish Talmud they became explicit. How on earth could these hints and slanders have arisen unless it was known that Mary was already pregnant when Joseph married her? Distasteful as this gossip is, it is corroborative evidence of the virgin birth.

Mary's response to the angelic announcement wins our immediate admiration: "I am the Lord's servant... May your word to me be fulfilled" (v. 38). Once God's purpose and method had been explained to her, she did not demur. She was entirely at God's disposal. She expressed her total willingness to be the virgin mother of the Son of God. Of course, it was an enormous privilege for her: "The Mighty One has done great things for me," she said (v. 49). Yet it was also an awesome and costly responsibility. It involved a readiness to become pregnant before she was married, and so expose herself to the shame and suffering of being thought an immoral woman.

To me the humility and courage of Mary in submitting to the virgin birth stand out in contrast to the attitudes of the critics who deny it. She surrendered her reputation to God's will. For us too what matters is that we allow God to be God and to do things his way, even if with Mary we thereby risk losing our good name.

For further reading: Luke 1:34–38

Bethlehem

SHE GAVE BIRTH TO HER FIRSTBORN, A SON. SHE WRAPPED HIM
IN CLOTHS AND PLACED HIM IN A MANGER, BECAUSE THERE WAS NO
GUEST ROOM AVAILABLE FOR THEM.

Luke 2:7

It is Luke who tells us the circumstances surrounding the birth of Jesus and how the son of David (Jesus) came to be born in the city of David (Bethlehem). He lays his emphasis on two particulars – a decree of Augustus, the famous emperor of Rome, and the behaviour of an anonymous innkeeper in Bethlehem. The emperor and the innkeeper were both – though quite differently and quite unknowingly – instruments of God's providential purpose.

On the one hand, Augustus, who reigned over the empire from 30 BC to AD 14, issued an edict that a census be taken of the whole population and that people must go to their own town in order to register. The census was doubtless with a view to taxation. As a result, Joseph and Mary journeyed from Nazareth to Bethlehem. It would have been unusual and unnecessary for Joseph to be accompanied by Mary, but probably he had resolved not to leave her behind in her advanced pregnancy.

On the other hand, no doubt relieved that their long journey was at last over, Joseph and Mary would have been devastated that the Bethlehem innkeeper could find no place for them to stay, except in what seems to have been a stable. When Mary's baby was born, she laid him in a manger, that is, in a feeding trough for animals. It was symbolic of the rejection that Jesus was later to experience.

Thus the emperor and the innkeeper both played their part in God's plan without knowing it. The emperor's edict brought Joseph and Mary to Bethlehem in fulfilment of prophecy (Mic. 5:2; Matt. 2:5–6). And the innkeeper, by reason of overcrowding in the town, ensured that the Saviour of the world was born appropriately not in a palace but in a stable, not in splendour but in obscurity and poverty.

For further reading: Luke 2:1–7

FRIDAY

The Shepherds

AND THERE WERE SHEPHERDS LIVING OUT IN THE FIELDS NEAR BY... AN
ANGEL OF THE LORD APPEARED TO THEM, AND... SAID TO THEM, "DO NOT
BE AFRAID. I BRING YOU GOOD NEWS THAT WILL CAUSE GREAT JOY FOR
ALL THE PEOPLE. TODAY... A SAVIOUR HAS BEEN BORN TO YOU; HE IS THE
MESSIAH, THE LORD."

Luke 2:8–11

Shepherds had a bad reputation in Israel; they were regarded as dishonest and unreliable. Yet it was to them that God chose to announce the most stupendous good news the world has ever heard, namely that the long-awaited Messiah had been born. How did they respond?

Firstly, they went to Bethlehem to see for themselves. Their reaction was neither one of credulity nor of incredulity, but of open-minded, unprejudiced inquiry. So "they hurried off" (v. 16), and they found what they were looking for. Truly "he who seeks finds" (Matt. 7:8).

Secondly, when they had seen Jesus, "they spread the word" concerning what they had seen and heard (v. 17). They could not keep the good news to themselves. They wanted everybody to know it.

Thirdly, "The shepherds returned, glorifying and praising God for all the things they had heard and seen" (v. 20). In other words, their experience issued in worship as well as in witness. But first, we read, they "returned." They did not spend the rest of their lives in the stable or loiter around the manger. Instead, they returned to the fields and the sheep, to their homes, their wives, and their children. But, although their jobs and their homes were the same, they themselves were not. They were new people in the old situation. They had been changed by seeing Jesus. There was a spirit of wonder and of worship in their hearts.

The discovery of Jesus Christ is still a transforming experience. It adds a new dimension to our old lifestyle. As Billy Graham often says, it "puts a new light in our eye and a new spring in our step."

For further reading: Luke 2:8–20

SATURDAY

The Fullness of Time

BUT WHEN THE SET TIME HAD FULLY COME, GOD SENT HIS SON...

Galatians 4:4

Why did the incarnation take place when it did – probably by our reckoning in 5 BC, about a year before the death of Herod the Great in 4 BC? Some two thousand years had passed since God called Abraham and promised through his family to bless all the families of the world. Why, then, did such a long time elapse between the promise and its fulfilment? Paul affirmed that God sent his Son "when the appointed time came" (Gal. 4:4 REB), but he gave no hint how the appointed time had been fixed.

Many speculations have been made, especially in regard to the sociopolitical situation at the time, and certainly several circumstances were favourable to the rapid spread and ready reception of the gospel.

Firstly, there was the *pax romana* in the empire. The legions were everywhere, keeping the peace and protecting travellers from brigands on land and pirates at sea. Secondly, Greek was the common language of the empire, and it was immensely helpful to evangelism that the Septuagint (the Old Testament in Greek) was available. Thirdly, there was widespread spiritual hunger. The old gods of Rome had lost their appeal. The mystery religions offered a kind of personal regeneration but were evidence rather of spiritual longings than of their satisfaction. Then there were the so-called God-fearers on the edge of the synagogue, who were attracted by Jewish monotheism and high ethical standards and with whom Paul regularly shared the gospel.

So it was that during a period of only ten years (AD 48–57) Paul saw the church established in the four Roman provinces of Galatia, Macedonia, Achaia, and Asia. He could claim, "So from Jerusalem all the way round to Illyricum, I have fully proclaimed the gospel of Christ" (Rom. 15:19). In many ways the time was ripe for world evangelization.

For further reading: Romans 15:23–29

PART II

FROM CHRISTMAS TO PENTECOST

AN OVERVIEW OF THE GOSPELS
(THE LIFE OF CHRIST)

January to April

We come now to the second section of the Christian calendar, which takes us from January to April/May, and so from Christmas to Pentecost, from the life of Israel to the life of Christ as it is recounted in the Gospels.

WEEK 18: RESPONSES TO CHRISTMAS

Whenever we think or speak of Christmas, we have in mind that epoch-making event by which God the eternal Son became a human being in Jesus Christ. But God went beyond the event to its announcement to the world. So now the question is how the world responded. We have already seen how the shepherds responded. This week we will consider other responses – by the Magi, Herod the Great, Simeon, and by later church leaders like the apostles Paul and John. Their responses were varied, ranging from acceptance to rejection, from the Magi's desire to worship Jesus to Herod's determination to destroy him. One might even say that the whole New Testament consists of responses to God's mighty act in Jesus Christ.

Sunday: The Visit of the Magi

Monday: The Rage of Herod

Tuesday: The Flight into Egypt

Wednesday: The Song of Simeon

Thursday: The Testimony of Paul

Friday: The Reflection of John

Saturday: The Challenge of John

Sunday

The Visit of the Magi

We... have come to worship him.
Matthew 2:2

Western churches celebrate 6 January as Epiphany, the manifestation of Christ to the Gentiles; the Eastern Orthodox churches celebrate this day as their Christmas.

The Magi seem to have been astrologer-priests from the ancient Persian Empire. Their visit to Jesus is beautifully complementary to that of the shepherds. The two groups could not have been more different from each other than they were. Racially the shepherds were Jews, while the Magi were Gentiles. Intellectually the shepherds were simple and untutored, while the Magi were scholars, wise men from the East. Socially the shepherds belonged to the world's have-nots, whereas the Magi (judging from the expensive gifts they brought) were wealthy.

Yet despite these barriers (racial, intellectual, and social), which normally separate people from one another, the Magi were united with the shepherds in their worship of the Lord Jesus, forerunners of millions of other Gentiles who have come to worship him.

This is the universal appeal of Jesus, irrespective of ethnicity. It brought the shepherds from their fields and the Magi from the East. It still acts like a magnet. It attracts people of all cultures. It is one of the most convincing evidences that Jesus is the Saviour of the world.

For further reading: Matthew 2:1–6

The Rage of Herod

HEROD IS GOING TO SEARCH FOR THE CHILD TO KILL HIM.

Matthew 2:13

In the end there are only two possible responses to Jesus Christ, which are epitomized in the contrasting figures of Herod the Great and the Magi. Herod's reaction was fully in keeping with his known character. His long reign was stained with blood. It was the Romans who had put him on the throne and called him "King of the Jews." But he was a foreigner; his father was an Edomite and his mother an Arabian princess. He had no right or title to the throne.

In consequence, Herod's throne was very insecure, and he lived in terror of rivals. When he saw one, he promptly had him or her liquidated. He killed his wife Mariamne; his mother, Alexandra; and his three sons Aristobulus, Alexander, and Antipater. He killed more than half the members of the Sanhedrin and sundry uncles, cousins, and other relatives. It is not surprising, therefore, that Josephus the Jewish historian called him "a pitiless monster" or that the Emperor Augustus said it was safer to be Herod's pig than his son. In our language he suffered from a severe paranoia. And now the Magi arrived asking where was he who was born "King of the Jews." Why, he, Herod, was the king of the Jews; who was this pretender?

In principle, the same situation prevails today. Many people perceive Jesus as a rival, a nuisance, an embarrassment, what C. S. Lewis called "a transcendental interferer." So we are faced with an alternative. Either we see Jesus as a threat and are determined like Herod to get rid of him, or we see him as the King of Kings and are determined like the Magi to worship him.

For further reading: Matthew 2:7–12

The Flight into Egypt

AN ANGEL OF THE LORD APPEARED TO JOSEPH IN A DREAM. "GET UP,"
HE SAID, "TAKE THE CHILD AND HIS MOTHER AND ESCAPE TO EGYPT."

Matthew 2:13

The Magi had left Jerusalem to begin their journey home, and Herod had been foiled in his plot to destroy the baby Jesus. So now Joseph was instructed to take Jesus and his mother and flee south into Egypt. There is something very poignant about the Son of God becoming a refugee baby and so identifying himself with the dispossessed people of the world.

But Matthew detects something else. He sees the flight into Egypt as a fulfilment of Scripture. "So was fulfilled what the Lord had said through the prophet: 'Out of Egypt I called my son'" (v. 15). It is not that these words from Hosea 11:1 were a literal prediction of the holy family's flight into Egypt, for their original reference was to the exodus. It is rather that Matthew sees in the story of Jesus a recapitulation of the story of Israel. This is apparent in at least four ways.

As Israel was oppressed in Egypt under the despotic rule of Pharaoh, so the infant Jesus became a refugee in Egypt under the despotic rule of Herod. As Israel passed through the waters of the Red Sea, so Jesus passed through the waters of John's baptism in the River Jordan. As Israel was tested in the wilderness of Zin for forty years, so Jesus was tested in the wilderness of Judea for forty days. And as Moses from Mount Sinai gave Israel the law, so Jesus from the Mount of Beatitudes gave his disciples the true interpretation and amplification of the law.

We can only marvel at the providence of God in this repetition of the pattern of sacred history.

For further reading: Hosea 11:1; Matthew 2:13–18

WEDNESDAY

The Song of Simeon

MY EYES HAVE SEEN YOUR SALVATION... A LIGHT FOR REVELATION TO THE
GENTILES, AND THE GLORY OF YOUR PEOPLE ISRAEL.

Luke 2:30, 32

We are introduced today to that godly old man named Simeon. He was eagerly awaiting the Messiah, and God had told him that he would not die before he had seen him. Moved by the Holy Spirit, he entered the temple courts at the precise moment that Joseph and Mary arrived there with their eight-day-old son. It was a marvellous example of divine synchronization.

Now Simeon had the spiritual discernment to recognize Jesus. He took him up in his arms, not just instinctively to give him a cuddle, but as a symbolic gesture of recognition, which he interpreted in his song. "Now, Master, you may let your servant go in peace, according to your word" (Luke 2:29 NAB).

Firstly, Simeon saw Jesus as *the salvation of God*. What his eyes had actually seen was Mary's child; what he said he had seen was God's salvation, the Messiah God had sent to liberate us from the penalty and prison of sin.

Secondly, Simeon saw Jesus as *the light of the world*, who would both enlighten the nations and bring glory to Israel. Consciously or unconsciously he echoed Isaiah 49:6, a verse that was later to have an important place in Paul's mission theology.

Thirdly, Simeon saw Jesus as *a cause of division*, a rock that some would stumble over and others would build on. He would cause some to rise and others to fall. Confronted by Jesus, neutrality is impossible.

The story of Simeon is a lesson in spiritual recognition. May God give us the discernment to see beneath surface appearances to the reality of Jesus Christ!

For further reading: Luke 2:25–35

THURSDAY

The Testimony of Paul

CHRIST JESUS CAME INTO THE WORLD TO SAVE SINNERS...
1 Timothy 1:15

The different responses to the coming of Christ were made not only by the immediate actors in the drama. We see them also in the later apostolic period, for example, in the apostles Paul and John. Today we listen to Paul: "Here is a trustworthy saying that deserves full acceptance: Christ Jesus came into the world to save sinners – of whom I am the worst" (v. 15). Paul claims that his statement of the gospel is reliable ("a trustworthy saying"), universal (it "deserves full acceptance"), historical ("Christ Jesus came into the world"), liberating (he came "to save sinners"), and personal ("I am the worst," because once the Holy Spirit convicts us of sin, we give up all odious comparisons).

I can never hear or read these words without thinking of Thomas Bilney, or "little Bilney" as he was called on account of his small stature. Elected in 1520 a Fellow of Trinity Hall, Cambridge, he was searching for peace but could not find it. But at last he wrote:

> I chanced upon this sentence of St. Paul – this one sentence, through God's instruction and inward working... did so exhilarate my heart, being before wounded with the guilt of my sins, and being almost in despair, that even immediately I seemed unto myself inwardly to feel a marvellous comfort and quietness, insomuch that "my bruised bones leaped for joy" (Psalm 51). After this, the Scripture began to be more pleasant unto me than honey or the honeycomb.

Bilney's most notable convert was Hugh Latimer, who later became the popular preacher of the English Reformation. Latimer greatly admired the courage with which Bilney went to the stake for his evangelical faith; he referred to him in his sermons as "Saint Bilney."

For further reading: 1 Timothy 1:12–17

FRIDAY

The Reflection of John

THE FATHER HAS SENT HIS SON TO BE THE SAVIOUR OF THE WORLD.

1 John 4:14

It is all but certain that the apostle John lived to a ripe old age and that he was the last surviving apostle. So it will be good to hear his mature reflection on the meaning and purpose of the incarnation: "The Father has sent his Son to be the Saviour of the world." It is a straightforward statement about Christmas in which the four nouns stand out: the *Father* sent the *Son* to be the *Saviour* of the *world*.

The world is John's term for godless society, which is displeasing to God and under his just judgment.

The Saviour indicates that the world needs salvation. For, though the words *sin* and *salvation* belong to a traditional vocabulary that embarrasses some and confuses others, we cannot jettison them. They express vital realities that it would be foolish to ignore. Salvation is freedom – freedom from guilt, judgment, self-centredness, fear, and death.

The Son is the Saviour we need, being both God and man, whose birth we celebrate at Christmas and whose death is the only ground on which God can forgive our sins today. For, to quote another of John's summary statements, God "sent his Son as an atoning sacrifice for our sins" (v. 10).

Moreover, *the Father* sent the Son to be the world's Saviour. The Son did not come of his own accord. Still less did he wrest salvation from a Father reluctant to give it. No, the Father sent him. The Father took the initiative in his great love. For in giving his Son, he was giving himself.

For further reading: 1 John 4:7–16

Saturday

The Challenge of John

YOU KNOW THAT HE APPEARED SO THAT HE MIGHT TAKE AWAY OUR SINS.

1 John 3:5

We come at the end of this week to one more response to Christmas, that is, one more reaction to the coming of Christ. It takes us back to the first letter of John and to what he wrote about the purpose of Christ's appearing.

The passage concerned is 1 John 3:4–9, in which John makes some extraordinary statements. He writes that the Christian does not sin and even cannot sin. On these words some have constructed a doctrine of sinless perfection. And all commentators have been perplexed by these statements, because they are not consistent with our experience. The fact is that we *do* sin, even after we have come to know Christ.

A careful examination of this text, however, suggests not that Christians do not and cannot commit sin but that we do not and cannot persist in it. So, whenever we *do* sin, we grieve and repent, for the whole tenor of our life is against sin and toward holiness. As Alfred Plummer wrote in his commentary, "Although the believer sometimes sins, yet not sin, but opposition to sin, is the ruling principle of his life."

But what will motivate us to forsake sin and pursue righteousness? John's answer is clear: it is to remember the purpose of Christ's appearing. He says so twice. "You know that he appeared so that he might take away our sins" (v. 5). Again, "The reason the Son of God appeared was to destroy the devil's work" (v. 8). If, therefore, Christ came in order to deal with our sin, it is inconceivable that we should continue to toy with it. Our response to Christmas is to live a life that is fully compatible with the reason he appeared on earth.

For further reading: 1 John 3:4–9

It is a wonderful providence of God that we have been given not one Gospel but four (not to mention the so-called apocryphal gospels that were written in the second century to promote a variety of heretical opinions). Jesus Christ is much too great and glorious a person to be captured by one author or depicted from one perspective. The Christ of the Gospels is a person with four faces, a diamond with four facets. We have no liberty either to turn the four into one by ironing out the individuality of each or to turn the one into four by exaggerating the individuality of each.

Sunday: Matthew, Part 1 – Jesus the Christ

Monday: Matthew, Part 2 – Jesus the Internationalist

Tuesday: Mark – Jesus the Suffering Servant

Wednesday: Luke, Part 1 – Jesus the Historical Figure

Thursday: Luke, Part 2 – Jesus the Saviour of the World

Friday: John, Part 1 – Jesus the Light of Human Beings

Saturday: John, Part 2 – Jesus the Giver of Life

Matthew, Part 1 – Jesus the Christ

ALL THIS TOOK PLACE TO FULFIL WHAT THE LORD HAD SAID THROUGH
THE PROPHET...

Matthew 1:22

Matthew presents Jesus as the Christ, the long-awaited Messiah, in whom the promises of God were being fulfilled. His favourite formula, which occurs eleven times in his Gospel, is some variation of this: "Now this took place that what was written in the prophets might be fulfilled."

It is appropriate, therefore, that Matthew should begin his Gospel with the genealogy of Jesus, in which he traces the royal line and specially emphasizes Abraham, the founding father of Israel, and David, the ancestor of the Messiah who would be "the son of David."

The theme of fulfilment is most clearly displayed in Jesus' inauguration of the kingdom of God. All four evangelists write that he proclaimed the kingdom, but Matthew had his special emphasis. In deference to Jewish reluctance to pronounce the sacred name of God, Matthew uses instead "the kingdom of heaven" (about fifty times). He also grasps that the kingdom is both a present reality and a future expectation.

One of Jesus' most remarkable sayings was recorded by Matthew, as also by Luke:

> Blessed are your eyes because they see, and your ears because they hear.
> For truly I tell you, many prophets and righteous people longed to see what
> you see but did not see it, and to hear what you hear but did not hear it.
> **Matthew 13:16–17**

In other words, the Old Testament prophets lived in the time of anticipation; the apostles were living in the time of fulfilment. Their eyes were actually seeing, and their ears actually hearing, what their predecessors had longed to see and hear. So Matthew does not portray Jesus so much as another prophet, one more seer in the long succession of the centuries, but rather as the fulfilment of all prophecy. Matthew also sees Jesus as confronting Israel with a final summons to repent and as already beginning to create a new Israel, his twelve apostles complementing the twelve tribes of Israel.

For further reading: Matthew 23:37–39

Matthew, Part 2 – Jesus the Internationalist

MANY WILL COME FROM THE EAST AND THE WEST, AND WILL TAKE
THEIR PLACES AT THE FEAST WITH ABRAHAM, ISAAC AND JACOB IN THE
KINGDOM OF HEAVEN.

Matthew 8:11

We saw yesterday that Matthew portrays a Jewish Jesus. Indeed, he proclaims him as the long-expected Messiah. The evidence for this Jewishness is indisputable. Jesus was steeped in the Old Testament. He saw himself as the fulfilment of all Old Testament prophecy.

More than that, Matthew records two occasions, which are not paralleled in the other Gospels, in which Jesus appears to be guilty of nationalism or ethnic prejudice. Firstly, referring to his own ministry, Jesus said, "I was sent only to the lost sheep of Israel" (15:24). Secondly, referring to the ministry of his disciples, he said to them, "Do not go among the Gentiles... Go rather to the lost sheep of Israel" (10:5–6).

But this was only a historical limitation. Jesus was giving Israel a last chance. But he added immediately that later his disciples would be "witnesses... to the Gentiles" (v. 18). And the same Matthew who recorded those sayings about Israel's "lost sheep" also recorded at the beginning of his Gospel the visit of the Gentile Magi, and at its end the great commission to "go and make disciples of all nations" (28:19). So, although Matthew's picture of Jesus is the most Jewish of the four pictures, it would be impossible to represent Jesus as guilty in any way of ethnic pride or prejudice. On the contrary, Jesus made it clear that the renewed Israel would be an international nation:

I say to you that many will come from the east and the west, and will take their places at the feast with Abraham, Isaac and Jacob in the kingdom of heaven.

Matthew 8:11

For further reading: Matthew 28:16–20

Tuesday

Mark - Jesus the Suffering Servant

HE [JESUS] THEN BEGAN TO TEACH THEM THAT THE SON OF MAN MUST
SUFFER MANY THINGS AND... BE KILLED AND AFTER THREE DAYS RISE
AGAIN.

Mark 8:31

The centre of Mark's Gospel is the cross of Christ. Once the Twelve had grasped who Jesus was and had confessed him as the Messiah, he began to teach them about the cross. It was a turning point in Jesus' ministry and so also in Mark's Gospel. Before this time Jesus had been fêted as a popular preacher and healer. But he had not come to be that kind of Messiah. So from now on he taught his disciples openly about the necessity of his sufferings and death. Mark records that on three more separate occasions Jesus solemnly predicted his death. Indeed, approximately one third of Mark's Gospel is devoted to his passion.

The essence of Jesus' teaching is found in his statement that "the Son of Man must suffer." Why must he suffer? What is the origin of his sense of compulsion? It is because the Scriptures must be fulfilled. Why, then, "the Son of Man"? By using this Hebraism for a human being, Jesus was referring to Daniel 7. In this vision "one like a son of man" (that is, a human figure) comes on the clouds and approaches the Ancient of Days (God). He is then given authority and sovereign power so that all people will serve him, and his kingdom will never be destroyed (Dan. 7:13–14).

Jesus adopted the title (Son of Man) but changed his role. According to Daniel, all nations would serve him. According to Jesus, he had come to serve, not to be served. In fact, Jesus did what nobody else had done: he fused the two Old Testament images, Isaiah's servant who suffers and Daniel's Son of Man who reigns. For first Jesus must bear our sins and only then rise and enter his glory.

For further reading: Mark 8:27–9:1

WEDNESDAY

Luke, Part 1 – Jesus the Historical Figure

SINCE I MYSELF HAVE CAREFULLY INVESTIGATED EVERYTHING FROM THE
BEGINNING, I TOO DECIDED TO WRITE AN ORDERLY ACCOUNT...

Luke 1:3

Luke wrote a two-volume work on the origins of Christianity, namely his Gospel and the Acts. And in his preface, which covers both books, he emphasizes the reliability of what he is writing. For he is absolutely clear that Jesus was no myth but a historical figure. So he sets out his case in five logical stages (vv. 1–4).

- Firstly, certain "things... have been fulfilled among us" (v. 1). These were the events of Jesus' ministry.
- Secondly, these events were seen by eyewitnesses who "handed down" what they had seen to others (v. 2).
- Thirdly, Luke, who was one of these, "carefully investigated everything from the beginning" (v. 3).
- Fourthly, Luke wrote down the result of his research, giving "an orderly account" of it (v. 3).
- Fifthly, there would be readers, including Theophilus, his distinguished patron, who would find in Luke's Gospel solid grounds for their faith.

But when did Luke pursue his investigations? For he was not one of the Twelve or an eyewitness. But later he enjoyed a two-year residence in Palestine while Paul was imprisoned in Caesarea (Acts 24:27). How did he occupy his time? We can only guess. Surely he travelled the length and breadth of the country, gathering material for his Gospel and for the early Jerusalem-based story of the Acts, visiting the sites associated with Jesus' ministry, familiarizing himself (as a Gentile) with Jewish culture, and interviewing eyewitnesses. These must have included the Virgin Mary, by now an elderly lady. For Luke tells Mary's story, including the intimacies surrounding Jesus' birth. These can have come only from Mary herself. All this establishes our confidence in the historical reliability of Luke's writings.

For further reading: Luke 1:1–4

Luke, Part 2 – Jesus the Saviour of the World

REPENTANCE FOR THE FORGIVENESS OF SINS WILL BE PREACHED IN HIS
NAME TO ALL NATIONS, BEGINNING AT JERUSALEM.
Luke 24:47

Yesterday we considered Luke as a historian; today we shall see him as a theologian and evangelist. What is his message? It is that Jesus is the Saviour of the world, reaching out to everybody irrespective of race, nationality, rank, age, or sex. So Luke deliberately places near the beginning of each of his volumes a statement of universality:

Luke 3:6 – "All people [*pasa sarx*] will see God's salvation."

Acts 2:17 – "I will pour out my Spirit on all people [*pasa sarx*]."

And throughout his Gospel he goes out of his way to show Jesus including those whom society often excludes.

Being a doctor, it is understandable that Luke should emphasize Jesus' compassion for the sick and suffering. But he also cared for women and children, the poor and needy, tax collectors and sinners, and especially Samaritans and Gentiles. In each case Luke's emphasis is stronger than that of the other evangelists.

Being a Gentile himself, Luke was a man of wide horizons. He never calls the waters of Galilee a sea, for he has himself sailed on the Great Sea (the Mediterranean), and by comparison he calls Galilee only a lake.

In the Acts Luke chronicles the three pioneer missionary journeys undertaken by his hero Paul, indicating the occasions when he was himself present as Paul's companion. The Acts records a triumphal progression from Jerusalem, the capital of Jewry, to Rome, the capital of the world. Wherever they went they proclaimed salvation (comprising forgiveness and the Spirit) as available in Christ to all people. And Luke records the apostle Peter's affirmation:

Salvation is found in no one else, for there is no other name under heaven
given to mankind by which we must be saved.
Acts 4:12

For further reading: Luke 24:44–49

John, Part 1 – Jesus the Light of Human Beings

THROUGH HIM ALL THINGS WERE MADE; WITHOUT HIM NOTHING WAS
MADE THAT HAS BEEN MADE. IN HIM WAS LIFE, AND THAT LIFE WAS THE
LIGHT OF ALL MANKIND.

John 1:3–4

Many people are troubled by the apparent remoteness of God. He seems to them distant, aloof, and unreal. They cry out with Job, "If only I knew where to find him!" (Job 23:3).

It is this image of an absentee God that John smashes to smithereens. In the prologue to his Gospel he writes of three comings of God into the world in Christ.

Firstly, *he was coming* into the world. It is a great mistake to suppose that the first time God came into the world was when he was born into it. No, he made the world and has never left it. He is "the true light that gives light to everyone," who "was coming into the world" (John 1:9). Thus, long before he came he was coming, giving to all both life and light. So everything beautiful, good, and true in the world we claim for Jesus Christ. People may not know this, for usually he preserves his incognito, but he is "the light of mankind" (v. 4). No human being is plunged in total darkness.

Secondly, *he came* into the world. "He came to that which was his own" (v. 11). He who had been coming to all people now came to his particular people. He who had been coming incognito now came in person, openly and publicly. The eternal Word became a human being. The tragedy is that the world did not recognize him.

Thirdly, *he still comes*. He comes now by his Spirit, and to those who receive him, who believe in his name, he gives the right to become God's children, born of God (v. 12).

A fourth coming could be added, although John does not mention it here. But later he records Jesus' promise, "*I will come back* and take you to be with me" (14:3, emphasis added).

So here are God's four comings. He was coming continuously as the light and life of human beings. He came on the first Christmas Day. He comes still, waiting for us to receive him, and he will come on the last day.

For further reading: John 1:1–14

Saturday

John, Part 2 – Jesus the Giver of Life

THESE [SIGNS] ARE WRITTEN THAT YOU MAY BELIEVE THAT JESUS IS THE
MESSIAH, THE SON OF GOD, AND THAT BY BELIEVING YOU MAY HAVE LIFE
IN HIS NAME.

John 20:31

John tells us that his ultimate purpose in writing his Gospel was that his readers might receive life through Christ. In order to receive life from Christ, they must believe in Christ, and in order to believe in Christ, John has selected certain signs that bear witness to Christ. Thus testimony leads to faith, and faith to life.

Indeed, John sees his Gospel primarily as testimony to Christ. It is almost as if his Gospel were a court scene and Jesus Christ were on trial. A succession of witnesses is called, beginning with John the Baptist, and the trial continues with seven miraculous signs, each of which is a dramatized claim.

1. Jesus turned water into wine, claiming to inaugurate a new order.
2. and 3. Jesus performed two healing miracles, claiming to give a new life.
4. Jesus fed five thousand people, claiming to be the Bread of Life.
5. Jesus walked on water, claiming that the powers of nature were under his authority.
6. Jesus gave sight to a man born blind, claiming to be the Light of the World.
7. Jesus raised Lazarus from death, claiming to be the resurrection and the life.

Yet there is another side to John's witness to Jesus. The seven signs, recorded in the first half of his Gospel, are signs of power and authority. In the second half of his Gospel, however, John records signs of weakness and humility – first in the washing of the disciples' feet and then in the cross, which John sees as the glorification of Jesus.

To sum up, John's Gospel is in two halves: part 1 is the Book of Signs, and part 2 is the Book of the Cross. But in both, throughout his Gospel, John is bearing witness to Jesus in order that his readers may believe in him and so receive life from him.

For further reading: John 20:30–31; 21:25

Week 20: The Years of Preparation

Although the data at the evangelists' disposal seem to have been slender, they tell us all we need to know about the years that elapsed between the birth and the baptism of Jesus. These are sometimes called "the hidden years" because they preceded his emergence on to the public stage. So we will be thinking this week about the childhood and boyhood of Jesus, his growth into maturity, his work at the carpenter's bench, and the witness borne to him by John the Baptist. Then, before his baptism, which marked the start of his public ministry, we will look at two private conversations he had (with Nicodemus and the Samaritan woman), which John records near the beginning of his Gospel.

Sunday: The Infancy of Jesus

Monday: The Boy in the Temple

Tuesday: The Hidden Years

Wednesday: The Carpenter's Shop

Thursday: The Witness of John the Baptist

Friday: The Encounter with Nicodemus

Saturday: The Encounter with the Samaritan Woman

The Infancy of Jesus

JOSEPH AND MARY TOOK HIM [JESUS] TO JERUSALEM TO PRESENT
HIM TO THE LORD...

Luke 2:22

Luke records more than the other evangelists about the infancy of Jesus. In particular, he refers to three events, or three things that were done to him, while he was still an infant.

Firstly, Jesus was circumcised when he was eight days old. Circumcision had been given to Abraham some two thousand years previously as a sign of the covenant that God had established with him and his descendants. It made Jesus a true son of Abraham (Gen. 17:12; Lev. 12:3).

Secondly, he was named Jesus, meaning "God is Saviour." Both Matthew and Luke record that an angel instructed Joseph and Mary before he was born to call him Jesus (Matt. 1:21; Luke 1:31). It indicated that he had come on a rescue mission.

Thirdly, Jesus was presented to the Lord in the temple in Jerusalem. Two distinct Old Testament rituals overlapped during this visit, one relating to the mother and the other to the child. On the one hand, once the prescribed forty days of ceremonial segregation were completed, Joseph and Mary offered the requisite sacrifices. Usually these were a lamb for a burnt offering and a pigeon for a sin offering. But Joseph and Mary availed themselves of the concession to poor people and brought two pigeons.

On the other hand, ever since the exodus, all firstborn males belonged to God but could be redeemed (Exod. 13:2). Once redeemed they could also be voluntarily presented to God for his service.

Thus Jesus was successively circumcised, named, and presented, and all three events were related to his mission in the world. His circumcision portrayed him as a son of Abraham, an authentic member of the covenant people of God. His name, Jesus, proclaimed him to be the heaven-sent Saviour of sinners. His presentation to God indicated that he was devoted to the service of God and ready to do his Father's will.

For further reading: Luke 2:21–24

The Boy in the Temple

WHY WERE YOU SEARCHING FOR ME?... DIDN'T YOU KNOW I HAD TO BE IN
MY FATHER'S HOUSE?

Luke 2:49

The only incident we know about in Jesus' boyhood is the highly significant story of how he got lost in the temple. The law required Israelite adults to go up to Jerusalem for the three main festivals – Passover, Harvest, and Ingathering (Exod. 23:14–17), although this duty was reduced to Passover only if the distance was too great to manage all three. Joseph and Mary went up annually at Passover, and on this occasion at least Jesus accompanied them. He was now twelve years old, and the following year at thirteen he would become *bar mitzvah* ("a son of the commandment"), assuming the spiritual responsibilities of an adult in the Jewish community.

How he got lost is not fully explained. It may have been that, because the men and women pilgrims were separated, Joseph and Mary each thought he was with the other. At all events, after three days they found him in the temple precincts, "sitting among the teachers, listening to them and asking them questions" (Luke 2:46). His hearers were "amazed" (v. 47) at his understanding, and his parents were "astonished" (v. 48) – verbs that are used elsewhere of the awe that people felt in Jesus' presence.

Especially striking, however, is what Jesus said, the first recorded words spoken by the Messiah. Notice two details of his speech.

Firstly, he called God his Father and the temple his Father's house. He thus corrected his mother, who had said to him, "Your father and I have been anxiously searching for you" (v. 48). Already Jesus was conscious of a special relationship with God as his Father.

Secondly, Jesus expressed a sense of compulsion: "Didn't you know I had to be in my Father's house?" (v. 49). Why *must* he be absorbed in this priority concern? No answer is given. But surely he must already have been aware of his mission as revealed in Scripture, and the Scriptures *must* be fulfilled.

For further reading: Luke 2:41–51

TUESDAY

The Hidden Years

AND JESUS GREW IN WISDOM AND STATURE, AND IN FAVOUR WITH GOD
AND MAN.

Luke 2:52

The graphic account of the loss and recovery of the boy Jesus in the temple precincts is, as we have seen, the only public incident that Luke records between his birth and his baptism. True, the apocryphal gospels try to fill in the gap. But they are all late, dating from the second century and therefore of dubious historical value. They are also either heretical or trivial in content, with one or two small exceptions. Luke's sober narrative is a welcome contrast.

So what was Jesus doing during those thirty years before his public ministry began? Answer: he was growing, or growing up, and so preparing for his mission. Luke tells us this in two "bridge" verses of chapter 2:

> *And the child grew and became strong; he was filled with wisdom, and the grace of God was on him… And Jesus grew in wisdom and stature, and in favour with God and man.*
>
> **Luke 2:40, 52**

Verse 40 is a bridge of twelve years, since in the preceding verse (v. 39) Jesus is still a baby, while in the following verse (v. 41) he has become twelve years old. Then verse 52 is a bridge of eighteen years, since in the preceding verse (v. 51) he is still twelve, while in the following verse (3:1) he has become thirty.

So during the two bridge periods of twelve and eighteen years he was growing physically, mentally, and spiritually. His body developed naturally. His mind expanded as he learned his lessons at home and at school. And he also grew in grace, becoming ever more pleasing to God and his neighbour.

Some people raise an objection here. If Jesus grew in these areas, they say, does it not inevitably mean that he was previously imperfect? No. We are claiming not that Jesus jumped straight from infancy to adulthood but that he grew and that at each stage he was perfect for that stage. For example, to say that he grew in favour with God does not mean he was previously out of favour but that at each stage he pleased God in accordance with his age. To insist on this growth is to guarantee the authentic humanness of Jesus.

For further reading: Hebrews 2:14–18

The Carpenter's Shop

WHERE DID THIS MAN GET THESE THINGS?... ISN'T THIS THE CARPENTER?

Mark 6:2-3

The word *carpenter* occurs only twice in the Gospels, once calling Jesus "the carpenter" and on the other occasion referring to him as "the carpenter's son." From this we deduce that Joseph had worked as a carpenter, that Jesus had been his apprentice, and that he took over from him, perhaps at Joseph's death.

Although the word *tektōn* could be used of any artisan or craftsman, it normally denoted a worker with wood. So Jesus will doubtless have made and repaired both household furniture and agricultural implements. J. E. Millais, the Pre-Raphaelite painter in the middle of the nineteenth century, can help us to visualize the inside of the carpenter's shop by his painting of that title. The child Jesus is at the centre of the picture. He has evidently injured himself with a nail, Joseph is leaning over to examine the wound, Mary is seeking to comfort Jesus with a kiss, and the youthful John the Baptist is carrying a bowl of water with which to bathe the injury. Jesus is leaning against the workbench, which seems to symbolize the altar of sacrifice.

Some of the Christian leaders of the early British labour movement derived inspiration from Jesus, for he dignified manual labour. James Stalker in his *Life of Jesus Christ* (1879) wrote:

> *It would be difficult to exhaust the significance of the fact that God chose for his Son, when he dwelt among men, out of all possible positions in which he might have placed him, the lot of a working man. It stamped men's common toils with everlasting honour.*

For further reading: Acts 20:33–35

The Witness of John the Baptist

THERE WAS A MAN SENT FROM GOD WHOSE NAME WAS JOHN. HE CAME AS
A WITNESS TO TESTIFY CONCERNING THAT LIGHT...

John 1:6–7

John the Baptist is often called Jesus' "forerunner" because, in fulfilment of a prophecy of Isaiah, he was sent in advance to "prepare the way for the Lord" (Mark 1:3). All four evangelists refer to his ministry, for they recognize its importance. In him the voice of prophecy, long silent, was heard again.

John's message was, "Repent, for the kingdom of heaven has come" (Matt. 3:2). In other words, the Messiah was about to arrive and inaugurate his rule. In order to be ready for his coming, the people must repent and receive John's baptism of repentance for the forgiveness of their sins. Many responded. Confessing their sins, they were baptized by him in the River Jordan.

John also gave a warning of judgment. He depicted the Messiah as having a winnowing fork in his hand, with which he will separate the wheat from the chaff.

But the characteristic ministry of the Messiah, according to the Baptist, would relate to salvation rather than judgment. These are John's words:

Look, the Lamb of God, who takes away the sin of the world... the one who
will baptise with the Holy Spirit.
John 1:29, 33

Putting these two verses together, we see that the characteristic work of Jesus is twofold. It involves a removal and a bestowal, a taking away of sin and a baptizing with the Holy Spirit. These are the two great gifts of Jesus Christ our Saviour – forgiveness and the Spirit. They are the two major blessings of the new covenant. They were promised by the prophets and confirmed by John the Baptist as gifts of the Messiah.

For further reading: John 1:29–34

FRIDAY

The Encounter with Nicodemus

JESUS REPLIED, "VERY TRULY I TELL YOU, NO ONE CAN SEE THE KINGDOM
OF GOD UNLESS THEY ARE BORN AGAIN."

John 3:3

Nicodemus is an outstanding example of a sincere seeker after the truth. If only there were more Nicodemuses in the world today – men and women who are prepared to lay aside apathy, prejudice, and fear and seek the truth with an honest and humble spirit! "Seek and you will find," Jesus promised (Matt. 7:7).

Jesus must have startled Nicodemus by telling him that he must be born again. What did he mean? Obviously he was not referring to a second physical birth or to an act of self-reformation. Nor can Jesus have been alluding to Christian baptism, since it was not instituted until after the resurrection. To be sure, baptism is the sign or sacrament of the new birth, but we must not confuse the outward sign with the inward thing signified. Baptism is a visible public dramatization of the new birth, which is itself an invisible and secret work of God, by which he gives us a new life, a new beginning.

Moreover (Jesus said), we *must* be born again. Without the new birth we can neither see nor enter God's kingdom. Nicodemus was religious, moral, educated, respectable, and courteous. He even believed in the divine origin of Jesus. But all this was not enough. He still needed to be born again.

So how does this new birth take place? From one point of view, it is entirely a work of God. Nobody has ever given birth to himself. So the new birth is a birth "from above," a birth "of the Holy Spirit." But from our side we have both to repent and to believe. Nicodemus could not bypass John's baptism of repentance. This was surely what Jesus meant by being "born of water." Then he must believe, putting his trust in Jesus the Messiah, who was the Saviour he needed.

For further reading: John 3:1–16

SATURDAY

The Encounter with the Samaritan Woman

[JESUS SAID,] "WHOEVER DRINKS THE WATER I GIVE HIM WILL NEVER
THIRST... [IT] WILL BECOME IN HIM A SPRING OF WATER WELLING UP TO
ETERNAL LIFE."

John 4:14

John began his Gospel with an affirmation that "the Word was God" (1:1) but went on
to affirm that "the Word became flesh" (v. 14). Now he illustrates from Jesus' encounter
with the Samaritan woman how vulnerable that humanity was. It was about twelve
noon when Jesus and his disciples reached Jacob's well, and the sun was at its hottest.
Jesus was tired after his morning's walk, so he sat by the well to rest. He was hungry
and so sent the disciples to the neighbouring village to buy food. He was also hot and
thirsty, so he asked the Samaritan woman for a drink. Thus Jesus was no superman
immune to the frailties of ordinary mortals. He was an authentic human being.

The other characteristic of Jesus that this story highlights is his attitude to tradition.
He was conservative in relation to Scripture, believing it to be the Word of God, but
radical in relation to tradition, knowing it to consist of only human words. A radical
is someone who is critical of all traditions and conventions, refusing to accept them
merely because they have been handed down from the past.

Now the Samaritan woman had a threefold conventional disability. Firstly, she
was a woman, and it was not done for a man to talk to a woman in public. But Jesus
did what wasn't done. Secondly, she was a Samaritan, and Jews did not associate with
Samaritans. Thirdly, she was a sinner, having had five husbands and now cohabiting
with a man to whom she was not married. But respectable people like rabbis did
not mix with sinners like her. Thus three times over Jesus did what wasn't done. He
deliberately breached the social conventions of the day. He was entirely free of gender
discrimination, ethnic prejudice, and moral priggishness. He loved and respected
everybody and shrank from nobody.

Thus Jesus was both conservative (in relation to Scripture) and radical (in relation
to culture) at the same time. It seems to me that we need a new generation of "RCs,"
standing now not for Roman Catholics but for radical conservatives.

For further reading: John 4:7–18

WEEK 21: THE PUBLIC MINISTRY

For approximately thirty years Jesus has been growing "in wisdom and stature, and in favour with God and man" (Luke 2:52). These were the years of his preparation. Now, however, the time has come for him to emerge out of the obscurity of the carpenter's shop into public life. So he went south to join the crowds who were flocking to listen to John the Baptist and to be baptized by him. Jesus' baptism was a kind of commissioning by the Father's voice and the Spirit's descent.

Fresh from this dramatic experience, he was grievously tempted by the devil to pursue his mission by avoiding the cross. After his temptations he began to proclaim the good news of the kingdom and to do mighty works of healing to validate his message. He soon became overwhelmed by the pressures of his work and was strengthened both by withdrawing to pray and by the Twelve, whom he called to be with him and share his ministry.

Sunday: The Baptism

Monday: The Temptations

Tuesday: The Good News

Wednesday: The Nazareth Manifesto

Thursday: The Healing Ministry

Friday: The Lord's Prayer Life

Saturday: The Call of the Twelve

The Baptism

AT THAT TIME JESUS CAME FROM NAZARETH IN GALILEE AND WAS
BAPTISED BY JOHN IN THE JORDAN.

Mark 1:9

John the Baptist's ministry had created a sensation. He found himself at the centre of a great spiritual revival. Large crowds converged on the lower reaches of the River Jordan, both to listen to his call to repentance and to be baptized. For judgment was imminent, he said, and he urged them to flee from the coming wrath.

Perhaps it was the news of this revival movement that convinced Jesus to leave his home, work, and relatives and to join it. It is not surprising, however, that when Jesus presented himself to John for baptism, John demurred. He had already spoken of Jesus as one mightier than he, the thongs of whose sandals he was not worthy to undo. So it would seem more appropriate for Jesus to baptize John than for John to baptize Jesus. But Jesus insisted.

It is also strange to us that Jesus should have asked for baptism. For John's was a baptism of repentance for the forgiveness of sins, whereas Jesus was without sin. Perhaps, therefore, he wished to identify with his people, knowing that one day he would bear their sins. At all events, John's baptism was an initiation into the purified remnant of Israel.

As Jesus emerged from the baptismal water, the heavens opened, the Spirit descended on him like a dove, and a voice cried, "This is my Son… with him I am well pleased" (Matt. 3:17). These words united two Old Testament Scriptures. Firstly, "this is my Son" echoes Psalm 2:7, where God declared the Davidic king to be his son. Secondly, "with him I am well pleased" echoes Isaiah 42:1, where God declared his pleasure in his servant. Thus Jesus was declared both Son and servant of God.

The baptism of Jesus was a beautiful trinitarian moment as the Father acknowledged the Son and the Spirit descended on him. It was the commissioning of Jesus, somewhat parallel to the call of the prophets, authorizing and equipping him for his mission.

For further reading: Matthew 3:13–17

The Temptations

THEN JESUS WAS LED BY THE SPIRIT INTO THE WILDERNESS TO BE
TEMPTED BY THE DEVIL.

Matthew 4:1

Jesus went straight from the waters of Jordan to the desert of Judea, where he was savagely tempted by the devil. The assault took two forms.

First came an assault on his identity, on who he was. The words of his Father were still ringing in his ears – "This is my Son" – when the voice from heaven was challenged by a voice from hell. The devil sneered, "*If* you are the Son of God… " (v. 6, emphasis added), implying that he was not. It was a deliberate attempt to sow in Jesus' mind the seeds of doubt. To counter them, Jesus must have kept repeating to himself the words of his Father, "This is my Son." Still today the devil attempts to undermine our self-conscious identity as God's children. For he is *diabolos*, the slanderer. We need to turn a deaf ear to him and listen instead to the great affirmations and promises of God in Scripture.

The devil's second assault was against the ministry of Jesus, against what he had come into the world to do. We saw yesterday that the heavenly voice identified Jesus not only as God's Son but also as God's servant, who would suffer and die for his people's sins. But the devil proposed other and less costly options. Why not win the world by satisfying its hunger, by a sensational display of power, or by striking a bargain with the devil – in each case bypassing the cross? The devil loves to persuade us that the end justifies the means.

Jesus refused to listen to the voice of the devil. Immediately, instinctively, vehemently, he rejected each temptation. There was no need to discuss or to negotiate. The matter had already been settled by Scripture ("It is written"); each time, he quoted an appropriate text from Deuteronomy 6 or 8. Still today there is a confusion of voices. The devil speaks through the secular culture surrounding us, and God speaks through his Word. Which shall we listen to? It is by our daily dogged discipline of Bible reading that we allow the devil's voice to be drowned by the voice of God. "Resist the devil, and he will flee from you" (James 4:7).

For further reading: Matthew 4:1–11

TUESDAY

The Good News

JESUS WENT INTO GALILEE, PROCLAIMING THE GOOD NEWS OF GOD.
"THE TIME HAS COME," HE SAID. "THE KINGDOM OF GOD HAS COME NEAR.
REPENT AND BELIEVE THE GOOD NEWS!"

Mark 1:14–15

These words are of particular interest, partly because they are the first recorded words of Jesus in his public ministry and partly because Mark twice calls them "good news." So what was the gospel according to Jesus? It consists of a statement followed by a summons.

The statement concerns the coming of the kingdom. Of course, Yahweh has always been King, ruling over both nature and history. Many times in the Old Testament we hear the splendid cry of faith, "Yahweh reigns." But the prophets predicted a time when he would establish a much more intimate kingdom than his general sovereignty in the world. The Messiah would inaugurate it. Characterized by righteousness and peace, it would extend throughout the world and last forever. It would offer a new life and a new community.

The good news was that this kingdom had drawn near. Jesus did not quite say that it had arrived, for its fullness was still to come. Yet already it was a present reality, for the time had been fulfilled, and he had ushered it in. Moreover, people could now "receive" or "enter" the kingdom. The way to do so was to repent and to believe, that is, to turn decisively away from all known sin and to turn in faith and commitment to Jesus as King.

This first proclamation of the gospel lays down a pattern for all true evangelism. We too need to make a statement (a thorough exposition of the good news of Christ crucified, risen, and reigning) and then issue a summons to people to come to him. The exposition and the exhortation belong essentially together.

For further reading: Matthew 9:35–38

WEDNESDAY

The Nazareth Manifesto

THE SPIRIT OF THE LORD IS ON ME, BECAUSE HE HAS ANOINTED ME TO
PROCLAIM GOOD NEWS TO THE POOR.

Luke 4:18

Matthew and Mark place Jesus' visit to the Nazareth synagogue later in his ministry. But Luke deliberately puts it at the very beginning of his ministry, because he sees it as a prophetic preview both of Jesus' message and of his rejection by his own people.

Jesus read the first two verses of Isaiah 61 and immediately claimed that Isaiah was referring to him. "Today this scripture is fulfilled in your hearing" (Luke 4:21). He was the Messiah, the anointed one, who had been commissioned to bring deliverance to four categories of people – the poor, the prisoners, the blind, and the oppressed.

The crucial question is whether the condition of these groups is spiritual or sociopolitical. Different answers are given. Some spiritualize the gospel, as if it offers only salvation from sin. Others politicize the gospel, as if it offers only liberation from oppression. But neither is satisfactory, for neither on its own does justice to the text. The spiritualizers forget that Jesus did fraternize with the poor, while the politicizers forget that the Greek word for *freedom* (v. 18) can also mean "forgiveness."

The only way to resolve this dilemma is to say that both are correct, since Jesus taught both. The poor in the Old Testament are both the humble poor who cry to God for mercy and the oppressed poor who need to be liberated. Further, "the gospel comes as good news to both. The spiritually poor, who... humble themselves before God, receive by faith the free gift of salvation... The materially poor and powerless find in addition a new dignity as God's children, and the love of brothers and sisters, who will struggle with them for their liberation from everything which demeans and oppresses them."[1]

What is true about the poor (both materially and spiritually) is also true of the prisoners, the blind, and the oppressed. The gospel is good news for them in both senses too.

For further reading: Luke 4:14–21

---

1   "The Manila Manifesto" (1980), in John Stott, ed., *Making Christ Known: Historic mission documents from the Lausanne Movement, 1974–1989* (Grand Rapids: Eerdmans, 1997), 234–35.

Thursday

The Healing Ministry

JESUS WENT THROUGHOUT GALILEE, TEACHING IN THEIR SYNAGOGUES,
PROCLAIMING THE GOOD NEWS OF THE KINGDOM, AND HEALING EVERY
DISEASE AND ILLNESS AMONG THE PEOPLE.

Matthew 4:23

The Gospel writers describe Jesus' ministry as threefold: teaching, preaching, and healing. Teaching and preaching are not hard to grasp or to imitate, but how are we to understand the ministry of healing?

Perhaps the place to begin is to affirm the goodness of God's creation. That is to say, disease was no part of God's original intention for the world, and it will be no part of his ultimate purpose either. In the new universe there will be neither sickness nor pain nor death nor tears (Rev. 21:4). Since, then, disease and death are alien intrusions into God's good world, doctors and nurses are right to wage war against them. Moreover, all healing is divine healing, since God has put into the human body remarkable therapeutic processes. For example, no sooner has an infection appeared than antibodies are created to fight it. It is this conviction that led Ambroise Paré, the Huguenot physician, to say, "I dressed the wound, but God healed it." The words are inscribed on a wall of the École de Médicine in Paris.

The Gospels make it plain, however, that the healing ministry of Jesus belonged to a different order. Like changing water into wine, multiplying loaves and fishes, and walking on water, Jesus' healings were supernatural demonstrations of the kingdom of God.

In trying to understand them, we will be wise to avoid opposite extremes. On the one hand, it would be absurd to put the Creator in a straitjacket and declare that miracles can't and don't happen. On the other hand, we have no liberty to say (as some do) that performing miracles is the normal Christian life. For however we define miracles, they certainly belong not to the normal but to the abnormal. If we claim to be able to heal the sick like Jesus, we need to remember that he healed without the use of medical or surgical means, without delay, degree, or remission, but immediately, completely, and permanently, and that even hostile eyewitnesses said, "We cannot deny it" (Acts 4:16).

For further reading: Acts 4:8–16

The Lord's Prayer Life

VERY EARLY IN THE MORNING, WHILE IT WAS STILL DARK, JESUS
GOT UP, LEFT THE HOUSE AND WENT OFF TO A SOLITARY PLACE,
WHERE HE PRAYED.

Mark 1:35

It is difficult for us to imagine how demanding Jesus' threefold ministry must have been. Mark gives us the outline of a sample day in Capernaum. It began with teaching, and Jesus amazed his hearers by the authority with which he spoke. News about him spread quickly over the whole region of Galilee, so that people flocked to him to be taught and healed. That evening after sunset, when it was cooler and he might have expected a meal and some rest, "the whole town gathered at the door" (v. 33), and he healed the sick. It sounds easy, but when later he healed a woman with a haemorrhage, we read that power went out of him. He must have felt drained. And most wearing of all was his confrontation with evil spirits. The kingdom of God had broken in; the devil's kingdom would not retreat without a fight.

I wonder what time Jesus went to bed that night. All we are told is that after a hectic day of ministry, he needed both physical and spiritual refreshment. So very early in the morning, Jesus got up and went off to a solitary place to pray.

Luke is the evangelist who took the greatest interest in this aspect of Jesus' behaviour. He mentions about ten particular occasions when Jesus prayed, several of which have no parallel in the other Gospels.

Jesus certainly knew Old Testament verses like Isaiah 40:31: "They that wait upon the LORD shall renew their strength" (KJV). And he sought this renewal in prayer. We also know how intimate his relation to his Father was from his use of the diminutive Aramaic form of address, "Abba." The late Professor Joachim Jeremias wrote, "Nowhere in the literature of the prayers of ancient Judaism… is this invocation of God as Abba to be found… Jesus on the other hand always used it when he prayed."[1] Thus renewed and refreshed from prayer, Jesus would return to the pressures of his busy ministry. It is this rhythm between prayer and ministry, renewal and engagement, that enabled Jesus to endure the strains of his ministry. And if he needed it, how much more do we?

For further reading: Mark 1:21–39

---

1   Joachim Jeremias, *The Central Message of the New Testament* (London: SCM, 1965), 16–17, 19–20, 21, 30.

SATURDAY

The Call of the Twelve

[JESUS] CALLED HIS DISCIPLES TO HIM AND CHOSE TWELVE OF THEM,
WHOM HE ALSO DESIGNATED APOSTLES...

Luke 6:13

Jesus' choice and call of the Twelve, according to Luke, took place after he had spent a whole night in prayer. He evidently knew that a decision of great importance was about to be made, for the Twelve were to fulfil a special role in the future. Two points are particularly noteworthy.

Firstly, *Jesus chose twelve*. He already had a number of followers or "disciples." But out of this wider group he chose twelve. There can be no doubt that the number chosen was deliberate. He saw the twelve apostles as equivalent to the twelve tribes of Israel. He and the apostles together would form the nucleus of a new and purified Israel.

The most striking feature of the list of the apostles is its extraordinary diversity. One dramatic example is that Matthew the tax collector (regarded as a traitor) and Simon the Zealot (an extreme nationalist) were fellow members of the apostolic band. Perhaps Jesus deliberately chose as his apostles men who were culturally different from one another in order to foreshadow the diversity that would always characterize his community.

Secondly, *Jesus designated them apostles*, or "sent ones." We need to recall the double background of this word. In the Old Testament the "sent ones" were the prophets. As Yahweh had sent his prophets, so Jesus was now sending his apostles. Then in rabbinic Judaism the "sent one" was the *shaliach* who was sent by the Sanhedrin to teach. Of him it was said that "the one sent by a person is as this person himself." That is, he carries with him the authority of the sender. It is in this regard that Jesus could later say to the Twelve, "He who receives you receives me" (Matt. 10:40 RSV) and "Whoever listens to you listens to me" (Luke 10:16).

In order to equip his apostles to speak in his name, Jesus appointed them "that they might be with him" as eyewitnesses, hearing his words and seeing his works, so that they might bear witness to what they had seen and heard (Mark 3:14; see also John 15:27). These implications of apostleship have an important bearing on the writing of the New Testament.

For further reading: Mark 3:13–19

Not only was Jesus a gifted teacher, but his favourite and distinctive medium of instruction was the parable. Basically the word *parable* means a comparison or simile, often in the form of a dramatic narrative, and usually conveying one main point, in contrast to the allegory, in which nearly every detail has its counterpart, as, for example, in the allegory of the vine and the branches.

The first function of Jesus' parables was to illustrate some truth, especially regarding the character, values, and coming of the kingdom of God. Secondly, they were intended to jolt his listeners into a decision of some kind. Thirdly, they concealed truth as well as revealing it, since "though seeing, they do not see; though hearing, they do not hear or understand" (Matt. 13:13). Failure to understand was not the purpose of the parables, but it was their consequence if the hearers hardened their hearts.

Sunday: The Parable of the Growing Seed

Monday: The Parable of the Sower

Tuesday: The Parable of the Wheat and the Weeds

Wednesday: The Three Lost and Found Parables, Part 1 – Gospel

Thursday: The Three Lost and Found Parables, Part 2 – Mission

Friday: The Parable of the Pharisee and the Tax Collector

Saturday: The Parable of the Good Samaritan

The Parable of the Growing Seed

A MAN SCATTERS SEED ON THE GROUND. NIGHT AND DAY, WHETHER HE
SLEEPS OR GETS UP, THE SEED SPROUTS AND GROWS... ALL BY ITSELF...

Mark 4:26–28

If we go by the chronology of Mark's Gospel, the parable of the growing seed was one of the very first. At that time the kingdom was tiny, consisting of only the few people who had heard Jesus preach the gospel and had responded to his summons. So this little parable was intended to reassure his followers and to bring them encouragement when the spread of the kingdom seemed slow.

In some important respects the kingdom grows as plants grow. A farmer scatters seed, and in due course, when the grain is ripe, he wields his sickle and reaps his crop. But between seedtime and harvest he does virtually nothing. Whether he sleeps or gets up makes no difference, for in either case the seed sprouts and grows.

As in nature, so in the kingdom of God. The kingdom has grown over the years to vast proportions, but its principle of growth remains the same.

Firstly, the kingdom grows *irresistibly*; nobody can stop its development. For a hidden power is at work causing "first the stalk, then the ear, then the full grain in the ear" (v. 28).

Secondly, the kingdom grows *imperceptibly*; we cannot watch it happening. It keeps on growing irrespective of our observation.

Thirdly, the kingdom grows *spontaneously*; we cannot contribute to its hidden process of growth. The soil produces grain "all by itself" (v. 28). The Greek word is *automatē*. Not, of course, that it is literally automatic, for it is by the secret operation of the Holy Spirit that the kingdom grows. The work is his, not ours.

For further reading: Mark 4:26–29

The Parable of the Sower

A FARMER WENT OUT TO SOW HIS SEED. AS HE WAS SCATTERING THE
SEED... [IT FELL ON DIFFERENT SOILS]... WHEN HE [JESUS] SAID THIS, HE
CALLED OUT, "HE WHO HAS EARS TO HEAR, LET HIM HEAR."
Luke 8:5, 8

It is not difficult to imagine a first-century Palestinian farmer at seedtime. With a wicker basket balanced on his left hip, he walks up and down his field, scattering seed rhythmically with his strong right arm.

To this parable Jesus added both his own explanation of it and his interpretative proverb: "He who has ears to hear, let him hear." For Jesus was describing his own teaching ministry as he broadcast the seed of the Word of God, and it was met with different receptions. Its enemies were the birds that ate it (the devil), the sun that scorched it (temptation and tribulation), and the thorns that choked it (wealth and worldliness). But the message of the parable does not end there. It follows a clear pattern. Four times we read that some seed fell, meaning (again four times) that four groups all heard the Word of God (v. 11). The basic question is what they did with it when they heard it. What reception did they give it?

Some give the Word no reception at all. It never penetrates their defences. They have a closed mind and a hard heart. They are extremely vulnerable to the devil. Others give the Word a shallow reception. True, they receive it with initial enthusiasm. For a short period they seem to be believers. But the seed never takes root; there is rock underneath their soil. Consequently, when the fierce glare of the sun (temptation and persecution) beats upon them, their spiritual life shrivels up.

Others give the Word a mixed reception. They receive the Word, but they receive other things in profusion as well; they can't discern between what is worldly and what is godly. They pride themselves on keeping an open mind – so open that they can keep nothing in it or out of it. In the end, business, pleasure, and wealth, like thorns, choke their spiritual life.

Yet others give the Word a wholehearted reception. They hold it fast and persevere. They give it priority. They nourish it. And it bears fruit.

For further reading: Luke 8:4–18

TUESDAY

The Parable of the Wheat and the Weeds

LET BOTH GROW TOGETHER UNTIL THE HARVEST.

Matthew 13:30

This parable introduces us to the strange phenomenon known as "nominal Christianity." That is, it is possible to be a Christian in name, not in heart, in appearance, not in reality.

The story is clear. There were two sowers, one a farmer and the other his enemy. There were two crops, one wheat and the other weeds. And there would be two harvests, for the weeds would be burned and the wheat garnered. But the same field is in mind throughout. The parable teaches three lessons.

Firstly, *the church is a mixed community.* Just as the field contained both wheat and weeds, so the church contains both believers and unbelievers. Some deny this. They point to verse 38, where Jesus says that "the field is the world." But the enemy sowed weeds "among the wheat" (v. 25), not in a different field, and in the end evildoers will be gathered out of the kingdom, that is, out of the community that acknowledges Jesus as King. So the church contains within its membership the true and the false. This justifies the distinction between the visible church (all baptized members) and the invisible church (all who truly belong to Jesus Christ).

Secondly, *the devil is at work in the church.* I am aware that some church leaders no longer believe in the devil. But Jesus did, and that should be enough for us. The devil infiltrates the church with his agents, who often look exactly like genuine believers. For the so-called weeds are darnel, which, at least in its early stages, is almost indistinguishable from wheat.

Thirdly, *the separation will take place at the end.* Counterfeit Christians will not be able to preserve their disguise forever. The Day of Judgment will unmask them. Meanwhile, we should not attempt to do God's sifting and separating work for him. This does not mean, however, that the church should be a totally inclusive community and that there is no room for discipline. Open heretics and open evildoers should be disciplined, but we cannot read hearts and must not pass judgment on those who profess and seem to be true believers.

For further reading: Matthew 13:24–30, 36–43

The Three Lost and Found Parables, Part 1 – Gospel

"THIS SON OF MINE WAS DEAD AND IS ALIVE AGAIN; HE WAS LOST AND IS FOUND." SO THEY BEGAN TO CELEBRATE.

Luke 15:24

Luke 15 must surely be among the best-known, best-loved chapters of the Bible, because it consists of the three lost-and-found parables – the lost sheep, lost coin, and lost son. They have been variously interpreted, however, and I must leave my readers to judge whether my emphasis on two truths is legitimate or not. We are to reflect on the gospel today and on mission tomorrow.

The parable of the lost son gives us a vivid account of human lostness. Here is everybody's autobiography. The son made a deliberate bid for independence. Demanding his inheritance was tantamount to wishing his father were dead. Then in the far country his self-will degenerated into self-indulgence. His lifestyle became extravagant and immoral. And when famine struck, he sank low enough to feed pigs (disgusting to Jews). No one lifted a finger to help him. He was bankrupt, hungry, and alone.

Meanwhile, his father's love for him never faltered. He missed him and longed for his return. This is grace, namely unmerited and unsolicited love. Moreover, God's love suffers for us. Some liberal critics argue that in the parable the father took no risk and felt no pain. Muslims too point at the parable and insist that the young man was saved without a Saviour, for the parable teaches forgiveness without atonement. But Dr Kenneth Bailey, an expert in Middle-Eastern culture, explains in *The Cross and the Prodigal* the significance of the parable. The whole village would have known that the son was in disgrace, deserving to be punished. But, instead of inflicting suffering on his son, the father bears it himself. A man of his age and position would always walk in slow, dignified steps and would never run anywhere. Yet here he is racing down the road, risking the ridicule of the whole village, and taking on himself the shame and humiliation due to his returning son. The father's coming down and going out hint at the incarnation. The humiliating spectacle in the village street hints at the meaning of the cross.

For further reading: Luke 15:11–24

THURSDAY

The Three Lost and Found Parables, Part 2 - Mission

NOW THE TAX COLLECTORS AND SINNERS WERE ALL GATHERING ROUND
TO HEAR JESUS. BUT THE PHARISEES... MUTTERED, "THIS MAN WELCOMES
SINNERS, AND EATS WITH THEM."

Luke 15:1-2

Luke's own editorial comment, describing the context in which the three parables were told, is too often overlooked. The tax collectors were despised both because they collaborated with the hated Roman occupation (or, in Galilee, worked for Herod Antipas) and because they were usually guilty of extortion. *Sinners*, on the other hand, was a term of abuse that the Pharisees gave to the common people ignorant of the law. The Pharisees ostracized both groups. So when Jesus associated with them, they were outraged. "This man welcomes sinners," they said in shocked horror. But Luke records this with his approval and even admiration. So should we. In fact, sinners are the only people Jesus welcomes. If he didn't, there would be no hope for us!

Jesus told his three lost-and-found parables in order to highlight the fundamental difference between himself and the Pharisees. He welcomed sinners; they objected and rejected them. They had a false notion of holiness. They thought they would be contaminated by contact, so they kept their distance. Jesus, however, fraternized with them freely and was even called "a friend of tax collectors and sinners" (Matt. 11:19). If Pharisees saw a prostitute approaching, they would gather their robes around them and shrink from her, but when a prostitute approached Jesus, he did not shrink from her but accepted her devotion.

So the question before us is whether we resemble Jesus or the Pharisees, whether we avoid contact with sinners or seek it. We must not misunderstand this. The fact that Jesus welcomed sinners does not mean that he condoned their sins. On the contrary, all three parables end on a note of repentance and celebration. Jesus rejected the opposite extremes of Pharisaism and compromise. There is joy in heaven, he said, over even one sinner who repents.

Because "this man welcomes sinners," we must welcome them too. Authentic mission is impossible without it.

For further reading: Luke 15:1-10

FRIDAY

The Parable of the Pharisee and the Tax Collector

I TELL YOU THAT THIS MAN [THE TAX COLLECTOR], RATHER THAN THE
OTHER [THE PHARISEE], WENT HOME JUSTIFIED BEFORE GOD.
Luke 18:14

Justification is a legal term, the opposite of *condemnation*. The Old Testament magistrates were instructed to justify the innocent and condemn the guilty. So we can imagine the indignation of the Pharisees when Jesus pronounced the sinful tax collector justified and the upright Pharisee condemned. Was Jesus daring to ascribe to God an action he had forbidden to human judges?

The two actors in the parable both went up to the temple to pray. But there the similarities end and the dissimilarities begin.

Firstly, they had an entirely different opinion of themselves. Five times the Pharisee used the personal pronoun *I*. But the tax collector used it only once and in the accusative, "God, have mercy on me, a sinner" (v. 13). This is the language of true penitence. Further, their different opinion of themselves was reflected in their posture. Both stood (in customary Jewish fashion). But the Pharisee stood erect, proud, and ostentatious, preoccupied with himself, whereas the tax collector "stood at a distance" (v. 13), eyes downcast and beating his breast.

Next, they had a different object of confidence for acceptance with God. The Pharisee trusted in himself that he was righteous, while the tax collector trusted in God's mercy alone.

Archbishop Thomas Cranmer in his 1552 Communion Service deliberately puts us where we belong, namely alongside the tax collector, "not weighing our merits but pardoning our offences through Jesus Christ," and saying that we do not presume to come to the Lord's table trusting in our own righteousness but in his "manifold and great mercies." This so-called prayer of humble access remains forever the language of the true penitent.

For further reading: Luke 18:9–14

SATURDAY

The Parable of the Good Samaritan

LOVE YOUR NEIGHBOUR AS YOURSELF.

Luke 10:27

This parable has been universally admired and variously interpreted. For example, many commentators ancient and modern, most famously Augustine, have regarded it as an allegory of our redemption. The good Samaritan is Jesus Christ our redeemer, who finds us half dead, dresses our wounds, commits us to the church (the inn), gives the innkeeper two silver coins (the sacraments), and promises to return. It's ingenious, and we may at least see the good Samaritan as a picture of redeeming love. But we have no liberty to allegorize every detail of the story. Instead, the parable throws light on what "love your neighbour" means.

Firstly, this parable is an illustration of *love*. Negatively, Moses gave examples of how, if we truly love our neighbour, we will neither neglect the poor, nor exploit wage earners, nor harm the deaf or the blind, nor pervert justice, nor use false weights or measures in business, nor harbor a grudge, nor take revenge, for all these are incompatible with "love your neighbour" (Lev. 19:18). Positively, we are to seek our neighbour's highest welfare.

Secondly, this parable gives us a definition of *neighbour*. Of all unlikely people, it was a Samaritan who came to the rescue of the robbers' victim. Samaritans were hated by Jews. Yet here is a Samaritan doing for a Jew what no Jew would ever dream of doing for a Samaritan. True neighbour love is reciprocal. It defines both who our neighbours are whom we are to serve and what being a neighbour to them will mean.

Though there are almost no Samaritans left in the world today, there are many people we may be tempted to despise and reject. I am thinking of people of another race, colour, or culture; homosexual persons who are victims of homophobia; or people of another faith, such as Muslims. Jesus' parable challenges us to overcome all such racial, social, sexual, and religious prejudices. I am not suggesting that we compromise our Christian beliefs and morals, but rather that we do not allow these to impede our active love for our neighbour. This is what "go and do likewise" (v. 37) will mean for us.

For further reading: Luke 10:25–37

Some people make the glib claim that they live by the Sermon on the Mount. One wonders if they have ever read it. More common is the opposite reaction, that the Sermon is a beautiful ideal but hopelessly unpractical, being unattainable. Tolstoy to some extent combined both responses, because on the one hand he longed to see the Sermon acted out, while on the other he acknowledged his personal failures.

The essence of the Sermon (which is likely to have been more a kind of extended summer school than a single homily) was Christ's call to his followers to be different from everybody else. "Do not be like them," he said (Matt. 6:8). The kingdom he has proclaimed is to be a counterculture, exhibiting a whole set of distinctive values and standards. So he speaks of righteousness, influence, piety, trust, and ambition and concludes with a radical challenge to choose his way.

Sunday: The Beatitudes

Monday: The Salt and the Light

Tuesday: Christ and the Law

Wednesday: The Six Antitheses

Thursday: Religious Practices

Friday: True and False Ambitions

Saturday: The Radical Choice

Sunday

The Beatitudes

Blessed are the poor in spirit, for theirs is the kingdom of heaven.

Matthew 5:3

We need to begin with three negatives. Firstly, Jesus is not encouraging us to be selective, for example, calling some to be meek and others to be merciful. No. All eight beatitudes, like all nine fruits of the Spirit, are to characterize Christ's followers. Secondly, Jesus is not prescribing a formula for mental health. True, *makarios* ("blessed") can mean "happy," but Jesus is making not a subjective judgment (what we feel) but an objective one (what God thinks). Thirdly, Jesus is not preaching salvation by good works but teaching how those already reborn by the Spirit will behave.

The poor in spirit are those who acknowledge that they are spiritually bankrupt. Their language is, "Nothing in my hand I bring, simply to your cross I cling." Those who mourn go further. It is not the loss of a loved one that they grieve but the loss of their integrity and self-respect. They are comforted by God's forgiveness. The meek (so the context suggests) are willing for others to think of them what they themselves say they are. The next stage is that they hunger and thirst for righteousness. A keen spiritual appetite marks the people of God.

If the first four beatitudes concern our relationship with God, the second four concern our relationship with others. Since our God is a merciful God, his people must be merciful too, loving and serving anybody in need, as the good Samaritan taught us last week. The next people to be blessed are the pure in heart, that is, the single-minded and the transparently sincere. Christians are also to be peacemakers. Then they will be called God's children, since their Father is the supreme peacemaker who made costly peace with us through the death of his Son (Col. 1:20). The eighth beatitude pronounces a blessing on those who are persecuted for the sake of righteousness. The persecution of Christians is increasing in several cultures today. It is an aspect of our Christian calling, Jesus taught, and puts us into a noble succession, since the prophets were persecuted before us.

So the counterculture of Jesus Christ is at odds with the cultures of the world. For Jesus congratulates those the world most pities and calls the world's rejects blessed.

For further reading: Matthew 5:1–12

The Salt and the Light

YOU ARE THE SALT OF THE EARTH... YOU ARE THE LIGHT OF THE
WORLD... LET YOUR LIGHT SHINE BEFORE OTHERS...
Matthew 5:13–14, 16

Salt and light are two of the commonest household necessities. Certainly Jesus must often have watched his mother use salt in the kitchen. In those days before refrigeration, salt was used mostly for preservative and antiseptic purposes. So Mary would have let fish and meat soak in salty water. And she would have lit the oil lamps when the sun went down.

Now these are the images Jesus chose to indicate the influence he intended his followers to exert in the world. What did he mean? What is it legitimate for us to deduce from his choice of metaphors? I suggest he was teaching four truths. Firstly, *Christians are radically different from non-Christians*. Both images set the two communities in contrast to one another. On the one hand, there is the world; on the other, there are you who are to be the dark world's light. Again, the world is like rotting meat and decaying fish, but you are to be its salt, hindering social decay. The two communities are as different from one another as light is from darkness and salt from decay.

Secondly, *Christians must penetrate non-Christian society*. Although spiritually and morally distinct, we are not to be socially segregated. A lamp does no good if it is stowed away in a cupboard, and salt does no good if it stays in the saltshaker. The light must shine into the darkness; the salt must soak into the meat. Both models illustrate the process of penetration.

Thirdly, *Christians can influence and change non-Christian society*. Salt and light are both effective commodities. They change their environment. When salt is introduced into meat, something happens; bacterial decay is hindered. Similarly, when the light is switched on, something happens; the darkness is dispelled. It is not only individuals who can be changed; societies also can be changed. Of course, we cannot perfect society, but we can improve it. History is full of examples of social improvement by Christian influence.

Fourthly, *Christians must retain their Christian distinctives*. The salt must retain its saltiness; otherwise it will be useless. Light must retain its brightness; otherwise it will never dispel the darkness. And what are our Christian distinctives? The rest of the Sermon on the Mount tells us.

For further reading: Matthew 5:13–16

TUESDAY

Christm *Christ and the Law*

DO NOT THINK THAT I HAVE COME TO ABOLISH THE LAW OR THE
PROPHETS; I HAVE NOT COME TO ABOLISH THEM BUT TO FULFIL THEM.

Matthew 5:17

People were very struck by Jesus' authority. "What is this?" they asked. "A new teaching!" In particular, they asked what the relation was between his authority and the authority of Moses' law.

To this question, spoken or unspoken, Jesus now gave a definitive answer. He had come not to abolish the Old Testament but to fulfil it, that is, to bring it to completion, to obey it, and to supply its true meaning. For it has a permanent validity. In consequence, greatness in the kingdom of God would be measured by obedience to the law. Jesus continued, "Unless your righteousness surpasses that of the Pharisees and the teachers of the law, you will certainly not enter the kingdom of heaven" (v. 20). On hearing this, the disciples must have been dumbfounded. For the scribes and Pharisees were the most righteous people on earth. As we have seen, they had calculated that the Old Testament contained 248 commandments and 365 permissions, and they claimed that they had kept them all. How could the disciples of Jesus be more righteous than the most righteous people on earth? The riddle is not hard to solve. Christian righteousness is greater than Pharisaic righteousness because it is deeper: it is a righteousness of the heart.

The rest of Matthew 5 consists of six parallel paragraphs, each of which contains a so-called antithesis introduced by the formula, "You have heard that it was said… But I tell you." With whom is Jesus contrasting himself? Many commentators have maintained that Jesus is setting himself against Moses. But this is definitely not so, for at least two reasons. Firstly, the formula Jesus used when quoting Scripture was, "It is written"; the formula, "It was said" introduced an oral tradition, not the written Scripture. Secondly, Jesus has just affirmed in unequivocal terms the lasting authority of Scripture (vv. 17–18); it is inconceivable that immediately afterward he should have contradicted Scripture and so have contradicted himself. No. He endorsed Scripture, insisted on its authority, and gave it its true meaning, as we will see tomorrow.

For further reading: Matthew 5:17–20

WEDNESDAY

The Six Antitheses

YOU HAVE HEARD THAT IT WAS SAID, "LOVE YOUR NEIGHBOUR AND HATE
YOUR ENEMY." BUT I TELL YOU, LOVE YOUR ENEMIES...
Matthew 5:43–44

We saw yesterday that what Jesus was contradicting in the six antitheses of Matthew 5 was not Scripture but tradition. All six antitheses are variations on the same theme. Because the scribes and Pharisees found the law burdensome, they tried to reduce its challenge by making its demands less demanding and its permissions more permissive. In this way they made the law more manageable. Let's take the fifth and sixth antitheses as our examples.

Here is the fifth: "You have heard that it was said, 'Eye for eye, and tooth for tooth.' But I tell you, do not resist an evil person" (vv. 38–39). An eye for an eye was an instruction to the judges of Israel. It expressed the *lex talionis*, the principle of an exact retribution as a maximum sentence. But the scribes and Pharisees extended it from the law courts (where it belonged) to the realm of personal relationships (to which it did not belong). They used it to justify revenge, which the law explicitly forbade.

Now the sixth antithesis: "You have heard that it was said, 'Love your neighbour and hate your enemy.' But I tell you: Love your enemies" (vv. 43–44). The scribes' quotation was a scandalous perversion of Scripture, for it added to the command to love our neighbour a corresponding command to hate our enemy, which is not in the Old Testament text. The teachers of the law asked themselves who their neighbour was whom they were obliged to love. Why, of course, they replied to themselves, their neighbour was their kith and kin in race and religion. So if they were required to love only their neighbour, it was tantamount to giving them permission to hate their enemy. But Jesus roundly condemned this casuistry. Our neighbour in the vocabulary of God, he insisted, includes our enemy.

If we love only those who love us, we are no better than unbelievers. If we love our enemies, however, it will be apparent that we are children of our heavenly Father, since his love is indiscriminate, giving rain and sunshine to all people alike. Alfred Plummer summed up the options: "To return evil for good is devilish. To return good for good is human. To return good for evil is divine."

For further reading: Matthew 5:43–48

THURSDAY

Religious Practices

BE CAREFUL NOT TO PRACTISE YOUR RIGHTEOUSNESS IN FRONT OF
OTHERS TO BE SEEN BY THEM.

Matthew 6:1

Jesus evidently assumed that his disciples would engage in the common practices of giving, praying, and fasting. For this trio of religious obligations expresses our duty to God (prayer), to others (giving), and to ourselves (fasting). The three paragraphs at the beginning of Matthew 6 follow an identical pattern. In vivid and humorous imagery Jesus paints a picture of hypocrites who practise their piety before men in order to be applauded by them. If you do this, he says, you will have received your reward in full, namely the applause you are hungry for. Instead, practise your piety in secret, for then your heavenly Father, who sees in secret, will reward you.

Jesus' first example is giving. He pictures a pompous Pharisee on his way to make a donation. In front of him march the trumpeters, blowing a fanfare, anxious to assemble an audience. For the hypocrite is an actor engaged in a theatrical performance. Instead, don't let your left hand know what your right is doing. That is, we are not even to be self-conscious in our giving, dwelling on it in a spirit of self-congratulation.

Jesus' second example is prayer. We are not to make a parade of our prayer habits but rather to enter our room, shut the door, and pray to our Father in secret. As nothing destroys prayer like side glances at human spectators, so nothing enriches it like a sense that God is watching. Our Father will reward us – not with some inappropriate reward but with what we most want, namely access into his presence.

Jesus' third example is fasting, which he took for granted in his disciples. The Bible suggests that fasting is not to be an isolated practice but is to be associated now with penitence, now with self-discipline, now with concern for the hungry, and now with special times of prayer for special needs. When we do fast, we are not to look dismal or disfigure our faces but to look normal, so that nobody will suspect that we are fasting.

The contrast is stark. Pharisaic piety is ostentatious, motivated by vanity, and rewarded by men; Christian piety is secret, motivated by humility, and rewarded by God.

For further reading: Matthew 6:1–18

FRIDAY

True and False Ambitions

BUT SEEK FIRST HIS [GOD'S] KINGDOM AND HIS RIGHTEOUSNESS, AND ALL
THESE THINGS WILL BE GIVEN TO YOU AS WELL.

Matthew 6:33

Jesus now contrasts what pagans seek and what Christians should seek first. What we seek is what we set before us as the supreme good to which we devote our lives. It is our preoccupation, our ambition. Jesus reduces the options to only two. Pagans are obsessed with their own material well-being (food, drink, and clothing), whereas Christians should be preoccupied above all with the reign and the righteousness of God and with their spread throughout the world.

Jesus begins with the negative. Three times he repeats his prohibition not to worry about material things. He is forbidding neither thought nor forethought, but rather anxious thought. For anxiety is incompatible with Christian faith. If God already takes care of our life and body, can we not trust him to take care of our food and clothing? Again, if God feeds the birds and clothes the lilies, can we not trust him to feed and clothe us?

At the same time, we must not misunderstand Jesus' teaching. Firstly, trusting God does not exempt us from working to earn our own living. The birds teach us this lesson. For how does God feed the birds? The answer is that he doesn't! Jesus was a keen observer of nature. He knew perfectly well that birds feed themselves. It is only indirectly that God feeds them by providing the wherewithal with which they feed themselves. Secondly, trusting God does not exempt us from calamity. True, not a single sparrow falls to the ground without our Father's permission. But sparrows do fall and get killed. So do human beings. So do airplanes.

Instead of being preoccupied with material things, the followers of Jesus are to seek first God's kingdom and God's righteousness. To seek God's kingdom is to proclaim Christ as King, so that people will submit to his rule. To seek God's righteousness is to remember that God loves righteousness and hates evil, so that, even outside the circle of the kingdom, justice is more pleasing to God than injustice, freedom than oppression, and peace than violence and war. In this double ambition our evangelistic and social responsibilities are combined, and the glory of God becomes our supreme concern.

For further reading: Matthew 6:25–34

SATURDAY

The Radical Choice

NOT EVERYONE WHO SAYS TO ME, "LORD, LORD," WILL ENTER THE
KINGDOM OF HEAVEN, BUT ONLY THE ONE WHO DOES THE WILL OF MY
FATHER WHO IS IN HEAVEN.

Matthew 7:21

Jesus sets before us, in the conclusion of the Sermon on the Mount, the radical choice between obedience and disobedience. Not, of course, that we can be saved by our obedience but that, if we have truly been saved, we will show it by our obedience.

Firstly, Jesus warns us of the danger of a merely verbal profession (vv. 21–23). To be sure, a verbal profession is essential. "Jesus is Lord" is the earliest, shortest, simplest of all Christian creeds. But if it is not accompanied by personal submission to the lordship of Jesus, it is useless. We may even hear on the last day the terrible words of Jesus: "I never knew you. Away from me, you evildoers" (v. 23).

Secondly, Jesus warns us of the danger of a merely intellectual knowledge. Whereas the contrast in verses 21–23 was between saying and doing, the contrast now is between hearing and doing (vv. 24–27). Jesus then illustrates it by his well-known parable of the two builders. It features a wise man who constructed his house on rock and a fool who could not be bothered with foundations and built his house on sand. As both got on with their building, a casual observer would not have noticed any difference between them, for the difference was in the foundations, and foundations are not seen. Only when a storm broke and battered both houses with great ferocity was the fatal difference revealed. In the same way, professing Christians (both the genuine and the spurious) look alike. Both appear to be building Christian lives. Both hear Christ's words. They go to church, read the Bible, and listen to sermons. But the deep foundations of their lives are hidden from view. Only the storm of adversity in this life and the storm of judgment on the last day will reveal who they are.

The Sermon on the Mount ends on the solemn note of radical choice. There are only two ways (narrow and broad) and only two foundations (rock and sand). On which road are we travelling? On which foundation are we building?

For further reading: Matthew 7:13–29

We return this week to Jesus' teaching on prayer, as recorded in Matthew 6:7–15. He now emphasizes that hypocrisy is not the only sin to avoid in prayer; "vain repetitions" (v. 7 KJV) or meaningless, mechanical utterance is another. The former is the folly of the Pharisee, the latter of the Gentile or pagan. Hypocrisy is a misuse of the *purpose* of prayer (diverting it from the glory of God to the glory of self); verbosity is a misuse of the very *nature* of prayer (degrading it from a real and personal approach to God into a mere recitation of words). So Jesus contrasts the pagan way of meaningless loquacity with the Christian way of meaningful communion with God, and he illustrates this by the beauty and balance of the Lord's Prayer.

Sunday: Pagan Prayer

Monday: Christian Prayer

Tuesday: Concern for God's Glory

Wednesday: Give Us Our Daily Bread

Thursday: Forgive Us Our Sins

Friday: Deliver Us from Evil

Saturday: Our Image of God

Pagan Prayer

AND WHEN YOU PRAY, DO NOT KEEP ON BABBLING LIKE PAGANS, FOR THEY
THINK THEY WILL BE HEARD BECAUSE OF THEIR MANY WORDS.

Matthew 6:7

The Greek verb *battalogeo* is variously rendered "to use vain repetitions," "to heap up empty phrases," and "to keep on babbling." It occurs nowhere else, and nobody knows for certain what it means. Some scholars think it was derived from a King Battus, who stuttered, or from another Battus who was the author of tedious and wordy poems. Most, however, regard it as an onomatopoeic expression, the sound of the word indicating its meaning. Just as *battarizo* meant "to stammer" and *barbaros* was a "barbarian," whose language the Greeks could not understand, so *battalogeo* might simply mean "to babble."

What, then, was Jesus prohibiting in prayer? Not all repetition, since he himself in Gethsemane kept on praying saying the same words, but rather all prayers that consist of words without meaning. It would certainly include prayer wheels and prayer flags. Also the mindless repetition of a mantra in transcendental meditation. Indeed, Maharishi Mahesh Yogi has himself expressed regret at his misleading choice of the word *meditation*, since true meditation always involves the conscious use of the mind. Christ's prohibition would also cover the use of the rosary, unless the telling of the beads genuinely aids thought instead of dispensing with it.

What about liturgical forms of worship? Are Anglicans guilty of *battalogia*? Yes, no doubt some of us are, if our mind wanders. But most of us find that the use of set forms aids concentration.

To sum up, what Jesus forbids his people is any kind of prayer with the mouth when the mind is not engaged. Pagans go through the pretense of prayer because they think that the more they say, the more likely they are to be heard. What an incredible notion! What kind of a God is this who is chiefly impressed by the mechanics and the statistics of prayer? "Do not be like them," Jesus says (v. 8).

For further reading: Matthew 6:5–8

Monday

Christian Prayer

Do not be like them [the pagans], for your Father knows what you need before you ask him.

Matthew 6:8

The reason why Christians are not to pray like pagans is that we believe in the living and true God. We are not to do as they do because we are not to think as they think. On the contrary, "your Father knows what you need before you ask him." He is neither ignorant of our needs nor hesitant to meet them. Why, then, should we pray? What is the point of prayer? Let Calvin answer our questions with his customary clarity:

> *Believers do not pray with the view to informing God about things unknown to him, or of exciting him to do his duty, or of urging him as though he were reluctant. On the contrary, they pray in order that they may arouse themselves to seek him, that they may exercise their faith in meditating on his promises, that they may relieve themselves from their anxieties by pouring them into his bosom; in a word that they may declare that from him alone they hope and expect, both for themselves and for others, all good things.*

If the praying of Pharisees was hypocritical and that of pagans mechanical, then the praying of Christians must be real – sincere as opposed to hypocritical, thoughtful as opposed to mechanical.

The so-called Lord's Prayer was given by Jesus as a model of what genuine Christian prayer is like. According to Matthew, he gave it as a pattern to copy ("Pray then like this" [v. 9 RSV]); according to Luke, as a form to use ("When you pray, say…" [Luke 11:2]). Indeed, we can use the prayer in both ways.

Jesus taught us to address God as "our Father in heaven" (v. 9). This implies first that he is personal. He may be, in C. S. Lewis' well-known expression "beyond personality," but he is certainly not less. Secondly, he is loving. He is not the kind of father we sometimes hear about – autocrat, playboy, drunkard – but one who fulfils the ideals of fatherhood in loving care for his children. Thirdly, he is powerful. What his love directs his power is able to perform. It is always wise, before we pray, to spend time recalling who he to whom we are coming is.

For further reading: Matthew 6:7–13

TUESDAY

Concern for God's Glory

OUR FATHER IN HEAVEN, HALLOWED BE YOUR NAME, YOUR KINGDOM
COME, YOUR WILL BE DONE, ON EARTH AS IT IS IN HEAVEN.

Matthew 6:9–10

The Lord's Prayer contains six petitions. The first three are concerned with the glory of God (his name, his kingdom, and his will), while the second trio is concerned with us and our needs (daily bread, forgiveness, and deliverance). A similar priority is recognized in the Ten Commandments, as the first five handle our duty to God and the second five our duty to our neighbour.

Today we will focus our attention on the glory of God in relation to his name, his rule, and his will. A name stands for the person who bears it, for his nature, character, and activity. So God's "name" is God himself as he has revealed himself. His name is already holy in that it is exalted above every other name. Yet we pray for its hallowing, that is, that it may be given the honour due to it in our lives, in the church, and in the world.

The kingdom of God is his royal rule, not so much in its absolute sovereignty over nature and history, but as it broke into the world with Jesus. To pray for its coming is to pray both that it may grow, as through the church's witness people submit to Jesus, and that it will be consummated when Jesus returns in glory.

Because God's will is the will of him who is perfect in knowledge, love, and power, it is folly to resist it and wisdom to discern, desire, and do it. We need to pray, therefore, that God's will may be done on earth as it is in heaven.

It is comparatively easy to repeat the words of the Lord's Prayer like a parrot, or indeed like a heathen "babbler." To pray them with sincerity, however, has revolutionary implications. Our priority becomes no longer the advancement of our own little name, kingdom, and will, but of God's. Whether we can pray these petitions with integrity is a searching test of the reality and depth of our Christian profession.

For further reading: Ephesians 1:3–14

Give Us Our Daily Bread

GIVE ME NEITHER POVERTY NOR RICHES, BUT GIVE ME ONLY MY DAILY
BREAD.

Proverbs 30:8

In the second half of the Lord's Prayer, the possessive adjective changes from *your* to *our*, as we turn from God's affairs to ours. Having expressed our burning concern for God's glory, we now express our humble dependence on his grace. Although our personal needs have been relegated to a secondary place, they have not been eliminated. To decline to mention them at all in prayer, on the ground that we don't want to bother God with such trivialities, is as great an error as to allow them to dominate our prayers.

Some early commentators could not believe that Jesus intended our first request to be for literal bread. It seemed to them inappropriate. So they allegorized the petition. Early church fathers like Tertullian, Cyprian, and Augustine thought the reference was either to the invisible bread of the Word of God (Augustine) or to the sacramental bread of Holy Communion. We should be thankful for the greater, down-to-earth understanding of the Reformers. Calvin called the spiritualizing of the fathers "exceedingly absurd." Luther wrote that bread was a symbol for "everything necessary for the preservation of this life, like food, a healthy body, good weather, house, home, wife, children, good government and peace."

The prayer that God will give us these things does not, of course, deny either that most people have to earn their own living or that we are commanded to feed the hungry ourselves. Instead, it is an expression of our ultimate dependence on God, who normally uses human means of production and distribution through which to fulfil his purposes. Moreover, it seems that Jesus wanted his followers to be conscious of a day-to-day dependence. The Greek adjective *epiousios* in "our daily bread" was so completely unknown to the ancients that Origen thought the evangelists had coined it. Whether it means "for the current day" or "for the following day," it is a prayer for the immediate future. We are to live a day at a time. To say grace before meals acknowledges this. It is a valuable Christian habit.

For further reading: Deuteronomy 26:1–11

THURSDAY

Forgive Us Our Sins

FORGIVE US OUR DEBTS, AS WE ALSO HAVE FORGIVEN OUR DEBTORS.
Matthew 6:12

Marghanita Laski, the well-known twentieth-century English novelist and critic, made no secret of her atheism. But one day, in a surprising moment of candor on television, she blurted out, "What I envy most about you Christians is your forgiveness; I have no one to forgive me." She was right. Forgiveness is at the heart of the gospel. Indeed, it is as indispensable to the life and health of the soul as food is to the body.

So the next petition in the Lord's Prayer is "Forgive us our debts." Sin is likened to a debt because it deserves to be punished and because when God forgives us he remits the penalty and drops the charge against us.

The addition of the words "as we also have forgiven our debtors" is further emphasized in verses 14 and 15, which follow the prayer and state that our Father will forgive us if we have forgiven others but will not forgive us if we refuse to forgive others. This certainly does not mean that our forgiveness of others earns us the right to be forgiven. It is rather that God forgives only the penitent, and that one of the chief evidences of true penitence is a forgiving spirit. Once our eyes have been opened to see the enormity of our offence against God, the injuries that others may have done to us appear by comparison extremely trifling. If, on the other hand, we have an exaggerated view of the offences of others, it proves that we have minimized our own. It is the disparity between the size of debts that is the main point of the parable of the unmerciful servant. Its conclusion is, "I cancelled all that debt of yours [which was huge]... Shouldn't you have had mercy on your fellow servant [whose debt was insignificant] just as I had on you?" (18:32–33).

For further reading: Matthew 18:23–35

FRIDAY

Deliver Us from Evil

AND LEAD US NOT INTO TEMPTATION, BUT DELIVER US FROM EVIL...

Matthew 6:13 KJV

These last two petitions of the Lord's Prayer are really one. They should probably be taken together as negative and positive aspects of the same prayer. But two problems confront us.

Firstly, the Bible tells us that God does not, even cannot, tempt us (James 1:13). So what is the point of praying that he will not do what he has promised never to do? Some answer by interpreting "tempting" as "testing." But a better explanation is to unite the two clauses of the prayer: to understand "lead us not into temptation" in the light of its counterpart "deliver us from evil," and to interpret "evil" as "the evil one." That is, it is the devil who is in view, who tempts God's people to sin, and from whom we need to be rescued.

Secondly, the Bible says that temptations and trials are good for us (James 1:2). If, then, they are beneficial, why should we pray not to be led into them? The probable answer is that this is a prayer more that we should overcome temptation than that we should avoid it. We could then paraphrase the petition: "Do not allow us so to be led into temptation that we fall to it, but rescue us from the evil one."

Looking back now, we can see that the three petitions of the Lord's Prayer are beautifully comprehensive. In principle they cover all our human need – material (our daily bread), spiritual (the forgiveness of our sins), and moral (our deliverance from evil). When we pray this prayer we are expressing our humble dependence on God in every area of our human life. Moreover, a trinitarian Christian is bound to see in these three petitions a veiled allusion to the three persons of the Trinity, since it is through the Father's creation and providence that we receive our daily bread, through the Son's atoning death that we receive the forgiveness of our sins, and through the Holy Spirit's indwelling power that we can be rescued from the evil one. No wonder some ancient manuscripts (though not the best) end with the doxology, attributing the kingdom, the power, and the glory to this triune God to whom alone they belong.

For further reading: 1 John 3:7–10

Saturday

Our Image of God

IF YOU, THEN, THOUGH YOU ARE EVIL, KNOW HOW TO GIVE GOOD GIFTS
TO YOUR CHILDREN, HOW MUCH MORE WILL YOUR FATHER IN HEAVEN
GIVE GOOD GIFTS TO THOSE WHO ASK HIM!

Matthew 7:11

Jesus seems to have given us in the Lord's Prayer a model of *real* prayer, *Christian* prayer, in distinction to the prayers of the Pharisees and the pagans. To be sure, one could recite the Lord's Prayer either hypocritically or mechanically or both. But if we mean what we say, then the Lord's Prayer becomes the divine alternative to both forms of false prayer.

The error of the hypocrite is selfishness. Even in his prayers he is obsessed with his own self-image and how he looks in the eyes of the beholder. But in the Lord's Prayer Christians are obsessed with God – with his name, his kingdom, and his will, not with theirs.

The error of the heathen is mindlessness. He just goes babbling on, giving voice to his meaningless liturgy. Over against this folly Jesus invites us to make all our needs known to our heavenly Father with humble thoughtfulness and so express our daily dependence on him.

So the fundamental difference between various kinds of prayer is the fundamentally different images of God that lie behind them. What kind of God is it who might be interested in such selfish and mindless prayers? Is God a commodity that we can use him to boost our own status, or a computer that we can feed words into him mechanically? From these unworthy notions we turn back with relief to the teaching of Jesus that God is our Father in heaven. We need to remember that he loves his children with the most tender affection, that he sees his children even in the secret place, that he knows his children's needs before they ask him, and that he acts on their behalf with his heavenly and kingly power. If we thus allow Scripture to fashion our image of God, we will never pray with hypocrisy but always with integrity, never mechanically but always thoughtfully, like the children of God we are.

For further reading: Matthew 7:7–11

WEEK 25: THE TURNING POINT

When we considered the temptations of Jesus, we saw that they were all attempts to persuade him to follow the way of popular acclaim and to deflect him from the way of the cross. The same temptation to disobedience and compromise dogged his footsteps.

It is this that explains Jesus' almost fierce command to people to keep silent about the miracles they had seen. It was what is called the "messianic secret." Jesus did not want people to know the fact of his messiahship until they were ready to grasp its nature.

But this week we come to the significant occasion when Peter for the first time made an explicit confession of Jesus as Messiah and then came to grasp – after protest – the necessity of the cross. It was the turning point in Jesus' ministry.

Sunday: Peter's Confession

Monday: The Necessity of the Cross

Tuesday: Taking Up the Cross

Wednesday: Finding Ourselves

Thursday: The Transfiguration

Friday: The Ransom Saying

Saturday: Greatness in the Kingdom of God

SUNDAY

Peter's Confession

"WHO DO YOU SAY I AM?" SIMON PETER ANSWERED, "YOU ARE THE
MESSIAH, THE SON OF THE LIVING GOD."
Matthew 16:15–16

The time had come for the disciples to make an unambiguous statement of their
faith in Jesus as Messiah. So he took them with him to the far north, to the village of
Caesarea Philippi, on the foothills of Mount Hermon and near the source of the River
Jordan. Here in privacy and solitude he asked them two questions. To his first question
about public opinion, they replied that people thought he was John the Baptist, Elijah,
Jeremiah, or another prophet. To his second question about who they thought he
was, Simon Peter, the leader and spokesman of the Twelve, blurted out, "You are the
Messiah." According to Matthew, Peter added, "the Son of the living God," although
probably using the title in its limited messianic sense. Then, as soon as Peter had borne
witness to Jesus, Jesus bore witness to Peter.

Firstly, Peter had come to his conviction not by human reasoning but by a revelation
of the Father.

Secondly, Peter was in some sense the rock on which the Messiah would build his
community, which would last forever. This is, of course, a controversial verse. But in
making up our minds about it, we would be wise to remember that throughout the
New Testament, Christ himself is the rock on which the church is built and that the
majority of early church fathers taught that the rock is the faith professed by Peter, not
Peter professing the faith.

Thirdly, Peter was given the keys of the kingdom, which he would later use
– historically speaking – to admit first the Jews, then the Samaritans, and then the
Gentiles into the kingdom of God.

One more point: no sooner had Peter made his confession of faith, than "Jesus
warned them not to tell anyone about him" (Mark 8:30). We will learn tomorrow that
this was the last time Jesus issued his command to silence, and why.

For further reading: Matthew 16:13–20

The Necessity of the Cross

HE [JESUS] THEN BEGAN TO TEACH THEM THAT THE SON OF MAN MUST
SUFFER MANY THINGS AND... BE KILLED... HE SPOKE PLAINLY ABOUT
THIS...

Mark 8:31–32

Before we come to the confrontation between Jesus and Peter, it may be helpful to fill in something of the historical background. For more than seven hundred years Israel had been oppressed by the successive empires of Assyria, Babylonia, Persia, Greece, and Rome – except for a brief intoxicating period under the Maccabees. At the turn of the first century, a number of apocalyptic movements arose, whose leaders made wild promises. Yahweh was about to intervene through the Messiah, they said; Israel's enemies would be destroyed in a violent and bloody conflict, and the messianic age of peace and freedom would dawn.

Galilee itself was a hotbed of such expectations, and some were focusing their hope on Jesus of Nazareth. Thus John records that "Jesus, knowing that they intended to come and make him king by force, withdrew again to a mountain by himself" (John 6:15). But Jesus had not come to be some kind of military Messiah. Hence the command to silence.

But now, once Peter had confessed Jesus as the Messiah, the disciples should be ready to learn about the sufferings of the Messiah. So Jesus "began to teach them [it was a new instruction] that the Son of Man must suffer many things and... be killed" (Mark 8:31). Moreover, he spoke this plainly and openly; there was no need for silence. Peter listened aghast and then exploded. "Never, Lord!... This shall never happen to you!" (Matt. 16:22). Peter would have been familiar with the figure of the Son of Man in Daniel chapter 7, who was given "authority, glory and sovereign power" (Dan. 7:14) so that all nations would worship him. How then could the Son of Man suffer? It was a contradiction in terms. So Peter was brash enough to rebuke Jesus, and Jesus now rebuked Peter. "Get behind me, Satan!" he said (Matt. 16:23). The same Peter who had received a divine revelation had now become an object of Satanic deception.

Still today the voice of Peter sometimes drowns the voice of Christ. For like Peter many people deny the necessity of the cross. The cross is still a stumbling block to human pride.

For further reading: Mark 8:31–33

TUESDAY

Taking Up the Cross

WHOEVER WANTS TO BE MY DISCIPLE MUST DENY THEMSELVES AND TAKE
UP THEIR CROSS AND FOLLOW ME.

Mark 8:34

It seems to me very remarkable that Jesus moved on from referring to *his* cross to referring to *ours*. It appears that somehow he already knew that he was going to be crucified. Now he says that if *anyone* wants to follow him, he *must* take up his cross. We cannot fail to observe the same note of necessity.

What did Jesus mean? According to H. B. Swete in his commentary on Mark's Gospel, to take up the cross is "to put oneself into the position of a condemned man on his way to execution." If we had lived in Roman-occupied Palestine in those days, and if we had seen a man carrying a crossbar, or *patibulum*, we would not have needed to run up to him and ask, "Excuse me, but what on earth are you doing?" No, we would have recognized him at once as a condemned criminal, because the Romans compelled those they condemned to death to carry their own cross to the place of crucifixion.

This was the imagery that Jesus chose to illustrate the meaning of self-denial. We need to rescue this vocabulary from being debased. We should not suppose that self-denial is giving up luxuries during Lent or that "my cross" is some personal and painful trial. We are always in danger of trivializing Christian discipleship, as if it were no more than adding a thin veneer of piety to an otherwise secular life. Then prick the veneer, and there is the same old pagan underneath. No, becoming and being a Christian involves a change so radical that no imagery can do it justice except death and resurrection – dying to the old life of self-centredness and rising to a new life of holiness and love. Paul was elaborating Jesus' vocabulary when he wrote, "I have been crucified with Christ" (Gal. 2:20) and, "Those who belong to Christ Jesus have crucified the flesh with its passions and desires" (Gal. 5:24).

One final thought: Luke added the adverb *daily* to the saying of Jesus: "Whoever wants to be my disciple must deny themselves and take up their cross *daily* and follow me" (Luke 9:23, emphasis added).

For further reading: Romans 8:12–14

WEDNESDAY

Finding Ourselves

FOR WHOEVER WANTS TO SAVE THEIR LIFE WILL LOSE IT, BUT WHOEVER
LOSES THEIR LIFE FOR ME AND FOR THE GOSPEL WILL SAVE IT.

Mark 8:35

Because this verse speaks of saving and losing our life, I used to think that it referred specifically to Christian martyrs who in dying for Christ would enter eternal life. But, although the verse may well include a reference to martyrdom, I now see that Jesus had a much wider application in mind than that. The language indicates this. The word translated "life" is *psuchē*, meaning "soul" or "self." Indeed, Luke renders Jesus' statement with the simple reflexive: "What good is it for someone to gain the whole world, and yet lose or forfeit their very self?" (Luke 9:25).

One might perhaps paraphrase Jesus' favourite epigram, which he seems to have used in several different contexts, in this way: "If you insist on holding on to yourself, and refuse to let yourself go, but determine to live for yourself, you will lose yourself. That is the way of death, not the way of life. But if you are willing to lose yourself, to give yourself away in love, in the service of the gospel, then in the moment of complete abandon, when you think you have lost everything, the miracle takes place and you find yourself."

In recent years several schools of psychology have developed that lay their emphasis on *self-actualization*. The word sounds promising in Christian ears until we remember that, according to Jesus, the only way to self-discovery is self-denial, and the only way to live is to die to our own self-centredness.

In two similar epigrams Jesus used commercial language, the language of profit, loss, and exchange. He asked two rhetorical questions, which remained unanswered. Firstly, what profit would there be in gaining the whole world (all the wealth, power, and fame it offers) and losing oneself? Secondly, what could anyone give in exchange for themself? Both questions emphasize the infinite value of the self in contrast to the value of the world. For one thing, it is impossible to gain the whole world. For another, if one could, it would not last, and while it did last, it would not satisfy.

For further reading: Luke 12:13–21

Thursday

The Transfiguration

SOME WHO ARE STANDING HERE WILL NOT TASTE DEATH BEFORE THEY
SEE THAT THE KINGDOM OF GOD HAS COME WITH POWER.

Mark 9:1

The evangelists seem to have understood this promise of Jesus as referring to his transfiguration, since they go on immediately to describe it. But how are we to interpret it? Four aspects may be mentioned.

Firstly, it was a *reassurance*. Jesus had shocked the Twelve by predicting his sufferings. But now he gives them a glimpse of his glory in order to assure them that through suffering the Messiah would enter into his glory.

Secondly, it was a *fulfilment*. It is, of course, highly significant that Moses and Elijah appeared to them and, according to Luke, talked with Jesus about his "exodus," that is, his death. They were representatives of the law and the prophets. They soon disappeared, however. Now that the reality had come, the shadows could fade away. In addition, the heavenly voice addressed Jesus in a composite sentence of three Old Testament phrases – "You are my son" (Ps. 2:7), "in whom I delight" (Isa. 42:1), "Listen to him" (Deut. 18:15). Thus Jesus was acclaimed in his three offices of Prophet, Priest, and King – the King who would rule over the nations, the Priest-servant who would offer himself in sacrifice for sin, and the Prophet who would complete the revelation of God.

Thirdly, it was an *anticipation*. According to Mark 9:9 Jesus commanded Peter, James, and John not to tell anyone what they had seen until after his resurrection. This was not a reversion to the messianic secret but a recognition that nobody could understand Jesus' transfiguration until after his resurrection. This was because his transfigured body was in fact his resurrection body in anticipation.

Fourthly, it was a *temptation*. This is a little speculative. But if Jesus' transfigured body was his resurrection body, presumably he could have stepped straight into glory without needing to die. But he didn't. Once again he resisted the temptation to avoid the cross. He deliberately came back to this life in order to die for our sins.

For further reading: 2 Peter 1:16–18

The Ransom Saying

THE SON OF MAN DID NOT COME TO BE SERVED, BUT TO SERVE, AND TO
GIVE HIS LIFE AS A RANSOM FOR MANY.

Mark 10:45

Mark records three distinct occasions on which Jesus predicted his sufferings and death. This is the third. It is especially important because it is our Lord's own interpretation of the cross; for it is reasonable to suppose that, if anybody understood the meaning of his death, he did.

To begin with, he emphasized that his death would be voluntary. Previously he had described it in the passive, namely that he would be betrayed, rejected, and killed. Now, however, he says that the Son of Man had come not to be served but to serve and to give himself. In other words, he had come not primarily to live his life but to give it as the culmination of a lifetime of service.

In particular, Jesus continued, he had come "to give his life as a ransom for many," which Paul later interpreted as meaning "for all" (1 Tim. 2:6). What, then, can we legitimately deduce from the ransom metaphor? Firstly, it indicates the gravity of our plight. We are likened to the slaves or captives of sin, who are unable to secure our release. Secondly, it indicates the value of the price paid for our liberation. As the apostle Peter wrote later, we have been redeemed not with silver or gold "but with the precious blood of Christ, a lamb without blemish or defect" (1 Pet. 1:19). The Passover is clearly in Peter's mind. As the firstborn Israelites were saved by the killing of a substitute lamb, so Christ died as our ransom in our place. Thirdly, it is implied that, having been purchased by Christ, we now belong to him. As Paul wrote to Titus, Jesus Christ "gave himself for us to redeem us from all wickedness and to purify for himself a people that are his very own" (Titus 2:14). So we are altogether his for time and eternity.

For further reading: Revelation 5:6–10

SATURDAY

Greatness in the Kingdom of God

WHOEVER WANTS TO BECOME GREAT AMONG YOU MUST BE YOUR SERVANT,
AND WHOEVER WANTS TO BE FIRST MUST BE SLAVE OF ALL.

Mark 10:43–44

When James and John, the sons of Zebedee, stood before Jesus, the antithesis between them was almost total. He had come to give and to serve; they wanted to get and to rule. The same choice faces us today.

Firstly, there is *the choice between self-seeking and self-sacrifice*. James and John said to Jesus, "We want you to do for us whatever we ask" (v. 35). Their request surely qualifies for inclusion in the *Guinness World Records* as the worst prayer ever prayed. For blatant self-centredness it would be hard to beat. They anticipated that there would be an unholy scramble for the best seats in the kingdom, so they judged it prudent to make an advance reservation. Their prayer was an attempt to bend God's will to theirs, whereas true prayer involves the surrender of our will to God's.

Secondly, there is *the choice between power and service*. They asked Jesus if they might sit on each side of him in the kingdom. What were they expecting to sit on? The floor? Cushions or stools? No, surely, on thrones. They came from a middle-class family, with servants to do their bidding. Perhaps they missed them and wanted to regain power to rule. In the world, Jesus commented, "their great men exercise authority over them. But it is not this way among you" (vv. 42–43 NASB). The new community of Jesus is organized on a different principle – service, not power, humility, not authority.

Thirdly, there is *the choice between suffering and security*. In leaving home and following Jesus, James and John had become vagrants. Did they regret leaving their comfortable home? In reply to Jesus' question, they claimed they could share his cup and his baptism, for they thought he was referring to the luxuries of the messianic banquet, whereas he was alluding to suffering and the way of the cross. Thus James and John coveted honour, power, and safety, while Jesus offered sacrifice, service, and suffering. With his dramatic words "not this way among you" Jesus indicated that there are two distinct communities in the world, with two distinct value systems. The symbol of one is the throne, but of the other the cross.

For further reading: Mark 10:35–45

Week 26: The Controversies of Jesus

There is no doubt that Christ was a controversialist. He was in constant debate with the religious leaders of his day. He disagreed with them, and they disagreed with him. So Mark, having given us an overview of Jesus' public ministry in his chapter 1, collected together in chapter 2 four controversies. What is particularly striking about them is that in each debate, explicitly or implicitly, Jesus advances a claim regarding his unique identity. After these four controversies we will look at three more (on tradition, divorce, and authority), which Mark includes in later chapters of his Gospel.

Sunday: The Debate Over Forgiveness

Monday: The Debate Over Fraternization

Tuesday: The Debate Over Fasting

Wednesday: The Debate Over the Sabbath

Thursday: The Debate Over Tradition

Friday: The Debate Over Divorce

Saturday: The Debate Over Paying Taxes

The Debate over Forgiveness

THE SON OF MAN HAS AUTHORITY ON EARTH TO FORGIVE SINS.

Mark 2:10

Mark tells the touching story of the paralytic who was both healed and forgiven. He was carried in by four of his friends, but the crowds made it impossible for them to reach Jesus. So the friends made a hole in the flat roof of the house and lowered the man on his stretcher through it. To everybody's surprise, instead of pronouncing him healed, Jesus pronounced him forgiven, for healing and forgiveness were twin blessings of the messianic kingdom.

At once the teachers of the law, who were sitting there, were indignant, saying, "Why does this fellow talk like that? He's blaspheming! Who can forgive sins but God alone?" (v. 7). In reply Jesus drew a parallel between the two blessings, but he added that he had first pronounced the paralytic forgiven because he wanted people to know that he had authority to forgive sins. Then he healed the paralytic, who got up and walked out in full view of them all, to everyone's amazement.

Some time later Luke records a similar incident. Jesus allowed a prostitute to anoint him with perfume, to wet his feet with her tears, and to cover them with kisses. When Jesus declared her forgiven, the guests at dinner said among themselves, "Who is this who even forgives sins?" (Luke 7:49).

So on two separate occasions Jesus forgave people's sins, saying, "Your sins are forgiven." In both cases the bystanders recognized Jesus' words as more than a declaration; they understood them as an absolution. And in both cases the witnesses were scandalized, for they knew that nobody can forgive sins except God alone.

For further reading: Mark 2:1–12

MONDAY

The Debate over Fraternization

IT IS NOT THE HEALTHY WHO NEED A DOCTOR, BUT THOSE WHO ARE ILL.
I HAVE NOT COME TO CALL THE RIGHTEOUS, BUT SINNERS.

Mark 2:17

In Mark's account of this second debate, the expression "tax collectors and 'sinners'" occurs three times. As we have seen (p. 188), tax collectors were universally disliked, even hated, at least by the local Jewish population in Galilee, firstly, because the taxes levied went into the coffers of Herod Antipas, secondly, because their work brought them into close contact with the Gentiles, and, thirdly, because it was their practice to extract as much as they could from their victims.

"Sinners" in this context were not just those who were disobedient to God's moral law (like all of us) but those who, whether through ignorance or intent, did not live according to the traditions of the scribes. Both groups were shunned by all respectable people, who would neither give hospitality to them nor receive hospitality from them, fearing ceremonial contamination. But Jesus deliberately and freely fraternized with them, having no such fears. He both called Levi-Matthew (a tax collector) to follow him and then accepted his invitation to a meal in his house, along with many other tax collectors and "sinners."

When the teachers of the law objected, Jesus responded by quoting a proverb, in which he likened himself to a doctor whose ministry was not to the healthy but to the sick, so that inevitably he would be found among those who needed him. When saying that he had come to call to repentance not the righteous but sinners, he meant not that some people are so righteous that they do not need salvation but that some people think they are. By "righteous" here he meant "self-righteous." Just as we do not go to the doctor unless we are sick and admit it, so we will not come to Christ unless we are sinners and admit it. Nothing keeps people out of the kingdom of God more effectively than pride or self-sufficiency.

For further reading: Mark 2:13–17

TUESDAY

The Debate over Fasting

HOW CAN THE GUESTS OF THE BRIDEGROOM FAST WHILE
HE IS WITH THEM?

Mark 2:19

Mark begins his account of the third debate by drawing attention to a difference between three groups of disciples. The disciples of John the Baptist and the disciples of the Pharisees, he writes, are fasting, but the disciples of Jesus are not. On the contrary, according to Luke, they "go on eating and drinking" (Luke 5:33). So some people came up to Jesus and asked him why the other two groups were fasting, while his disciples were not.

Jesus replied with a counterquestion: "How can the guests of the bridegroom fast while he is with them? They cannot, so long as they have him with them" (Mark 2:19). Some commentators understand this as a proverb for inappropriate action. For example, it would be as inappropriate for us to do this or that as it would for guests to fast during the wedding festivities.

But personally I think that a mini allegory is intended. Jesus the bridegroom was with them. So this was a time of joyful celebration. It would therefore be wholly inappropriate for them to fast at that time. "But the time will come," Jesus continues, "when the bridegroom will be taken from them" (v. 20). "Taken" or "taken away" could be an allusion to his violent death. True, he had not yet plainly predicted his sufferings, yet it seems that he already had an inkling of them. On that day, when he will be taken from them, they will grieve and fast. As we saw in the Sermon on the Mount, Jesus seems to have assumed that giving, praying, and fasting would all be part of the Christian life.

Not that fasting is always associated with grief. For although in one sense the bridegroom has been taken away from us, in another he has returned to us in the Holy Spirit, and our grief has been turned into joy (John 16:20–22).

For further reading: Mark 2:18–20

WEDNESDAY

The Debate over the Sabbath

THE SABBATH WAS MADE FOR MAN, NOT MAN FOR THE SABBATH. SO THE
SON OF MAN IS LORD EVEN OF THE SABBATH.

Mark 2:27–28

The fourth debate between Jesus and the religious leaders was over the Sabbath and what it was lawful or unlawful to do on the Sabbath. Mark records two incidents, both of which happened on the Sabbath.

The first took place in some grain fields, in which Jesus allowed his disciples as they walked to pluck and eat some heads of grain. Now the law specifically prohibited reaping on the Sabbath (Exod. 34:21); the oral tradition declared plucking equivalent to reaping, and therefore the disciples were guilty (in the eyes of the scribes) of a serious violation of the law. But Jesus appealed to Scripture. He reminded them that when David and his companions were hungry, they ate the consecrated bread in the tabernacle, which it was lawful only for the priests to eat. But Scripture did not condemn them, which shows that Scripture is less rigid in its application of the law than the Pharisees were. Jesus concluded with the great pronouncements that "the Sabbath was made for man [that is, for our enjoyment], not man for the Sabbath," and that he was himself "Lord even of the Sabbath," because he had authority to interpret it correctly.

The second incident took place in the synagogue, in which Jesus on the Sabbath healed a man with a shriveled hand. He told the man to stand up publicly in front of everyone. Then he asked the bystanders, "Which is lawful on the Sabbath: to do good or to do evil, to save life or to kill?" (3:4). Nobody answered, for there was more in Jesus' question than was first apparent. He was exposing their hypocrisy. For, whereas Jesus was planning to do good and to heal on the Sabbath, they were full of evil thoughts and, Mark tells us, "began to plot... how they might kill Jesus" (v. 6).

Looking back over the series of four mini debates or conflict stories, which Mark has brought together, we see that they not only preserve valuable teaching but depict Jesus in his supremacy. We see him as the Son of Man with authority to forgive sin, as the physician of our souls, as the bridegroom who fills his guests with joy, and as the Lord even of the Sabbath.

For further reading: Mark 2:23–3:6

THURSDAY

The Debate over Tradition

YOU HAVE A FINE WAY OF SETTING ASIDE THE COMMANDS OF GOD IN
ORDER TO OBSERVE YOUR OWN TRADITIONS!

Mark 7:9

Some Pharisees and law teachers had come from Jerusalem. Gathering around Jesus, they were horrified to see that his disciples were eating their food with unclean hands. This was a question not of hygiene but of ceremonial purity according to the tradition of the elders. "And they observe many other traditions," Mark explains to his Gentile readers, "such as the washing of cups, pitchers and kettles" (v. 4).

So the Pharisees lived under the authority of traditions handed down from generation to generation. And they followed them slavishly, even if they came into collision with Scripture. It is this for which Jesus criticized them. Three times he repeated the same criticism, using almost the same words – for example, "You have let go of the commands of God and are holding on to human traditions" (v. 8). Jesus clearly regarded tradition as the word of people and Scripture as the Word of God. The Pharisees were allowing their traditions to stifle the Word of God instead of allowing the Word of God to reform their traditions.

This was the main issue during the Reformation. The medieval Catholic Church had smothered the Word of God with a mass of unbiblical traditions. So, just as Jesus swept away the traditions of the elders, the Reformers swept away the traditions of the medieval church, that the Word of God might be supreme. The Reformers taught the supremacy of Scripture over tradition. And Reformed churches still do, including the Anglican Church. It is often said that the Anglican Church has a threefold authority – Scripture, tradition, and reason. But this is not so. To be sure, tradition and reason have a vital role to play in the elucidation of Scripture. But what shall we do when Scripture, tradition, and reason are in conflict? The answer is that Scripture has supreme authority. The followers of Jesus are called to a radical nonconformity to tradition and convention in order to honour the supremacy of Scripture and the lordship of Jesus Christ.

For further reading: Mark 7:1–13

FRIDAY

The Debate over Divorce

HAVEN'T YOU READ... THAT AT THE BEGINNING THE CREATOR "MADE
THEM MALE AND FEMALE," AND SAID, "FOR THIS REASON A MAN WILL
LEAVE HIS FATHER AND MOTHER AND BE UNITED TO HIS WIFE, AND THE
TWO WILL BECOME ONE FLESH"?

Matthew 19:4–5

Once again some Pharisees came to Jesus to test him. According to Matthew, their question was this: "Is it lawful for a man to divorce his wife for any and every reason?" (v. 3). It was a test question about the grounds for divorce and has a modern ring about it. But it was an old question too. During the first century BC the rival Pharisaic parties led by Rabbi Shammai and Rabbi Hillel respectively were debating this very question. Rabbi Shammai was strict, maintaining that divorce was permissible only for a serious sexual offence. Rabbi Hillel, on the other hand, was lax, arguing that a man might divorce his wife for even the most trivial offences, such as that she was quarrelsome or a bad cook. So the Pharisees wanted to embroil Jesus in this rabbinic debate. Whose side was Jesus on?

Jesus did not give the Pharisees a direct answer to their question about divorce; instead, he spoke to them about marriage. He referred them back to Genesis 1 and 2, drawing their attention to the two facts that human sexuality is a divine creation and human marriage a divine institution. For he bracketed two texts (Gen. 1:27; 2:24) and made God the author of both. For the same Creator who "at the beginning... 'made them male and female'" (Matt. 19:4) also said (in the biblical text), "For this reason a man will leave his father and mother and be united to his wife, and the two will become one flesh" (v. 5). "Therefore," Jesus said, adding his personal endorsement, "what God has joined together [literally, "yoked together"], let man not separate" (v. 6). This teaching is unambiguous. The marriage bond is more than a human contract; it is a divine yoke. Although Moses permitted divorce for a serious offence, Jesus called it a concession to the hardness of human hearts: "It was not this way from the beginning" (v. 8). In my own pastoral ministry I have found Jesus' priority a very helpful rule. Whenever anybody asks to come and talk with me about divorce, I decline – until we have first talked about marriage and reconciliation.

For further reading: Matthew 19:3–9

SATURDAY

The Debate over Paying Taxes

GIVE BACK TO CAESAR WHAT IS CAESAR'S AND TO GOD WHAT IS GOD'S.

Mark 12:17

The question whether loyal Jews should pay taxes to the emperor or not was a contentious and emotional political issue in those days. At one extreme were the fanatical zealots like Judas the Galilean, who in AD 6 led a revolt against Rome and whose battle cry was, "No tribute to the Romans." Much more moderate were the Pharisees, who resented but justified payment, while the Herodians supported a policy of payment. A mixed group (divided over payment but united in opposition to Jesus) came to him one day with their trick question: "Is it right to pay the poll-tax to Caesar or not?" (v. 14). It put him on the horns of a dilemma. If he said no, he would be in imminent danger of arrest and worse. If he said yes, he would immediately lose popular support.

Jesus asked for a silver denarius and then inquired whose image and superscription it bore. "Caesar's," they replied. In fact, the image would have been that of Tiberius, who was emperor at the time, while the superscription would have read in Latin, "Tiberius Caesar, son of the divine Augustus, high priest."

In enunciating his famous epigram that Caesar's things belong to Caesar and God's things to God, Jesus was not saying that there are two self-contained and independent spheres (one Caesar's and the other God's), for everything that is Caesar's is ultimately God's. He was rather saying that God's people must give to Caesar (or literally "give back," as if repaying a debt) the recognition that was due to him. For they could not enjoy the blessings of Roman rule (like peace, justice, education, and roads) and contribute nothing in return. Yet there were limits to what was owed to Caesar. God-fearing Jews could certainly not take part in the cult of the emperor. The deification of the state did not end with the Roman Empire. Still today there are totalitarian régimes of both the left and the right that demand an uncritical allegiance, which Christians cannot possibly give. They still go to prison and torture, labour camp and death rather than compromise their loyalty to God. Christians are loyal citizens, giving to Caesar what is Caesar's, but they reserve their worship for God alone, giving to God what is God's.

For further reading: Mark 12:13–17

For six weeks we have been reflecting on some of the main words and works of Jesus during his public ministry. We come now to his final week on earth, which is usually called Holy Week. It begins with Jesus' triumphal entry into Jerusalem (Palm Sunday) and ends with his crucifixion (Good Friday). It is immediately noteworthy that the evangelists devote a disproportionate amount of space to Jesus' final week – in Luke's case a quarter of his Gospel, in the case of Matthew and Mark about a third, and in John's Gospel as much as a half. This shows how important the Gospel writers regard the events surrounding Jesus' death.

Sunday: The Triumphal Entry into Jerusalem

Monday: The Cleansing of the Temple

Tuesday: The Parable of the Tenants

Wednesday: The Error of the Sadducees

Thursday: The Little Apocalypse

Friday: The Anointing by Mary

Saturday: The Motivation of Judas

SUNDAY

The Triumphal Entry into Jerusalem

As he [Jesus] approached Jerusalem and saw the city,
he wept over it...

Luke 19:41

Jesus' entry into Jerusalem is recorded by all four evangelists, although each adds details that the others omit. Jesus had evidently made up his mind to fulfil what stood written of him in Zechariah 9, namely that a future king of Judah would ride into Jerusalem bringing salvation, yet not with swashbuckling bravado nor on a prancing warhorse, but humbly and meekly on the back (of all creatures!) of a donkey. Thus he would "proclaim peace to the nations" (Zech. 9:10).

This incident bears all the signs of having been prearranged and even stage managed. Probably on a previous visit Jesus had arranged with friends in Bethany to lend him their donkey, releasing it on the agreed password "The Master needs it." Then the crowds entered into the drama, spreading their clothes on the donkey's back and on the road and breaking into spontaneous cheering.

Having passed through the villages of Bethany and Bethphage, the cavalcade rounded the brow of the Mount of Olives, and suddenly Jerusalem came into view, with its glittering pinnacles and the spacious courts of the temple. Here, it seems, as the shouts of the crowd died down, to everybody's astonishment and embarrassment Jesus burst into tears. Through his sobs he uttered a prophetic lament over the city, predicting its destruction because it did not recognize the time of God's visitation.

It is surely remarkable that, at the very moment when Jesus warned the city of judgment, he was weeping over it in love. Divine judgment (which is the main theme throughout Holy Week) is a solemn, awesome reality. But the God who judges is the God who weeps. He is not willing that any should perish. And when in the end his judgment falls on anybody (as Jesus said it will), God's eyes will be full of tears.

For further reading: Luke 19:41–44

The Cleansing of the Temple

HE [JESUS] SAID, "IS IT NOT WRITTEN: 'MY HOUSE WILL BE CALLED A
HOUSE OF PRAYER FOR ALL NATIONS'? BUT YOU HAVE MADE IT 'A DEN OF
ROBBERS'."

Mark 11:17

As soon as Jesus entered Jerusalem, so Mark tells us, and before he took any action, he went to the temple and "looked around at everything" (v. 11). Then, because it was late, he and the Twelve went out of the city for the night. Thus Jesus had time to reflect on what he had seen and what had profoundly shocked him, namely the commercialism of the sanctuary of God, the very centre of the religious life of Israel.

The business of the money changers related to the half-shekel temple tax and to the merchants who were selling cattle and sheep for the sacrifices. This lucrative business had become a monopoly in the hands of the high priests and had led to the gross exploitation of poor pilgrims. It had turned God's house of prayer into a den of thieves, as Jesus said, quoting from Isaiah and Jeremiah. So he acted with calculated violence. John says he made a whip of cords, which it seems clear he used on the animals ("both sheep and cattle" [John 2:15]), not on human beings. In addition, he overturned the tables used by the money changers and the vendors of doves. He also prevented people from carrying merchandise through the temple courts.

The portrait that the evangelists are painting of Jesus has now received a further perspective. For the Christ who rode into Jerusalem in humility, and who wept over the city on account of its wilful blindness, now brandishes a whip, a symbol of judgment. It is only after we have seen the tears in his eyes that we are ready to see the whip in his hand.

For further reading: Mark 11:15–18

TUESDAY

The Parable of the Tenants

LAST OF ALL, HE SENT HIS SON TO THEM. "THEY WILL RESPECT MY SON,"
HE SAID. BUT... THEY... KILLED HIM.

Matthew 21:37–39

As the final week progressed, the authorities' hostility to Jesus grew, and the themes of confrontation and judgment clarified. A striking example of this is the so-called parable of the tenants that, however, is an allegory, not a parable.

The landowner who planted a vineyard and provided it with a wall, a winepress, and a watchtower is evidently God himself, whose vineyard is Israel as in Isaiah 5. He did everything within his power to make his people fruitful in good works. The tenant farmers, to whom the owner rented his vineyard, are the religious leaders of Israel. In due course, when the vintage was ripe, the owner sent his servants (the prophets) to collect the fruit, but the tenants seized, beat, stoned, and killed them. So the owner sent more servants, but they were ill-treated in the same way. Last of all, he sent his son to them. "They will respect my son," he said to himself. Instead, the tenants killed him.

In conclusion, Jesus asked his hearers a straight question, which compelled them to make a moral judgment against themselves, since by their answer they condemned themselves. Indeed, Matthew explicitly says so: "When the chief priests and the Pharisees heard Jesus' parables, they knew he was talking about them" (Matt. 21:45). Here is Jesus' question: "What will he [the landowner] do to those tenants?" (v. 40). They replied, "He will bring those wretches to a wretched end... and he will rent the vineyard to other tenants, who will give him his share of the crop" (v. 41).

"Therefore I tell you," Jesus said, "the kingdom of God will be taken away from you [Israel] and given to a people [the Gentiles] who will produce its fruit" (v. 43).

For further reading: Matthew 21:33–41

WEDNESDAY

The Error of the Sadducees

JESUS REPLIED, "YOU ARE IN ERROR BECAUSE YOU DO NOT KNOW THE
SCRIPTURES OR THE POWER OF GOD."
Matthew 22:29

The Pharisees and the Sadducees were in constant debate and disagreement with each other. For example, the Pharisees had constructed an elaborate theology of the afterlife, but the Sadducees rejected it, teaching that our souls and bodies die together. More basic were their different attitudes to Scripture, both of which Jesus criticized. The Pharisees *added* to Scripture (their traditions); the Sadducees *subtracted* from Scripture (its supernatural element).

During Holy Week some Sadducees came to Jesus with a trick question based on the law of levirate marriage. This ruled that if a husband died childless, his brother must marry the widow. "Well," the Sadducees said, "there were once seven brothers. They all died childless until finally the woman also died. So whose wife would she be in the next life, since all seven had married her?" (author's paraphrase). One can see the smirk on the Sadducees' faces. They thought they were being frightfully clever and could ridicule belief in an afterlife as an absurdity.

Jesus began and ended his reply with a clear statement that the Sadducees were in error, indeed, "badly mistaken" (Mark 12:27). Moreover, their error was due to their ignorance. They knew neither the Scriptures nor the power of God.

As an example of the Sadducees' ignorance of Scripture, Jesus referred them to the incident of the burning bush and what was implicit in God's announcing himself as the God of Abraham, Isaac, and Jacob. God had established with the patriarchs a unique covenant of love. Did the Sadducees really think that such a covenant relationship could be broken by death? Still today many errors in the church are due to ignorance of or disrespect for the Scriptures.

The more basic cause of the Sadducees' error, however, was another kind of ignorance. They assumed that if there were an afterlife, it would be the same kind of life as before. It seems not to have occurred to them that God could create another order of being in which marriage has been abolished. They were ignorant of the power of God.

For further reading: Mark 12:18–27

Thursday

The Little Apocalypse

TRULY I TELL YOU, THIS GENERATION WILL CERTAINLY NOT PASS AWAY
UNTIL ALL THESE THINGS HAVE HAPPENED.

Mark 13:30

Sitting one day on the Mount of Olives, Jesus and his disciples enjoyed the panoramic view across the Kidron Valley to Herod's temple. It had already been about fifty years in building, and it was still not quite finished. Nevertheless, it was a spectacular sight. "What massive stones!" commented the disciples, "What magnificent buildings!" (v. 1). Yet to their astonishment Jesus responded that not a single stone would survive the temple's coming destruction. This was the beginning of the so-called little apocalypse recorded in Mark 13, Matthew 24, and Luke 21, in which Jesus peered into the future. Our difficulty in interpreting this discourse is that Jesus was looking ahead both to the immediate future (the fall of Jerusalem and destruction of the temple in AD 70) and to the ultimate future (the Parousia and the end of history). The two events were to some extent intertwined in Jesus' teaching, so it is not always clear to which he was alluding.

Immediate signs would include the rise of false messiahs, wars and rumours of wars, earthquakes, and famines. But these, Jesus said, were "the beginning of birth-pains" (v. 8); the end was not yet. Other signs heralding the end would include persecution and martyrdom, the worldwide preaching of the gospel, family divisions, and great convulsions in the sun, the moon, and the stars, which is familiar apocalyptic imagery for sociopolitical upheavals. And then people would "see the Son of Man coming in clouds with great power and glory" (v. 26). Indeed, that generation would not pass away until "all these things" (the heralding signs) had taken place. In contrast to "all these things," however, nobody knows that day or that hour, not even the Son himself.

The main emphasis of the little apocalypse is not to be found in any programme of signs and events but in Jesus' repeated summons (seven times in Mark 13) to be alert and ready for his coming, since nobody knows when it will take place. "What I say to you," Jesus concludes, "I say to everyone: 'Watch!'" (v. 37).

For further reading: Mark 13

FRIDAY

The Anointing by Mary

SHE POURED PERFUME ON MY BODY BEFOREHAND TO PREPARE
FOR MY BURIAL.

Mark 14:8

Another dramatic, well-remembered incident took place in the village of Bethany one evening during Holy Week. Jesus was having dinner as the guest of one known as Simon the Leper, whose leprosy had, of course, been healed. As Jesus was reclining at the meal, a woman approached him from behind. Mark preserves her anonymity, but John identifies her as Mary of Bethany, one of the two sisters of Lazarus, who had recently been raised from the dead (John 12:1–8). Mary had brought with her an alabaster jar of very expensive perfume. She broke the jar and poured the perfume over Jesus' head. Is it possible that her anointing of him was her way of acknowledging him as the Messiah? But the bystanders were indignant over the waste. The ointment, they protested, could have been sold for a whole year's wages and the proceeds given to the poor. They rebuked her sharply.

But Jesus came to her defence. From his words we can learn five truths of rich significance. Firstly, she had done to him not a wasteful thing but "a beautiful thing" (Mark 14:6), expressing her wholehearted devotion to him. Secondly, she was not in any way demeaning the poor but was daring to put Jesus above them. Thirdly, she had done what she could, according to her resources, while recognizing that other people serve Jesus in other ways. Fourthly, she had poured perfume over his body, anticipating the anointing it would receive at the time of his burial. Fifthly, she and her act of generous love would be remembered wherever the gospel would be preached throughout the world.

Mary's act of self-sacrifice is deliberately set in relief by Mark against the dark background of Judas's act of treachery, to which we come tomorrow.

For further reading: Mark 14:1–11

SATURDAY

The Motivation of Judas

THEN JUDAS ISCARIOT, ONE OF THE TWELVE, WENT TO THE CHIEF PRIESTS
TO BETRAY JESUS TO THEM.

Mark 14:10

It is true that the betrayal of Jesus by Judas was seen by the early church as a fulfilment of Scripture (see Ps. 41:9; John 17:12), and that it took place after Satan had first "prompted" and then "entered into" Judas (John 13:2, 27). Yet these facts do not exonerate Judas. Neither biblical prophecy nor Satanic influence robbed him of personal responsibility for his action. At the last minute in the upper room Jesus made a final appeal to him (John 13:25–30), and when Judas rejected it, Jesus said: "Woe to that man who betrays the Son of Man!" (Matt. 26:24).

What then can have been Judas's motivation? The evangelists focus on his love of money. John tells us that he was treasurer of the apostolic band and that he was a thief, helping himself to the contents of their common purse. No wonder he was horrified by Mary's lavish extravagance. He seems to have gone straight to the priests in order to recoup some of the loss. He bargained with them and settled on thirty silver coins, the ransom price of a common slave.

Another motive for Judas's betrayal may have been political rather than commercial. There has been much speculation about the meaning of Judas's surname, Iscariot. Some believe it was a place name and that he was "a man from Kerioth," a village south of Hebron. Others think that Iscariot was a corruption of *sikarios*, an assassin (from *sica*, a dagger), and that Judas was a member of the *sikarii*, a fanatical terrorist group mentioned by Josephus, the first-century Jewish historian. Was Judas a militant nationalist, then, longing for the liberation of Israel from Roman domination and disillusioned with Jesus as a messianic failure? It is possible, but the evidence is not strong enough for us to be sure.

The evangelists, as we have seen, set Mary and Judas in stark contrast – Mary's uncalculating generosity and Judas's coldly calculated bargain. Incensed by Mary's waste of a year's wages, Judas sold Jesus for barely a third that amount. Truly "the love of money is a root of all kinds of evil" (1 Tim. 6:10).

For further reading: John 13:1–2, 18–30

Week 28: The Upper Room

Jesus had evidently made up his mind to spend his last evening in a private meal with his disciples, for he had made arrangements with a friend to lend him his guest room, which Jesus described as "a large room upstairs, furnished and ready" (Mark 14:15). According to the Synoptic evangelists, this was the Passover meal that followed the sacrificing of the Passover lambs, for Jesus spoke of his eagerness to eat the Passover with them (Luke 22:15). According to John, however, Jesus died on the cross a day earlier at the very time that the Passover lambs were being killed. Various attempts have been made to harmonize these two chronologies. The best seems to be to declare both correct, each having been observed by a different group – either the Pharisees and the Sadducees or the Galileans and the Judeans. We will have the privilege this week of watching Jesus wash his disciples' feet and inaugurate the Lord's Supper. We will also listen both to his teaching about the Holy Spirit and to his prayers for his disciples.

Sunday: The Foot Washing

Monday: The Lord's Supper

Tuesday: The Two Comings of Christ

Wednesday: The Vine and the Branches

Thursday: The Advantages of Jesus' Departure

Friday: The Ministry of the Spirit of Truth

Saturday: The Lord's Prayer for His Own

The Foot Washing

HE [JESUS] GOT UP FROM THE MEAL, TOOK OFF HIS OUTER CLOTHING,
AND WRAPPED A TOWEL ROUND HIS WAIST... HE POURED WATER INTO A
BASIN AND BEGAN TO WASH HIS DISCIPLES' FEET, DRYING THEM WITH THE
TOWEL THAT WAS WRAPPED ROUND HIM.

John 13:4–5

During supper Jesus washed his disciples' feet and told them to follow his example. Some Christians have copied him literally. Popes and patriarchs, kings and queens still do on Maundy Thursday. Some Protestant churches (e.g., the Mennonites) also incorporate a foot washing in their communion service. Others believe that Jesus was not so much instituting a ceremony as referring to a common cultural practice. Transposing it into our culture, Jesus meant that if we love one another, we will serve one another, and no service will be too menial or dirty for us to do.

But the foot washing was more than an example of humble service; it was also a parable of salvation. At first Peter refused to let Jesus wash his feet. In that case, Jesus said, Peter could not be in fellowship with him. Next Peter requested the washing of his hands and head as well. Jesus responded, "He who has bathed does not need to wash, except for his feet, but he is clean all over" (John 13:10 RSV).

It is quite clear from this that the washing was a picture of salvation and that it was in two stages, first a bath and then a regular washing of the feet. The social custom behind this distinction was familiar. Before going out to have dinner in a friend's house, the guest would take a bath. Then, walking barefooted or in sandals, his feet would get dirty again. So on arrival a slave would wash his feet. But he would not need another bath.

Just so, when we first come to Jesus Christ in repentance and faith, we are given a bath. Theologically, it is called "justification" (receiving a new status) or "regeneration" (experiencing a new birth), both of which are dramatized in baptism, which is unrepeatable. Then, because we continue to fall into sin and get spattered with mud in the dirty streets of the world, what we need is not another justification or regeneration or baptism but a daily forgiveness, symbolized in our regular attendance at the Lord's Supper. So Peter made two opposite mistakes. First, he protested against being washed at all. Then he asked for a bath, whereas all he needed was a washing of his feet. May God enable us to grasp the distinction!

For further reading: John 13:1–15

The Lord's Supper

WHENEVER YOU EAT THIS BREAD AND DRINK THIS CUP, YOU PROCLAIM THE LORD'S DEATH UNTIL HE COMES.

1 Corinthians 11:26

During the meal in the upper room Jesus took bread, broke it, and gave it to his disciples saying, "This is my body given for you; do this in remembrance of me" (Luke 22:19). Then after the meal he took a cup of wine and gave it to them saying, "This cup is the new covenant in my blood, which is poured out for you" (Luke 22:20). These are immensely significant words and actions, for they tell us Jesus' own view of his death. Three truths stand out.

The first is the centrality of his death. Jesus was giving instructions for his own memorial service. They were to eat bread and drink wine in memory of him. Moreover, the bread would stand not for his living body but for his body given for them and the wine for his blood shed for them. In other words, death would speak from both the elements. So it was by his death that he wished to be remembered.

The second truth we learn from the Lord's Supper concerns the purpose of Jesus' death. According to Matthew, the cup stood for "my blood of the covenant, which is poured out for many for the forgiveness of sins" (Matt. 26:28). This is the truly fantastic claim that through the shedding of his blood in death God would establish the new covenant promised through Jeremiah (Jeremiah 31), one of whose greatest promises was the forgiveness of sins.

The third truth taught by the Lord's Supper concerns the need for us to appropriate personally the benefits of Jesus' death. For in the drama of the upper room the disciples were not spectators only but participants. Jesus not only broke the bread but gave it to them to eat. Similarly, he not only poured out the wine but gave it to them to drink. Just so, it was not enough for Christ to die; we have to make the blessings of his death our own. The eating and the drinking were, and still are, a vivid acted parable of receiving Christ as our crucified Saviour and of feeding on him in our hearts by faith.

The Lord's Supper, as instituted by Jesus, was evidently not meant to be a slightly sentimental "forget me not"; it was rather a drama rich in spiritual significance.

For further reading: Jeremiah 31:31–34

The Two Comings of Christ

IF I GO AND PREPARE A PLACE FOR YOU, I WILL COME BACK AND
TAKE YOU TO BE WITH ME… I WILL NOT LEAVE YOU AS ORPHANS;
I WILL COME TO YOU.

John 14:3, 18

At the beginning of John 14, and again near its end, Jesus tells his disciples, "Do not let your hearts be troubled" (vv. 1, 27). He is alluding to a form of heart trouble from which the whole world suffers and that no cardiologist on earth is able to cure. What John records in this chapter is the Great Physician's diagnosis and prescription. One might even entitle the chapter "Spiritual Heart Trouble: its Causes and Cure." Its cause was the imminent departure of the disciples' Master; it was this prospect of being abandoned by Jesus that gave them heart trouble, and the cure was faith in his promised comings.

Christ's ultimate coming on the last day is the topic of the first fourteen verses, although they are also applicable to our death. Jesus promises, (1) "I am going… to prepare a place for you" (v. 2) so that death for believers is like going home, (2) "I will come back" (v. 3), (3) "I will… take you to be with me" (v. 3), and (4) "I am the way and the truth and the life" (v. 6). It is a beautiful thought that he who is our destination is also our forerunner, our escort, and our path.

Verses 15–26, however, refer to Christ's intermediate coming. The fact that he was coming in the future did not imply that he would abandon them meanwhile. On the contrary, he would send the Holy Spirit, or, better, he would come himself in the person of the Holy Spirit. But to whom would he come? He would show himself to his lovers, and his lovers prove their love by their obedience (v. 21).

In the last five verses (vv. 27–31) John returns to the theme of Christ's imminent departure. Again Jesus tells them not to be troubled or afraid. Instead, he said to them "*Shalom!*" "Peace!" Matthew Henry wrote of this with his customary charm:

When Christ was about to leave the world he made his will; his soul he committed to his Father; his body he bequeathed to Joseph of Arimathea; his clothes fell to the soldiers; his mother he left to the care of John. But what should he leave to his disciples, that had left all for him? Silver and gold he had none; but he left them that which was infinitely better, his peace.

For further reading: John 14:1–31

The Vine and the Branches

I AM THE VINE; YOU ARE THE BRANCHES. IF YOU REMAIN IN ME
AND I IN YOU, YOU WILL BEAR MUCH FRUIT; APART FROM ME YOU CAN
DO NOTHING.

John 15:5

In his allegory of the vine and the branches, Jesus was almost certainly thinking about Israel, the choice vine that Yahweh had planted in Canaan, and assuming the continuity between Israel and God's new community. The essential message of the allegory is plain, namely that it is just as much God's purpose for his people to be fruitful as it is the function of the vine to produce grapes.

It is surprising how many Christians imagine that to be fruitful means to be successful in winning people for Christ. And evangelism is indeed a very important part of our Christian calling. But if we compare Scripture with Scripture, the grapes in God's vineyard were justice and righteousness, whereas in the New Testament the fruit of the Spirit is Christlikeness. See Isaiah 5; Galatians 5:22–23; and Colossians 1:10.

What, then, are the secrets of fruitfulness? The first is the pruning of the vine. God is an indefatigable gardener. He prunes every fruit-bearing branch so that it may bear more fruit. This pruning is surely a picture of suffering. And pruning is a drastic process. The bush or shrub is cut right back, usually in the autumn. To the uninitiated it looks extremely cruel. Sometimes only a stump is left – naked, jagged, scarred, and mutilated – but when the spring and summer return, there is much fruit. The painful pruning knife has evidently been in safe hands. Some form of suffering is virtually indispensable to holiness.

The second secret of fruitfulness is the "abiding" of the branches in the vine. In essence to be a Christian is to be "in Christ," organically united to Christ. So to abide in Christ is to maintain and develop an already existing relationship. Moreover, it is a reciprocal relationship, since we abide in Christ and Christ in us. For Christ to abide in us we must let him do so, allowing him to be increasingly what he is, our Lord and our Life Giver. But for us to abide in Christ, Bishop J. C. Ryle put it like this:

Abide in me. Cling to me. Stick fast to me. Live the life of close and intimate communion with me. Get nearer and nearer to me. Roll every burden on me. Cast your whole weight on me. Never let go your hold on me for a moment.

For further reading: John 15:1–8

Thursday

The Advantages of Jesus' Departure

Nevertheless I tell you the truth: it is to your advantage
that I go away...

John 16:7 RSV

How could it possibly have been to the apostles' advantage that Jesus should leave them? They had had three marvellous years in his company. We look upon them with envy. If only we could have been with Jesus! If only we could have watched him feed the hungry, heal the sick, and raise the dead! What can Jesus have meant?

Well, the apostles experienced two major drawbacks. Firstly, while Jesus was with them on earth, his presence was localized. So they were sometimes separated from one another, for example, when they were in the boat and he was praying on the mountain. They could not enjoy uninterrupted fellowship with him. Suppose, then, that he had not gone away. Let me update how Henry Drummond, the nineteenth-century Scottish author and evangelist, put it: Suppose Jesus was still in Jerusalem. Every ship and plane would be crowded with Christian pilgrims. Suppose you were in one of them. With much difficulty you land. But every road is congested. Between you and Jerusalem lies a dark, seething mass of people. You have come to see Jesus, but you will never see him.

It was to avoid just such a frustration that Jesus went away and sent the Holy Spirit to take his place. For what the Holy Spirit has done is to universalize the presence of Jesus and to make him accessible to everybody everywhere.

The apostles' second disadvantage was that while Jesus was with them on earth, his presence was not only local but also external. He was unable to enter their personality or change them from within, getting at the source of their thoughts, motives, and desires.

But later he would be able to, Jesus said, "for he dwells with you, and will be in you" (14:17 RSV). Thus the Holy Spirit internalizes the presence of Jesus so that Christ dwells by his Spirit in our hearts and transforms us into his likeness. It is, therefore, greatly to our advantage that Jesus went away, for in his place the Holy Spirit came. And the Holy Spirit has made the presence of Jesus no longer local but universal, no longer external but internal. The Spirit both universalizes and internalizes the presence of Jesus Christ.

For further reading: John 16:5–11

The Ministry of the Spirit of Truth

I HAVE MUCH MORE TO SAY TO YOU, MORE THAN YOU CAN NOW BEAR.
BUT WHEN HE, THE SPIRIT OF TRUTH, COMES, HE WILL GUIDE YOU INTO
ALL THE TRUTH.

John 16:12–13

Central to the upper room discourse are two promises relating to the teaching ministry of the Spirit of truth. Firstly, the Spirit of truth "will remind you of everything I have said to you" (14:26). Although Christians with bad memories have sometimes claimed this promise, its primary reference was to the apostles. For three years Jesus had taught them. Now he is concerned that this rich patrimony of truth should be preserved. He had done the teaching; the Holy Spirit would do the reminding. The promise was fulfilled in the writing of the Gospels.

Secondly, the Spirit of truth "will guide you into all truth" (16:13 KJV) or "into all the truth." I doubt if any biblical text has suffered so much misinterpretation as this one. The question at issue concerns the identity of the "you" in the promise, "He will guide *you* into all the truth." Roman Catholics apply it to the pope and the college of bishops regarded as the apostles' successors, the Orthodox to the church and its living tradition, liberal theologians to the climate of educated opinion, and Pentecostals to every Spirit-filled believer. But reformed and evangelical Christians insist that "you" must refer to the apostles gathered around Jesus in the upper room. The pronoun *you* occurs three times in John 16:12–13: "I have much more to say to *you*, more than *you* can now bear. But when he, the Spirit of truth, comes, he will guide *you* into all the truth" (emphasis added). Of these, the first two *you*s definitely refer to the apostles. So the third must also, since we cannot change the identity of the "you" in the middle of the sentence. Thus Jesus regarded his teaching ministry as incomplete. He had much more that he wanted to teach the apostles, but they were incapable of receiving it all. So the Holy Spirit would complete what Jesus had left incomplete. He would lead the apostles into all the truth that he wanted them to know, a promise fulfilled in the writing of the Acts, the letters, and the Revelation.

Thus the Holy Spirit had both a reminding and a supplementing ministry, both being fulfilled in the writing of the New Testament.

For further reading: John 15:26–27; 16:12–15

SATURDAY

The Lord's Prayer for His Own

JESUS... LOOKED TOWARDS HEAVEN AND PRAYED:
"FATHER, THE HOUR HAS COME."

John 17:1

John 17 is one of the most profound chapters of the Bible. Whole books have been written to expound it. Thomas Manton, for example, at one time Oliver Cromwell's chaplain, preached forty-five sermons on it. When published as a book, it ran to more than 450 pages. So what can we hope to accomplish in a mere 350 words? After praying for himself, that he might be glorified on the cross, Jesus prays for his own people.

Firstly, Jesus prays for the *truth* of the church, literally that the Father would keep his people in his name or, better, "true to his name" (v. 12 JB). It is a prayer that his people will be faithful to the revelation that he has given them.

Secondly, Jesus prays for the *holiness* of the church. His prayer is not that we will withdraw from the world but that, while remaining in the world, we will be kept from the evil one (v. 15).

Thirdly, Jesus prays for the *mission* of the church. "As you sent me into the world, I have sent them into the world" (v. 18). Moreover, he makes his mission the model of ours. For as he entered our world, so we are to enter other people's worlds. Authentic mission is incarnational mission.

Fourthly, Jesus prays for the *unity* of the church, and this unity has two aspects. Firstly, it is unity with the apostles. "I pray not only for *these* [the apostles], but for *those* also who through their words will believe in me. May they *all* be one" (vv. 20–21 JB, emphasis added). "All" must be a combination of "these" and "those." It is a prayer that there will be a historical continuity between the apostles and the postapostolic church, that the church in every age will be truly apostolic, loyal to the teaching of the New Testament. Secondly, it is a unity with the Father and the Son (v. 21).

Here, then, is the double unity for which Jesus prayed. It is a unity with the apostles (a common truth) and a unity with the Father and the Son (a common life). Structures are important. But more important still is a unity of truth and life.

For further reading: John 17

The Last Supper ended with a hymn, probably Psalms 115–118, which concluded the "Hallel" and so the Passover meal.

Jesus and the Twelve (though now without Judas) then walked together to an orchard called Gethsemane on the Mount of Olives, where they regularly spent the night. Here Jesus experienced an agony of distress, which helps us to understand what he was about to suffer on the cross. There then followed in succession his betrayal by Judas, his denial by Peter, and his trials before the Sanhedrin, Herod, and Pilate, leading up to the terrible mocking and scourging to which he was subjected by the soldiers.

Sunday: The Agony in the Garden

Monday: The Betrayal by Judas

Tuesday: The Denial by Peter

Wednesday: The Trial Before the Sanhedrin

Thursday: The Trial Before Pilate

Friday: The Vacillations of Pilate

Saturday: The Responsibility for Jesus' Death

The Agony in the Garden

HE [JESUS] BEGAN TO BE DEEPLY DISTRESSED AND TROUBLED.
"MY SOUL IS OVERWHELMED WITH SORROW TO THE POINT OF DEATH,"
HE SAID TO THEM.

Mark 14:33–34

Jesus' agony in the olive orchard provides a vivid example of the paradox of his person. On the one hand, we see his human hunger for the companionship and prayer support of his friends, together with the recognition that his will could be distinct from his Father's ("Not my will, but thine, be done" [Luke 22:42 KJV]). On the other hand, even in the midst of his pain, he spoke to God in the unique intimacy of the address "*Abba*, Father" (Mark 14:36).

But what was his distress? The Greek words deserve to be more vividly translated than they are in the NIV. The REB is better. It reads, "Horror and anguish overwhelmed him, and he said to them, 'My heart is ready to break with grief'" (vv. 33–34). And Luke alone adds, with his medical interest, that "his sweat was like drops of blood falling to the ground" (Luke 22:44). Jesus referred to his coming ordeal as a "cup" from which he shrank in dread. Was it simply death? Socrates met his end in the prison cell in Athens in a very different mood. He drank his cup of hemlock, Plato wrote, "without trembling… very cheerfully and quietly." So was Socrates braver than Jesus? No, all the evidence is against this. Jesus' physical and moral courage had not for a moment wavered. In that case their cups must have been filled with different poisons. The cup that Jesus ardently longed to avoid was neither the physical pain of crucifixion nor the mental anguish of desertion by his friends but the spiritual horror of bearing the sins of the world. In the Old Testament the cup was a regular symbol of God's wrath. For example, Isaiah described Jerusalem after its destruction as having "drunk from the hand of the LORD the cup of his wrath" (Isa. 51:17).

From the agony in the garden Jesus emerged with a resolute determination to go to the cross. Though John does not include an account of Gethsemane, he does include a saying that the other evangelists do not: "Shall I not drink the cup the Father has given me?" (John 18:11).

For further reading: Mark 14:32–42

MONDAY

The Betrayal by Judas

THEN THE MEN STEPPED FORWARD, SEIZED JESUS AND ARRESTED HIM.
Matthew 26:50

We tried the week before last to penetrate into the motivation of Judas. Today we watch the unfolding of his plot to betray Jesus. The whole story illustrates the interweaving of divine purpose and human action in the providence of God.

Coming out of his ordeal in the olive grove of Gethsemane, Jesus is clear in his mind that there is no alternative to the cross and is surrendered to it in his will. "What shall I say?" he asks. "'Father, save me from this hour?' No, it was for this very reason I came to this hour. Father, glorify your name!" (John 12:27–28). So Jesus is ready for the next stage in the drama. A detachment of armed soldiers, sent by the chief priests and led by Judas, arrives at the garden, for Judas was familiar with this rendezvous. He had also given them the prearranged signal of a kiss. Jesus' only protest was that he was not leading a rebellion but had been teaching daily in the temple courts, where they could have arrested him.

But Peter was in no mood to submit to Jesus' arrest. As at Caesarea Philippi, so here he still rejected the concept of a Messiah who would suffer and die. This time he did not only expostulate; he took impetuous action. He drew his sword and slashed the right ear of the high priest's servant Malchus. Jesus told him to sheathe his sword and added, "Do you think I cannot call on my Father, and he will at once put at my disposal more than twelve legions of angels? But how then would the Scriptures be fulfilled that say it must happen in this way?" (Matt. 26:53–54).

It is most impressive to see Jesus deliberately putting himself under the authority of the Old Testament Scriptures. He must be betrayed, arrested, rejected, condemned, and ultimately killed. Why must these things take place? Because the Scriptures said so.

For further reading: Matthew 26:47–56

Tuesday

The Denial by Peter

THEN PETER REMEMBERED THE WORD JESUS HAD SPOKEN TO HIM:
"BEFORE THE COCK CROWS TWICE YOU WILL DISOWN ME THREE TIMES."
AND HE BROKE DOWN AND WEPT.

Mark 14:72

On their way to Gethsemane Jesus had predicted that Peter would disown him. But the impetuous Peter had vehemently denied the very possibility: "Even if I have to die with you," he said, "I will never disown you" (v. 31). Yet he did the very thing he declared he would never do.

All four evangelists record Peter's denial of Jesus, although it is not altogether easy to harmonize their different accounts. It seems, however, that each of the three challenges and each of the three denials became more serious than its predecessor. They all took place in or near the courtyard of the high priest's house. One might summarize them as follows:

Firstly, an anonymous servant girl accused Peter of being "with that Nazarene , Jesus" (v. 67), but Peter insisted that he did not know what she was talking about.

Secondly, another girl involved others in affirming that Peter was himself "one of them" but Peter denied it on oath.

Thirdly, a group of bystanders went up to Peter and challenged him directly, saying, "Surely you are one of them, for you are a Galilean" (v. 70). Then Peter began to curse and swear and even (some commentators suggest) call down a curse on Jesus. At this a cock crowed, and Jesus looked straight at Peter. Then Peter remembered what Jesus had said to him and broke down and wept.

We must not minimize the seriousness of Peter's denials. But nor must we underestimate the greatness of God's forgiving and transforming grace. In due course Peter was restored and became a rocklike leader in the church.

For further reading: Mark 14:66–72

WEDNESDAY

The Trial Before the Sanhedrin

THE CHIEF PRIESTS AND THE WHOLE SANHEDRIN WERE LOOKING FOR
EVIDENCE AGAINST JESUS SO THAT THEY COULD PUT HIM TO DEATH...

Mark 14:55

Scholars are still debating some details of the four trials Jesus endured – before Annas, Caiaphas, Herod, and Pilate. It seems clear, however, that he was taken straight from Gethsemane to a late-night, informal, and preliminary hearing by Jewish leaders chaired by Annas, who, we are told, was himself an ex-high priest and Caiaphas's father-in-law. His reputation was that he was a covetous old man who had made himself rich by the commercial abuse of the temple. Jesus was interrogated about his followers and his teaching but declined to answer the questions put to him on the grounds that his words and deeds were already well known.

Next, probably early the following morning, Jesus was brought before a plenary session of the Sanhedrin, which was the supreme court responsible for political, legal, and religious affairs in Jerusalem. The purpose of this meeting was to formulate an accusation against Jesus that could be submitted to the Roman court presided over by Pilate. Pilate would not be interested in trivial ecclesiastical offences against Jewish law but only in revolutionary claims that might threaten public security. So Caiaphas, who as high priest presided over meetings of the Sanhedrin, directly challenged Jesus on whether he was the Messiah. In response Jesus not only affirmed "I am" but quoted both Daniel 7 and Psalm 110:1 as fulfilled in him, thus claiming to have universal dominion and to share the throne of God. No wonder Caiaphas accused him of blasphemy and so as deserving of death.

We cannot help contrasting the behaviour of Peter (yesterday) and Jesus (today). Peter denied Jesus, but Jesus, while refusing to answer frivolous questions, courageously affirmed his messiahship before the highest Jewish court in the land.

For further reading: Mark 14:53–65

Thursday

The Trial Before Pilate

THEN THE JEWISH LEADERS TOOK JESUS FROM CAIAPHAS TO THE PALACE
OF THE ROMAN GOVERNOR... SO PILATE CAME OUT TO THEM AND ASKED,
"WHAT CHARGES ARE YOU BRINGING AGAINST THIS MAN?"

John 18:28–29

Rome had a worldwide reputation for the justice of its law courts. It is in keeping with its impartial legal procedures that the session began. Pilate asked what charges Jesus' accusers were bringing against their prisoner. In reply the Jewish leaders accused Jesus of three offences: of "subverting our nation," of forbidding the payment of taxes to Caesar, and of claiming to be "Messiah, a king" (Luke 23:2). The first two charges seemed somewhat imprecise, but the third was a serious indictment of treason. It also raised Pilate's suspicions. The prisoner did not look like a king. What kind of a king was he? His kingly rule, Jesus explained, was to bear witness to the truth.

One of the striking features of the evangelists' narrative is Pilate's repeated declaration of Jesus' innocence. After the preliminary hearing, for example, Pilate said, "I find no basis for a charge against this man." Next, after Herod had sent Jesus back to Pilate, Pilate affirmed: "I... have found no basis for your charges against him. Neither has Herod" (Luke 23:14–15). Then when the crowd demanded his death, Pilate responded to them, "I have found in him no grounds for the death penalty" (Luke 23:22). Pilate's wife then created a dramatic diversion by sending him a message: "Don't have anything to do with that innocent man" (Matt. 27:19). Her reason was that she had had a bad dream about him. Finally, Pilate took water and washed his hands in front of the crowd, saying, "I am innocent of this man's blood" (Matt. 27:24).

Thus on five distinct occasions Pilate is recorded as having declared Jesus innocent. This was, of course, deliberate. While Christianity remained a *religio illicita* in the Roman Empire, it was important to establish the innocence of Jesus. The evangelists did it by quoting no less a person than Pontius Pilate, the procurator of the Roman province of Judea.

For further reading: John 18:28–38

FRIDAY

The Vacillations of Pilate

WANTING TO SATISFY THE CROWD, PILATE RELEASED BARABBAS TO THEM.
HE HAD JESUS FLOGGED, AND HANDED HIM OVER TO BE CRUCIFIED.

Mark 15:15

Pontius Pilate, procurator of Judea, was an able administrator but sometimes insensitive to Jewish scruples. In the Gospels we see him impaled on the horns of a dilemma, torn between justice and expediency. On the one hand (as we saw yesterday), he knew Jesus was innocent, and he said so repeatedly. On the other hand, he feared the consequences if he did not yield to the mob. The evangelists depict him as "wanting to release Jesus" (Luke 23:20) and "wanting to satisfy the crowd" (Mark 15:15). But he found that he could not fulfil both wants simultaneously. It is fascinating to watch him wriggling in his painful predicament. He tried four ways of avoiding a clear decision.

Firstly, he tried to shift the responsibility to somebody else. Discovering that Jesus came from Galilee and was therefore in Herod's jurisdiction, he sent him to Herod for trial. But Herod found no basis for the charges against Jesus.

Secondly, he tried to do the right thing (release Jesus) for the wrong reason (because of the Passover custom), freeing Jesus as an act of clemency instead of an act of justice.

Thirdly, he tried to satisfy the crowd with half measures, having Jesus flogged instead of crucified.

Fourthly, he tried to persuade the crowd of his integrity (by washing his hands publicly) even while contradicting it (by sending Jesus to the cross). Each was a subterfuge, an attempt to avoid a commitment by compromise.

Why was Pilate so weak, such a moral coward? John tells us. The Jews kept shouting to him: "If you let this man go, you are no friend of Caesar" (John 19:12). That settled it. The issue was plain. He had to choose between two kings. To his everlasting shame, he made the wrong choice. He chose to be a friend of Caesar and an enemy of all reason and justice. His name has been immortalized in the clause of the creed that declares that Jesus "suffered under Pontius Pilate."

For further reading: John 19:4–16

SATURDAY

The Responsibility for Jesus' Death

THE CHIEF PRIESTS... BOUND JESUS, LED HIM AWAY AND HANDED HIM
OVER TO PILATE.

Mark 15:1

Who was responsible for Jesus' death? We Christians are often accused of anti-Semitism because (it is alleged) we try to fasten the blame onto the Jews, especially the Jewish leaders. But responsibility for the crucifixion of Jesus is spread much more widely than to a single group of people. The evangelists make it plain that Judas, the priests, Pilate, the crowd, and the soldiers all played a significant part in the drama. Moreover, in each case more than a hint of motivation is suggested. Judas was moved by greed, the priests by envy, Pilate by fear, the crowd by hysteria, and the soldiers by callous duty. We recognize the same mixture of sins in ourselves.

The same Greek verb is used of each stage. The word is *paradidōmi*, which can mean to deliver, to hand over, to give up, and even to betray. Thus Judas handed Jesus over to the priests. The priests handed him over to Pilate. Pilate handed him over to the will of the crowd, and the crowd handed him over to be crucified.

But this is only the human side of the story. Jesus insisted that his death was a voluntary act on his part, so that he handed himself over to it: "No one takes it [my life] from me, but I lay it down of my own accord" (John 10:18). And in some passages the verb *paradidōmi* reappears. For example, "the Son of God... loved me and gave himself for me" (Gal. 2:20).

Still, however, there is one more perspective to consider, namely the action of God the Father in giving up his Son to death. For example, God is described as "he who did not spare his own Son, but gave him up for us all" (Rom. 8:32).

Finally, there is one passage in which the divine and human aspects of Jesus' death are brought together. Peter preached, "This man was handed over to you by God's deliberate plan and foreknowledge; and you, with the help of wicked men, put him to death" (Acts 2:23). Here the death of Jesus is attributed equally to the purpose of God and the wickedness of men. No attempt is made to resolve the paradox. Both statements are true.

For further reading: Acts 4:27–28

WEEK 30: THE END

We have spent several weeks following the public ministry of Jesus from his baptism to his arrest and have considered some samples of his teaching as well. Last week we watched while his ordeal of suffering began. Betrayed by Judas and denied by Peter, he was also subjected to interrogation in both a Jewish and a Roman court. Now this week, before we listen to Jesus' seven words from the cross, we need to gain an overview of his sufferings and death, beginning with the story of Barabbas and of Simon of Cyrene and continuing with Jesus' crucifixion, death, and burial.

Sunday: Barabbas the Brigand

Monday: Simon of Cyrene

Tuesday: The Crucifixion

Wednesday: The New Temple

Thursday: The Sufferings of the Christ

Friday: The Burial of Jesus

Saturday: A Dead Christ?

SUNDAY

Barabbas the Brigand

NOW IT WAS THE CUSTOM AT THE FESTIVAL TO RELEASE A PRISONER
WHOM THE PEOPLE REQUESTED.

Mark 15:6

We know nothing about Barabbas except what we read in the Gospels. But all four evangelists tell his story. Putting the different pieces of evidence together, it appears that he was a notorious criminal and political prisoner. He had taken part recently in an insurrection in the city and was both a robber and a murderer. In our terms, he was a terrorist who was now on death row awaiting execution.

The evangelists also refer to the procurator's custom of granting a Passover amnesty to a prisoner chosen by the people. Pilate saw in this tradition a way of escape from his personal dilemma. He suggested to the crowd that they should choose Jesus. But to his great consternation, they chose Barabbas instead, thus foiling his plan.

It is hard to imagine Barabbas's incredulity when his cell door was flung open and he was called out not to execution but to freedom. He must have stumbled out dumbfounded into the bright sunshine of a spring day. He was not only released but, in a sense, redeemed.

Perhaps Barabbas also felt (as we do) the anomaly of his position. The one who had given sight to the blind and had laid his hands on little children was to be crucified, while the ruffian who deserved his sentence was to go scot-free. The apostle Peter referred to this topsy-turvy situation in the second sermon he preached to the crowd in Jerusalem. They had killed the author of life, he said, while asking for a murderer to be released for them (Acts 3:14–15).

Christians see in the story of Barabbas more than an anomaly; we also see a parable of our redemption. For each of us resembles Barabbas. Like him we deserve death. But like him we have escaped death because Jesus died in our place. If curiosity drew Barabbas to Calvary (though this is purely speculative), perhaps he watched Jesus dying and said to himself, "He is dying in my place." Perhaps the sight even touched, softened, and redeemed him.

For further reading: Mark 15:6–15

Monday

Simon of Cyrene

AS THE SOLDIERS LED HIM AWAY, THEY SEIZED SIMON FROM CYRENE...
AND PUT THE CROSS ON HIM AND MADE HIM CARRY IT BEHIND JESUS.

Luke 23:26

Jesus must have been worn out. He had had to endure several trials without sleep, together with a merciless flogging and much abuse. And now by Roman tradition he had to carry his own cross, or at least its crossbar, to the place of execution. It seems that he stumbled under its weight. True, none of the evangelists says so, but Christian tradition does. And this may explain why the soldiers laid hold of Simon of Cyrene and transferred the cross to his shoulders, compelling him to carry it. The church has always honoured Simon for this act of kindness, even if he was forced to do it.

It seems clear that Simon and his family became believers. For Mark identifies him as "the father of Alexander and Rufus" (Mark 15:21), which indicates that they were well known in the church of Rome by the time Mark's Gospel was published there. "Simeon called Niger [black]," a leader in the church of Antioch, may have been the same man (Acts 13:1), and the Rufus and his mother whom Paul greeted in Rome (Rom. 16:13) may well have been the same family. All this suggests that the Simon who carried the cross for Jesus was a black African from what we call Libya.

It is interesting to reflect how three of the major actors in the drama of the passion were related to the cross. We could say that Judas *caused* the cross, because his treachery led straight to it; Barabbas *escaped* the cross, gaining his freedom at Jesus' expense; and Simon *bore* the cross, carrying it for Jesus. Moreover, these three are not incompatible with Christian experience today. Like Judas we have caused the cross by our greed and duplicity. Like Barabbas we have escaped the cross through him who died in our place. And like Simon we are called to take up our cross every day and follow Christ.

For further reading: Luke 9:18–26

TUESDAY

The Crucifixion

THEY BROUGHT JESUS TO THE PLACE CALLED GOLGOTHA...
AND THEY CRUCIFIED HIM.

Mark 15:22, 24

Cicero in one of his speeches described crucifixion as "a most cruel and disgusting punishment." He added later that the very word *cross* should be far removed not only from the person of a Roman citizen but also from his thoughts, his eyes, and his ears. It is neither surprising nor accidental, therefore, that the evangelists are very restrained in what they write. All they say is that "here they crucified him," without giving any descriptive details.

Nevertheless, we know from other sources that the prisoner was laid on his back; that his hands, wrists, or arms were nailed to the *patibulum* (crossbeam); and that the cross was then hoisted to an upright position and dropped into a hole dug for it.

Pilate then had a "title" in Aramaic, Latin, and Greek fixed above Jesus' head, which read "Jesus of Nazareth, the King of the Jews." The Jewish leaders tried to persuade Pilate to change the wording to the effect that Jesus *claimed* to be the King of the Jews, but Pilate refused.

Gradually the crowd of sightseers thinned out. The soldiers gambled for Jesus' clothes, and the women watched, weeping. Some priests and lawyers also stayed, mocking him: "He saved others... but he can't save himself! He's the king of Israel! Let him come down now from the cross, and we will believe in him. He trusts in God. Let God rescue him now if he wants him" (Matt. 27:42–43). Part of what they were saying was literally true. He could have exercised his divine power and come down from the cross, but what he could not do was save himself and them at the same time. In order to save them he must remain on the cross and die.

So "the cross" soon came to refer not so much to a form of execution as to the gospel of salvation. The apostle Paul could write, "May I never boast except in the cross of our Lord Jesus Christ" (Gal. 6:14).

For further reading: 1 Corinthians 1:17–25

WEDNESDAY

The New Temple

Here is one more piece of abuse that the Jewish leaders hurled at Jesus while he hung on the cross. It concerned his teaching about the temple, and it deserves our meditation today.

The place to begin is our Lord's respectful attitude to the temple as the house of God. He, of course, knew the history of Israel. He was well acquainted with the sequence of events from the tabernacle in the desert, to the first temple built by Solomon, to the second temple begun after the Babylonian exile, to Herod's temple still under construction. In each of these buildings there was an inner sanctuary, or Holy of Holies, in which the Shekinah glory, the symbol of God's presence, could be seen. Thus God dwelt in the midst of his people, and the temple was the focus of their spiritual life.

But Jesus was shocked by the contemporary desecration of the temple by its use for commerce. The house of prayer had become a den of thieves. So Jesus did more than cleanse the temple; he foretold its destruction and replacement. "Destroy this temple," he said, "and I will raise it again in three days" (John 2:19). His hearers entirely misinterpreted his meaning. They protested that the Jerusalem temple had already been under construction for forty-six years; how could he possibly rebuild it in three days? The claim was absurd. But John explained that Jesus was referring to his resurrection body, which would become a new temple, the focus of the new messianic community. In the future, even when only two or three of his disciples met in his name, he would be among them (Matt. 18:20).

Jesus' contemporaries never forgot this saying of his. The false witnesses reminded the Sanhedrin of it. And while he was on the cross the priests mocked his prophecy of a new temple. The New Testament letters, however, unfold Jesus' prophecy. The old temple was destroyed in AD 70, but now Jesus' messianic and resurrected community is the new temple, the dwelling place of God by his Spirit (see 1 Cor. 3:16).

For further reading: Ephesians 2:11–22

The Sufferings of the Christ

HE [JESUS] SAID TO THEM, "... DID NOT THE MESSIAH HAVE TO SUFFER
THESE THINGS AND THEN ENTER HIS GLORY?"

Luke 24:25–26

Why did Matthew in particular lay such stress on the sufferings of Jesus? That he should emphasize the cross is understandable, for Christ died for our sins, and his cross is the heart of the gospel. But why the emphasis on his passion, that is, on his sufferings?

Firstly, suffering identified Jesus as the true Messiah. He had plainly taught that the Son of Man must suffer many things and enter his glory through suffering. So, since the distinctive of Matthew's Gospel is to portray Jesus as the fulfilment of the Old Testament, he draws attention to it in the passion story. Was Jesus betrayed and deserted by his friends? It was in fulfilment of Psalm 41:9: "Even my close friend, someone I trusted, one who shared my bread, has lifted up his heel against me." Was he painfully oppressed and repudiated? It was in fulfilment of Isaiah 53:3: "He was despised and rejected by mankind, a man of suffering, and familiar with pain." Did he maintain a dignified silence before his judges? It was in fulfilment of Isaiah 53:7: "He was led like a lamb to the slaughter, and as a sheep before its shearers is silent, so he did not open his mouth." Was he flogged, punched, slapped, and spat on? It was in fulfilment of Isaiah 50:6: "I offered my back to those who beat me, my cheeks to those who pulled out my beard; I did not hide my face from mocking and spitting." All these, Matthew implies, were signs of the true Messiah, the suffering servant of the Lord.

Secondly, suffering also identifies the messianic community. For example, the eighth beatitude recorded by Matthew declares persecution to be a necessary characteristic of the Messiah's followers. This is still true today. According to Paul Marshall, in his well-documented book *Their Blood Cries Out*, there were between 200 and 250 million Christians being persecuted for their faith in 1997, and a further 400 million living under serious restrictions of religious liberty. Thus suffering is the badge of both the Messiah and his disciples.

For further reading: 1 Peter 2:13–25

The Burial of Jesus

JOSEPH OF ARIMATHEA... TOOK DOWN THE BODY, WRAPPED IT IN THE
LINEN, AND PLACED IT IN A TOMB CUT OUT OF ROCK.

Mark 15:43, 46

According to Jewish law, the body of an executed criminal might not be left hanging all night; it had to be buried before the sun went down (Deut. 21:22–23). This is where Joseph of Arimathea enters the story.

Joseph was what we would call a senator, a senior member of the Sanhedrin, and he had become a secret believer in Jesus. Taking his courage in both hands, he asked Pilate for the body of Jesus, for crucified criminals would normally be thrown into a common grave or left to the dogs and the vultures. Pilate was surprised to hear that Jesus was already dead, but the centurion on duty assured him that it was so. Consequently, Joseph and (according to John) Nicodemus buried the body of Jesus, laying it on a stone slab in Joseph's tomb while the women watched.

The first reason why the burial of Jesus became part of the gospel is that his burial attested the reality of his death (1 Cor. 15:3–4). Jesus did not merely swoon or appear to die. The women did not go to the wrong tomb. No grave robbers could have interfered with the body. No, if the body disappeared and the tomb was empty, it was because it had been resurrected, that is, simultaneously raised and changed. There could be no alternative explanation.

Secondly, the burial is part of the gospel because it indicates the bodily nature of the resurrection. The person who was raised and seen is none other than the person who died and was buried. So the resurrection was neither a hallucination nor a resuscitation but an objective supernatural event by which the process of decomposition was arrested and the dead body of Jesus was both raised and changed.

For further reading: Mark 15:42–47

SATURDAY

A Dead Christ?

But GOD RAISED HIM FROM THE DEAD, FREEING HIM FROM THE AGONY
OF DEATH, BECAUSE IT WAS IMPOSSIBLE FOR DEATH
TO KEEP ITS HOLD ON HIM.

Acts 2:24

The burial of Jesus is part of the gospel, as we saw yesterday, because it affirms both the reality of his death and the bodily nature of his resurrection. We must therefore hold fast to these truths. At the same time, we must also insist that the Christ we worship is not the dead and buried Christ but the Christ who is resurrected and alive. Yet even some professing Christians seem to believe in a Jesus who is more dead than alive.

As an illustration of this, I allude to the thesis developed by Dr John Mackay in his famous book entitled *The Other Spanish Christ*. Mackay spent twenty years as a missionary in Peru and later became a distinguished president of Princeton Theological Seminary. In his book he retold the terrible story of the Spanish conquistadors who vanquished and colonized Latin America's native people by brute force at the beginning of the sixteenth century. The picture of Jesus that Spanish Catholicism introduced into the continent was a figure of tragedy. Of one particular picture, Mackay wrote, "He is dead for ever... This Christ... does not rise again."

It is surely very striking that about fifty years after John Mackay was in Peru, the late Henri Nouwen visited it. Both men – the Presbyterian missionary and the Roman Catholic priest – came to the same conclusion. Nouwen wrote in his diary about Peruvian Catholicism:

> *Nowhere did I see a sign of the resurrection, nowhere was I reminded of the truth that Christ overcame sin and death, and rose victorious from the grave. All was Good Friday. Easter was absent... The nearly exclusive emphasis on the tortured body of Christ strikes me as a perversion of the Good News into a morbid story that intimidates... people, but does not liberate them.*[1]

John Mackay and Henri Nouwen were surely right. The good news is that Christ crucified is now risen. Hallelujah!

For further reading: Acts 2:22–32

---

1   Henri Nouwen, *Graçias: A Latin American Journal* (Maryknoll, NY: Orbis, 1983), 105.

Week 31: The Seven Words from the Cross

Last week we followed Jesus to crucifixion and burial and watched this climax through the eyes of onlookers. This week we will seek to gain an insider's view of what was happening through the eyes of Jesus himself. He spoke seven short but significant sentences from the cross, which together throw light on the cross. No one evangelist records them all. Matthew and Mark preserve only one (the cry of dereliction), while of the remaining six, Luke records three and John three. The church has cherished these so-called seven words from the cross as disclosing the otherwise unknown thoughts of Jesus. None of them was uttered in bitterness or complaint. As we will see, each is an expression either of his great love for us, or of his dreadful work of sin bearing, or of his final triumph and victory.

Sunday: His Prayer for His Executioners

Monday: His Salvation of a Criminal

Tuesday: His Commendation of His Mother

Wednesday: His Cry of Dereliction

Thursday: His Agony of Thirst

Friday: His Shout of Triumph

Saturday: His Final Surrender

SUNDAY

His Prayer for His Executioners

JESUS SAID, "FATHER, FORGIVE THEM, FOR THEY DO NOT KNOW WHAT
THEY ARE DOING."

Luke 23:34

The first three words from the cross portray Jesus the example. They express the love he showed to others. "Do not weep for me," he had said earlier (v. 28). Nor did he weep for himself. He did not dwell in self-pity on his pain and loneliness nor on the gross injustice that was being done to him. Indeed, he had no thought for himself, only for others. He had nothing left now to give away; even his clothes had been taken from him. But he was still able to give people his love. The cross is the epitome of his self-giving – as he showed his concern for the men who crucified him, the mother who bore him, and the penitent thief who was dying at his side.

His first word was his prayer for the forgiveness of his executioners. Think how remarkable this was. His physical and emotional sufferings had already been almost intolerable. But now he had been stripped and laid on his back, and the rough hands of the soldiers had wielded their hammers clumsily. Surely now he will think of himself? Surely now he will complain against God like Job, or plead with God to avenge him, or exhibit a little self-pity? But no, he thinks only of others. He may well have cried out in pain, but his first word is a prayer for his enemies. The two criminals beside him curse and swear. But not Jesus. He practises what he has preached in the Sermon on the Mount: "Love your enemies, do good to those who hate you, bless those who curse you, pray for those who ill-treat you" (Luke 6:27–28).

For whom, then, was he praying? No doubt especially for the Jewish leaders who had rejected their Messiah. In answer to Jesus' prayer, they were granted a forty-year reprieve, during which many thousands repented and believed in Jesus. Only in AD 70 did the judgment of God fall on the nation, when Jerusalem was taken and its temple destroyed.

For further reading: Matthew 18:21–35

MONDAY

His Salvation of a Criminal

JESUS ANSWERED HIM [THE PENITENT THIEF], "TRULY I TELL YOU, TODAY
YOU WILL BE WITH ME IN PARADISE."
Luke 23:43

All four evangelists tell us that three crosses were erected at Golgotha ("the place called the Skull" [v. 33]) that fateful morning. They make it plain that Jesus was on the middle cross, while two robbers ("criminals" according to Luke) were crucified on either side of him.

At first both thieves joined in the chorus of hate to which Jesus was now subjected (Matt. 27:44). Only one continued, however, hurling insults at Jesus and challenging him to save himself and them. But the second thief rebuked him saying, "Don't you fear God… since you are under the same sentence? We are punished justly… But this man has done nothing wrong" (Luke 23:40–41). Then, turning to Jesus, the penitent robber said, "Jesus, remember me when you come into your kingdom" (v. 42).

This ascription of kingship to Jesus is remarkable indeed. No doubt the penitent thief had heard the priests mocking Jesus' claim to be the king of Israel, and he had probably read the inscription over his head, "This is Jesus of Nazareth, the King of the Jews." He had also seen Jesus' quiet, regal dignity. At all events, he had come to believe that Jesus was a king. He had also heard Jesus' prayer for the forgiveness of his executioners, and forgiveness is what he knew he needed, since he confessed that he was being punished justly.

To his cry to be remembered Jesus replied, "Truly I tell you, today you will be with me in paradise" (v. 43). There were no recriminations. He was not reproached that he repented only at the eleventh hour. No doubt was cast on the genuineness of his repentance. Jesus simply gave this penitent believer the assurance he longed for. He promised him not only entry into paradise, involving the joy of Christ's presence, but an immediate entry that very day. And he assured him of these things with his "Truly I tell you," the last time he used this familiar formula. I imagine that, during the long hours of pain that followed, the forgiven thief stayed his heart and mind on the sure and saving promise of Jesus.

For further reading: Luke 23:32–43

His Commendation of His Mother

HE [JESUS] SAID TO HER [HIS MOTHER], "WOMAN, HERE IS YOUR SON,"
AND TO THE DISCIPLE [JOHN], "HERE IS YOUR MOTHER."
John 19:26–27

Perhaps Jesus closed his eyes as he bore the brunt of the first onslaught of pain. Perhaps as it subsided a bit he opened them again. At all events, as he looked down from the cross, he saw a little group of faithful women and the apostle John ("the disciple whom he loved" [v. 26]). And then he saw his mother. She was, of course, very precious to him from a human point of view. True, she had not always understood him, and once or twice he had had to speak to her firmly when she stood in the way of his doing his Father's will. Nevertheless, she was his mother. He had been conceived in her womb by the supernatural operation of the Holy Spirit. She had given birth to him, laid him in a manger, and cared for him during his childhood. It would have been she who taught him the biblical stories of the patriarchs, kings, and prophets, and the plan and purpose of God. She had also set him a radiant example of godliness.

Now we read that "near the cross of Jesus stood his mother" (v. 25). Gracious, sorrowing lady! It is hard to imagine the depth of her grief as she watched him suffer. Old man Simeon's prophecy was being fulfilled that a sword would pierce her own soul (Luke 2:35).

Jesus thinks not of his pain but of hers. He is determined to spare her the anguish of seeing him die. So he avails himself of a right that scholars tell us a crucified man had, even from the cross, namely to make a testamentary disposition. Using the terminology of family law, he put her under John's protection and care and put John under hers. Immediately John took her away to his Jerusalem home.

Looking back over the first three words from the cross, we are amazed at the unselfishness of Jesus. He had no thought for himself. In spite of the pain and shame he was experiencing, he prayed for the forgiveness of his enemies, he promised paradise to a penitent criminal, and he provided for his bereaved mother. This is love, and Scripture says to us, "Live a life of love, just as Christ loved us and gave himself up for us" (Eph. 5:2).

For further reading: John 19:25–27

WEDNESDAY

His Cry of Dereliction

FROM NOON UNTIL THREE IN THE AFTERNOON DARKNESS CAME OVER ALL
THE LAND. ABOUT THREE IN THE AFTERNOON JESUS CRIED OUT IN A LOUD
VOICE... "MY GOD, MY GOD, WHY HAVE YOU FORSAKEN ME?"

Matthew 27:45–46

If the first three words from the cross portray Jesus as our example, the fourth (and later the fifth) portray him as our sin bearer. The crucifixion took place at about 9 a.m., and the first three words from the cross seem to have been spoken near the beginning of this period. Then there was silence. At about noon, when the sun was at the meridian, an inexplicable darkness stole over the countryside. It cannot have been a natural eclipse of the sun, because the Feast of the Passover took place at full moon. No, it was a supernatural phenomenon, perhaps intended by God to symbolize the horror of great darkness into which the soul of Jesus now plunged. It lasted three hours, during which no word escaped the lips of the suffering Saviour. He bore our sins in silence.

Then suddenly, at about 3 p.m., Jesus broke the silence and spoke the remaining four words from the cross in rapid succession, beginning with, "My God, my God, why have you forsaken me?" This terrible cry is recorded by Matthew and Mark alone, and in the original Aramaic – "*Eloi, Eloi, lama sabachthani?*" The onlookers who said, "He's calling Elijah" (v. 47) were almost certainly jesting; no Jews could have been so ignorant of Aramaic as to make that foolish blunder.

Everybody agrees that Jesus was quoting from Psalm 22:1. But why did he quote it and declare himself forsaken? Logically there can be only two explanations. Either Jesus was mistaken and not forsaken or he was telling the truth and was forsaken. For myself I reject the first explanation. To me it is inconceivable that Jesus, in the moment of his greatest surrender, could have been mistaken and that his sense of godforsakenness was imaginary. The alternative explanation is simple and straightforward. Jesus was not mistaken. The situation on the cross was of God forsaken by God – and the estrangement was due to our sins and their just reward. And Jesus expressed this terrible experience of godforsakenness by quoting the only Scripture that foretold it and that he had perfectly fulfilled.

For further reading: Galatians 3:6–14

His Agony of Thirst

JESUS SAID, "I AM THIRSTY."

John 19:28

At the time of his crucifixion Jesus was offered wine to drink mixed with gall, but after tasting it, he refused to drink it (Matt. 27:34), perhaps because he was determined to be in full possession of his senses while suffering for us on the cross. Hours later, however, on emerging from the godforsaken darkness, and knowing that the end was near, Jesus said, "I am thirsty." In response the bystanders soaked a sponge in wine vinegar (the Roman soldiers' common drink) and lifted it on a stalk of hyssop to Jesus' lips.

This is the only word from the cross that expressed Jesus' physical pain. He spoke it, the evangelist added, that the Scripture might be fulfilled. Indeed, it had been prophesied twice in the Psalms. In Psalm 22:15 it is written, "My strength is dried up like a potsherd, and my tongue sticks to the roof of my mouth," while in Psalm 69:21 we read, "They put gall in my food and gave me vinegar for my thirst."

It would be a mistake to suppose, however, that a literal physical thirst exhausts the significance of Jesus' fifth cry from the cross. His thirst, like the darkness, was also surely figurative. If the darkness of the sky symbolized the darkness in which our sins enveloped Jesus, and if the death of his body was to symbolize his spiritual death, then his thirst symbolized the torment of separation from God. Darkness, death, and thirst. What are these but what the Bible calls hell – outer darkness, the second death, and the lake of fire – all expressing the horror of exclusion from God? This is what our Saviour suffered for us on the cross.

Thirst is an especially poignant symbol, because Jesus had earlier said, "Let anyone who is thirsty, come to me and drink" (John 7:37). But he who slakes our thirst himself now experiences on the cross a ghastly thirst. He longs, like the rich man in the parable, that Lazarus will dip the tip of his finger in water and cool his tongue. Thus Jesus thirsted on the cross that we might never thirst again (Rev. 7:16).

For further reading: Luke 16:19–31

FRIDAY

His Shout of Triumph

WHEN HE HAD RECEIVED THE DRINK, JESUS SAID, "IT IS FINISHED."
John 19:30

In the first three words from the cross we saw Jesus as our example, and in the fourth and fifth as our sin bearer. Now in the last two cries he appears as the conqueror, for they express the victory that he has won for us.

One could perhaps claim that the words of the sixth cry ("It is finished") are the most momentous ever spoken. Already in anticipation Jesus had claimed that he had completed the work he had come into the world to do (17:4). So next he makes a public declaration of it. His cry is not the despairing groan of one who is dying in resignation and defeat. It is a shout, according to Matthew and Mark, uttered "in a loud voice" (Matt. 27:50), proclaiming a resounding victory.

The Greek verb (*tetelestai*) is in the perfect tense, indicating an achievement with lasting results. It might be rendered, "It has been and remains forever accomplished." For Christ has made what the letter to the Hebrews calls "one single sacrifice for sins" (Heb. 10:12 NJB) and what Cranmer in the Book of Common Prayer called "a full, perfect and sufficient sacrifice, oblation and satisfaction for the sins of the whole world." In consequence, because Christ has finished the work of sin bearing, there is nothing left for us to do, or even to contribute.

And to demonstrate the satisfactory nature of what Christ has done, the veil of the temple was torn down "from top to bottom" (Matt. 27:51) in order to show that the hand of God had done it. This curtain had hung for centuries between the outer and the inner sanctuaries as an emblem of the inaccessibility of God to sinners, for no one might penetrate beyond the veil into the presence of God except the high priest on the Day of Atonement. But now the veil was torn in half and discarded, for it was needed no longer. The worshippers in the temple courts, gathered that afternoon for the evening sacrifice, were dramatically informed of another and a better sacrifice by which they could draw near to God.

For further reading: Hebrews 10:11–14, 19–25

SATURDAY

His Final Surrender

JESUS CALLED OUT WITH A LOUD VOICE, "FATHER, INTO YOUR HANDS
I COMMIT MY SPIRIT." WHEN HE HAD SAID THIS, HE BREATHED HIS LAST.

Luke 23:46

None of the evangelists says that Jesus "died." They seem deliberately to avoid the word. They do not want to give the impression that in the end death claimed him and that he had to yield to its authority. Death did not claim him as its victim; he seized it as its victor.

Between them the evangelists use four different expressions, each of which places the initiative in the process of dying in Jesus' own hands. Mark says he "breathed his last" (Mark 15:37), and Matthew that he "gave up his spirit" (Matt. 27:50), while Luke records his words, "Father, into your hands I commit my spirit" (Luke 23:46). But John's expression is the most striking, namely that "he bowed his head and gave up his spirit" (John 19:30). The verb is again *paradidōmi*, which was used of Barabbas, the priests, Pilate, and the soldiers who "handed over" Jesus. But now John uses it of Jesus himself, handing over his spirit to the Father and his body to death. Notice that before he did this he "bowed his head." It is not that he first died, and then his head fell forward onto his chest. It was the other way around. The bowing of the head was his final act of surrender to the will of his Father. So by word and deed (bowing the head and declaring that he was handing over his spirit), Jesus indicated that his death was his own voluntary act.

Jesus could have escaped death right up to the last minute. As he said in the garden, he could have summoned more than twelve legions of angels to rescue him. He could have come down from the cross, as his mockers challenged him to do. But he did not. Of his own free will and deliberate choice he gave himself up to death. It was he who determined the time, the place, and the manner of his departure.

The last two words from the cross ("finished" and "I commit my spirit") proclaim Jesus as the conqueror of sin and death. We must come humbly to the cross, deserving nothing but judgment, pleading nothing but mercy, and Christ will deliver us from both the guilt of sin and the fear of death.

For further reading: Hebrews 2:14–18

WEEK 32: THE MEANING OF THE CROSS

We have been following the dramatic story of the sufferings and death of the Messiah and have listened carefully to his seven words from the cross. This week we are going to delve a bit more deeply into the meaning of his death. Not that we will discover a single explanation of its purpose. On the contrary, the cross is a diamond with many facets. Yet we will try from these to gain a full and balanced understanding of why he died. First, however, we need to grasp the central importance that is attached to the cross in the New Testament and so in the life and witness of the church.

Sunday: The Centrality of the Cross

Monday: The Example of Jesus

Tuesday: An Atonement for Sin

Wednesday: A Revelation of Love

Thursday: Victory through the Cross

Friday: The Cross and Suffering

Saturday: The Cross and Mission

The Centrality of the Cross

I RESOLVED TO KNOW NOTHING WHILE I WAS WITH YOU EXCEPT JESUS
CHRIST AND HIM CRUCIFIED.

1 Corinthians 2:2

Anybody who investigates Christianity for the first time is immediately struck by its emphasis on the death of Jesus and, as we have already seen, especially by the disproportionate amount of space that the evangelists devote to the last week of his life.

The Gospel writers had learned this emphasis from Jesus himself. On three separate and solemn occasions Jesus predicted his death, saying, "The Son of Man must suffer many things... and... be killed" (Mark 8:31). It *must* happen, he insisted, because it had been foretold in the Old Testament Scriptures. Jesus also referred to his death as his "hour," the hour for which he had come into the world. At first he repeated that it was "not yet," but at last he was able to say that "the hour has come."

Perhaps most striking of all is the fact that Jesus made deliberate provision for how he wished to be remembered. He instructed his disciples to take, break, and eat bread in memory of his body to be broken for them, and to take, pour out, and drink wine in memory of his blood to be shed for them. Death spoke from both elements. No symbolism could be more self-evident. How did he want to be remembered? Not for his example or his teaching, not for his words or works, not even for his living body or flowing blood, but for his body given and blood shed in death.

So the church has been right in its choice of symbol for Christianity. It could have chosen any one of several options – for example, the crib, symbolizing the incarnation; or the carpenter's bench, speaking of the dignity of manual labour; or the towel, symbol of humble service; or others. But it passed them by in favour of the cross.

The choice of the cross as the supreme Christian symbol was all the more remarkable because in Greco-Roman culture the cross was an object of shame. How, then, could the apostle Paul say that he gloried in it? This is the question to which we will seek an answer this week.

For further reading: 1 Corinthians 1:17–25

The Example of Jesus

TO THIS YOU WERE CALLED, BECAUSE CHRIST SUFFERED FOR YOU,
LEAVING YOU AN EXAMPLE, THAT YOU SHOULD FOLLOW IN HIS STEPS.

1 Peter 2:21

Once Peter had acknowledged Jesus as the Messiah, Jesus began to teach the disciples that he must suffer. But Peter violently disagreed. "No, Lord," he shouted, "this will never happen to you." But now in his thinking, some thirty years later, the death of Jesus, which had seemed to him inconceivable, has become indispensable.

We need to recall the historical background to Peter's letter. Christianity was still an illegal religion, and the neurotic emperor Nero was known to be hostile to it. Already there were spasmodic outbursts of persecution. Peter is especially concerned for Christian slaves in non-Christian households. They must bear unjust suffering patiently, he says. Why? Because this is part of a Christian's calling. Why? Because Jesus, though sinless, suffered for us but did not retaliate, leaving us an example, that we should follow in his steps.

The Greek word for *example* here is unique in the New Testament. It denotes a teacher's copybook on which children trace their letters when learning to write. So Peter is urging us to copy the example of Jesus and also to follow in his steps. This is a poignant appeal from Peter's pen, since he had boasted that he would follow Jesus to prison and to death, whereas in the event he had followed him only at a distance. Now recommissioned, however, Peter is determined to follow the way of the cross and bear unjust suffering patiently.

A question arises in our minds, however. If we submit to unjust suffering, is there no place for justice? Are we to allow evildoers to trample all over us and so encourage evil to flourish? No. First Peter 2:23 answers our question. It tells us both that Jesus did not retaliate and that "he entrusted himself [and his cause] to him who judges justly." In other words, the reason we are called to non-retaliation is not because evil should be allowed to triumph but because it is not our responsibility to punish it. It is the responsibility of the just Judge both now through the law courts and ultimately on judgment day. Thus love and justice are not incompatible; they complement one another, as we see in the example of Jesus.

For further reading: 1 Peter 2:18–23

TUESDAY

An Atonement for Sin

FOR CHRIST ALSO SUFFERED ONCE FOR ALL, THE RIGHTEOUS FOR THE UNRIGHTEOUS, TO BRING YOU TO GOD.

1 Peter 3:18

This is one of the great New Testament texts about the cross. It tells us the major reason why Christ died. We have seen that he died as a martyr to his own greatness and as an example of how to bear suffering patiently. Now we need to penetrate more deeply into the meaning and purpose of the cross.

Firstly, *Christ died to bring us to God.* Behind this statement lies the assumption that we are separated from God and need to be brought back to him. And this is so. All our sense of alienation and of homesickness can be traced ultimately to our estrangement from God, and our estrangement is due to our sin. As Isaiah put it, "Your iniquities have separated you from your God; your sins have hidden his face from you" (Isa. 59:2). What, then, did Christ do to remedy this situation?

Secondly, *Christ died for sins, the righteous for the unrighteous.* To understand this, we need to recall that sin and death are riveted to one another from the beginning to the end of the Bible as an offence and its just reward. "The wages of sin is death" (Rom. 6:23). But Jesus committed no sins for which atonement needed to be made. So if he died for sins, it must have been our sins, not his, for which he died. As Peter put it, he died for sins, "the righteous for the unrighteous" (1 Pet. 3:18), the innocent for the guilty. It is this that justifies our conviction that Jesus' death was substitutionary. That is, he died as our substitute. We deserved to die; he died instead. And because he took our place, bore our sin, and died our death, we may be freely forgiven.

Thirdly, *Christ died for sins once for all.* The adverb *hapax* ("once") means not "once upon a time" but "once and for all." It expresses the absolute finality of what Christ did on the cross. It is because he had paid the full penalty for our sins that he could cry out, "It is finished." So what is there left for us to do? Nothing! We can contribute nothing to what Christ has done. All we can do is to thank him for what he has done and rest in his finished work.

For further reading: Hebrews 9:23–28

A Revelation of Love

BUT GOD DEMONSTRATES HIS OWN LOVE FOR US IN THIS: WHILE WE WERE
STILL SINNERS, CHRIST DIED FOR US.

Romans 5:8

How can we believe in the love of God when there appears to be so much evidence to contradict it? The apostle Paul spells out in Romans 5 two major means by which we become sure that God loves us. The first is that he "has poured out his love into our hearts by the Holy Spirit, whom he has given us" (v. 5). The second is that "God demonstrates his own love for us in this: While we were still sinners, Christ died for us" (v. 8). How, then, can we doubt God's love? To be sure, we are often profoundly perplexed by the tragedies of life. But God has both proved his love for us in the death of his Son and poured his love into us by the gift of his Spirit. Objectively in history and subjectively in experience, God has given us good grounds for believing in his love. The integration of the historical ministry of God's Son (on the cross) with the contemporary ministry of his Spirit (in our hearts) is one of the most wholesome and satisfying features of the gospel.

What the Bible does is not solve the problem of suffering but give us the right perspective from which to view it. Then, whenever we are torn with anguish, we will climb the hill called Calvary and, from that unique vantage ground, survey the calamities of life.

What makes suffering insufferable is not so much the pain involved as the feeling that God doesn't care. We picture him lounging in a celestial armchair, indifferent to the sufferings of the world. It is this slanderous caricature of God that the cross smashes to smithereens. We are to see him not on a comfortable chair but on a cross. For the God who allows us to suffer once suffered himself in Jesus Christ, and he continues to suffer with us today. There is still a question mark against human suffering, but over that mark we boldly stamp another mark – the cross.

For further reading: Romans 8:28–39

Thursday

Victory Through the Cross

THEY TRIUMPHED OVER HIM BY THE BLOOD OF THE LAMB.
Revelation 12:11

It is impossible to read the New Testament without being struck by the atmosphere of joyful confidence that pervades it. It stands out in relief against the rather insipid religion that often passes for Christianity today. There was no defeatism in the early Christians. Victory, conquest, triumph, and overcoming – this was the vocabulary of those first followers of Jesus. They attributed this victory to the cross.

Yet any contemporary observer who saw Christ die would have listened with astonished incredulity to the claim that the Crucified was a conqueror. Look at him there, spread-eagled on his cross, robbed of all freedom, pinned and powerless. It appears to be total defeat.

But the Christian claim is that the reality is the opposite of the appearance. What looked like the defeat of goodness by evil was more certainly the defeat of evil by goodness. Overcome there, Jesus was himself overcoming. The victim was the victor, and the cross is still the throne from which he rules the world.

In vivid imagery the apostle Paul describes how the powers of evil surrounded Jesus and closed in around him on the cross, how he stripped them from himself, disarmed them, and made a public spectacle of them, triumphing over them by the cross (Col. 2:15). What precise form this cosmic battle took is not explained. But we do know that Jesus resisted the temptations to avoid the cross, to retaliate, and to resort to worldly power. He remained uncompromised.

The theme of victory through the cross, which the ancient Greek fathers and later Latin fathers celebrated, was lost by some medieval theologians but recovered by Martin Luther at the Reformation. This was the thesis of Gustav Aulen, a Swedish theologian, in his influential book *Christus Victor*. He was right to recover this somewhat neglected motif. Yet we must not make the opposite mistake, emphasizing the theme of triumph at the expense of the themes of atonement and revelation.

For further reading: Revelation 12:1–12

FRIDAY

The Cross and Suffering

I WANT TO KNOW CHRIST – YES, TO KNOW THE POWER OF HIS
RESURRECTION AND PARTICIPATION IN HIS SUFFERINGS.

Philippians 3:10

The fact of suffering undoubtedly constitutes the single greatest challenge to the Christian faith. Sensitive spirits ask if it can possibly be reconciled with God's justice and love. Philip Yancey has gone further and uttered the unutterable that we may have thought but to which we may never have dared to give voice. He wrote in his book *Where Is God When It Hurts?* "If God is truly in charge... why is he so capricious, unfair? Is he the cosmic sadist who delights in watching us squirm?"

Instead, Scripture assures us that our God is a suffering God, being himself far from immune to suffering. We need to see him weeping over the impenitent city of Jerusalem and dying on the cross. I venture to quote something I wrote in *The Cross of Christ*:

> I could never myself believe in God, if it were not for the cross. The only
> God I believe in is the One Nietzsche ridiculed as "God on the cross." In the
> real world of pain, how could one worship a God who was immune to it? I
> have entered many Buddhist temples in different Asian countries and stood
> respectfully before the statue of the Buddha, his legs crossed, arms folded,
> eyes closed, the ghost of a smile playing round his mouth, a remote look on
> his face, detached from the agonies of the world. But each time after a while
> I have had to turn away. And in imagination I have turned instead to that
> lonely, twisted, tortured figure on the cross, nails through hands and feet,
> back lacerated, limbs wrenched, brow bleeding from thorn-pricks, mouth
> dry and intolerably thirsty, plunged in God-forsaken darkness. That is the
> God for me! He laid aside his immunity to pain. He entered our world of
> flesh and blood, tears and death. He suffered for us. Our sufferings become
> more manageable in the light of his.

As P. T. Forsyth put it, "The Cross of Christ... is God's only self-justification in such a world as ours."

For further reading: Hosea 11:8–9

SATURDAY

The Cross and Mission

VERY TRULY I TELL YOU, UNLESS A GRAIN OF WHEAT FALLS TO THE
GROUND AND DIES, IT REMAINS ONLY A SINGLE SEED. BUT IF IT DIES, IT
PRODUCES MANY SEEDS.

John 12:24

Among the pilgrims in Jerusalem there were some Greeks. Evidently, neither the philosophy of Greece nor the religion of Judaism had satisfied them. They were still spiritually hungry. So they came to Philip (perhaps because of his Greek name) and asked him, "Sir... we would like to see Jesus" (v. 21). Jesus' reply to their question was indirect but clear in its implications: "The hour has come for the Son of Man to be glorified" (v. 23). In other words, those Greeks had asked at precisely the right time, for he was about to be glorified, that is, revealed in all his glory. That hour we know from elsewhere was the hour of his death.

Jesus went on to develop an agricultural metaphor. If a seed remains in the dry, warm security of the granary, it will never reproduce itself. It has to be buried alive in the cold, dark grave of the soil. There it has to die. Then out of its wintry grave the springtime grain will sprout. One could sum it up in a simple rhyme: "If it clings to its own, it will remain all alone, but if it dies, it multiplies." Of this fundamental principle the cross of Jesus is history's supreme example. If he had clung to life, the world would have died. But because he died in the godforsaken darkness, there is life for the world.

Tony Lambert in his book *The Resurrection of the Chinese Church* wrote, "The reason for the growth of the church in China... is inextricably linked to the whole theology of the cross. The stark message of the Chinese Church is that God uses suffering... to pour out revival and build his church."

Another link between the cross and mission was Jesus' claim, "I, when I am lifted up from the earth, will draw all people to myself" (v. 32). His promise seems to combine the literal and the figurative. The primary reference is clearly to his being lifted up on the cross (v. 33), and indeed the cross exerts its own magnetism. But he is also lifted up figuratively whenever he is faithfully proclaimed. We rejoice in the universal appeal of Christ crucified, an appeal that is irrespective of ethnicity, nationality, class, gender, and age.

For further reading: John 12:20–33

WEEK 33: THE RESURRECTION APPEARANCES

"The Lord has risen" (Luke 24:34). This is the universal Easter faith, which affirms the objective historical reality of Jesus' resurrection. It is perhaps sufficient to make a threefold confession. Firstly, the tomb was empty, and no adequate alternative to the resurrection has ever explained the disappearance of the body. Secondly, the Lord was seen, and the appearances do not fit what we know of hallucinations. Thirdly, the disciples were changed people. Only the resurrection can account for their transformation from doubt to faith, cowardice to courage, and sorrow to joy.

This week we are going to take a fresh look at the six major appearances that are recorded in the Gospels. Their very variety confirms their veracity.

Sunday: Mary Magdalene

Monday: The Emmaus Walk

Tuesday: The Upper Room

Wednesday: Doubting Thomas

Thursday: The Recommissioning of Peter

Friday: The Great Commission According to Luke

Saturday: Paul's Summary of the Resurrection Appearances

Mary Magdalene

"He [Jesus] asked her, "Woman, why are you crying?"... Jesus said, "Do not hold on to me..."

John 20:15, 17

It is a marvellous providence of God that the first person to whom the risen Lord revealed himself was a woman and that a woman was also the first person he commissioned to proclaim the gospel of the resurrection to others. Is this not a deliberate affirmation of womanhood at a time when women were not regarded as reliable witnesses? This privileged woman was Mary Magdalene. The Gospels do not tell us much about her. But we do know that she stayed by the cross to the bitter end and that she followed the funeral cortège to the garden and saw Jesus buried. Some thirty-six hours later she and other women returned and found the tomb opened and the body gone. She ran back to alert Peter and John. They raced to the tomb, and she followed them at a more leisurely pace. By the time she arrived, they had gone and she was alone.

John paints two dramatic little cameos. In the first Mary was weeping, especially because she thought she had lost the only man who had ever treated her with dignity, love, and respect. The light had gone out of her life. But Jesus had not left her, as she thought. On the contrary, he was there at her side, risen, but she did not know it.

In the second cameo Mary was clinging to him. And Jesus said to her, "Do not hold on to me, because I have not yet ascended" (v. 17 NRSV). Many people ask why Jesus should have invited the apostles to handle him while forbidding Mary to hold on to him. The answer is that holding and handling are different actions. The apostles were invited to handle him in order to verify that he was not a ghost; the reason Mary was forbidden to hold on to him was that her gesture symbolized the wrong kind of relationship. The best translation would perhaps be, "Stop clinging on to me." She had to learn that she could not resume the old familiar friendship she had previously enjoyed. Once he had ascended, a new relationship would become possible.

As we picture Mary weeping and Mary clinging, we see the contrasting mistakes that she made. She wept because she thought she had lost him altogether. She clung to him because she thought she had got him back just as he had been to her before.

For further reading: John 20:10–18

The Emmaus Walk

THEN THE TWO TOLD WHAT HAD HAPPENED ON THE WAY, AND HOW JESUS
WAS RECOGNISED BY THEM WHEN HE BROKE THE BREAD.

Luke 24:35

The walk to Emmaus, a village seven or eight miles northwest of Jerusalem, is one of the most vivid of Easter stories. It took place during the afternoon of Easter Day. One disciple is identified as Cleopas; the other may well have been his wife. As they walked, they talked about the amazing events that had taken place in Jerusalem recently. And as they talked, the risen Jesus joined them.

Notice what Luke tells us about their eyes. According to verse 16, their eyes were kept from recognizing him; according to verse 31, their eyes were opened and they recognized him. The question is, what happened to make the difference? And how can our eyes be opened as theirs were?

Firstly, we can know Christ through the Scriptures. Jesus reproved them for being so slow to believe the prophets, and then he took them through the three main divisions of the Old Testament – the Law, the Prophets, and the Psalms (v. 44), explaining their teaching about the sufferings and glory of the Messiah. As Jesus had said earlier, "The Scriptures… bear witness to me" (John 5:39 RSV). So we need to look for Christ in all the Scriptures. As we do so, our hearts will burn within us.

Secondly, we can know Christ through the breaking of bread. The Emmaus disciples may have seen the scars in his hands or recognized his voice. But it seems more likely that those four verbs Luke uses rang a bell in their memory, that he took bread, gave thanks, broke it, and gave it to them. It was then that their eyes were opened and they knew him. As they said later, "Jesus was recognised by them when he broke the bread" (Luke 24:35). Many Christians have testified to a similar experience. One example is John Wesley's mother, Susanna. When the words of administration were spoken to her one day, she confessed, "The words struck through my heart and I knew God for Christ's sake had forgiven me all my sins."

Here, then, are two major ways by which Cleopas and his companion came to recognize the risen Lord, and by which we may know him today – through the Scriptures and through the breaking of bread, through the Word and the sacrament.

For further reading: Luke 24:13–35

TUESDAY

The Upper Room

JESUS CAME AND STOOD AMONG THEM AND SAID, "... PEACE BE WITH YOU!
AS THE FATHER HAS SENT ME, I AM SENDING YOU."
John 20:19, 21

This is John's version of the Great Commission. It is surrounded by four short, sharp sentences, which he addressed to his disciples. Firstly, Jesus gave them *an assurance of peace*. It was the evening of the first Easter Day, and the apostles had assembled behind locked doors, full of fear. Then Jesus came and stood in their midst and spoke peace to their troubled minds and consciences. Of course, *shalom* was the conventional greeting, but there is more than convention here. Then he showed them his hands and his side, confirming his word with a sign, as in the Lord's Supper.

Secondly, Jesus gave them *a model of mission*: "As the Father has sent me, I am sending you" (v. 21). Jesus' mission involved the incarnation, which has been described as "the most spectacular example of cross-cultural identification in the history of the world." It was total identification, though without any loss of identity, for in becoming one of us, he did not cease to be himself. And now he sends us into the world as the Father had sent him. All authentic mission is incarnational mission. That is, it entails entering other people's worlds.

Thirdly, Jesus gave them *a promise of the Holy Spirit*. He breathed on them and said, "Receive the Holy Spirit" (v. 22). They were not to go out on their own. Mission without the Holy Spirit is impossible. It is he who equips and empowers us for evangelism. Elsewhere Jesus told the disciples to wait for the Spirit to come. His breathing on them was an acted parable confirming the promise that they would later receive.

Fourthly, Jesus gave them *a gospel of salvation*: "If you forgive anyone's sins, their sins, they are forgiven; if you do not forgive them, they are not forgiven" (v. 23). It is another controversial sentence, and on it the Roman Catholic Church has based the claim that its priests have judicial authority to hear confessions and grant absolution. But on no single occasion did the apostles either require confession or grant absolution. Instead, they preached the gospel of salvation with authority, promising forgiveness to those who believed and warning of judgment to those who refused.

For further reading: John 20:19–23

Doubting Thomas

BLESSED ARE THOSE WHO HAVE NOT SEEN AND YET HAVE BELIEVED.

John 20:29

Soon after the publication of his controversial book *The Satanic Verses*, Salman Rushdie said in an interview, "Doubt, it seems to me, is the central condition of a human being in the twentieth century." The patron saint of this era of doubt is the apostle Thomas. "Doubting Thomas" we call him sympathetically, almost affectionately. Consider his pilgrimage:

Firstly, *Thomas the absentee*. On Easter Day, in the evening, for whatever reason, Thomas was absent and so missed the blessing of seeing the risen Lord. It is a calculated risk to be an irregular churchgoer. But the following Sunday Thomas was back in his place, and the blessing he missed on the first Sunday he received on the second!

Secondly, *Thomas the sceptic*. When the other disciples told Thomas that they had seen the Lord, Thomas should have believed them. Indeed, Jesus reproved Thomas and pronounced a blessing on those who have not seen and yet believe. There are two main ways by which we come to believe anything. The first is by our own empirical investigation; the second is by accepting the testimony of reliable witnesses. So when the others said, "We have seen the Lord" (v. 25), Thomas should have believed them, since he knew they were honest and sober witnesses. Just so, if everybody today insisted on seeing and touching the risen Lord, there would be no believers. Instead, millions have come to faith on the testimony of those who did see and touch. The reasonableness of faith depends on the credibility of the witnesses.

Thirdly, *Thomas the believer*. Thomas not only believed but worshipped, saying, "My Lord and my God!" (v. 28). And tradition adds that he later went to Parthia, Persia, and India as a missionary. Indian Christians tell us that he planted the church in Kerala and was martyred in Madras.

The ground of Christian faith is still the testimony of the apostolic eyewitnesses. We believe in Jesus Christ today not because we have seen him but because they have. Hence the vital importance of the New Testament, which contains the witness of the apostles. They say to us in writing what they first said to Thomas in speech: "We have seen the Lord."

For further reading: John 20:24–29

Thursday

The Recommissioning of Peter

PETER WAS HURT BECAUSE JESUS ASKED HIM THE THIRD TIME, "DO YOU
LOVE ME?" HE SAID, "LORD, YOU KNOW ALL THINGS; YOU KNOW THAT I
LOVE YOU." JESUS SAID, "FEED MY SHEEP."

John 21:17

Is it possible for backsliders to be restored, for those who have denied Christ to be given another chance? These questions greatly exercised the early church during the systematic persecutions of the third and early fourth centuries. What should be done with the lapsed? The church has tended to oscillate between extreme laxity (never disciplining anybody) and extreme severity (refusing restoration even to the penitent).

How Jesus treated Peter after he had denied him is an object lesson in reinstatement and recommissioning. To begin with, Jesus seems to have carefully chosen the context in which the restoration would take place. He had already met Peter in Jerusalem, but he chose the familiar surroundings of Galilee as the appropriate place. Seven of the apostles went fishing, we are told, waiting for Jesus to meet them according to his promise. The similarity of what happened next to an earlier incident on the lake of Galilee (the fruitless fishing expedition, the instruction to fish in another place, and the huge catch) must have helped John to recognize Jesus on the lakeside and Peter to dive in and swim to the shore. It looks like a deliberate restaging of the first time Jesus commissioned Peter.

After breakfast on the beach came the interview Peter was dreading. Three times he had denied Jesus. So three times Jesus asked him the same question: "Do you love me?" And three times Jesus recommissioned him, saying, "Feed my sheep." Older commentators made much of the two Greek verbs for *love*. But we do not know what Aramaic words Jesus used, and the two Greek verbs have varied emphases.

The important point is that Jesus asked Peter, "Do you love me?" He asked Peter not about the past but about the present, not about words or deeds but about Peter's attitude of heart. Love for Christ takes priority, because it is forgiven sinners who love much. Following each profession of love came Jesus' word of recommissioning. What is clear is that Peter's denial, serious though it was, did not disqualify him. Jesus not only reinstated Peter in the favour of God but also recommissioned him for the service of God.

For further reading: John 21:1–17

The Great Commission According to Luke

THIS IS WHAT IS WRITTEN: THE MESSIAH WILL SUFFER AND RISE FROM
THE DEAD ON THE THIRD DAY, AND REPENTANCE FOR THE FORGIVENESS
OF SINS WILL BE PREACHED IN HIS NAME TO ALL NATIONS, BEGINNING AT
JERUSALEM.

Luke 24:46–47

Today we reflect on Luke's version of the Great Commission. In it the risen Lord summarizes the gospel in five truths, each of which is double. Firstly, there is *the double event*, namely the death and resurrection of the Messiah (v. 46). The good news begins with history. It was an event before it could become an experience.

Secondly, there is *the double proclamation*. On the basis of the name of Christ crucified and resurrected, forgiveness (the gospel offer) and repentance (the gospel demand) are proclaimed. True, the gospel is a free offer, but what is free is not always cheap. We cannot turn to Christ without simultaneously turning from evil.

Thirdly, there is *the double scope*. The gospel is to be made known "to all nations, beginning at Jerusalem" (v. 47). That is, in opening the door of faith to the Gentiles, God did not close it on the Jews. We must firmly reject the extraordinary teaching of a "two-track" gospel, which maintains that there is no need for Jews to believe in Jesus because they already have their own covenant with Abraham. But everybody needs to come to Christ!

Fourthly, there is *the double accreditation of the gospel*. On the one hand, there is the Old Testament witness to the Messiah (vv. 44, 46), while on the other, "you [the apostles] are witnesses of these things" (v. 48). Thus the death and resurrection of Jesus have in the Old and New Testaments a double attestation.

Fifthly, there is *the double mission*. The Great Commission involved a double sending (v. 49) – the sending to them of the Holy Spirit and the sending of them into the world. The two missions go together, for the Holy Spirit is a missionary Spirit.

Thus the risen Lord has given us a beautifully balanced and comprehensive account of the gospel. We are commissioned to proclaim repentance and forgiveness on the basis of him who died and was raised, to all humankind (Gentiles and Jews), according to the Scriptures (Old and New Testaments), in the power of the Spirit given to us. Let's keep these things together.

For further reading: Luke 24:44–49

Saturday

Paul's Summary of the Resurrection Appearances

FOR WHAT I RECEIVED I PASSED ON TO YOU AS OF FIRST IMPORTANCE:
THAT CHRIST DIED FOR OUR SINS ACCORDING TO THE SCRIPTURES, THAT
HE WAS BURIED, THAT HE WAS RAISED ON THE THIRD DAY ACCORDING TO
THE SCRIPTURES, AND THAT HE APPEARED...

1 Corinthians 15:3–5

Paul here identifies the gospel that was preached by the apostles and received by the Corinthians, on which they had taken their stand and by which they were being saved. It concerned the truths of the death and resurrection of Christ. Firstly, these truths are *central* truths. Of course, other truths are important, such as Christ's virgin birth, sinless life, mighty works, glorious ascension, continuing reign, and future return, but the death and resurrection of Jesus are "of first importance." Secondly, these truths are *historical* truths. They are not myths but verifiable historical events, which can be pinpointed on the calendar, as indicated by the telltale phrase "on the third day."

Thirdly, these truths are *physical* truths. That is, Christ died, and to demonstrate the physical reality of his death, he was buried. Then he rose, and to demonstrate the physical reality of his resurrection, he was seen, and Paul lists his appearances to three individuals and three groups. Moreover, all four events (death, burial, resurrection, and appearances) must have been equally physical. That is, the Jesus who was raised and seen was the same Jesus who had died and was buried. Some say that Paul did not believe in the empty tomb. But if it was Jesus' buried body that was raised and seen, then the tomb must have been empty. So *resurrection* is not a synonym for life after death. The resurrected and transformed body of Jesus was the first bit of the material universe to be redeemed, and it is a pledge that the whole will one day be transformed.

Fourthly, these truths are *biblical* truths, for both took place "according to the Scriptures," witnessed to by the prophets of the Old Testament and the apostles of the New. An encounter with the risen Lord was an essential qualification for the apostolate (9:1; 15:8). Fifthly, these truths are *theological* truths – events of huge significance. We deserved to die for our own sins, but he died our death instead of us. How great is his love! The death and resurrection of Christ (central, historical, physical, biblical, and theological truths) constitute the gospel. If this foundation is lost, the whole superstructure will collapse.

For further reading: 1 Corinthians 15:1–11

What we need to ask now is not whether the resurrection happened but whether it matters whether it happened. For if it happened, it happened nearly two thousand years ago. How can an event of such remote antiquity have any great significance for us today? Why on earth do Christians make such a song and dance about it? Is it not irrelevant?

No, my argument this week is that the resurrection resonates with our human condition. It speaks to our needs in a way that no other distant event does or could do. It is the mainstay of our Christian assurance regarding the past, the present, and the future.

It is striking that in the very earliest days of the church the Jewish leaders "were greatly disturbed because the apostles were teaching the people, proclaiming in Jesus the resurrection of the dead" (Acts 4:2). This does not mean that the apostles had changed their minds about the gospel and were focusing no longer on the cross but on the resurrection. The cross remained at the centre of the gospel, but of course, it was the cross as confirmed by the resurrection.

Sunday: The Verdict Reversed

Monday: The Assurance of Forgiveness

Tuesday: The Symbol of Power

Wednesday: The Conquest of Death

Thursday: The Resurrection of the Body

Friday: Our Living Hope

Saturday: Worldwide Mission

The Verdict Reversed

THE GOD OF OUR ANCESTORS RAISED JESUS FROM THE DEAD – WHOM YOU
KILLED BY HANGING HIM ON A CROSS. GOD EXALTED HIM TO
HIS OWN RIGHT HAND AS PRINCE AND SAVIOUR...
WE ARE WITNESSES OF THESE THINGS...

Acts 5:30–32

It is hard for us to grasp the disciples' deep disillusion when their Master was crucified. They had come to believe in him as their nation's long-awaited Messiah. But ever since his arrest in the garden, things had gone from bad to worse, and their faith had steadily eroded. The Jewish leaders had contrived his rejection to their own intellectual and legal satisfaction. They had committed him to a further trial before Pilate, who in the end bowed to the will of the people. Then he was condemned to the humiliation and pain of crucifixion.

Thus one after another the courts had condemned Jesus. In each case the verdict had gone against him, and on the cross no last-minute reprieve had been granted. So finally his lifeless body was lifted from the cross and carried to Joseph's grave to be buried. The last straw was when a great stone was rolled across the mouth of the tomb and sealed, and Pilate set a guard, as he put it, to make it as secure as they could (Matt. 27:65).

So that was it: a dead and buried corpse, a sealed and guarded tomb, weeping women keeping watch nearby, and shattered dreams. As the Emmaus disciples said, "We had hoped that he was the one who was going to redeem Israel" (Luke 24:21).

Death had taken Jesus beyond human help. Only a miracle could remedy the situation now. Only a resurrection. And it was by a resurrection that God intervened. As a result, the same pattern developed in the early sermons of the apostles. We find it in the first Christian sermon ever preached (Acts 2), in the second (Acts 3), in the third (Acts 5), in Peter's sermon before Cornelius (Acts 10), and in Paul's sermon in Pisidian Antioch (Acts 13): "You killed him. God raised him. We are witnesses." It expresses the first and most basic significance of the resurrection, namely that by raising Jesus, God decisively reversed the verdict passed on him by human beings and validated him as truly the Son of God and Saviour.

For further reading: Acts 2:22–36

Monday

The Assurance of Forgiveness

If Christ has not been raised, your faith is futile; you are still in your sins.

1 Corinthians 15:17

The second significance of the resurrection is that it assures us of God's forgiveness. We have already noted that forgiveness is both one of our basic human needs and one of God's best gifts through the gospel. I have read the statement of the head of a large English mental hospital: "I could dismiss half my patients tomorrow if they could be assured of forgiveness." For all of us have a skeleton or two in some dark cupboard – memories of things we have thought, said, or done, of which in our better moments we are thoroughly ashamed. Our conscience nags, condemns, even torments us.

Several times during his public ministry Jesus spoke words of forgiveness and peace, and in the upper room he referred to the communion cup as his "blood of the covenant... poured out for many for the forgiveness of sins" (Matt. 26:28). Thus he linked our forgiveness with his death.

That is what Jesus said. But how can we know that he was correct, that he achieved by his death what he said he would achieve, and that God has accepted his death in our place as a full, perfect, and sufficient sacrifice for our sins? The answer is that, if he had remained dead, we would never have known. Rather, without the resurrection we would have to conclude that his death was a failure. The apostle Paul saw this logic clearly. The terrible consequences of no resurrection, he wrote, would be that the apostles are false witnesses, believers are unforgiven, and the Christian dead have perished. But in fact, Paul continued, Christ was raised from the dead, and by raising him, God has assured us that he approved of his sin-bearing death, that he did not die in vain, and that those who trust in him receive a full and free forgiveness. The resurrection validates the cross.

For further reading: 1 Corinthians 15:12–20

TUESDAY

The Symbol of Power

THAT YOU MAY KNOW... HIS INCOMPARABLY GREAT POWER... [WHICH] HE
EXERTED WHEN HE RAISED CHRIST FROM THE DEAD...

Ephesians 1:18–20

The resurrection of Jesus Christ also assures us of God's power. For we need God's power in the present as well as his forgiveness of the past. Is God really able to change human nature, to make cruel people kind and sour people sweet? Is he able to take people who are dead to spiritual reality and make them alive in Christ? Yes, he really is! He is able to give life to the spiritually dead and transform us into the likeness of Christ.

But how can these claims be substantiated? Only because of the resurrection. Paul prays that the eyes of our heart may be enlightened, so that we may know "his incomparably great power for us who believe" (v. 19). How may we know this? In addition to the inward illumination of the Holy Spirit, God has given us an outward, public, objective demonstration of it in the resurrection. For the power available for us today is the very same power "he exerted when he raised Christ from the dead" (v. 20). The resurrection is thus portrayed as the supreme evidence in history of the creative power of God.

We are always in danger of trivializing the gospel, of minimizing what God is able to do for us and in us. We speak of becoming a Christian as if it were no more than turning over a new leaf and making a few superficial adjustments to an otherwise secular life. But no, becoming and being a Christian, according to the New Testament, is an event so radical that no language can do it justice except death and resurrection – death to the old life of self-centredness and resurrection to a new life of love. In brief, the same God of supernatural power who raised Jesus from physical death can raise us from spiritual death. We know he can raise *us* because we know that he raised *him*. Now our prayer is that in every aspect of our lives we may "know Christ... [and] the power of his resurrection" (Phil. 3:10).

For further reading: Ephesians 1:15–23

The Conquest of Death

CHRIST JESUS... HAS DESTROYED DEATH AND HAS BROUGHT LIFE AND
IMMORTALITY TO LIGHT THROUGH THE GOSPEL.

2 Timothy 1:10

The most fantastic of all Christian claims is that Jesus Christ rose from the dead. It strains our credulity to the limit. Human beings have tried with all possible ingenuity both to defy and to deny death. But only Christ has claimed to conquer it, that is, to defeat it in his own experience and to deprive it of its power over others.

In our day, at least in the West, nobody exemplifies the widespread *angst*, and especially the fear of death, more dramatically than the tragi-comedian Woody Allen. He regards death and dissolution with terror. It has become an obsession with him. True, he is still able to joke about it. "It's not that I'm afraid to die," he famously quips. "I just don't want to be there when it happens." He calls death "absolutely stupefying."

Jesus Christ, however, rescues his disciples from this horror. Consider one of his great "I am" sayings: "I am the resurrection and the life. The one who believes in me will live, even though they die; and whoever lives by believing in me will never die" (John 11:25–26). These verses contain a double promise of Jesus to his followers. The believer who lives will never die, because Christ is their life, and death will seem to them only a trivial episode. The believer who dies, however, will live again, because Christ is their resurrection. Thus Christ is both the life of those who live and the resurrection of those who die. Christ transforms both life and death.

It is said of Henry Venn, the eighteenth-century evangelical Anglican vicar, that when he was told he was dying, his joy at dying kept him alive another fortnight! Such a fearless, joyful attitude to the onset of death is possible only because of the resurrection of Jesus Christ and his conquest of death.

For further reading: John 11:17–44

Thursday

The Resurrection of the Body

THE LORD JESUS CHRIST... WILL TRANSFORM OUR LOWLY BODIES SO THAT
THEY WILL BE LIKE HIS GLORIOUS BODY.

Philippians 3:20–21

Christ's conquest of death also indicates the nature of resurrection. Firstly, the risen Lord was not a resuscitated corpse. We do not believe that our bodies will be miraculously reconstituted out of the identical material particles of which they are at present composed. Jesus performed three resuscitations during his ministry, restoring to this life the son of the widow of Nain, Jairus's daughter, and Lazarus. One understands the sympathy that C. S. Lewis expressed for Lazarus. "To be brought back," he wrote, "and have all one's dying to do again was rather hard." But Jesus' resurrection was not a resuscitation. He was raised to an altogether new plane of existence in which he was no longer mortal but "alive for ever and ever" (Rev. 1:18).

Secondly, our Christian hope of resurrection is not merely the survival of the soul. As Jesus himself said, "It is I myself! Touch me and see; a ghost does not have flesh and bones, as you see I have" (Luke 24:39). So the risen Lord was neither a revived corpse nor an immaterial ghost. Instead, he was raised from death and simultaneously changed into a new vehicle for his personality. Moreover, our resurrection body will be like his, and his was a remarkable combination of continuity and discontinuity. On the one hand, there was a clear link between his two bodies. The scars were still there in his hands, feet, and side, and Mary Magdalene recognized his voice. On the other hand, his body passed through the grave clothes, out of the sealed tomb, and through locked doors. So it evidently had new and undreamed-of powers.

The apostle Paul illustrated this combination from the relation between seeds and flowers. The continuity ensures that each seed produces its own flower. But the discontinuity is more striking, since out of a plain and even ugly little seed will spring a fragrant, colourful, and elegant flower. "So will it be with the resurrection of the dead" (1 Cor. 15:42). To sum up, what we are looking forward to is neither a resuscitation (in which we are raised but not changed) nor a survival (in which we are changed into a ghost but not raised bodily) but a resurrection (in which we are both raised and changed, transfigured and glorified simultaneously).

For further reading: 1 Corinthians 15:35–38

FRIDAY

Our Living Hope

IN HIS GREAT MERCY HE [GOD] HAS GIVEN US NEW BIRTH INTO A LIVING
HOPE THROUGH THE RESURRECTION OF JESUS CHRIST FROM THE DEAD...

1 Peter 1:3

The Christian hope focuses not only on our individual future (the resurrection of the body) but also on our cosmic future (the renewal of the universe). This promise is all the more relevant today in view of global warming and the threat of environmental disaster. On the whole, however, we Christians tend to think and talk too much of an ethereal heaven and too little about the new heaven and the new earth. Yet the whole of Scripture is shot through with this wider and more material expectation. Scripture begins with the original creation of the universe and ends in its last chapters with the creation of a new universe. And in between, the perspective is overshadowed by this Alpha and Omega, this Beginning and End.

The first outspoken expression of this is God's word in Isaiah 65: "See, I will create new heavens and a new earth" (v. 17). Then Jesus himself spoke of the *palingenesia*, literally "the new birth," but translated by the NIV "the renewal of all things" (Matt. 19:28). In the rest of the New Testament the three major apostolic authors (Paul, Peter, and John) all allude to the same theme. Paul writes that the whole creation will one day be liberated from its bondage to pain and decay (Rom. 8:18–25). Peter prophesies that the present heavens will be replaced by a new heaven and earth, which will be the home of righteousness and peace (2 Pet. 3:7–13).

Next, John writes that he saw the same replacement, together with the New Jerusalem, coming down out of heaven from God (Rev. 21:1–2). And in the same chapter John writes that the kings of the earth and the nations will bring their glory into the city, though "nothing impure will ever enter it" (Rev. 21:27). We need to be cautious in our interpretation of these verses, but they seem to mean that human culture will not all be destroyed but, once purged of every taint of evil, will be preserved to beautify the New Jerusalem.

To sum up, just as in the resurrection of the body, so in the renewal of the universe, the old will not all be destroyed but will be transformed. This is our living hope through the resurrection of Jesus Christ from the dead (1 Pet. 1:3).

For further reading: Romans 8:18–25

SATURDAY

Worldwide Mission

THEN JESUS CAME TO THEM AND SAID, "ALL AUTHORITY IN HEAVEN AND
ON EARTH HAS BEEN GIVEN TO ME. THEREFORE GO AND MAKE DISCIPLES
OF ALL NATIONS..."

Matthew 28:18–19

It is important to observe that the Great Commission to go and make disciples of all nations stems from the resurrection. Only after Jesus had risen could he claim universal authority, and only then could he exercise it in sending his disciples into the world. It was the resurrection that made the difference.

This was the thesis of Johannes Blauw, formerly Secretary of the Netherlands Missionary Council, in his book *The Missionary Nature of the Church*. He pointed out that in the Old Testament the prophets' vision of the last days was of a pilgrimage of the nations to Jerusalem, for Mount Zion would be exalted above all mountains, and all nations would flow into it like a river.

In the New Testament, however, the direction is reversed. The prophets' "centripetal missionary consciousness" is now replaced by a "centrifugal missionary activity." That is, instead of the nations flowing into the church, the church now goes out to the nations. And what was the turning point? It was the resurrection. The resurrected Lord Christ, who could claim universal authority, could exercise his authority in commanding his disciples to go. "Mission," Blauw concludes, "is the summons of the lordship of Christ."

The essential link between the universal authority of Jesus and the universal commission of the church pervades Scripture. For example, we see it in Daniel 7, where the Son of Man is given authority so that all nations will worship him. We also see it in Philippians 2:9–11, where we are told that God has super-exalted Jesus and given him the name above every name, that is, the rank above every rank, in order that every knee should bow to him and every tongue confess him Lord. If God wants universal homage to be given to the risen Lord, we must want it too.

For further reading: Matthew 28:16–20

PART III

FROM PENTECOST TO THE PAROUSIA

AN OVERVIEW OF THE ACTS, THE LETTERS, AND THE REVELATION (LIFE IN THE SPIRIT)

May to August

We have looked into the Old Testament and followed the life of Israel. We have looked into the Gospels and followed the life of Christ. We come now to the third section of the Bible, namely the Acts, the letters, and the Revelation, which will enable us to follow the life of the church.

Without the Acts, the New Testament would be seriously impoverished. For although we have four accounts of Jesus, we have only this one account of the early church. So the Acts occupies an indispensable place in the Bible. In it Luke tells us of the ascension of Jesus and the coming of the Spirit, of the ministries of Stephen and Philip, and of the dramatic conversions of Saul and Cornelius, after which Peter fades into the background and Luke's hero Paul dominates the stage.

But the Acts does more than provide a narrative of these events. Its value is also in the inspiration that it brings us. Calvin was right to call it "a kind of vast treasure."

Sunday: Luke's Two Volumes

Monday: The Promise of the Spirit

Tuesday: The Ascension of Jesus

Wednesday: Waiting and Praying

Thursday: Replacing Judas

Friday: The Pentecost Event

Saturday: The Trinity

SUNDAY

Luke's Two Volumes

IN MY FORMER BOOK, THEOPHILUS, I WROTE ABOUT ALL THAT
JESUS BEGAN TO DO AND TO TEACH UNTIL THE DAY HE WAS TAKEN
UP TO HEAVEN...

Acts 1:1–2

It is almost universally believed that Luke's "former book" was his Gospel. Indeed, what Luke has bequeathed to us is not so much two books as two parts of one book. Certainly, the preface to his Gospel introduces both parts. In it, as we have already seen, Luke refers to certain events that had taken place, which the apostles had witnessed and passed on to the next generation, which Luke himself had "carefully investigated ... from the beginning" (Luke 1:3), and which he had decided to put into writing. As an educated doctor he wrote polished Greek, and since on several occasions he was Paul's travelling companion (drawing attention to his presence by slipping into an unobtrusive "we"), he was an eyewitness of numerous events in the Acts. A. N. Sherwin-White, formerly reader in ancient history at Oxford University, reached this conclusion: "For Acts the confirmation of historicity is overwhelming."[1]

A caution is appropriate at this point, however. In reading the Acts we must not idealize the early church as if it had no blemishes. As we shall see, it had many.

What, then, shall we call this book that we are going to study for the next seven weeks? The popular title is "The Book of Acts" and is justified by a fourth-century codex. But it is hardly appropriate, since it does not indicate whose acts are in mind. "Acts of the Holy Spirit" makes a valid point but omits the human beings through whom the Spirit was working. The traditional title since the twentieth century has been "The Acts of [the] Apostles" with or without the definite article, and certainly apostles dominate the stage. But none of these does justice to the book's first verse, which attributes the recorded works and words to Jesus. The most accurate (though cumbersome) title would be something like "The Continuing Words and Deeds of Jesus by His Spirit through His Apostles."

For further reading: Luke 1:1–4

---

1 A. N. Sherwin-White, *Roman Society and Roman Law in the New Testament* (Oxford: Oxford University Press, 1963), 25.

The Promise of the Spirit

YOU WILL RECEIVE POWER WHEN THE HOLY SPIRIT COMES ON YOU;
AND YOU WILL BE MY WITNESSES... TO THE ENDS OF THE EARTH.

Acts 1:8

During the forty days that elapsed between Easter Day and Ascension Day, Jesus focused his teaching on two main topics, namely the kingdom of God and the Spirit of God whose coming he, his Father (in the Old Testament), and John the Baptist had all promised. It also seems that Jesus related those two topics to each other, as the prophets had done in the Old Testament, affirming that the outpouring of the Spirit would be one of the major blessings of the Messiah's kingdom. But the apostles' understanding of these things seems to have been confused, as is evident from what they asked Jesus. "Lord, are you at this time going to restore the kingdom to Israel?" (v. 6). Their question was full of errors.

Firstly, in asking about a restoration of the kingdom, it is clear that the apostles were still dreaming of a political liberation from Rome. But in his reply Jesus spoke of the Holy Spirit giving them power to witness. The kingdom of God is his rule in the lives of his people. It is spread by witnesses, not soldiers, through a gospel of peace, not a declaration of war.

Secondly, in asking about a restoration to Israel, it is evident that the apostles were still cherishing narrow, nationalistic aspirations. They hoped Jesus would give back to Israel her lost national independence, which the Maccabees had recovered for a brief intoxicating period in the second century BC. In his reply Jesus broadened their horizons. Their witness would indeed begin in Jerusalem and continue in nearby Judea, but it would radiate out "to the ends of the earth."

Thirdly, in asking whether Jesus was going to restore the kingdom to Israel "at this time," they were being presumptuous, as they already knew the answer. Jesus first told them that it was not for them to know times or dates, which the Father had fixed by his own authority, and then told them what they could know, namely that they were to witness in the power of the Spirit in ever-widening circles. In fact, the whole interim period between Pentecost and the Parousia (however long or short) was to be filled with the worldwide mission of the church.

For further reading: Acts 1:1–8

TUESDAY

The Ascension of Jesus

AFTER HE SAID THIS, HE WAS TAKEN UP BEFORE THEIR VERY EYES, AND A
CLOUD HID HIM FROM THEIR SIGHT.

Acts 1:9

There is widespread skepticism whether the ascension of Jesus was a literal, historical event. Surely, critics say, it belongs to a prescientific cosmology in which heaven was regarded as "up there," so that Jesus had to be "taken up" in order to get there. Must we not therefore demythologize the ascension? Then we can retain the truth that Jesus went to the Father, while at the same time stripping it of its primitive mythological clothing.

But there are two main reasons why we should reject this attempt to discredit the ascension as a literal event. Firstly, as we noted last Sunday, Luke relies heavily on the testimony of eyewitnesses. He does so here. Jesus was taken up "before their very eyes" until a cloud hid him "from their sight." As they were "looking intently" into the sky, the two angels spoke of their having "seen" him go into heaven (v. 10). Five times in this very brief account Luke stressed that the ascension took place visibly and was verified by eyewitnesses.

Secondly, the visible ascension had a readily intelligible purpose. It is not that Jesus needed to take a journey in space. It is silly to represent him as the first cosmonaut. No, in the transition from his earthly to his heavenly state, he could perfectly well have vanished, as on other occasions, and gone to the Father secretly and invisibly. The reason for a public and visible ascension is surely that he wanted the disciples to know that he had gone for good. During the forty days, he had kept appearing, disappearing, and reappearing. But now this interim period was over. This time his departure was final. So they were not to wait around for his next resurrection appearance. Instead, they were to wait for someone else, the Holy Spirit.

There was something fundamentally anomalous about their gazing up into the sky when they had been commissioned to go to the ends of the earth. It was the earth, not the sky, that was to be their preoccupation. Their calling was to be witnesses, not stargazers.

For further reading: Acts 1:9–12

WEDNESDAY

Waiting and Praying

THEY ALL JOINED TOGETHER CONSTANTLY IN PRAYER...

Acts 1:14

After Jesus had left them, the apostles walked back to Jerusalem "with great joy" (Luke 24:52) and waited for ten days until the Holy Spirit came. Luke tells us how they occupied their time during those days before Pentecost. In his Gospel he says that "they stayed continually at the temple, praising God" (Luke 24:53), whereas according to the Acts, "they all joined together constantly in prayer" in the room in which they were lodging. It was a healthy combination: continuous praise in the temple and continuous prayer in the home.

Who were these people who met together in praise and prayer? They numbered about 120, we are told. They included the eleven surviving apostles, whom Luke lists with only minor variations from the list he has given in his Gospel. In addition, he mentions "the women" (Acts 1:14), presumably meaning Mary Magdalene, Joanna, Susanna, and others who had supported Jesus and the apostles financially and who had found the tomb empty. Next, and separately, as occupying a position of particular honour, Luke adds "Mary the mother of Jesus" (v. 14), whose unique role in the birth of Jesus he has described in the first two chapters of his Gospel. "His brothers" are mentioned last (v. 14); they had probably come to faith because of the private resurrection appearance that Jesus had granted to James the Lord's brother (1 Cor. 15:7).

All these (the apostles, the women, and the mother and brothers of Jesus), together with the rest who made the number up to 120, "joined together constantly in prayer." Their praying was both united and persevering. No doubt the grounds of their unity and perseverance were the command and promise of Jesus. He had promised to send the Holy Spirit, and he had commanded them to wait for him to come and only then to begin their witness. From this we learn that God's promises do not render prayer superfluous. On the contrary, it is only God's promises that give us both the warrant to pray and the confidence that he will hear and answer our prayers.

For further reading: Acts 1:12–14

Thursday

Replacing Judas

IT IS NECESSARY TO CHOOSE ONE OF THE MEN WHO HAVE BEEN
WITH US... FOR ONE OF THESE MUST BECOME A WITNESS WITH US
OF HIS RESURRECTION.

Acts 1:21–22

Only one other event is recorded between the ascension and Pentecost, namely the appointment of another apostle to replace Judas. Peter stood up among the believers and quoted from Psalms 69 and 109 as biblical warrant for this act, especially Psalm 109:8: "May another take his place of leadership." It is instructive to note the three qualifications for what Peter called "this apostolic ministry" (Acts 1:25).

The first was *a personal appointment by Jesus*. Matthias was appointed not by the church but by Christ, as the Twelve had been (Luke 6:13). True, the 120 nominated two candidates, and they later cast lots, a method sanctioned by the Old Testament but not used after Pentecost. Essentially, however, they sought God's will by prayer. For though Jesus had gone to heaven, he was still accessible by prayer and was also the "heart knower." So they prayed, "Show us which of these two you have chosen" (Acts 1:24).

The second qualification was *an eyewitness experience of Jesus*. Mark and John had both made it plain why Jesus had chosen the Twelve. It was "that they might be with him" (Mark 3:14) and that in consequence they might testify to him (John 15:27). Similarly, Peter said: "It is necessary to choose one of the men who have been with us the whole time the Lord Jesus was living among us, beginning from John's baptism to the time when Jesus was taken up from us" (Acts 1:21–22). The third qualification was *a resurrection appearance of Jesus*, which is why Paul qualified (1 Cor. 9:1; 15:8–9). Judas's replacement must also have seen the risen Lord so that he might become a witness, with the other apostles, of his resurrection (Acts 1:22).

The stage is now set for the day of Pentecost. The apostles have received Christ's commission and seen his ascension. The apostolic team is complete again, ready to be his chosen witnesses. Only one thing is missing: the Spirit has not yet come. Though the place left vacant by Judas has been filled by Matthias, the place left vacant by Jesus has not yet been filled by the Spirit.

For further reading: Acts 1:15–26

The Pentecost Event

EXALTED TO THE RIGHT HAND OF GOD, HE [JESUS] HAS RECEIVED FROM THE FATHER THE PROMISED HOLY SPIRIT AND HAS POURED OUT WHAT YOU NOW SEE AND HEAR.

Acts 2:33

The day of Pentecost was a multifaceted event. Firstly, it was the final act of the saving ministry of Jesus before the Parousia, and in that respect it was as unrepeatable as Christmas Day, Good Friday, Easter Day, and Ascension Day. Next, it was the inauguration of the new era of the Spirit. Thirdly, it equipped the apostles for their unique teaching role. And fourthly, it can be understood as the first revival, in which God visited his people in mighty power.

Luke's narrative begins with a brief and matter-of-fact account of what happened. The Spirit of God came upon the waiting disciples, and his coming was accompanied by three supernatural signs – a sound like violent wind, what looked like tongues of fire, and speech in other languages. But what was the *glossolalia* that they spoke? Firstly, it was not the result of intoxication, as a small minority jested. Secondly, it was not (as some have suggested) a miracle of hearing. True, "each one heard their own language being spoken" (v. 6), but it was a phenomenon of hearing only because it had first been a phenomenon of speaking. Thirdly, it was not a case of incoherent speech that Luke mistook to be language. Fourthly, and positively, according to Luke, it was a supernatural ability to speak a recognizable language (that they had never learned) in which to proclaim the wonders of God.

Luke is at pains to emphasize the cosmopolitan nature of the crowd that gathered. Although they were all Jews from the dispersion, staying in Jerusalem, they came "from every nation under heaven" (v. 5), that is, from the Greco-Roman world situated round the Mediterranean basin. All the nations were, of course, not present literally, but they were representatively, for Luke deliberately includes in his list descendants of Shem, Ham, and Japheth, and has given us in Acts 2 a "table of nations" comparable to the one in Genesis 10. Ever since the early church fathers, commentators have seen the blessing of Pentecost as a deliberate and dramatic reversal of the curse of Babel. At Babel human languages were confused, and the nations were scattered; in Jerusalem the language barrier was supernaturally overcome as a sign that the nations would now be gathered together in Christ.

For further reading: Acts 2:1–13

The Trinity

THEREFORE GO AND MAKE DISCIPLES OF ALL NATIONS,
BAPTISING THEM IN THE NAME OF THE FATHER AND OF THE SON
AND OF THE HOLY SPIRIT...

Matthew 28:19

It was not until the ninth century that the first Sunday after Pentecost was popularly celebrated as Trinity Sunday. It is a very appropriate arrangement, which Cranmer cemented in his 1549 Prayer Book. For we have followed the church calendar through the Old Testament (the story of God the Father-Creator) and from Christmas to Easter (the story of Jesus), reaching a climax in the coming of the Spirit. It has been a historical unfolding of the Trinity.

I have myself found it helpful for many years, at the very beginning of each day, to recite the following trinitarian liturgy, which begins with praise and ends in prayer:

Almighty and everlasting God,
Creator and Sustainer of the universe, I worship you.
Lord Jesus Christ,
Saviour and Lord of the world, I worship you. Holy Spirit,
Sanctifier of the people of God, I worship you.
Glory be to the Father, and to the Son, and to the Holy Spirit.
As it was in the beginning, is now and ever shall be, world without end.
Amen.

Heavenly Father, I pray that this day
I may live in your presence and please you more and more.
Lord Jesus Christ, I pray that this day
I may take up my cross and follow you.
Holy Spirit, I pray that this day your fruit may ripen in
my life – love, joy, peace, patience, kindness, goodness, faithfulness,
gentleness and self-control.
Holy, blessed and glorious Trinity, three persons and one God,
have mercy upon me.
Amen.

For further reading: Ephesians 2:18

Luke records in the Acts nineteen significant Christian speeches, constituting about 25 per cent of his book. Nobody imagines that these speeches are verbatim accounts of what was said on each occasion. For one thing, they are too brief to be complete. For example, Peter's Pentecost sermon as recorded by Luke would have taken only about three minutes to deliver.

Liberal scholars in recent years have gone to the opposite extreme and argued that ancient historians like Thucydides invented speeches and inserted them into the mouths of their chief characters, and that Luke will have followed the same convention.

But conservative scholars have challenged this thesis. It fails to do justice to the historical conscience of Thucydides or to the claim of Luke to be recording carefully researched material. Rejecting both extremes of literalism and skepticism, it is better to regard the Acts speeches as reliable summaries of what was said on each occasion.

Sunday: Peter's Quotation from Joel

Monday: Jesus' Life and Ministry

Tuesday: Jesus' Death

Wednesday: Jesus' Resurrection

Thursday: Jesus' Exaltation

Friday: Jesus' Salvation

Saturday: The Gospel for Today

Peter's Quotation from Joel

THIS IS WHAT WAS SPOKEN BY THE PROPHET JOEL: "IN THE LAST DAYS,
GOD SAYS, I WILL POUR OUT MY SPIRIT ON ALL PEOPLE. YOUR SONS AND
DAUGHTERS WILL PROPHESY…"

Acts 2:16–17

What Luke has described in Acts 2:1–13 Peter now explains. The extraordinary phenomenon of Spirit-filled believers declaring God's wonders in foreign languages is the fulfilment of Joel's prediction that God would pour out his Spirit on all humankind.

Peter's exposition is similar to what in the Dead Sea Scrolls is called a *pesher*, that is, an interpretation of an Old Testament passage in the light of its fulfilment. So Peter introduces his sermon with the words "this is that" (v. 16 KJV). He deliberately changes Joel's "afterward" (Joel 2:28) to "in the last days," in order to emphasize that with the Spirit's coming the last days have come. He also reapplies the passage to Jesus, so that "the Lord" who brings salvation is no longer Yahweh but Jesus, who saves from sin and judgment everyone who calls on his name (v. 21).

It is the unanimous conviction of the New Testament authors that Jesus inaugurated the last days or messianic age and that the final proof of this was the outpouring of the Spirit, since this was the Old Testament promise of promises for the end time. This being so, we must be careful not to requote Joel's prophecy as if we are still awaiting its fulfilment. This is not how Peter understood and applied the text. The whole messianic era, which stretches between the two comings of Christ, is the age of the Spirit in which his ministry is one of abundance. The verb *pour out* seems to illustrate the generosity of God's gift of the Spirit (neither a drizzle nor even a shower but a tropical downpour), its finality (for what has been poured out cannot be gathered again), and its universality (widely distributed among the different groupings of humankind, irrespective of gender, age, or rank).

"And [they] will prophesy": that is, the universal gift (the Spirit) will lead to a universal ministry (prophecy). Clearly this is not a reference to the gift of prophecy, which only some receive. Rather, all God's people are prophets in the sense that all of us enjoy the knowledge of God through Christ by the Spirit.

For further reading: Acts 2:14–21

MONDAY

Jesus' Life and Ministry

FELLOW ISRAELITES, LISTEN TO THIS: JESUS OF NAZARETH WAS A MAN
ACCREDITED BY GOD TO YOU BY MIRACLES...

Acts 2:22

We saw yesterday that Peter applied Joel's prophecy to Pentecost. The best way to understand Pentecost, however, is not through the Old Testament prediction but through the New Testament fulfilment, not through Joel but through Jesus.

As Peter summoned the people of Israel to listen to him, his very first words following the quotation from Joel were "Jesus of Nazareth." In all evangelism it should be the same. Our chief and overriding responsibility is to point people to Jesus. In every evangelistic proclamation, the wise evangelist keeps bringing the conversation back to the person and work of Jesus Christ. As the apostle Paul was later to write at the beginning of Romans, the gospel of God concerns the Son of God. As T. R. Glover wrote in *The Jesus of History*, "Jesus remains the very heart and soul of the Christian movement, still controlling men, still capturing men."

Having named the name (of Jesus), Peter went on to tell his story in six stages, the first of which being his life and ministry: he "was a man accredited by God." This expression is very striking. We cannot claim that Peter was already affirming the divine-human person of Jesus. Nevertheless, Peter did sense that there was about Jesus both a human and a divine reality.

Moreover, Peter emphasized God's attestation of Jesus by bringing together the three New Testament words for the miracles that God performed publicly through him, namely *miracles, wonders,* and *signs.* The first word, *miracles (dunameis),* indicates their nature; they were exhibitions of God's power *(dunamis).* The second word, *wonders (terata),* indicates their consequence; they aroused amazement in those who witnessed them. Then the third word, *signs (sēmaia),* indicates their purpose; they were intended to have significance, to signify the claims of the Messiah.

For further reading: Acts 10:38–39

TUESDAY

Jesus' Death

THIS MAN WAS HANDED OVER TO YOU BY GOD'S DELIBERATE PLAN AND
FOREKNOWLEDGE; AND YOU... PUT HIM TO DEATH...

Acts 2:23

In this first Christian sermon ever preached, which we are considering this week, Peter moved straight from the life to the death of Jesus. The contrast is very marked, for "this man," whom God had accredited by miracles, they had put to death. More remarkable still is the way Peter attributed the responsibility for Jesus' death. On the one hand, Jesus had been "handed over" to them, not by Judas (although the same verb is used in the Gospels in reference to Judas's betrayal) but "by God's deliberate plan and foreknowledge." On the other hand, they, "with the help of wicked men" (v. 23) (presumably the Romans), put him to death by nailing him to the cross. Thus the same event, namely the death of Jesus by crucifixion, was attributed by Peter simultaneously to the purpose of God and the wickedness of people.

No fully developed doctrine of the atonement is yet expressed; it was too early for that. Nevertheless, already important indicators have begun to appear, due no doubt to Jesus' teaching about his death, which he would have given the apostles after his resurrection. Firstly, Peter already understood that in some way through Jesus' death God's saving purpose was being worked out.

Secondly, Peter had also begun to understand that human evil and divine providence were not incompatible with each other. God forwards his purposes even through the wickedness of people.

Thirdly, Peter describes Jesus as having been "put... to death by nailing him to the cross" (v. 23). Not long afterward, however, in Peter's second speech, he will describe Jesus' death not as being nailed to the cross but as being hanged on a tree (Acts 5:30 KJV). And that will be a profoundly theological statement, indicating that in his death Jesus bore in our place the curse of the broken law. As Paul was later to write, "Christ redeemed us from the curse of the law [that is, from the judgment that the law pronounces on those who break it] by becoming a curse for us" (Gal. 3:13). Thus the apostles Peter and Paul are at one in seeing the cross as a tree, the place of a curse.

For further reading: Galatians 3:10–14

Jesus' Resurrection

GOD HAS RAISED THIS JESUS TO LIFE, AND WE ARE ALL WITNESSES OF IT.

Acts 2:32

Having stated that Jesus had been put to death by men, Peter went on to say that God had raised him from the dead. He also made three statements about the resurrection of Jesus.

Firstly, God had freed him "from the agony of death" (v. 24). The Greek word for *agony* means "birth pains," so the resurrection was pictured as a regeneration, a new birth out of death into life.

Secondly, "it was impossible for death to keep its hold on him" (v. 24). Peter affirmed this moral impossibility without explaining it.

Thirdly, Peter saw in Psalm 16 a prediction of the Messiah's resurrection. In it the psalmist expressed his confidence that he would not be abandoned to death or corruption, but instead would be shown the path of life. But this prediction could not refer to David, since David had died and been buried, and his tomb was still there in Jerusalem. So, since David was a prophet, and since he knew that God had promised to set a distinguished descendant on his throne, he spoke of the resurrection of the Messiah (Acts 2:30–31).

Peter's use of Scripture may sound strange to us until we remember that all Old Testament Scripture bears witness to Christ, especially to his death, resurrection, and worldwide mission. That is its character and purpose. Jesus himself had said so both before and after his resurrection. In consequence, his disciples came naturally to read the Old Testament Christologically and to understand Old Testament references to God's anointed and David's royal descendants as finding their fulfilment in Jesus.

Having quoted Psalm 16 and applied it to the resurrection of Jesus, Peter concluded, "We are all witnesses of it" (Acts 2:32). Thus the spoken testimony of the apostles and the written predictions of the prophets converged. Or, as we would say, the Old and New Testament Scriptures together coincided in their witness to the resurrection of Christ.

For further reading: Acts 2:24–32

Jesus' Exaltation

THEREFORE LET ALL ISRAEL BE ASSURED OF THIS: GOD HAS MADE THIS
JESUS, WHOM YOU CRUCIFIED, BOTH LORD AND MESSIAH.

Acts 2:36

Peter now jumps straight from Jesus' resurrection from the dead to his exaltation to God's right hand. From this position of supreme honour and executive authority, having received the promise from the Father, Jesus has poured out the Spirit.

Peter again clinches his argument with an apt Old Testament quotation. As he has applied Psalm 16 to the Messiah's resurrection, so he now applies Psalm 110 to the Messiah's ascension:

The Lord said to my Lord:
"Sit at my right hand
until I make your enemies
a footstool for your feet."

Acts 2:34–35

David did not ascend to heaven any more than he had been preserved from decay by resurrection. Yet he designates as "my lord" him whom Yahweh had instructed to sit at his right hand. Jesus had already applied this verse to himself when he was teaching in the temple courts. He asked the Jewish leaders how David could call the Messiah "Lord" while at the same time he was David's son (Mark 12:35–37). It is significant that both the apostle Paul and the writer to the Hebrews also applied Psalm 110 to Jesus some time later (1 Cor. 15:25; Heb. 1:13).

Peter's conclusion is that all Israel should be assured that this same Jesus, whom they had repudiated and crucified, God had now made "both Lord and Christ" (Acts 2:36). Not, of course, that Jesus became Lord and Christ only at the time of his ascension, for throughout his public ministry he was (and indeed claimed to be) both. It is rather that now God had exalted him to be in reality and power what he already was by right.

For further reading: Acts 2:33–36

FRIDAY

Jesus' Salvation

REPENT AND BE BAPTISED, EVERY ONE OF YOU, IN THE NAME OF JESUS
CHRIST FOR THE FORGIVENESS OF YOUR SINS. AND YOU WILL RECEIVE
THE GIFT OF THE HOLY SPIRIT.

Acts 2:38

Conscience stricken, Peter's hearers asked anxiously what they must do. Peter replied that they must repent, completely changing their minds about Jesus, and be baptized in his name, submitting to the humiliation of baptism (which Jews regarded as necessary for Gentile converts only) and submitting to it in the name of the very person they had previously rejected. This would be a clear public token of their repentance and also of their faith, since Peter later called them believers.

Then they would receive two free gifts of God – the forgiveness of their sins (even of the sin of rejecting God's Christ) and the gift of the Holy Spirit to regenerate, indwell, and transform them. For they must not think that the Pentecostal gift was for the apostles alone, or for the 120 disciples who had waited ten days for the Spirit to come, or for any elitist group, or even for that generation alone. God had not placed any such limitation on his offer and gift. On the contrary, the promise or gift or baptism of the Spirit (interchangeable terms) was for those also who were listening to Peter's speech and for their children in subsequent generations, indeed, for all who were far off (whether Jews of the dispersion or even the Gentile world), in fact, for all without exception whom the Lord would call to him. For the gift of God is coextensive with the call of God.

Next came Peter's final appeal: "Save yourselves from this corrupt generation" (v. 40). Peter was not asking for private and individual conversions only but for a public identification with other believers, thus transferring their membership to the messianic community.

The amazing response to Peter's appeal is now recorded. About three thousand people accepted his message and were baptized. According to Peter's promise, they must have received forgiveness and the Spirit, although this time apparently with no supernatural signs. At least, Luke makes no mention of phenomena like wind or fire or languages.

For further reading: Acts 2:37–41

The Gospel for Today

FOR WHAT I RECEIVED I PASSED ON TO YOU AS OF FIRST IMPORTANCE:
THAT CHRIST DIED FOR OUR SINS ACCORDING TO THE SCRIPTURES...
THAT HE WAS RAISED ON THE THIRD DAY ACCORDING TO THE
SCRIPTURES...

1 Corinthians 15:3–4

I have myself found it an aid to faithfulness to express the apostles' message in the following terms. Firstly, *the gospel events*. Although the apostles rehearsed the whole saving career of Jesus, including his life and ministry, his exaltation, and his future coming, they concentrated on his death and resurrection both as historical happenings and as significant saving events. Secondly, *the gospel witnesses*. The apostles appealed to a twofold evidence to authenticate Jesus so that in the mouth of two witnesses the truth might be established (Deut. 19:15). The first was the Old Testament Scriptures, and the second was the testimony of the apostles themselves. "We are witnesses," Peter kept repeating. Thus the one Christ has a double attestation. We have no liberty to preach a Christ of our own fantasy or even to focus on our own experience, since we were not eyewitnesses of the historical Jesus. Our responsibility is rather to speak of the authentic Christ of the Old and New Testament Scriptures. The primary witnesses are the prophets and apostles; our witness is always secondary to theirs.

Thirdly, *the gospel promises*. The gospel is good news not only of what Jesus did by his death and resurrection but also of what he offers us as a result, namely the forgiveness of our sins (to wipe away the past) and the gift of the Spirit (to make us new people). Together these constitute salvation or freedom; they are both publicly signified in baptism. Fourthly, *the gospel conditions*. What the gospel demands is a radical turn from sin to Christ, which takes the form inwardly of repentance and faith, and outwardly of baptism. By these things we change allegiance, as we are transferred into the new community of Jesus. Here, then, is our fourfold message – two events (Christ's death and resurrection), as attested by two witnesses (prophets and apostles), on the basis of which God makes two promises (forgiveness and the Spirit) on two conditions (repentance and faith, with baptism). There is a wholeness about the biblical gospel.

For further reading: 1 Corinthians 15:1–11

Although I believe that my readers come from different churches or denominations, at least two things surely unite us. Firstly, we are all committed to the church. At least, I hope we are. I hope that none of my readers is that grotesque anomaly – an unchurched Christian – for the New Testament knows nothing of such a monster! No, we are not only committed to Christ, we are committed to the body of Christ. Indeed, we cannot be one without the other. For the church lies at the centre of the purpose of God. God's purpose, conceived in a past eternity, being worked out in history, to be perfected in a future eternity, is not just to save isolated individuals and so perpetuate our loneliness, but rather to call out a people for himself and to build his church. Indeed, Christ died for us not only to redeem us from sin but to purify for himself a people who are enthusiastic for good works (Titus 2:14). So, then, the reason we are committed to the church is that God is.

Secondly, we are all concerned for the renewal of the church. In many parts of the world the church is spreading rapidly, but it is often growth without depth. There is much superficiality everywhere. We need to recover the biblical vision of a renewed church.

Sunday: God's Vision for His Church

Monday: Study

Tuesday: Fellowship

Wednesday: Sharing

Thursday: Worship

Friday: Evangelism

Saturday: The Marks of a Living Church

God's Vision for His Church

THEY DEVOTED THEMSELVES TO THE APOSTLES' TEACHING AND TO
FELLOWSHIP, TO THE BREAKING OF BREAD AND TO PRAYER.

Acts 2:42

What is God's vision for his church? Luke tells us. Having described what happened on the day of Pentecost, and having supplied an explanation of it through Peter's Christ-centred sermon, Luke goes on to show us the effects of Pentecost by giving us a beautiful little cameo of the Spirit-filled church in Jerusalem. Of course, the church did not begin that day. It is incorrect to call the day of Pentecost the birthday of the church. For the church as the people of God goes back at least four thousand years to Abraham. What happened at Pentecost was that the remnant of God's people became the Spirit-filled body of Christ.

What, then, are the distinguishing marks of a living church? To answer this question we have to go back to the beginning and take a fresh look at the first Christian church in Jerusalem. At the same time, it is essential that we are realistic. We have a tendency to romanticize the early church. We look at it through tinted spectacles. We speak of it in whispers, as if it had no faults. Then we miss the rivalries, the hypocrisies, the immoralities, and the heresies that troubled the early church as they trouble the church today.

Nevertheless, one thing is certain. The early church, for all its excesses and failures, had been deeply and radically stirred by the Holy Spirit.

So we come back to our question: What did that first-century church look like? What evidences did it give of the presence and power of the Holy Spirit? If we can answer these questions, we will be well on the way to discovering the marks of a living church in the twenty-first century.

For further reading: John 17:6–26

MONDAY

Study

THEY DEVOTED THEMSELVES TO THE APOSTLES' TEACHING...
Acts 2:42

Luke focuses on four marks of the Jerusalem church. The first is very surprising; we would probably not have chosen it. It is that a living church is a learning church. "They devoted themselves to the apostles' teaching." This is the very first thing Luke tells us. The Holy Spirit, we might say, opened a school in Jerusalem that day. The schoolteachers were the apostles, whom Jesus had appointed and trained. And there were three thousand pupils in the kindergarten. It was a truly remarkable situation.

We note that those new Spirit-filled converts were not enjoying a mystical experience that led them to neglect their intellect, despise theology, or stop thinking. On the contrary, they concentrated on receiving instruction. I do not hesitate to say that anti-intellectualism and the fullness of the Spirit are mutually incompatible. For who is the Spirit? Jesus called him "the Spirit of truth," so that wherever he is at work, truth matters.

Notice also that those believers did not suppose that, because they had received the Holy Spirit, he was the only teacher they needed and they could dispense with human teachers. No, they sat at the apostles' feet. They were eager to learn all they could. They knew that Jesus had appointed them teachers. So they submitted to the apostles' authority, which was authenticated by miracles. For if verse 42 tells us of the apostles' teaching, verse 43 tells us that the apostles did many signs and wonders. Similarly, some years later Paul referred to his miracles as "the marks of a true apostle" (2 Cor. 12:12).

How is it possible, then, for us to devote ourselves to the apostles' teaching and submit to their authority? For we have to insist that there are no apostles in the church today. To be sure, there are bishops, pioneer missionaries, and other church leaders, and we might perhaps call their ministries apostolic. But there are no apostles who have an authority comparable to that of the apostles Peter, John, and Paul. So the only way we can submit to the apostles' authority is to submit to their teaching in the New Testament, for it is there that it has come down to us in its definitive form. Fidelity to the apostles' teaching is the very first mark of an authentic church.

For further reading: 1 Timothy 4:1–13

TUESDAY

Fellowship

IF WE WALK IN THE LIGHT, AS HE IS IN THE LIGHT, WE HAVE FELLOWSHIP
WITH ONE ANOTHER...

1 John 1:7

If the first mark of a living church is study, the second is fellowship, and today and tomorrow we will focus on this topic. "They devoted themselves to the apostles' teaching and to the fellowship" (Acts 2:42). This is the well-known Greek word *koinōnia*, which expresses our common Christian life, what we share as Christian believers. It bears witness to two complementary truths, namely what we share *in* and what we share *out*.

Firstly, *koinōnia* expresses what we share in together, especially the grace of God. "Our fellowship," wrote the apostle John, "is with the Father and with his Son, Jesus Christ" (1 John 1:3), and the apostle Paul added "the fellowship of the Holy Spirit" (2 Cor. 13:14). So authentic fellowship is trinitarian fellowship, our common participation in the Father, the Son, and the Holy Spirit. Many factors separate us – ethnicity, nationality, culture, gender, and age – but we are united in having the same heavenly Father, the same Saviour and Lord, and the same indwelling Spirit. It is our common share in him and in his grace that makes us one.

Secondly, *koinōnia* expresses what we share out together. *Koinōnia* is the word Paul used to refer to the collection he was organizing among the Greek churches for the benefit of the poverty-stricken churches in Judea. And the adjective *koinōnikos* means "generous."

It is on this aspect of the word that Luke concentrates:

All the believers were together and had everything in common. They sold property and possessions to give to anyone who had need.

Acts 2:44–45

These are very disturbing verses. We tend to jump over them rather quickly in order to avoid their challenge. We will face them tomorrow.

For further reading: Acts 4:32–35

Sharing

ALL THE BELIEVERS WERE TOGETHER AND HAD EVERYTHING IN COMMON
[*KOINŌNIA*].

Acts 2:44

A few miles east of Jerusalem at that time the Essene leaders of the Qumran community were committed to the common ownership of property, and the members of the monastic community handed over all their money and possessions when they were initiated.

Certainly Jesus does call some to total voluntary poverty, like the rich young ruler, Saint Francis of Assisi and his followers, and Mother Teresa and her sisters, maybe to witness to the truth that a human life does not consist in the abundance of our possessions. But not all Jesus' followers are called to this. The prohibition of private property is a Marxist, not a Christian, doctrine. Besides, even in Jerusalem the selling and the giving were voluntary, for we read in verse 46 that they "broke bread in their homes." In their homes? But I thought they had all sold their homes and their furniture! Apparently not. And the sin of Ananias and Sapphira recorded in Acts 5 was not that they kept back part of their property but that they kept part while pretending to give it all. Their sin was not greed but deceit. The apostle Peter was clear in his words to Ananias: "Didn't it belong to you before it was sold? And after it was sold, wasn't the money at your disposal?" (Acts 5:4). In other words, all Christians have to make a conscientious decision before God how we use our possessions.

Nevertheless, we must not avoid the challenge of this passage. Those early Christians loved one another, which is hardly surprising, since the first fruit of the Spirit is love. In particular, they cared for their impoverished brothers and sisters, so they shared with them their goods. This principle of voluntary Christian sharing is surely a permanent one. Those of us who live in affluent circumstances must simplify our economic lifestyle, not because we imagine that this would solve the macroeconomic problems of the world, but out of solidarity with the poor.

So a Spirit-filled church is a generous church. Generosity has always been a characteristic of the people of God. Our God is a generous God; his people must be generous too.

For further reading: Acts 5:1–11

Thursday

Worship

THEY DEVOTED THEMSELVES... TO THE BREAKING OF BREAD
AND TO PRAYER.

Acts 2:42

We have seen that a living church is a learning and a caring church. It is also a worshipping church. "The breaking of bread" is evidently a reference to the Lord's Supper, though probably with a fellowship meal included, and "prayer" is more literally "the prayers," alluding to prayer services or prayer meetings. What strikes me most about the worship of the early church is its balance in two respects.

Firstly, their worship was both formal and informal; for it took place both in the temple and in their homes (v. 46). We note that the first believers did not immediately abandon the institutional church. Doubtless they were anxious to reform it according to the gospel, for they knew that its sacrifices had been fulfilled in the sacrifice of Christ. But they continued to attend the traditional prayer services that must have had a degree of formality. They also supplemented these with more informal home meetings and with their own distinctively Christian worship or Eucharist. We should not polarize between the structured and the unstructured, the liturgical and the spontaneous. The early church had both. So should we. Every congregation of any size should break itself into small groups.

Secondly, the early church's worship was both joyful and reverent. There is no doubt about their joy. The Greek word *agalliasis* in verse 46 denotes an exuberant outburst of joy. For the fruit of the Spirit is joy, and sometimes a more uninhibited joy than our ecclesiastical traditions encourage. When I attend some church services, I think I have come to a funeral by mistake. Everybody is dressed in black. Nobody smiles or talks. The hymns or songs are played at the pace of a snail or a tortoise, and the whole atmosphere is lugubrious. But Christianity is a joyful religion, and every meeting or service should be a celebration of joy. At the same time, the early church's worship was never irreverent. Yet today, if some church services are funereal, others are flippant. But if joy is a mark of authentic worship, so is reverence. "Everyone was filled with awe" (v. 43). The living God had visited Jerusalem, and they bowed down before him in that mixture of wonder and humility we call worship.

For further reading: Psalm 95

FRIDAY

Evangelism

AND THE LORD ADDED TO THEIR NUMBER DAILY THOSE WHO
WERE BEING SAVED.

Acts 2:47

So far we have considered the study, fellowship, and worship of the early church, for it is to these three activities that Luke says they devoted themselves. Yet these are aspects of the church's interior life; they tell us nothing about its outreach to the world.

This illustrates the great danger of textual preaching, that is, of isolating a text from its context. Acts 2:42 is a very popular text for preachers. Millions of sermons have been preached on it, as if it gave a comprehensive account of the church. But on its own it presents a disastrously unbalanced picture of the church. Verse 42 gives the impression that the early church was interested only in studying at the feet of the apostles, caring for its own members, and worshipping God. In other words, it was living in a ghetto, preoccupied with its own domestic life and ignoring the plight of the lonely and the lost outside.

But this was not the case. The early Christians were also committed to mission. But it is not until verse 47 that we learn this. Verse 47 corrects the imbalance of verse 42, for it teaches us three lessons about the early church's evangelism. Firstly, the Lord Jesus himself did it. "The Lord added to their number." Doubtless he did it through the preaching of the apostles, the everyday witness of church members, and their common life of love. But he did it. Only he can open the eyes of the blind, unstop the ears of the deaf, give life to the dead, and so add people to the church.

Secondly, Jesus did two things together: "The Lord added to their number... those who were being saved." He did not add people to the church without saving them, nor save them without adding them to the church. Salvation and church membership still go together.

Thirdly, he did both daily. Those early Christians did not regard evangelism as an occasional activity. Day by day people were being added to the church. We need to recover this expectation today.

For further reading: 1 Thessalonians 1:1–10

SATURDAY

The Marks of a Living Church

THEY... ATE TOGETHER WITH GLAD AND SINCERE HEARTS, PRAISING GOD
AND ENJOYING THE FAVOUR OF ALL THE PEOPLE.

Acts 2:46–47

Looking back over the four marks of a living church, which Luke has singled out, it is now clear that they concern the relationships of the early Christians. Firstly, *they were related to the apostles*. They devoted themselves to the apostles' teaching. They sat at the apostles' feet and submitted to their authority. A living church is an apostolic church, committed to believe and obey the teaching of the apostles.

Secondly, *they were related to each other*. They devoted themselves to the fellowship. They loved each other. A living church is a caring church. Thirdly, *they were related to God*. They worshipped God in the breaking of bread and the prayers, formally and informally, with joy and with reverence. A living church is a worshipping church.

Fourthly, *they were related to the world*. They reached out in witness and mission. A living church is an evangelizing church.

Some years ago in the capital city of a Latin American republic I was introduced to a group of Christian students who had dropped out of the church. They called themselves *Cristianos Descolgados*, "unhooked Christians." They had visited every church in their city and had been unable to find what they were looking for. What was that? To my astonishment, without knowing Luke's picture, they went straight through his four marks. They were looking for a church in which:

1. The Bible was taught.
2. There was a loving, caring fellowship.
3. There was sincere and humble worship.
4. There was a compassionate outreach to the world outside.

There is no need for us to wait for the Holy Spirit to come. He did come on the day of Pentecost, and he has never left the church. But we need to humble ourselves before him and seek his fullness, direction, and power. For then our churches will at least approximate to Luke's beautiful ideal in apostolic teaching, loving fellowship, living worship, and outgoing, ongoing evangelism.

For further reading: Acts 2:37–47

Luke has painted an idyllic picture of the early Christian community in Jerusalem. Commissioned by Christ and empowered by the Spirit, the church was about to set sail on her great missionary voyage. But almost immediately a perilous storm blew up that threatened to engulf her.

Alternatively, we might say that, if the chief actor in the story of Acts 1 and 2 was the Holy Spirit, the chief actor in Acts 3 to 6 seems to have been Satan. True, he is mentioned by name only once (5:3), but his malevolent activity may be discerned throughout.

The devil's crudest tactic was physical violence or persecution; he tried to crush the church by force. Next, he resorted to moral corruption, attempting to infiltrate the church through the deceit of Ananias and Sapphira. His third and subtlest tactic was social distraction. He tried to deflect the apostles from their priority tasks of preaching and prayer. If he had succeeded, and the apostles had given up preaching, an untaught church would have been exposed to every wind of false teaching. So these were the devil's three weapons – persecution, corruption, and distraction. He has not changed his tactics.

Sunday: The Healing of the Lame Man

Monday: Peter's Second Sermon

Tuesday: The Outbreak of Persecution

Wednesday: The Continuance of Persecution

Thursday: Ananias and Sapphira

Friday: A Problem and its Solution

Saturday: A Vital Principle

The Healing of the Lame Man

IT IS JESUS' NAME... THAT COMPLETELY HEALED HIM, AS YOU CAN ALL
SEE.

Acts 3:16

What triggered the opposition of the Jewish authorities was the healing of the lame man outside one of the temple gates, together with Peter's second sermon, which followed it.

Peter and John the apostles were going up to the temple at three o'clock one afternoon, which was the hour of prayer. It was observed by all pious Jews like Daniel and God fearers like Cornelius. The apostles' arrival at the temple coincided with the arrival of a man lame from birth who was being carried, presumably by friends and relatives, so that he could beg from those who came to worship. The beggar's post, Luke says, was "the temple gate called Beautiful" (v. 2). Commentators mostly identify this as the Nicanor Gate, which was the temple's main eastern entrance. According to Josephus, being made of Corinthian brass, it "greatly excelled those that were only covered over with silver and gold." It was about seventy-five feet high and had huge double doors.

But at the foot of this magnificent structure the lame man sat begging. Luke's medical interest is betrayed in the brief clinical history he gives. The patient was a congenital case, he tells us; he had never walked. He was now more than forty years old, and he was so severely disabled that he had to be carried and put down every day to beg. But when Peter told him in the name of Jesus of Nazareth to get up and walk, an orthopedic miracle took place. His feet and ankles became strong – so strong and agile that he jumped to his feet and began to walk, which he had never done before. Not only so, but he now accompanied Peter and John into the temple, walking, leaping, and praising God. It was an outstanding fulfilment of the messianic prophecy: "Then will the lame leap like a deer" (Isa. 35:6).

A crowd quickly gathered. For they saw him "walking and praising God" (Acts 3:9). They recognized him as the same man who had been a familiar sight for decades, since he had sat there every day begging. "And they were filled with wonder and amazement at what had happened to him" (v. 10).

For further reading: Acts 3:1–10

Peter's Second Sermon

PETER... SAID TO THEM: "... THE GOD OF ABRAHAM, ISAAC AND JACOB,
THE GOD OF OUR FATHERS, HAS GLORIFIED HIS SERVANT JESUS."

Acts 3:12–13

Astonished by the healing of the lame man, which they had witnessed, a crowd assembled in one of the temple cloisters. Peter seized the opportunity to preach. Just as the Pentecost event had been the text for his first sermon, so the healing of the cripple became the text for his second. Both were mighty acts of the exalted Christ. Both were signs that proclaimed him Lord and Saviour. Both aroused the crowd's amazement.

Peter began by ascribing all the credit to Jesus. He went on to declare with outspoken courage that they had disowned him (by killing him) but God had vindicated him (by raising him).

Perhaps the most remarkable feature of Peter's sermon is its Christ-centredness. He directed the crowd's attention away from both the healed cripple and the apostles themselves to the resurrected and exalted Christ. In his testimony to Jesus, he attributed to him a cluster of significant titles, beginning with "Jesus Christ of Nazareth" (v. 6) and continuing with "[God's] servant" (v. 13), "the Holy and Righteous One" (v. 14), "the author of life" (v. 15), and "the prophet like [Moses]" (v. 22). Next, Peter calls on the crowd to repent so that they may inherit the blessings of repentance – especially forgiveness and refreshment until Christ comes to consummate all things. These Christ-centred promises were already foreshadowed in the Old Testament, and Peter mentioned some of them. It is impressive that he regards the many and varied strands of Old Testament prophecy as a united testimony.

This comprehensive witness to Jesus as rejected by people but vindicated by God, as the fulfilment of all Old Testament prophecy, as demanding repentance and promising blessing, and as the author and giver of life, physically to the healed cripple and spiritually to all those who believe, aroused the indignation and antagonism of the authorities. The devil cannot endure the exaltation of Jesus Christ. So he stirred up the Sanhedrin to persecute the apostles.

For further reading: Acts 3:11–26

TUESDAY

The Outbreak of Persecution

[THE AUTHORITIES] SEIZED PETER AND JOHN... AND... PUT THEM IN JAIL.

Acts 4:3

Luke makes it plain that the persecution of the apostles was initiated by the Sadducees. They were the ruling class of wealthy aristocrats, who had several reasons for resenting the teaching of the apostles. Because they were not expecting a Messiah, they were exasperated by the apostles' testimony to Jesus. Because they rejected the supernatural, "they were greatly disturbed because the apostles were... proclaiming in Jesus the resurrection of the dead" (v. 2). Because they collaborated with the Romans, they feared the subversive influence of the Christian movement, and they were determined to stop it spreading. They regarded the apostles as both agitators and heretics.

So Peter and John were arrested, jailed, and the following morning brought before the Sanhedrin, including Annas and Caiaphas, who had figured prominently in the trial and condemnation of Jesus. Was history to repeat itself? The court's interrogation began with a direct question to the defendants: "By what power or what name did you do this?" (v. 7). Peter replied without hesitation that it was by the name of Jesus of Nazareth, whom they had killed and God had raised. He then moved on from healing to salvation and declared that Jesus was the one and only Saviour (v. 12).

The court forbade Peter and John to preach or teach "in this name," which they were reluctant even to pronounce (v. 17). But the apostles said they could not help speaking about what they had seen and heard. The court threatened them further and let them go.

Immediately the apostles went to their own people, reported everything that had happened, and then turned to prayer. Having been bold in witness, they were now bold in prayer. Before they uttered any petition, however, they filled their minds with the God they were praying to. They called him *Despotēs*, "sovereign Lord," and they then reminded themselves that he is the God of creation, of revelation, and of history. Only now, with their vision of God clarified, and they themselves humbled before him, were they ready to pray, not for their safety, but that they might preach the gospel "with great boldness" (v. 29) and that God would confirm his Word with signs and wonders.

For further reading: Acts 4:23–31

The Continuance of Persecution

THE APOSTLES LEFT THE SANHEDRIN, REJOICING BECAUSE THEY HAD
BEEN COUNTED WORTHY OF SUFFERING DISGRACE FOR THE NAME.

Acts 5:41

Angered by the failure of their first assault on the apostles, the authorities resolved to take further action. This time they arrested most if not all the apostles and put them in the public jail. But during the night an angel rescued them and told them to preach the gospel in the temple courts, which they did. In their defence the apostles were concerned to uplift Christ, whom God had raised and exalted. The Council were infuriated by this outspoken testimony to Jesus and wanted to put them to death.

But at this point the widely respected Pharisee Gamaliel made a diplomatic intervention. Using two earlier rebels as precedents (whose historical details are uncertain), he advised the Council to leave the apostles alone, since if their activity was of human origin, it would fail, whereas if it were from God, it could not be stopped; rather, the Council would be found fighting against God. We should not, however, credit Gamaliel with an invariable principle, since at least in the short run evil sometimes triumphs, while good sometimes fails.

The Council accepted Gamaliel's advice, had the apostles flogged, repeated the order not to speak in the name of Jesus, and let them go. The apostles' reaction arouses our admiration. Their backs cruelly lacerated and bleeding, they nevertheless left the Sanhedrin rejoicing that they were counted worthy to suffer shame for the Name (v. 41). Luke has now completed his account of the two waves of persecution that broke over the infant church. In the first the Council issued a prohibition and a warning, which led the apostles to pray for boldness to go on preaching. In the second the Council repeated the prohibition and flogged them, which led to their praising God for the honour of suffering dishonour for Christ.

The devil has never given up his attempt to destroy the church by force. Still today in many cultures the church is being persecuted. But we don't need to fear for its survival. As Tertullian wrote in his Apology, "Kill us, torture us, condemn us, grind us to dust... The more you mow us down, the more we grow; the seed is the blood of Christians."

For further reading: John 12:20–26

Thursday

Ananias and Sapphira

Didn't it belong to you before it was sold? And after it was sold, wasn't the money at your disposal?

Acts 5:4

The story of the deceit and death of Ananias and Sapphira is important partly because it illustrates Luke's honesty as a historian (he did not suppress this sordid episode) and partly because it throws light on the interior life of the early church (it was not all romance and righteousness). Several commentators have suggested a parallel between Ananias and Achan – the Achan who stole money and clothing after the destruction of Jericho. Here is F. F. Bruce's comment: "The story of Ananias is to the Book of Acts what the story of Achan is to the Book of Joshua. In both narratives an act of deceit interrupts the victorious progress of the people of God."

It seems that Ananias and Sapphira had conspired to commit some kind of misappropriation. But Luke concentrates rather on their hypocrisy. They brought to the apostles only a proportion of the sale of their property, while pretending to bring it all. They wanted the credit for generosity without the inconvenience of it. So they told a brazen lie. Peter saw behind their hypocrisy the subtle activity of Satan. So he confronted Ananias: "How is it that Satan has so filled your heart that you have lied to the Holy Spirit…? You have not lied just to human beings but to God" (vv. 3–4). Ananias dropped dead under the judgment of God, and so did Sapphira some three hours later.

There are at least two valuable lessons to learn from this tragic story. Firstly, we perceive the gravity of their sin. Luke records in his Gospel Jesus' denunciation of hypocrisy. If the hypocrisy of Ananias and Sapphira had not been publicly exposed and punished, the ideal of an open fellowship in the church would have been destroyed from the beginning.

Secondly, we learn the necessity of church discipline. The church has tended to oscillate in this area between extreme severity (disciplining members for even the most trivial offences) and extreme laxity (exercising no discipline at all, even for the most serious offences). It is a good general rule that secret sins should be dealt with secretly, private sins privately, and only public sins publicly.

For further reading: Acts 5:1–11

Friday

A Problem and its Solution

WE WILL TURN THIS RESPONSIBILITY OVER TO THEM AND WILL GIVE OUR ATTENTION TO PRAYER AND THE MINISTRY OF THE WORD.

Acts 6:3–4

The devil's next attack was the cleverest of the three. Having failed to overcome the church by either persecution or corruption, he now tried distraction. If he could preoccupy the apostles with social administration (which, though essential, was not their calling), they would neglect their God-given responsibilities to preach and to pray, and so leave the young church without adequate defence against false doctrine.

A regrettable *goggysmos* (a grumbling complaint) had broken out between the two groups called *Hellenistai* (Grecian Jews) and *Hebraioi* (Hebraic Jews). In particular the *Hellenistai* were complaining against the *Hebraioi* that their widows were being neglected in the daily distribution of food. The apostles saw that the problem was deeper than one of cultural tension. The administration was threatening to occupy all their time and so inhibit them from the work that Christ had specifically entrusted to them, namely preaching and teaching, with prayer.

So the Twelve wisely called a church meeting and shared the problem with the disciples. It would not be right, they said, for them to neglect the ministry of the Word in order to wait on tables. It was a question of calling. So they proposed that the church members should choose seven men, full of wisdom and the Spirit, to whom the apostles could delegate the care of the widows. Then they (the apostles) would be able to give priority to preaching and prayer. This delegation of social work to the Seven may be the origin of the diaconate, although they are not called *diakonoi*.

The church saw the point of the apostles' plan and put it into effect, choosing seven men, all with Greek names, and all Spirit-filled believers, including Stephen and Philip. They were presented to the apostles, who prayed for them and commissioned and authorized them to exercise this ministry by the laying on of hands. The immediate problem was solved.

For further reading: Acts 6:1–6

Saturday

A Vital Principle

So Christ himself gave the apostles, the prophets, the
evangelists, the pastors and teachers, to equip his people for
works of service, so that the body of Christ may be built up...

Ephesians 4:11–12

A vital principle is illustrated in the appointment of the Seven. It is this. Although God calls all his people to ministry, he calls different people to different ministries, and those who are called to the ministry of the Word and prayer must on no account allow themselves to be distracted from these priorities. It is surely deliberate that the work of the Twelve and the work of the Seven are both called *diakonia*, meaning "ministry" or "service." The former is "the ministry of the word" (Acts 6:4) or pastoral work, while the latter is the ministry of tables (v. 2, literally "to serve tables") or social work. Both are Christian ministries. Both require spiritual people to exercise them, and both can be full-time ministries. The only difference between them lies in the form their ministry takes, requiring different gifts and different callings. We do a great disservice to the church when we refer to the pastorate as "the ministry." The use of the definite article implies that we think the ordained pastorate is the only ministry there is. But *diakonia* is a generic word for service; it lacks specificity until a descriptive adjective is added – pastoral, social, political, medical, educational, and many others. We need to recover this vision of the wide diversity of ministries to which God calls his people.

In particular, it is vital for the health and growth of the church that pastors and people in the local congregation learn this lesson. The apostles were not too busy for ministry, but were preoccupied with the *wrong* ministry. So are many pastors today. Instead of concentrating on the ministry of the Word, they have become overwhelmed with administration. Sometimes it is the pastor's fault (he wants to keep all the reins in his own hands), and sometimes the people's (they want him to be a general factotum). In either case, the consequences are disastrous. The standards of preaching and teaching decline, and the laypeople cannot exercise their God-given roles. As a direct result of the action of the apostles, "the word of God spread" and "the number of disciples... increased rapidly" (v. 7). But of course! The spread of the Word and the growth of the church go hand in hand.

For further reading, see Luke's six summaries of growth: Acts 6:7; 9:31; 12:24;
16:5; 19:20; 28:30–31

After the coming of the Spirit and the counter-attack of Satan (whose overthrow Luke has celebrated [Acts 6:7]), the church is almost ready to initiate its worldwide mission. So far it has been limited to Jews and restricted to Jerusalem. Now, however, the Holy Spirit is about to thrust his people out into the wider world, and the apostle Paul (Luke's hero) is to be God's chosen instrument to pioneer this development. But first, in the next six chapters of the Acts, Luke explains how the foundations of the Gentile mission were laid by two remarkable men (Stephen the martyr and Philip the evangelist), followed by two remarkable conversions (of Saul the Pharisee and Cornelius the centurion). These four men, each in his own way, together with the apostle Peter, through whose ministry Cornelius was converted, made an indispensable contribution to the global expansion of the church.

Sunday: Stephen's Witness

Monday: Stephen's Martyrdom

Tuesday: Philip in Samaria

Wednesday: Philip and an Ethiopian Leader

Thursday: The Conversion of Saul – its Cause

Friday: The Conversion of Saul – its Effects

Saturday: The Conversion of Cornelius

Stephen's Witness

[Men] began to argue with Stephen. But they could not stand up against the wisdom the Spirit gave him as he spoke.

Acts 6:9–10

Stephen was one of the Seven, and Luke declares him to be full of the Spirit, wisdom, grace, faith, and power. Yet surprisingly, he provoked some Jewish opposition. He was accused of speaking "blasphemous words against Moses and against God" (v. 11). When he was brought before the Sanhedrin, the accusation turned out to be that Stephen "never stops speaking against this holy place and against the law" (v. 13). This was, of course, a very serious charge, since the temple and the law were the Jews' most precious and sacred possessions.

Some commentators have criticized Stephen's speech before the Council as being rambling, dull, irrelevant, and even incoherent. But this is a superficial judgment. In particular, Stephen argued that the great figures of the Old Testament never imagined that God could be imprisoned in man-made buildings. Stephen picked out four major epochs, dominated by four major characters, in order to prove his point. Firstly, God appeared to Abraham in idolatrous Mesopotamia. Secondly, God was with Joseph in an Egyptian prison. Thirdly, God was with Moses in all three periods of his life. Fourthly, although David and Solomon built the temple, they knew very well that the Most High does not dwell in buildings. Thus, the single thread that runs through Stephen's speech is that Yahweh is a pilgrim God. His presence cannot be localized. He is always on the move, calling his people out in fresh adventures and always accompanying them as they go.

As for the law (Stephen's second topic), he turns the tables on his judges. It is not he who shows disrespect for God's law; it is they. They are "stiff-necked people", with "uncircumcised" hearts and ears (7:51), just like their fathers. They are resisting the Holy Spirit and rejecting God's Messiah.

For further reading: Acts 6:8–15

Stephen's Martyrdom

WHILE THEY WERE STONING HIM, STEPHEN PRAYED, "LORD JESUS,
RECEIVE MY SPIRIT." THEN HE FELL ON HIS KNEES AND CRIED OUT, "LORD,
DO NOT HOLD THIS SIN AGAINST THEM." WHEN HE HAD SAID THIS, HE
FELL ASLEEP.

Acts 7:59–60

Stephen's death was full of Christ. Following his speech, Luke records three further sentences that he spoke. Firstly, he said, "Look… I see heaven open and the Son of Man standing at the right hand of God" (v. 56). Perhaps Jesus had stood up to welcome his first martyr. Unwilling to listen to Stephen's exaltation of Jesus, the Council rushed at him, dragged him out of the city and began to stone him. Now he uttered his second sentence: "Lord Jesus, receive my spirit" (v. 59). His prayer was similar to that which Jesus prayed just before he died, "Father, into your hands I commit my spirit" (Luke 23:46). Thirdly, when Stephen fell on his knees, he cried out, "Lord, do not hold this sin against them" (Acts 7:60). This was reminiscent of Jesus' first words from the cross, which Luke has also recorded.

There were, in fact, several parallels between the death of Jesus and the death of Stephen. In both cases, false witnesses were produced and the charge was one of blasphemy. In both cases, too, each prayed for the forgiveness of his executioners and for the reception of his spirit. Luke concludes his narrative with the words "he fell asleep" (v. 60) – "an unexpectedly beautiful and peaceful description of so brutal a death," wrote F. F. Bruce.

What interests many people most about Stephen is that he was the first Christian martyr. Luke's main concern lies elsewhere, however, namely with the vital role Stephen played in the development of the worldwide Christian mission. His teaching showed already from the Old Testament that God was tied to his people, not to buildings. So now Jesus was ready to accompany his people wherever they went. This assurance is indispensable to mission. God has bound himself to his church (promising that he will never leave it) and to his Word (promising that it will never pass away). But God's church means people, not buildings, and God's Word means Scripture, not traditions. As long as these essentials are preserved, the buildings and the traditions can, if necessary, go. We must not allow them to imprison the living God or to impede his mission in the world.

For further reading: Acts 7:54–60

Philip in Samaria

PHILIP WENT DOWN TO A CITY IN SAMARIA AND PROCLAIMED THE
MESSIAH THERE.

Acts 8:5

It is difficult for us to conceive how bold Philip's action was in evangelizing Samaritans, for the hostility between Jews and Samaritans had lasted about a thousand years. But Jesus had told his followers to include Samaria within the area of their witness (1:8). So Philip preached Christ in a Samaritan city, and many believed and were baptized. But when the apostles in Jerusalem heard that Samaria had received the Word of God, they sent two of their number (Peter and John) to investigate. On arrival they discovered (we are not told how) that the Samaritans had received the gospel and baptism without receiving the Holy Spirit. So the apostles prayed for them and laid their hands on them, and they received the Spirit. Did Luke understand the Samaritans' divided experience as normal or as abnormal? Opposite answers are given. According to some Christians, initiation into Christ is a two-stage experience, either baptism followed by episcopal confirmation or regeneration followed by baptism with the Spirit as a second and subsequent experience.

According to other Christians, however, initiation into Christ is a single-stage experience comprising repentance and faith, new birth, baptism, and the gift of the Spirit. If this is correct, then the Samaritan experience of two stages was abnormal. For the apostles' normal teaching was that all believers receive the Spirit when they believe (Acts 2:38; Rom. 8:9), and their normal practice was not to send an apostolic delegation to evaluate the work of evangelists.

So why did they do it on this occasion? And why, in any case, was the Spirit not given to the Samaritans when they believed? The most natural explanation of the delayed gift of the Spirit in the case of the Samaritans is that this was the first time that evangelism had taken place outside Jerusalem and inside Samaria. This is the importance of the incident in Luke's unfolding story. It was a crucial moment. Would the long-standing rift between Jews and Samaritans be perpetuated in the Christian community? Is it not reasonable to suggest that it was in order to avoid such a disaster that God deliberately withheld his Spirit until the apostles had endorsed Philip's policy? The apostles' action was effective. A Samaritan schism within the church was avoided.

For further reading: Acts 8:14–17

Wednesday

Philip and an Ethiopian Leader

Then Philip began with that very passage of Scripture and told him the good news about Jesus.

Acts 8:35

This story is so well known that perhaps it does not need to be rehearsed in detail. Suffice it to say that, after his visit to Samaria, Philip received a fresh commissioning, this time to go south to the desert road that led ultimately to Egypt. Providentially, he met an Ethiopian public official who was evidently Jewish, for he was returning in his chariot from one of the annual festivals in Jerusalem and had the Isaiah scroll open on his lap. Out of Isaiah 53 Philip told him the good news of Jesus and at his request baptized him.

Luke has deliberately brought together two examples of Philip's evangelistic labours. The similarities between them are obvious; it is the differences that are instructive, especially in the people evangelized and the methods employed. Take the people evangelized. They were different in race, rank, and religion. The Samaritans were of mixed race, half Jewish and half Gentile, and Asiatic, while the Ethiopian seems to have been a black African, though Jewish by birth or conversion. As for rank, the Samaritans are likely to have been ordinary citizens, whereas the Ethiopian was a distinguished public servant in the employment of the crown. That brings us to religion. The Samaritans revered Moses but rejected the prophets, whereas the Ethiopian had a strong attachment to Judaism and was reading one of the very prophets the Samaritans rejected. Yet despite their differences in racial origin, social class, and predisposing religious condition, Philip presented them with the same good news of Jesus.

Consider next the methods Philip employed. His mission to the Samaritans was an early example of "mass evangelism," for the crowds heard his message, saw his signs, paid attention to him, believed, and were baptized (vv. 6, 12). Philip's conversation with the Ethiopian, however, was a conspicuous example of "personal evangelism," for here was one man sitting alongside another man and talking to him out of the Scriptures, privately and patiently, about Jesus. It is noteworthy that the same evangelist was adaptable enough to use both methods, namely public proclamation and private testimony. But, although he could alter his method, Philip did not alter his message.

For further reading: Acts 8:26–40

The Conversion of Saul – its Cause

HE FELL TO THE GROUND AND HEARD A VOICE SAY TO HIM,
"SAUL, SAUL, WHY DO YOU PERSECUTE ME?"

Acts 9:4

Is the conversion of Saul intended to be a model of Christian conversion today? The answer is yes, but only if we distinguish between the dramatic outward accompaniments and the essential inward experience. It is not necessary for us to be blinded by a flash of divine lightning, but it is necessary for us to have a personal encounter with Jesus Christ and to surrender to him.

What stands out of the narrative is the sovereign grace of God. Saul did not "decide for Christ" (to use our modern jargon); it was Christ who decided for him and laid hold of him. The evidence for this is indisputable. Luke's narrative begins with a reference to Saul "still breathing out murderous threats" (v. 1), probably depicting him as a wild and ferocious beast. He was in no mood to consider the claims of Christ. His mind was poisoned with prejudice. But within a few days he would be a converted and baptized Christian! Yet we need to make two qualifications.

Firstly, God's grace in the conversion of Saul was not sudden. To be sure, "suddenly a light… flashed around him" (v. 3), but this was by no means the first time that Christ had spoken to him; it was rather the culmination of a process. Jesus said that it was hard for him to "kick against the goads" (26:14), thus likening Saul to a stubborn bullock and himself to a farmer using a goad to break him in. What were these goads? They would include his conscience, the persistent rumours that Jesus had risen from the dead, the witness of Stephen, and above all, his doubts. As Carl Jung said, "Fanaticism is found only in individuals who are compensating secret doubts."

Secondly, God's grace in the conversion of Saul was not compulsive. The Christ who appeared to him did not turn him into a robot or compel him to act as if in a hypnotic trance. On the contrary, Jesus asked Saul the probing question, "Why do you persecute me?" (22:7). And Saul answered with two counter-questions, "Who are you, Lord?" and, "What shall I do?" (vv. 8, 10). His response was rational, conscientious, and free. Thus the cause of Saul's conversion was sovereign grace, but sovereign grace is gradual and gentle. Divine grace does not trample on human personality.

For further reading: Acts 9:1–9

FRIDAY

The Conversion of Saul – its Effects

THE LORD TOLD HIM [ANANIAS], "GO TO THE HOUSE OF JUDAS ON
STRAIGHT STREET AND ASK FOR A MAN FROM TARSUS NAMED SAUL,
FOR HE IS PRAYING."

Acts 9:11

It is wonderful to see the transformation that took place in Saul, especially in his relationships. Firstly, he had a new reverence for God, as evidenced by his praying. Of course, as a Pharisee he had often prayed before, or at least said prayers, both publicly and privately. But now he experienced a new access to God through Christ and a new sense of God's Fatherhood as the Holy Spirit bore witness with his spirit that he was a child of God. As R. G. H. Lenski, the Lutheran commentator, has expressed it, "The raging lion has been changed into a bleating lamb."

Secondly, he had a new relationship to the church. When Ananias visited Saul and laid hands on him, he addressed him as "Brother Saul" or "Saul my brother." I never fail to be moved by these words. They must have sounded like music in Saul's ears. What? Was the archenemy of the church to be received as a brother? Yes! So he got up and was baptized into the Christian community. Some three years later in Jerusalem the disciples were at first skeptical of his conversion. It was Barnabas who introduced Saul to the apostles. Thank God for Ananias in Damascus and Barnabas in Jerusalem. If it had not been for the welcome they secured for Saul, the whole course of church history would have been different.

Thirdly, Paul had a new responsibility to the world. Already on the Damascus road Jesus had told him that he was appointed to bear witness to what he had seen and heard. And Ananias confirmed his commissioning as apostle to the Gentiles. He was also warned that he would suffer. In fact, he had to be smuggled out of Damascus and then flee from Jerusalem. Thus the story of Saul's conversion, which began with his leaving Damascus with official accreditation from the high priest to arrest Christians, ends with his leaving Jerusalem as a fugitive himself.

There are many Sauls in the world today, people richly endowed with gifts of intellect and character, stubborn, even fanatical in their rejection of Christ. We need more holy expectation that such people can be first converted and then be transformed in all their relationships. Let's magnify the grace of God.

For further reading: Acts 9:19–30

SATURDAY

The Conversion of Cornelius

SO THEN, EVEN TO GENTILES GOD HAS GRANTED REPENTANCE
THAT LEADS TO LIFE.

Acts 11:18

It is difficult for us to grasp the impassable gulf that yawned in those days between Jews and Gentiles. No orthodox Jew would ever enter a Gentile's house, let alone sit down at the table with him. We saw in Acts 8 how God prevented a Jewish-Samaritan schism in the church; how will he now prevent a Jewish–Gentile schism?

The story is told twice in Acts – firstly by Luke in chapter 10 and secondly by Peter at the beginning of chapter 11. We will follow the latter. It has been well said that the principal subject of Acts 10 and 11 is not the conversion of Cornelius but the conversion of Peter (from his racial prejudice). Peter told the Jerusalem church what had happened. It was only by four successive hammer blows of revelation that God convinced Peter not to call anybody unclean (10:28).

The first hammer blow was *the divine vision* of a sheet let down from heaven containing clean and unclean animals, reptiles, and birds, while God's voice told Peter to kill and eat. The second was *the divine command* to accompany the three men who had come from Cornelius, without hesitation or distinction, even though they were Gentiles. The third was *the divine preparation*, namely that an angel had told Cornelius to fetch Peter. Thus God was working at both ends, in Cornelius and in Peter, deliberately arranging for them to meet by granting to each on successive days a special, independent, and appropriate vision. The fourth and final hammer blow was *the divine action*. While Peter was still speaking, the Holy Spirit came on the Gentile audience. This has often been described as the Gentile Pentecost, corresponding to the Jewish Pentecost that had taken place in Jerusalem.

These four hammer blows of revelation were all aimed deftly at Peter's racial prejudice. Together they demonstrated conclusively that God had welcomed Gentile believers into his family on equal terms with believing Jews. The right deduction was immediately made: since God had given the same gift of the Spirit to Gentiles and Jews, the church must give them an equal welcome. If God had given them Spirit baptism, the church might not deny them water baptism. "God does not show favouritism" (10. 34).

For further reading: Acts 11:1–18

"God has given even to the Gentiles the repentance that leads to life" (Acts 11:18 NRSV). This was an epoch-making declaration by the conservative Jewish leaders of the Jerusalem church. God himself had put the matter beyond dispute by bestowing his Spirit on a Gentile household. So the inclusion of the Gentiles is to become Luke's main theme in the rest of Acts, and with chapter 13 he will begin to chronicle Paul's amazing missionary exploits. Before this, however, he gives his readers two vignettes, which form a transition from the conversion of the first Gentile (through Peter) to the systematic evangelization of Gentiles (through Paul). In the first, the expansion of the church northward is depicted, and the scene is Antioch. In the second (12:1–25), opposition to the church by King Herod Agrippa I is depicted, and the scene is Jerusalem. This is Luke's final Peter story before his leadership role is taken over by Paul and Jerusalem is eclipsed by the goal of Rome.

Sunday: Expansion and Opposition

Monday: Paul's First Missionary Journey

Tuesday: The Jerusalem Council

Wednesday: Mission in Macedonia

Thursday: Paul in Athens

Friday: Paul in Corinth

Saturday: Paul in Ephesus

Expansion and Opposition

SOME OF THEM, HOWEVER... WENT TO ANTIOCH AND BEGAN TO SPEAK TO
GREEKS ALSO, TELLING THEM THE GOOD NEWS ABOUT THE LORD JESUS.

Acts 11:20

Luke now tells us that some evangelists went northwest to the coast, reaching as far as
Phoenicia, Cyprus, and Antioch. They preached, he adds, "only among Jews" (v. 19).
But some who came to Antioch spoke "to Greeks also" (v. 20). It is uncertain whether
they were pagan Greeks, Greek-speaking Jews, or some kind of mixture. Antioch
was certainly a highly appropriate venue for the first international church and the
springboard for the worldwide Christian mission, for it was a huge cosmopolitan city.

News of this development reached the leaders of the Jerusalem church. As they had
sent Peter and John to investigate the Samaritan situation, so now they sent Barnabas
to Antioch. He saw the evidence of God's grace in changed lives and encouraged the
converts to remain true to the Lord. He also went on to Tarsus and brought Saul to
Antioch to teach the large numbers of converts.

But this significant church growth was not unchallenged. Expansion was followed
by opposition. Enter King Herod Agrippa I, son of Herod the Great. He had the
apostle James beheaded and the apostle Peter imprisoned. It was a serious crisis. But
the church members gave themselves to prayer, and Peter was miraculously released.
Next morning, on the very day on which Peter was to have been tried and probably
executed, he was nowhere to be found. Herod's plan had been foiled.

Luke goes on to document Herod's final overthrow. The people of Tyre and Sidon,
who had quarreled with the king, sought an audience with him and sued for peace. On
the appointed day he harangued the crowd, who shouted, "This is the voice of a god,
not of a man" (12:22). Immediately, since he had usurped the honour due to God, he
was struck down and died.

Luke now adds one of his summary verses: "But the word of God continued to
spread and flourish" (v. 24). Luke's artistry is evident. The chapter opens with James
dead, Peter in prison, and Herod triumphing; it closes with Herod dead, Peter free, and
the Word of God triumphing. Such is the power of God to overthrow hostile human
plans and to establish his own plans in their place.

For further reading: Acts 12:1–5

MONDAY

Paul's First Missionary Journey

THE HOLY SPIRIT SAID, "SET APART FOR ME BARNABAS AND SAUL FOR THE
WORK TO WHICH I HAVE CALLED THEM."

Acts 13:2

Barnabas and Saul, with John Mark, were commissioned as missionaries by the leaders of the church in Antioch. At each of their future stopping places Luke records something of note. In Cyprus (Barnabas's home) the proconsul himself believed. At Perga John Mark deserted them and went home. On arrival in Pisidian Antioch, as we know from his letter to the Galatians, Paul was suffering from a debilitating illness, perhaps malaria, which had damaged his eyesight. Yet here Paul and Barnabas took the radical step of turning to the Gentiles.

The missionaries now journeyed about a hundred miles southeast to Iconium, where large numbers of Jews and Gentiles believed. In Lystra, following the healing of a cripple, the superstitious crowd now tried to worship them, but Paul urged them to turn from their idolatry to the living God of creation. Next, the crowd turned against Paul, stoned him, and dragged him out of the city, thinking he was dead. Worship one moment and a lynching the next! Such is the fickleness of the crowd. But Paul revived, and the following morning his poor battered body began the sixty-mile trudge to Derbe, where large numbers again believed. Paul and Barnabas now retraced their steps, revisiting the churches they had planted and encouraging the young disciples. On arrival back in Syrian Antioch, they gathered the church together and "reported all that God had done through them" (14:27).

What was Paul's missionary policy? As Roland Allen wrote in his famous book *Missionary Methods: St. Paul's or Ours?* "Nothing can alter or disguise the fact that St. Paul did leave behind him at his first visit complete churches." On what foundations, then, did his indigenization policy rest? There were three. Firstly, Paul exhorted the new converts to "remain true to the faith" (v. 22). That is, there was a cluster of central truths that he calls "the faith" and that he had taught them. Secondly, Paul and Barnabas "appointed elders [plural] for them in each church" (v. 23). Thirdly, Paul and Barnabas committed them to the Lord, convinced that he was able to look after his own people. Thus the young churches had the apostles to teach them, pastors to shepherd them, and the Holy Spirit to guide and protect them. With this threefold provision the churches could safely be left.

For further reading: Acts 14:21–28

TUESDAY

The Jerusalem Council

SOME... [BELIEVING] PHARISEES... SAID, "THE GENTILES MUST BE
CIRCUMCISED AND REQUIRED TO KEEP THE LAW OF MOSES."
THE APOSTLES AND ELDERS MET TO CONSIDER THIS QUESTION.

Acts 15:5–6

It had been assumed that Gentile converts would be absorbed into Israel by circumcision. But now something quite new was happening, something that disturbed and even alarmed many. Converts were being welcomed into fellowship by baptism without circumcision. We must be clear about the point that was at issue. A pressure group we call either "Judaizers" or "the circumcision party" arrived in Antioch claiming authorization by the apostles and insisting that without circumcision there was no salvation. In other words, faith in Jesus was not enough; converts must add to their faith circumcision. They must let Moses complete what Jesus had begun and let the law supplement the gospel. Paul was absolutely outraged by this contradiction of the gospel. Were Gentile believers a sect of Judaism or authentic members of a multiracial family? So a council was convened in Jerusalem, with James the Lord's brother in the chair. First, the apostle Peter reminded the Council how through his ministry Cornelius and his family had been converted and received the Spirit, making no distinction. Next, the Council listened with great respect to Paul and Barnabas, who gave an account of their missionary journey. Finally, James quoted from the prophet Amos. It was the combination of prophetic witness and apostolic experience that convinced him. His conclusion was that they should not make it difficult for Gentiles who were turning to God, but instead ask them to respect Jewish consciences by abstaining from four practices.

There is debate as to whether the four practices are moral or cultural. If moral they were idolatry, murder and immorality, omitting the fourth (the meat of strangled animals) as the Western text does. But these are such grave sins that it would not be necessary for a special decree to ban them. In this case, the practices banned were cultural – eating idol meats, drinking blood, eating non-kosher food, and marrying within the prohibited degrees (see Lev. 17 and 18). Three of these relate to diet and could inhibit table fellowship between Jews and Gentiles. We may say, then, that the Jerusalem Council secured a double victory – a victory of truth in confirming the gospel of grace, and a victory of love in preserving the fellowship by sensitive concessions to Jewish scruples.

For further reading: Acts 15:19–29

WEDNESDAY

Mission in Macedonia

DURING THE NIGHT PAUL HAD A VISION OF A MAN OF MACEDONIA
STANDING AND BEGGING HIM,
"COME OVER TO MACEDONIA AND HELP US."

Acts 16:9

The most notable feature of Paul's second missionary expedition is that for the first time the good seed of the gospel was planted in European soil. Luke tells us of Paul's vision or dream, in which a Macedonian stood begging for help. Some have conjectured that he was none other than Luke himself, whom Paul had just met and whose presence is affirmed by the first of his "we" sections.

During the mission in Philippi, Luke tells us of three interesting converts. The first was Lydia, a wealthy businesswoman from Thyatira, in whose house the church later met. The second was an anonymous slave girl who made money for her masters by fortune-telling. And the third was the Roman jailer who asked what he must do to be saved. It would be hard to imagine three more different people. Racially, socially, and psychologically, they were worlds apart. Yet they were united in Christ, even if Paul's exhortations to unity in his letter to the Philippians may betray some tensions in the church.

From Philippi the missionaries moved on south to Thessalonica, the capital of the Roman province of Macedonia. For three Sabbaths running, Paul reasoned with people out of the Scriptures, explaining and proving that the Messiah had to suffer and rise from the dead. Next, he proclaimed Jesus, telling the story of his birth, life, death, and resurrection. Then he put two and two together, identifying the Jesus of history with the Christ of Scripture, saying, "This Jesus, whom I proclaim to you is the Christ" (17:3 RSV). Unbelieving Jews soon started a riot, and the missionaries had to be smuggled out of the city by night. They then journeyed to Berea. Luke immediately tells us that the Bereans were more open-minded than the Thessalonians in that they examined the Scriptures daily to see if what Paul was saying was true.

One particular aspect of both the Thessalonian and the Berean missions was people's serious attitude to the Scriptures. For example, Paul in Thessalonica reasoned, explained, proved, proclaimed, and persuaded, while in Berea the Jews diligently examined the Scriptures. As Bengel wrote, "A characteristic of the true religion is that it suffers itself to be examined into."

For further reading: Acts 17:1–4, 10–11

Thursday

Paul in Athens

While Paul was waiting for them [Silas and Timothy] in Athens,
he was greatly distressed to see that the city was full of idols.

Acts 17:16

There is something enthralling about Paul in Athens, the great Christian apostle alone amid the glories of ancient Greece. As he walked through the city he was "greatly distressed" or "provoked" (RSV) by the idolatry he saw. It is the very verb used in the Septuagint of God's reaction to idolatry. Athenian idols aroused in Paul deep stirrings of jealousy for the name of God. So he reasoned in the synagogue and in the marketplace with those who were there. Then a group of Epicurean and Stoic philosophers began to dispute with him. One cannot help admiring how versatile Paul was in sharing the gospel with different kinds of people. His dialogue with the philosophers led to an invitation to address the world-famous, supreme council of Athens, the Areopagus.

Paul took as his text or point of contact the altar he had found inscribed "to an unknown god." He claimed to proclaim to them the god they ignorantly worshipped. Paul then portrayed him as the Creator of the universe, the Lord of heaven and earth; as the Sustainer of life who therefore does not need to be sustained; as the Ruler of nations, determining their times and places; as the Father of human beings, whose offspring we are (as the Stoic philosopher Aratus had said); and as the Judge of the world, who has overlooked past ignorance but now commands everybody everywhere to repent, having appointed the Judge and raised him from the dead. Some jeered; others believed.

It is the comprehensiveness of Paul's message that is impressive. He proclaimed God in his fullness as Creator, Sustainer, Ruler, Father, and Judge. All this is part of the gospel, or, at least, the necessary prolegomena to the gospel. Many people are rejecting our gospel today, not because they perceive it to be false, but because they perceive it to be trivial. They are looking for an integrated worldview that makes sense of all their experience. We learn from Paul that we cannot preach the gospel of Jesus without the doctrine of God, or the cross without the creation, or salvation without judgment, or vice versa. Today's world needs a bigger gospel, the full gospel of Scripture, what Paul later in Ephesus was to call "the entire plan of God" (20:27 NAB).

For further reading: Acts 17:22–31

FRIDAY

Paul in Corinth

AFTER THIS, PAUL LEFT ATHENS AND WENT TO CORINTH.

Acts 18:1

It seems to have been Paul's deliberate policy to move purposefully from one strategic city centre to the next. So Luke depicts him visiting Athens, Corinth, and Ephesus, three major cities of the Greco-Roman world.

"After this [following his Areopagus speech and its aftermath], Paul left Athens and went to Corinth" (v. 1). It was about this journey that Paul later wrote, "I resolved to know nothing while I was with you except Jesus Christ and him crucified. I came to you in weakness with great fear and trembling" (1 Cor. 2:2–3). Some commentators explain Paul's resolve in this way. His sermon to the philosophers had been a flop, being too intellectual and focused on the creation instead of the cross. So on his way to Corinth he repented and determined to preach the cross alone. But Luke gives no hint that he thinks Paul's sermon a flop. On the contrary, he records it as a model of Paul's preaching to intellectuals. Besides, he did preach the cross, because he preached the resurrection, and you cannot preach one without the other. Further, some did believe, and Paul did not change his tactics when he reached Corinth.

No, the reason for Paul's anxiety and resolve was different. It was surely the pride and immorality of the Corinthian people that intimidated him, since the cross comes into direct collision with both. The Corinthians were proud of their city (its wealth, culture, and games) and of its prestige as capital of the province of Achaia, taking precedence even over Athens. But the cross undermines all human pride. Corinth was also associated in everybody's mind with immorality, as *korinthiazai* meant to practise immorality. On the flat summit of the Acrocorinth behind the city stood the temple of Aphrodite or Venus, the goddess of love, and a thousand of her female slaves roamed the city's streets by night as prostitutes. But the gospel of Christ crucified summoned the Corinthians to repentance and holiness. It is in this way that Christ's cross, in its call for self-humbling and self-denial, was a stumbling block to proud and sinful Corinthians. Hence Paul's weakness, fear, and trembling.

For further reading: 1 Corinthians 2:1–5

SATURDAY

Paul in Ephesus

ALL THE JEWS AND GREEKS WHO LIVED IN THE PROVINCE OF ASIA HEARD
THE WORD OF THE LORD.

Acts 19:10

The pattern of Paul's evangelistic ministry in Ephesus was similar to that in Corinth. He began in the synagogue, but when the gospel was rejected, he moved to a secular venue.

Looking back, we can learn from Paul in Corinth and Ephesus some important lessons about the where, the how, and the when of urban evangelism.

Firstly, we notice *the secular places Paul chose* – in Corinth the house of Titius Justus and in Ephesus the lecture hall of Tyrannus. Still today religious people need to be evangelized in religious buildings (church being equivalent to synagogue), but secular people can better be reached in secular buildings, for example, through home evangelism or lecture evangelism.

Secondly, consider *the reasoned presentation Paul made*. Luke uses two verbs four times each, one meaning to argue (*dialegomai*) and the other to persuade (*peithō*). "This man... is persuading the people," the Jews complained to Gallio (18:13). In both synagogue and lecture theatre Paul combined argument and persuasion so that his approach was serious, well reasoned, and convincing. Of course, arguments are no substitute for the Holy Spirit, but then trust in the Holy Spirit is no substitute for arguments. The Spirit of truth brings people to faith in Jesus not in spite of the evidence but because of the evidence when he opens their minds to attend to it.

Thirdly, note *the extended periods Paul stayed* – two years in Corinth and three in Ephesus. His use of the hall of Tyrannus is particularly remarkable. The accepted text reads that he lectured daily for two years. But the Bezan text adds "from the fifth hour to the tenth," that is, from eleven in the morning to four o'clock in the afternoon. Assuming that Paul kept one day in seven for rest and worship, a daily five-hour lecture six days a week for two years comes to 3,120 hours of gospel argument! No wonder Luke comments that "all the residents of [the province of] Asia, both Jews and Greeks, heard the word of the Lord" (19:10 NRSV).

For further reading: Acts 19:8–10

Week 41: The Long Journey to Rome

Luke now narrates how Paul left Ephesus and then travelled from place to place until he reached Jerusalem (Acts 21:17). True, Luke has let us into the secret that Paul was intending after visiting Jerusalem to head for Rome (19:21). Nevertheless, it is Jerusalem that filled his vision at this stage. In fact, it seems clear that Luke sees a parallel between Jesus' journey to Jerusalem (which is prominent in his first volume) and Paul's journey to Jerusalem (which he describes in his second). Of course, the mission of Jesus was unique. Yet the correspondence between the two journeys seems too close to be a coincidence. Like Jesus, Paul travelled to Jerusalem with a group of his disciples, opposed by hostile Jews who plotted against his life.

Like Jesus, Paul made or received three successive predictions of his "passion" or sufferings, including his being handed over to the Gentiles. Like Jesus Paul declared his readiness to lay down his life and expressed his abandonment to the will of God. Like Jesus, Paul was determined to complete his ministry and not be deflected from it. We should not press the details, but surely Luke intends his readers to see Paul following in his Master's footsteps.

Sunday: Paul Addresses the Ephesian Elders

Monday: Paul in Jerusalem

Tuesday: Paul the Prisoner

Wednesday: Paul the Defendant

Thursday: Paul the Witness

Friday: Rome at Last!

Saturday: The Providence of God

Paul Addresses the Ephesian Elders

KEEP WATCH OVER... ALL THE FLOCK OF WHICH THE HOLY SPIRIT HAS
MADE YOU OVERSEERS. BE SHEPHERDS OF THE CHURCH OF GOD, WHICH
HE BOUGHT WITH HIS OWN BLOOD.

Acts 20:28

On his way to Jerusalem Paul and his companions stopped at the port of Miletus and sent a message to the elders of the Ephesian church to meet them there. In addressing them, Paul developed the pastoral metaphor relating to shepherds, sheep, and wolves.

Firstly, he described *the example of the shepherd*, namely himself. There had been an extraordinary degree of thoroughness in his ministry. He had been thorough in his teaching (the whole counsel of God), thorough in his outreach (the whole population of Ephesus), and thorough in his methods (public in the hall of Tyrannus and private from house to house). Thus he had shared all possible truth with all possible people by all possible means. He could claim to be innocent of the blood of all people.

Secondly, Paul described *the invasion of wolves* (false teachers). Wolves hunt both singly and in packs, and sheep are defenceless against them. So the apostle urges the shepherds to be on their guard. For a double task is given to the shepherds of Christ's flock, namely to feed the sheep and to rout the wolves, that is, to teach the truth and combat error. This emphasis is unpopular today. It is frequently said that we must always be positive in our teaching and never negative. But those who say this are in disagreement with our Lord Jesus and his apostles, who both refuted error themselves and urged us to do the same.

Thirdly, Paul emphasized *the value of the sheep* (the people). For they are the church of God the Father, purchased with the blood of Christ, while the Holy Spirit appoints their overseers. This splendid trinitarian truth should have a profound effect on our ministry. For sheep are not at all the clean and cuddly creatures they look from a distance but are subject to unpleasant pests. I hesitate to apply the metaphor too literally! But some church members are a great trial to their pastors (and vice versa). So how shall we persevere in loving and serving them? Answer: by remembering how precious they are – so valuable, in fact, that the three persons of the Trinity are all involved in caring for them.

For further reading: Acts 20:17–38

MONDAY

Paul in Jerusalem

WHEN WE ARRIVED AT JERUSALEM, THE BROTHERS AND SISTERS RECEIVED
US WARMLY. THE NEXT DAY PAUL AND THE REST OF US
WENT TO SEE JAMES...

Acts 21:17–18

When Paul and his travel companions arrived in Jerusalem, they went to see James. James was still the recognized leader of the worldwide Jewish Christian community, which now numbered many thousands. In depicting Paul and James face-to-face, each flanked by some supporters, Luke presents his readers with a dramatic situation, fraught with both risk and possibility. For James and Paul were the representative leaders of two Christianities, Jewish and Gentile. And during the years since they last met, both movements had grown considerably, under God's good hand. The confrontation could have been painful. But both men had a conciliatory spirit. Take James first. As Paul gave a detailed report of what God had done among the Gentiles through his ministry, there was no murmur of disapproval. They praised God together.

But Paul was also anxious to be conciliatory and showed it in two ways. The first (although for some reason Luke does not mention it until Acts 24:17) was the presentation to the Jewish church of the offerings collected from the Greek churches. Perhaps Paul had already presented this gift privately. He saw it not just as an expression of love for the needy but as a tangible symbol of Jewish–Gentile solidarity in the body of Christ. Luke concentrates, however, on the second example of Paul's conciliatory spirit, namely the positive way in which he responded to the proposal James put to him. Because of the large number of Jewish Christians in Jerusalem, all of whom were zealous for the law, it was important to quash the rumour that was spreading, namely that Paul was teaching *Jewish* Christians to turn away from Moses and to declare circumcision and law observance unnecessary. (What he should teach *Gentile* converts had been settled at the Council of Jerusalem.) So James proposed that Paul should engage in certain purification rites, not as an obligation, but as a concession to Jewish Christian scruples. Paul took appropriate action immediately.

We can only thank God for the generosity of spirit displayed by both James and Paul. They were already agreed doctrinally (that salvation is by grace in Christ through faith) and ethically (that Christians must obey the moral law); the issue between them concerned culture, ceremony, and tradition.

For further reading: Acts 21:17–26

TUESDAY

Paul the Prisoner

SEIZING PAUL, THEY DRAGGED HIM FROM THE TEMPLE, AND IMMEDIATELY
THE GATES WERE SHUT.

Acts 21:30

So far Luke has portrayed his hero on the offensive, taking bold initiatives to evangelize most of Asia Minor and Greece. But now he found himself on the defensive. Following Paul's three epic missionary journeys, Luke describes his five trials – before a Jewish crowd, the Sanhedrin, Felix, Festus, and King Agrippa II. This narrative takes up nearly two hundred verses in our English Bibles. Why such detail? One of his major themes has been the relations between Jews and Gentiles. And now in Acts 21 to 23 he depicts the reaction to the gospel of these two communities. The two themes of Jewish opposition and Roman justice are interwoven in Luke's narrative, with the Christian apostle caught between them, the victim of the one and the beneficiary of the other.

Luke shows no sign of anti-Semitism; he is simply recording the facts. He documents the Jews' determination to get rid of Paul. Luke's statement that when the mob dragged Paul out of the temple, "immediately the gates were shut" (21:30) was more than a fact. The slammed gates symbolized the final Jewish rejection of the gospel. Paul's policy of turning to the Gentiles had been justified.

Luke's second and corresponding theme is Roman justice. He presents the Roman authorities as friends of the gospel, not enemies. Luke has already shown how the magistrates in Philippi actually apologized to Paul and Silas for maltreating them, how Gallio in Corinth refused even to listen to Jewish accusations against Paul, and how the town clerk in Ephesus declared the Christian leaders innocent and dismissed the angry crowd. And now in Jerusalem Claudius Lysias, the military tribune, twice rescued Paul from being lynched, exempted him from a brutal interrogation by torture on discovering that he was a Roman citizen, and protected him from a Jewish murder plot.

This protection by Roman justice was even more clear in Paul's trials. Although accused by the Jews, Paul was tried and exonerated by the Romans. The same had been true in the parallel trials of Jesus. Three times in the case of Jesus, and three times in the case of Paul, the accused was declared not guilty in a court of law. The legality of the Christian faith had been established.

For further reading: Acts 22:22–29

Paul the Defendant

I HAVE DONE NOTHING WRONG AGAINST THE JEWISH LAW OR AGAINST
THE TEMPLE OR AGAINST CAESAR.

Acts 25:8

Luke enables us to follow Paul's three successive trials – before the procurators Felix and Festus and King Agrippa II. He portrays him in two guises – first and negatively as a defendant, then secondly and positively as a witness.

Before Felix Paul vigorously denied the charge of sectarianism and of trying to desecrate the temple. He emphasized the continuity of his gospel with the Old Testament Scriptures. He served the God of their fathers with a good conscience. He believed everything written in the Law and the Prophets. He cherished a firm hope in the fulfilment of God's promises about the Messiah. Not apostasy but continuity summed up his attitude to Moses.

Before Festus, who succeeded Felix, Paul rejected the charge of sedition. He had not been responsible for any breaches of the peace. So certain was he that he had done nothing against Caesar that he judged it necessary to appeal to Caesar in order to clear himself. He could say, "I have done nothing wrong against the Jewish law or against the temple or against Caesar" (v. 8). Not anarchy but loyalty summed up his attitude to Caesar.

Before Agrippa and his queen Bernice no fresh charges were produced. Paul seems rather to be responding to the unspoken question of why the Jews were so anxious to get rid of him. It had to do with his ministry to the Gentiles, to which, however, he was inescapably committed out of obedience to the vision and voice of Jesus.

Paul's three defences were successful. Neither Felix nor Festus nor Agrippa found him guilty. Instead, each indicated that he was innocent of the charges. Paul was not content with this, however. He went further. He proclaimed in court his three-fold loyalty – to Moses and the prophets, to Caesar, and above all to Jesus Christ, who met him on the Damascus road. This was his self-defence. He was a faithful Jew, a faithful Roman, and a faithful Christian.

For further reading: Acts 25:1–12

Paul the Witness

I HAVE APPEARED TO YOU TO APPOINT YOU AS A SERVANT AND AS A
WITNESS...

Acts 26:16

Luke's purpose in describing the three court scenes was not just apologetic; it was evangelistic as well. During his two years of imprisonment, which had interrupted his missionary career, Paul must have felt very frustrated. But when opportunities for witness were given him, he seized them with confidence and courage. The main examples Luke gives are his private interview with Felix and his public confrontation with Agrippa.

Felix has been described as one of the worst of Roman officials. He was well known for his cruelty, lust, and greed. He seems to have had no moral scruples. But Paul was not afraid of him. Since he spoke to him about righteousness, self-control, and future judgment (24:25), it is reasonable to suppose that he rebuked the procurator for his sins. He also spoke to him of faith in Jesus.

As for the trial before Agrippa, Paul was not overawed by the show of pomp and power that marked that occasion or by the assembly of notable personages in court. "See what an audience is gathered together for Paul!" exclaimed Chrysostom. But Paul made no attempt to ingratiate himself with the authorities. He wanted the king's conversion, not his favour. Three times Luke has Paul repeating the elements of the gospel in the king's hearing (26:18, 20, 23). Each time Paul thus repeated the gospel in court, he was in fact deliberately preaching it to the court. Festus might call him mad, but Paul knew that he was "speaking the sober truth" (v. 25 RSV).

Thank God for Paul's courage! Kings and queens, governors and generals did not daunt him. Jesus had warned his disciples that they would be "brought before kings and governors" on account of his name and had promised that on such occasions he would give them "words and wisdom" (Luke 21:12, 15). Jesus had also told Ananias (who had presumably passed the information on) that Paul was his "chosen instrument" to carry his name "before the Gentiles and their kings and to the people of Israel" (Acts 9:15). These predictions had come true, and Paul had not failed.

For further reading: Acts 26:12–23

FRIDAY

Rome at Last!

AND SO WE CAME TO ROME.
Acts 28:14

Many readers of Acts 27 have commented on the precision and vividness of Luke's narrative. It is surely due to the fact that Luke himself accompanied Paul throughout their voyage from Caesarea to Rome and so could draw on his daily log of their progress. His accuracy has been vouched for by a certain James Smith, a Scottish yachtsman of thirty years' experience, who had familiarized himself with the weather patterns of the Mediterranean and wrote up his findings in his book *The Voyage and Shipwreck of Saint Paul*. The early days of their voyage around the eastern shores of the Mediterranean were uneventful. But, unable to find a safe and suitable berth on Crete in which to harbor for the winter, they sailed on in the open sea until a northeasterly wind of hurricane force caught them, and they drifted helplessly for fourteen days until they were grounded on Malta. The islanders looked after them for the three winter months, and then they set sail for Italy. Some Christian brothers heard that they were coming and walked about thirty miles along the Appian Way to welcome them.

In Rome Paul was permitted to live in his own lodgings, though under the surveillance of a soldier. He invited the Jewish leaders to meet him and assured them that he had done nothing against the Jewish people or customs and that the Romans had wanted to let him go. The leaders replied that they had heard nothing against him but that they would like to learn more about his beliefs. So on the appointed day they met him, and he proclaimed the kingdom of God and taught about the Lord Jesus Christ, doubtless arguing for the identification of the historical Jesus with the biblical Christ. Paul's audience was divided, but because of the hardness of Jewish hearts, Paul for the fourth time turned decisively to the Gentiles, for, he added, "They will listen!" (v. 28). For two whole years they came to Paul and listened to him.

The final words of the Acts are adverbial expressions meaning "with all boldness" and "without hindrance." They describe the freedom that the gospel enjoyed, with neither internal nor external restraint. They speak of a wide-open door, through which we in our day now have to pass.

For further reading: Acts 28:17–31

The Providence of God

I HOPE TO SEE YOU [IN ROME] WHILE PASSING THROUGH AND THAT YOU
WILL ASSIST ME ON MY JOURNEY THERE [TO SPAIN].

Romans 15:24

What is the importance of Acts 27 and 28? Answer: it concerns the providence of God. It illustrates the truth that "there is no wisdom, no insight, no plan that can succeed against the LORD" (Prov. 21:30). This providential activity of God is seen in these chapters in two complementary ways, firstly in bringing Paul to Rome and secondly in bringing him there as a prisoner. It was an unexpected combination of circumstances.

First, Luke intends us to marvel with him over the safe conduct of Paul to Rome. Jesus had said to him in Jerusalem, "Take courage! As you have testified about me in Jerusalem, so you must also testify in Rome" (Acts 23:11). Yet circumstance after circumstance seemed calculated to make this impossible. He was arrested and imprisoned, threatened with assassination, nearly drowned in the Mediterranean, almost killed by soldiers, and poisoned by a snake. And behind all these incidents demonic forces (symbolized in the raging sea) were at work, seeking to prevent Paul from reaching his God-planned, God-promised destination. But God obstructed the devil's purpose. It is exciting to watch. Will Paul make it? Yes, he will! He does! But Paul arrived a prisoner. How was this compatible with the providence of God? God's promise had been that Paul would *testify* in Rome, meaning before Caesar (Acts 27:24), and this could not have happened unless Paul had arrived in Rome as a prisoner on trial.

There is another way, however, that Paul's confinement ennobled his witness. For as a result he has bequeathed to posterity three major prison letters, Philippians, Ephesians, and Colossians. I am not saying that he needed time in jail to get his writing done! But in God's providence there is something distinctive about those prison letters. They set forth more powerfully than anywhere else the supreme, sovereign, undisputed, and unrivalled lordship of Jesus Christ. The person and work of Christ are now given cosmic proportions, for through Christ God has created and redeemed all things. In addition, having humbled himself to the cross, he has been exalted by God to the highest place, and God has put all things under his feet. Through his prison experience Paul's perspective was adjusted, his horizon extended, his vision clarified, and his witness enriched.

For further reading: Colossians 1:15–18

For the next seven weeks we will be reviewing the twenty letters of the New Testament, and then for the final four weeks of the year we will seek to grasp the main themes of the book of Revelation.

Our studies in the New Testament letters will inevitably be inadequate, since in some cases we give only a day or two to important letters. Yet it may be helpful to try to gain an overview of the letters and so of the life in the Spirit that they depict.

We begin with the letter to the Galatians because I believe it to have been Paul's first letter, addressed to the churches of the four cities he visited on his first missionary journey. The main reason for this belief is that Galatians contains no reference to the Council of Jerusalem and its decrees, although they would have been directly relevant to the controversy that had erupted in the Galatian churches. So surely it must be dated before the Council, even probably written while Paul was on his way up to the Council. One senses the apostle's hot indignation that the Judaizers were undermining his apostolic authority and perverting the gospel of grace.

The letters to the Thessalonians, on the other hand, were written after Paul's visit to Thessalonica during his second missionary journey. Because he had had to be smuggled out of the city by night and had not returned, his enemies had launched a smear campaign against him. It is evident that at least in 1 Thessalonians Paul was defending himself against the accusations of his detractors.

Sunday: No Other Gospel

Monday: Authentic Freedom

Tuesday: The Fruit of the Spirit

Wednesday: Placarding Christ Crucified

Thursday: Evangelism Through the Local Church

Friday: Metaphors of Ministry

Saturday: Glory Revealed

No Other Gospel

I AM ASTONISHED THAT YOU ARE SO QUICKLY DESERTING THE ONE WHO
CALLED YOU TO LIVE IN THE GRACE OF CHRIST AND ARE TURNING TO A
DIFFERENT GOSPEL – WHICH IS REALLY NO GOSPEL AT ALL.

Galatians 1:6–7

Returning from the four Galatian cities evangelized during their first missionary journey, Paul and Barnabas reported to the church of Syrian Antioch how God had "opened a door of faith to the Gentiles" (Acts 14:27). And they stayed a long time with the disciples in Antioch.

Luke writes that during this period, however, "some men came down from Judea to Antioch and were teaching the brothers: 'Unless you are circumcised, according to the custom taught by Moses, you cannot be saved'" (Acts 15:1). This is surely the same event as that referred to in Galatians 2:12: "certain men came from James" (that is, claiming to come from James, although later he asserted that they lacked his authorization [Acts 15:24]). One can imagine the heated debate the visitors caused. They were Judaizers, and they were undermining the gospel. For they were insisting that faith in Jesus was not enough for Gentile converts; they must also keep the law, that is, allow Moses to complete what Jesus had begun. Even the apostle Peter was won over by their teaching, so (as Paul told the Galatians) he had to confront Peter publicly, since the truth of the gospel was at stake (Gal. 2:11–16). But Peter's defection was temporary. By the time of the Council of Jerusalem, he had recovered his equilibrium.

Meanwhile, some of these Judaizing "troublemakers" had reached the Galatian cities and were teaching the same distorted message. They were also having some success, to Paul's astonishment. So serious was the situation that he castigated it as a desertion on their part and called down a solemn judgment on anyone (angelic or human, including himself) who perverted the gospel from the good news of grace (God's free and unmerited favour) to a religion of works righteousness. He even went so far as to say that if we could gain our salvation by obedience to the law, then "Christ died for nothing" (v. 21). That is, if we say we can manage on our own and win our salvation by ourselves, we are implying that the cross was not necessary. Paul begins and ends with a reference to grace (1:3; 6:18). The gospel is good news of God's free grace; there is no other gospel.

For further reading Galatians 1:6–9

Monday

Authentic Freedom

IT IS FOR FREEDOM THAT CHRIST HAS SET US FREE. STAND FIRM, THEN, AND DO NOT LET YOURSELVES BE BURDENED AGAIN BY A YOKE OF SLAVERY.

Galatians 5:1

The New Testament portrays Jesus Christ as the supreme liberator and the Christian life as a life of freedom. Jesus himself had said to some believing Jews, "If you hold to my teaching, you are really my disciples. Then you will know the truth, and the truth will set you free" (John 8:31–32). But what is Christian freedom? It begins with emancipation from the awful bondage of having to win our salvation by obedience to the law. It includes freedom from guilt and from a guilty conscience, the unutterable joy of forgiveness, acceptance and access to God, and the whole experience of mercy without merit. But Christian freedom is not freedom from all restrictions and restraints.

Firstly, it is not freedom to indulge our fallen, self-centred nature. "You, my brothers, were called to be free," Paul wrote. "But do not use your freedom to indulge the flesh" (Gal. 5:13). So our freedom in Christ is not to be used as a pretext for self-indulgence. For if we live in the Spirit, we will not gratify the desires of the sinful nature (v. 16).

Secondly, Christian freedom is not freedom to exploit our neighbour. Rather, "serve one another… in love" (v. 13). There is a powerful paradox here. So far from having liberty to ignore, neglect, or abuse our neighbours, we are commanded to love them and through love to serve them. So from one point of view Christian freedom is a form of slavery – not slavery to our selfish nature but to our neighbour. We are free in relation to God but slaves in relation to each other.

Thirdly, Christian freedom is not freedom to disregard the law, for "the entire law is fulfilled in keeping this one: 'Love your neighbour as yourself'" (v. 14). The apostle does not say that if we love our neighbour, we can dispense with the law but that we will fulfil it.

Authentic freedom is not freedom to indulge our fallen nature but to control it, not freedom to exploit our neighbours but to serve them, and not freedom to disregard the law but to fulfil it.

For further reading: Galatians 5:1–15

TUESDAY

The Fruit of the Spirit

BUT THE FRUIT OF THE SPIRIT IS LOVE, JOY, PEACE, FORBEARANCE,
KINDNESS, GOODNESS, FAITHFULNESS, GENTLENESS AND SELF-CONTROL.
Galatians 5:22–23

The Holy Spirit not only is holy in his nature and character but works for the holiness of his people. Firstly, there are *two opposing combatants* – the flesh, meaning our inherited, fallen, twisted nature, and the Spirit, meaning the indwelling Holy Spirit himself. Moreover, the combatants have contrasting desires. So our Christian personality is a battle ground of opposing forces.

Secondly, there are *two opposing lifestyles* to which the two combatants lead. The acts of the sinful nature are obvious and very unpleasant. Paul lists fifteen of them and adds that the list is not exhaustive. They fall into four categories, namely sex, religion, society, and drink. But there is another lifestyle, as beautiful as the other is ugly. Love, joy, and peace characterize our relationship with God; patience, kindness, and goodness our relationship with others; and faithfulness, gentleness, and self-control our mastery of ourselves. They seem to be a portrait of Jesus and are identified as the fruit of the Spirit, since like fruit they grow naturally and steadily.

Thirdly, there are *two opposing attitudes*. That is, we are called to repudiate our sinful nature and surrender to the Holy Spirit. Indeed, those who belong to Christ Jesus have (already) crucified their sinful nature with its passions and desires (v. 24). That is, we have taken this evil, slimy, slippery thing called our sinful nature and have nailed it to the cross. Now we must leave it there. We must also surrender to the Holy Spirit and walk in step with him. These opposing attitudes are to be decisive, complete, and continuous. We are not to keep returning to the scene of crucifixion. It is similar in our attitude to the Holy Spirit. We need to cultivate the things of the Spirit by our wise use of our Sundays, our daily disciplined private devotion, our regular public worship and attendance at the Lord's Supper, and our involvement in Christian service. For these are God-given means of grace, that is, channels through which God's grace comes to us, and a major secret of sanctification.

For further reading: Galatians 5:16–26

Placarding Christ Crucified

BEFORE YOUR VERY EYES JESUS CHRIST WAS
CLEARLY PORTRAYED AS CRUCIFIED.

Galatians 3:1

Paul described his preaching ministry in the Galatian cities as a public placarding of Christ crucified. Of course, the Galatians had not seen Jesus die. Nor had Paul. But through the preaching of the cross Paul had brought the past into the present and made the historical event of the cross a contemporary reality. In consequence, the Galatians could now see the cross in their imagination, could understand that Christ had died for their sins, and could kneel before the cross in great humility and receive from his hands the gift of eternal life, absolutely free and utterly undeserved.

But his preaching of the cross, as Paul was later to elaborate in 1 Corinthians, is a stumbling block to human pride, for it insists that we cannot achieve our salvation by anything we do. Indeed, we cannot even contribute to it. Salvation is a totally noncontributory gift of God. As Archbishop William Temple put it, "The only thing of my very own which I contribute to my redemption is the sin from which I need to be redeemed."

It is in this connection that Paul contrasted himself with the false teachers, the Judaizers. They preached circumcision (apostolic shorthand for self-salvation by obedience to the law) and so escaped persecution for the cross of Christ (6:12). He, on the other hand, preached Christ crucified (salvation through Christ alone) and so was always being persecuted (5:11).

The same choice faces all Christian communicators today. Either we flatter people and tell them what they want to hear (about their ability to save themselves) – we develop a pussy-cat ministry, stroking them until they purr with pleasure – or we tell them the truth they do not want to hear (about sin, guilt, judgment, and the cross) and so arouse their hostility. In other words, either we are unfaithful in order to be popular or we are willing to be unpopular in our determination to be faithful. I doubt very much if it is possible to be faithful and popular at the same time. Paul saw the need to choose. So should we.

For further reading: Galatians 5:11; 6:11–18

THURSDAY

Evangelism Through the Local Church

OUR GOSPEL CAME TO YOU... YOU WELCOMED THE MESSAGE...
THE LORD'S MESSAGE RANG OUT FROM YOU...
1 Thessalonians 1:5–6, 8

Paul began his first letter to the Thessalonians by reminding them of his visit. He described it in three stages. Firstly, *"our gospel came to you"* (v. 5). It came with words (because it has a specific content). But not with words only, for words spoken in human weakness need to be confirmed with divine power. The gospel also came to them with deep conviction. If *power* describes the objective impact of the preaching, *conviction* describes the subjective state of the preachers. Moreover, the truth of the Word, the conviction with which it was spoken, and the power of its impact all stemmed from the Holy Spirit. Truth, conviction, and power are still three essential characteristics of authentic Christian preaching.

Secondly, *"you welcomed the message"* (v. 6). There had been severe suffering, for the true gospel always arouses hostility, but there is also joy when the gospel is received. The same Holy Spirit who gave power to those who preached the gospel gave joy to those who received it. He was working at both ends of the communication process. The converts also became imitators of Christ and his apostles and a model to believers because they had been transformed.

Thirdly, *"the Lord's message rang out from you"* (v. 8). The Greek verb can mean to sound, ring, peel, or boom. Chrysostom thought that Paul was likening the preaching of the gospel to the sound of a loud trumpet. At all events, the gospel proclaimed by the Thessalonians made a loud noise that seemed to reverberate through the hills and valleys of Greece.

Two points stand out in this first chapter of 1 Thessalonians. Firstly, the church that receives the gospel must pass it on. Nothing is more impressive than the sequence "our gospel came to you"–"you welcomed the message" – "the Lord's message rang out from you." This seems to be God's simplest plan for the spread of the good news throughout the world. Secondly, the church that passes on the gospel must embody it. The news of the transformation of the Thessalonians was spreading automatically, and the missionaries even felt redundant.

For further reading: 1 Thessalonians 1:1–10

Friday

Metaphors of Ministry

You ARE WITNESSES, AND SO IS GOD, OF HOW HOLY, RIGHTEOUS AND
BLAMELESS WE WERE AMONG YOU WHO BELIEVED.

1 Thessalonians 2:10

Paul's surreptitious night-time departure from Thessalonica and his failure to return aroused a lot of criticism, making it necessary for him to defend himself, which he did by a series of vivid metaphors.

He wrote first of the faithfulness of *a steward*: "We speak as those approved by God to be entrusted with the gospel" (v. 4). It is true that the word *steward* does not occur in the text, but the concept of stewardship is implicit, since Paul had been put in trust with the gospel.

Secondly, "We proved to be gentle among you, as *a mother* tenderly cares for her own children" (v. 7 NASB). Yes, and not only gentle, but affectionate and sacrificial as well. It is wonderful that Paul, who was tough in mind and character, should have referred to his ministry in these feminine terms.

Thirdly, "We dealt with each of you as *a father* deals with his own children" (v. 11, emphasis added). The apostle seems to be thinking of a father's educational role, teaching by both word and example.

Fourthly, Paul mentions the boldness of *a herald*. To herald (*kerysso*) is the commonest New Testament word for preaching. "We preached the gospel of God to you," Paul writes (v. 9).

The faithfulness of a steward, the gentleness of a mother, the encouragement of a father, and the boldness of a herald. From these four metaphors of ministry we learn the two major responsibilities of those who are called to pastoral ministry. The first is our responsibility to the Word of God, as stewards to guard it and heralds to proclaim it. And the second is our responsibility to the people of God, as their mother and father to love and encourage them. Or we could say that the two chief marks of pastoral leaders should be truth and love in combination. How is this possible? Only by the indwelling of the Holy Spirit, for he is the Spirit of truth, and the first fruit of the Spirit is love.

For further reading: 1 Thessalonians 2:1–13

SATURDAY

Glory Revealed

WE PRAY THIS SO THAT THE NAME OF OUR LORD JESUS MAY BE GLORIFIED
IN YOU, AND YOU IN HIM...

2 Thessalonians 1:12

Paul's two letters to the Thessalonians are well known for their many references to the Parousia, that is, the personal, visible, and glorious return of Christ. In fact, each of their eight chapters contains a mention of it. Particularly striking is the recurring reference in the second letter's first chapter to the glory of Christ.

Firstly, *the Lord Jesus will be revealed in his glory* (v. 7). True, the word *glory* is missing from this verse, but the implication is there. The Parousia will be no paltry sideshow but rather an event of awe-inspiring cosmic splendour.

Secondly, *the Lord Jesus will be glorified in his people* (v. 10). That is, the revelation of his glory will not be objective only (so that we will see it) but also in his people (so that we will share it). The two glorifications (his and ours) will take place simultaneously, though the apostle's emphasis is not so much on the glorification of the saved as on the glorification of the Saviour in the saved.

Thirdly, *those who deliberately reject Christ will be excluded from his glory* (vv. 8–9). Their terrible fate is described as both destruction and exclusion. The implied tragedy is that human beings made by God, like God, and for God should spend eternity without God, irrevocably banished from his presence. Instead of shining with the glory of Christ, their light will be extinguished in outer darkness. Here, then, is the solemn alternative that the apostle sets before us. It is either participation in or exclusion from the glory of Jesus Christ.

Fourthly, *meanwhile, Jesus Christ must begin to be glorified in us* (v. 12). The glorification of Jesus in his people and their consequent glorification are not a transformation that is entirely reserved for the last day. The process begins now. Indeed, it must begin now if it is to be brought to its proper end when Christ comes. That day will not suddenly reverse the processes that are going on now; it will rather confirm and complete them.

For further reading: 2 Thessalonians 1:1–12

Paul's letter to the Romans, although a genuine letter, is also a kind of Christian manifesto of freedom through Jesus Christ. It is the fullest and grandest statement of the gospel in the New Testament. It proclaims freedom from the wrath of God revealed against all ungodliness, freedom from "the dark little dungeon of our own ego" (Malcolm Muggeridge), freedom from ethnic conflict, freedom from death and the fear of death, freedom from pain and decay in the future redeemed universe, and freedom to live in love for God and our neighbour.

Romans has also had an enormous influence on the church, not least at the time of the Reformation. Luther called it "really the chief part of the New Testament, and... truly the purest gospel." Calvin added that if we understand it, "we have an open door to all the most profound treasures of Scripture." And William Tyndale, the father of the English Bible, described it as "the principal and most excellent part of the New Testament... and also a light and a way in unto the whole Scripture."

Above all, it contains Paul's own commitment to the gospel. In verses 14–16 of the first chapter he writes, "I am a debtor... I am eager... I am not ashamed of the gospel." May we experience the same eagerness!

Sunday: Universal Sin and Guilt

Monday: Divine Demonstration in the Cross

Tuesday: Dead to Sin, Alive in Christ

Wednesday: The Steadfast Love of God

Thursday: God's Plan for Jews and Gentiles

Friday: Transformed Relationships

Saturday: The Weak and the Strong

Universal Sin and Guilt

THEREFORE NO ONE WILL BE DECLARED RIGHTEOUS IN GOD'S SIGHT
BY THE WORKS OF THE LAW;
RATHER, THROUGH THE LAW WE BECOME CONSCIOUS OF OUR SIN.

Romans 3:20

Nothing keeps people away from Christ more than their inability to see their need of him or their unwillingness to admit it. It is this plain and unpopular principle that lies behind Romans 1:18–3:20. Paul demonstrates the universality of human sin and guilt by dividing the human race into several sections and by accusing them one by one. He shows that each group has failed to live up to the knowledge they have. Instead, they have deliberately suppressed and even contradicted it. Therefore they are guilty and without excuse. Nobody can plead innocence, because no one can plead ignorance.

Firstly, Paul portrays *depraved Gentile society* in its idolatry, immorality, and antisocial behaviour (1:18–32).

Secondly, Paul addresses *critical moralizers* (whether Gentiles or Jews), who profess high ethical standards and apply them to everybody except themselves (2:1–16).

Thirdly, Paul turns to *self-confident Jews*, who boast of their knowledge of God's law but do not obey it (2:17–3:8).

Fourthly, Paul encompasses *the whole human race* and concludes that we are all guilty and without excuse before God (3:9–20).

This is the point to which the apostle has been relentlessly moving, namely that "every mouth may be silenced" and that the whole world may be "held accountable to God" (v. 19).

How, then, should we respond to Paul's devastating exposure of human sin and guilt? Not, I think, by changing the subject and talking instead of the need for self-esteem, nor by blaming our behaviour on our genes, our nurturing, or our culture, but by accepting the divine diagnosis of our condition and by accepting responsibility for it too. Only then shall we be ready for the great "but now" of Romans 3:21, in which Paul begins to explain how God has intervened through Christ and his cross for our salvation.

For further reading: Romans 3:9–31

Monday

Divine Demonstration in the Cross

He did this to demonstrate his justice... But God demonstrates
his own love for us...

Romans 3:25; 5:8

All human beings of every race and rank, the immoral and the moralizing, Jews and Gentiles, are without exception sinful, guilty, inexcusable, and speechless before God. That was the terrible human predicament we considered yesterday. There was no ray of light, no flicker of hope, no prospect of rescue. "But now," Paul suddenly breaks in, God himself has intervened. After the long dark night a new day has dawned. It is a fresh revelation, and it focuses on Christ and his cross. Romans 3:21–26 is a tightly packed paragraph, which Charles Cranfield has called the "centre and heart" of this part of the letter, while Leon Morris goes further and writes that this paragraph may be "possibly the most important single paragraph ever written." For here great terms like *propitiation* or *atonement, redemption,* and *justification* occur.

But I will concentrate on what Paul writes about the demonstration of God's justice and love. The apostle draws a deliberate contrast between the past and the present, between sins committed previously (which God in his forbearance left unpunished) and the present in which God has acted to demonstrate his justice. It is a contrast between the divine forbearance that postponed the punishment and the divine justice that exacted it in Christ and his cross.

According to Romans 5:8, however, there was another demonstration on the cross: "But God demonstrates his own love for us in this: while we were still sinners, Christ died for us." Here *demonstrate* is really too weak a word; *prove* would be better. To grasp this, we need to remember that the essence of loving is giving and that the degree of love is measured partly by the costliness of the gift to the giver and partly by the worthiness or unworthiness of the recipient. By these standards, God's love in Christ is absolutely unique. For in sending his Son to die for sinners, he was giving everything, his very self, and giving himself for those who deserved nothing from him except judgment.

We cannot understand the cross unless we have seen it as a double demonstration – of God's justice and God's love.

For further reading: Romans 5:1–11

TUESDAY

Dead to Sin, Alive in Christ

WHAT SHALL WE SAY, THEN? SHALL WE GO ON SINNING, SO THAT GRACE
MAY INCREASE?

Romans 6:1

Twice in Romans 6 (vv. 1, 15) we hear Paul's imaginary critic asking the same question: Does Paul mean by his teaching that we may go on sinning so that God's grace may go on forgiving? Both times the apostle responds with an outraged "By no means!" Christians who ask such a question show that they have never understood the meaning of either their baptism (vv. 1–14) or their conversion (vv. 15–23).

Did they not know that their baptism signified union with Christ in his death, that his death was a death unto sin (meeting its demand and paying its penalty), and that they had shared in his resurrection too? By union with Christ they were themselves dead to sin but alive to God. How, then, could they go on living in what they had died to? It was similar with their conversion. Had they not decisively offered themselves to God as his slaves? How, then, could they contemplate lapsing into their old slavery to sin? Our baptism and conversion have both closed the door on the old life and opened a door to a new life. It is not impossible for us to go back, but it is inconceivable that we should. Far from encouraging sin, grace prohibits it.

It is not enough for us to utter our outraged negative "By no means!" We have to go further and confirm this negative with a reason, namely the necessity of remembering who we are on account of our conversion (inwardly) and our baptism (outwardly). We are one with Christ (vv. 1–14), and we are slaves of God (vv. 15–23). How, then, could we willfully persist in sin and presume on grace? The very thought is intolerable and a complete contradiction in terms. So we should constantly be reminding ourselves who we are. We need to learn to talk to ourselves and ask ourselves questions: "Don't you know who you are? Don't you know that you are united to Christ and enslaved to God?" We need to go on pressing ourselves with such questions until we reply to ourselves, "Yes, I *do* know who I am, a new person in Christ; and by the grace of God I mean to live accordingly."

For further reading: Romans 6:1–23

The Steadfast Love of God

I AM CONVINCED THAT NEITHER DEATH NOR LIFE, NEITHER ANGELS NOR
DEMONS,... NEITHER HEIGHT NOR DEPTH, NOR ANYTHING ELSE IN ALL
CREATION, WILL BE ABLE TO SEPARATE US FROM THE LOVE OF GOD THAT
IS IN CHRIST JESUS OUR LORD.

Romans 8:38–39

Romans 8 is without doubt one of the best-known chapters of the Bible, especially its last twelve verses. Here the apostle soars to sublime heights. Having described the chief privileges of justified believers – peace with God, union with Christ, freedom from the law, and life in the Spirit – Paul's great Spirit-directed mind now sweeps over the whole plan and purpose of God from a past eternity to an eternity still to come.

He begins with *five unshakeable convictions* (v. 28) – that God is at work in our lives, that he works for the good of his people, that he does it in all things, for those who love him, and have been called according to his purpose. We know these five things, Paul writes, even though we do not always understand them. Next come *five undeniable affirmations* (vv. 29–30), which elaborate what Paul means by God's "purpose." They refer to God's people whom God foreknew (meaning that he set his love on them), whom he predestined to be conformed to the likeness of his Son, whom he also called to himself through the gospel, whom he justified, and finally whom he glorified. Our glorification is expressed in a past tense, because of its certainty, even though it is still future. Thus Paul moves steadily on from stage to stage. Finally come *five unanswerable questions*:

Question 1: "If God is for us, who can be against us?" (v. 31). *Question 2*: "He who did not spare his own Son, but gave him up for us all – how will he not also, along with him, graciously give us all things?" (v. 32). *Question 3*: "Who will bring any charge against those whom God has chosen? It is God who justifies" (v. 33). *Question 4*: "Who is the one who condemns?... Christ Jesus who died – more than that, who was raised to life – is at the right hand of God and is also interceding for us" (v. 34). *Question 5*: "Who shall separate us from the love of Christ?" (v. 35).

Here, then, are five convictions about God's providence, five affirmations about his purpose, and five questions about his love, which together bring us fifteen assurances about him. We urgently need them today, since nothing in our world seems stable any longer.

For further reading: Romans 8:28–39

Thursday

God's Plan for Jews and Gentiles

AGAIN I ASK: DID THEY STUMBLE SO AS TO FALL BEYOND RECOVERY?
NOT AT ALL!

Romans 11:11

Throughout the first half of his letter Paul has forgotten neither the ethnic mix of the Roman church nor the tensions that kept surfacing between the Jewish Christian minority and the Gentile Christian majority. The time has now come for him to address head-on the underlying theological problem. How is it that the Jewish people as a whole have rejected their Messiah? Uniquely privileged by God, how could they remain entrenched in their prejudices?

Paul gives a double answer to these questions. To begin with, Jewish unbelief was due to God's purpose of election. But it was also attributable to Israel's own obstinate disobedience. In particular, she stumbled over the stumbling stone, namely Christ and his cross. This tension between divine election and human rebellion constitutes a contradiction that our finite minds cannot fathom. But we must affirm both truths, even if we cannot reconcile them.

In Romans 11 Paul looks into the future and declares that Israel's fall is neither total, since there is a believing remnant, nor final, since God has not rejected his people and they will recover (vv. 1–11). He then goes on to develop his allegory of the olive tree and teaches two lessons from it. The first is a warning to the Gentiles (the wild olive shoot that has been grafted in) not to presume or boast (vv. 17–22). The second is a promise to Israel (the natural branches) that if they do not persist in unbelief, they will be grafted back in again (vv. 23–24). Paul's vision for the future (which he calls a "mystery" [v. 25] or revelation) is that the full number of both Jews and Gentiles will be gathered in (vv. 12, 25). Indeed, God will have mercy on them all (v. 32), not meaning everybody without exception but rather both Jews and Gentiles without distinction. It is not surprising that this prospect leads Paul to break out into a doxology, in which he praises God for the depth of both his riches and his wisdom (vv. 33–36).

For further reading: Romans 11:25–36

Transformed Relationships

DO NOT CONFORM TO THE PATTERN OF THIS WORLD,
BUT BE TRANSFORMED BY THE RENEWING OF YOUR MIND.
Romans 12:2

Paul now makes an eloquent appeal to his readers. He bases it on the mercies of God that he has been expounding, and he calls for both the consecration of our bodies and the renewal of our minds. He sets before us the stark alternative that has always and everywhere confronted the people of God, either to conform to the pattern of this world or to be transformed by renewed minds that discern God's "good, pleasing and perfect will" (v. 2). The choice is between the world's fashion and the Lord's will.

In the chapters that follow, it becomes clear that God's good will is concerned with all our relationships, which are radically changed by the gospel. Paul treats eight of them. For example, we are to cultivate a sober estimate of ourselves and to exercise our gifts for the benefit of the body of Christ. But the most challenging exhortation is the call to love our enemies (vv. 17–21). Echoing the teaching of Jesus, Paul writes that we are not to repay evil for evil but to be careful to do what is good. We are not to take revenge but rather to leave the punishment of evil to God.

It is important to keep together the two texts that both refer to the wrath of God. According to Romans 12:19 we are not to take revenge but "leave it to the wrath of God" (RSV). According to Romans 13:4 the magistrate is one of "God's servants, agents of wrath to bring punishment on the wrongdoer." We human beings as private individuals are to love and serve our enemies. We are not authorized to take the law into our own hands and punish offenders. The punishment of evil is God's prerogative, and during the present age he exercises it through the law courts.

For further reading: Romans 12:14–13:5

SATURDAY

The Weak and the Strong

ACCEPT THE ONE WHOSE FAITH IS WEAK,
WITHOUT QUARRELLING OVER DISPUTABLE MATTERS.

Romans 14:1

Our relationship with the weak is the one Paul treats at greatest length (14:1–15:13). They are evidently weak in faith or conviction rather than in will or character. So if we are trying to picture a weaker brother or sister, we must envisage not a vulnerable Christian easily overcome by temptation but a sensitive Christian full of indecision and scruples. What the weak lack is not strength of self-control but liberty of conscience. The weak in Rome must have been mainly Jewish Christians, who believed they should still observe both the food laws and the feasts and fasts of the Jewish calendar. Paul himself was one of the strong and identifies with their position. His educated conscience assures him that foods and days are matters of secondary importance. At the same time, he refuses to ride roughshod over the sensitive consciences of the weak. His overall exhortation to the church is to accept the weak as God has done (14:1, 3) and to accept one another as Christ has done (15:7). The strong must not despise, browbeat, or condemn the weak or damage them by persuading them to act against their conscience.

The most notable feature of Paul's instructions is that he grounds them on his Christology, and in particular on the death, resurrection, and Parousia of Jesus. The weak are brothers and sisters for whom Christ died. Christ rose to be their Lord, and we have no right to interfere with his servants. He is also coming to be our judge, so we should not play the role of judge ourselves. We should also follow the example of Christ, who did not please himself but became a servant, indeed, a servant of both Jews and Gentiles. So Paul leaves his readers with a beautiful vision of the weak and the strong, Jewish believers and Gentile believers, who are bound together by such a spirit of unity that "with one mind and one voice" they might glorify God together (15:6).

For further reading: Romans 15:1–13

WEEK 44: THE TWO LETTERS TO CORINTH

It is difficult to reconstruct Paul's visits and letters to Corinth, which helped to cement his relationship to the members of the Corinthian church. It is clear, however, that strong bonds of Christian affection united him to them. It was natural for him to address them as "my dear children" (1 Cor. 4:14). For though they may have had "ten thousand guardians" (v. 15) to discipline them, they did not have many fathers to love them, whereas Paul had become their father through the gospel (see vv. 14–21).

It is interesting to compare the Roman and Corinthian letters. Romans is an orderly, carefully constructed unfolding of the gospel, while the two Corinthian letters were ad hoc documents, responding to the perceived needs of the Corinthians and answering some of their questions. Perhaps as many as twenty topics are handled in 1 and 2 Corinthians – theological, ethical, pastoral, and personal. Although they address real problems in first-century Corinth, Paul's instruction is remarkably relevant to the needs of the church in many cultures today.

Sunday: Power Through Weakness

Monday: The Debate About Idol Meats

Tuesday: The Spirit of Unity

Wednesday: Paul's Travel Plans

Thursday: Supernatural Dimensions of Evangelism

Friday: Good News of Reconciliation

Saturday: Grace and Giving

SUNDAY

Power Through Weakness

BUT WE HAVE THIS TREASURE IN JARS OF CLAY TO SHOW THAT
THIS ALL-SURPASSING POWER IS FROM GOD AND NOT FROM US.

2 Corinthians 4:7

One of the overriding themes of the Corinthian correspondence is power through weakness; there are eight distinct expressions of it in the two letters.

Of course, the lust for power has been a characteristic of the human story ever since Adam and Eve were offered power in exchange for disobedience. Still today the pursuit of money, fame, and influence is a concealed drive for power. We see it in politics and in public life, in big business and industry, in the professions and the media, and even in the church and in parachurch organizations. Power! It is more intoxicating than alcohol, more addictive than drugs. It was Lord Acton, the nineteenth-century British politician, who composed the epigram, "Power tends to corrupt; absolute power corrupts absolutely." He was a Roman Catholic who in 1870 strongly opposed the decision of the First Vatican Council to attribute infallibility to the pope. He saw it as power corrupting the church.

The Bible contains clear warnings about the use and abuse of power, and Paul insisted on his theme of power through weakness, divine power through human weakness. In the first two chapters of 1 Corinthians, he gives three striking examples of the same principle.

We see it first in the gospel itself, for the weakness of the cross is the saving power of God (1 Cor. 1:17–25). Secondly, we see power through weakness in the Corinthian converts, for God had chosen weak people to shame the strong (1 Cor. 1:26–31). Thirdly, power through weakness is exhibited in Paul the evangelist, since he had come to Corinth "in weakness with great fear and trembling" but also "with a demonstration of the Spirit's power" (1 Cor. 2:1–5).

Thus the gospel, the converts, and the preacher (or the evangel, the evangelized, and the evangelist) all exhibited the same principle that God's power operates best in human weakness. For God chose a weak instrument (Paul) to bring a weak message (the cross) to weak people (the socially despised). But through this triple weakness the power of God was – and still is – displayed.

For further reading: 1 Corinthians 1:18–2:5

Monday

The Debate About Idol Meats

NOW ABOUT FOOD SACRIFICED TO IDOLS: WE KNOW THAT
"WE ALL POSSESS KNOWLEDGE". BUT KNOWLEDGE PUFFS UP
WHILE LOVE BUILDS UP.

1 Corinthians 8:1

Today's text plunges us into one of the hottest debates that rocked the first-century Christian church. Were the followers of Jesus permitted to eat meat that, before it was sold in the butcher's shop, had been used in a pagan sacrificial ritual? Or was the eating of such meat tantamount to idolatry?

The opponents in the debate (whom we met last Saturday) were the weak and the strong. On the one hand, those with a strong conscience were theologically well educated. They knew that idols were nothing, so they had no qualms about eating. And they were right. But they had little respect for the weak. They bulldozed their way through other people's consciences. In their case their knowledge needed to be tempered with love. On the other hand, those with a weak conscience, probably just converted from idolatry, were anxious above everything to serve God faithfully. They would not even touch idol meats. They were right in their resolve to have nothing to do with idols. But their theology was weak. In their case their love for God needed to be strengthened by sound knowledge. The strong needed more gentleness, and the weak more understanding.

The key expression is that "knowledge puffs up while love builds up" (v. 1). Knowledge brings freedom (vv. 4–8). We know there is only one God, and our monotheism brings us freedom of conscience and of action. But some people do not have this knowledge and therefore do not have this freedom. Therefore love limits freedom (vv. 9–13). If someone with a weak conscience sees you (a person of knowledge) defiantly eating in an idol's temple, he might be emboldened to follow your example and so wound his conscience.

From this ancient debate two permanent truths stand out. First, *consciences must be respected*. They are not infallible. They need to be educated, but they must not be violated. We must never ride roughshod over other people's consciences. Secondly, *love limits liberty*. Our conscience, educated by the Word of God, gives us great freedom of action. Yet this does not allow us to assert our freedom at other people's expense. Knowledge gives freedom, but love limits it.

For further reading: 1 Corinthians 8:1–13

TUESDAY

The Spirit of Unity

JUST AS... MANY PARTS FORM ONE BODY, SO IT IS WITH CHRIST.
FOR WE WERE ALL BAPTISED BY ONE SPIRIT SO AS TO FORM ONE BODY –
WHETHER JEWS OR GENTILES, SLAVE OR FREE – AND WE WERE ALL GIVEN
THE ONE SPIRIT TO DRINK.

1 Corinthians 12:12-13

We know from 1 Corinthians 1 that the Corinthian church was torn apart by factions, and it is against this background of division that we can best understand today's text. Paul's emphasis is that there is only one Holy Spirit and that he is the Spirit of unity. Seven or eight times in the first half of chapter 12 he is called either "the one Spirit" or "the same Spirit." Paul enforces this by making three strong and unifying statements.

Firstly, all believers have been *illumined* by one and the same Spirit to say "Jesus is Lord" (vv. 1–3). Still today this is a reliable test to apply to any person or movement. The characteristic work of the Holy Spirit is to glorify Jesus. We must never separate the second and third persons of the Trinity.

Secondly, all believers have been *enriched* by one and the same Spirit with different gifts (vv. 4–11). There are five lists of spiritual gifts in the New Testament. Added together, there are at least twenty-one of them, and some are quite ordinary, like administrative gifts, doing works of mercy, and giving money. Their purpose is "for the common good" (v. 7), and the more they build up the church, the more important they are (14:12).

Thirdly, all believers have been *baptized* with one and the same Spirit into the body of Christ (vv. 12–13). It is well known that Pentecostal and charismatic Christians regard the baptism of the Spirit as a second experience, subsequent to conversion and new birth, that some Christians have received and others have not (though all may). But our text appears to contradict this teaching. For here, according to the apostle Paul, we have all been baptized with the one Spirit and have all drunk of the same Spirit. The gift of the Spirit, portrayed now as a baptism and now as drinking, is the privilege of all believers. "If anyone does not have the Spirit of Christ, they do not belong to Christ" (Rom. 8:9).

For further reading: 1 Corinthians 12:1–13

Paul's Travel Plans

I HOPE TO SPEND SOME TIME WITH YOU, IF THE LORD PERMITS.
BUT I WILL STAY ON AT EPHESUS UNTIL PENTECOST...

1 Corinthians 16:7-8

Paul is in Ephesus, the capital of Asia, but intends to travel through Macedonia to Corinth and then hopes to take the collection money to Jerusalem. This journey is at least thirteen hundred miles as the crow flies and considerably more by ship.

Notice that the apostle made his plans in two complementary ways. On the one hand, all his plans were subject to the will and purpose of God. His conditional clause "if the Lord permits" was not the artificial addition of the words "God willing" to every sentence but a genuine submission of his plans to Christ. On the other hand, in making plans, Paul used his common sense and took into consideration all relevant circumstances. For example, he wanted to go to Jerusalem because of the symbolic importance of the gift he would take with him. On his way he would like to spend adequate time (winter) in Corinth, seeking to bring peace to a divided church and waiting until winter storms would end and make the sea navigable again. On his way to Corinth he planned to pass through Macedonia, visiting Philippi, Thessalonica, and Berea. Meanwhile, he wanted to stay in Ephesus until Pentecost (about June), partly because "a great door for effective work" (v. 9) had opened for him (in the hall of Tyrannus) and partly because many were opposing him. Thus each stage of his journey had reasons. He would spend spring in Ephesus, summer in Macedonia, and autumn and winter in Corinth, sailing for Jerusalem the following spring. It is impressive that Paul handled his travel plans by a judicious combination of divine guidance and common sense.

The lesson we learn from 1 Corinthians 16 is that all life belongs to God, and that nothing is outside the sphere of his interest. Dualism, or the divorce of things sacred from things secular, has been a disastrous tendency throughout church history. The apostle Paul was emphatically not guilty of it. In 1 Corinthians 15 he handled sublime resurrection truth, while in chapter 16 he handled everyday affairs. He lived in both worlds simultaneously.

For further reading: 1 Corinthians 16:1-9

Thursday

Supernatural Dimensions of Evangelism

GOD, WHO SAID, "LET LIGHT SHINE OUT OF DARKNESS," MADE HIS LIGHT
SHINE IN OUR HEARTS TO GIVE US THE LIGHT OF THE KNOWLEDGE OF
GOD'S GLORY DISPLAYED IN THE FACE OF CHRIST.

2 Corinthians 4:6

Second Corinthians 3–4 is a classical passage on the pastoral ministry. In it Paul introduces the supernatural dimensions of evangelism. "The god of this age [the devil]," he tells us, has blinded the eyes of unbelievers (v. 4). And faced with their blindness, we are helpless. For it is not given to us to open the eyes of the blind. A thick veil lies over their minds so that they cannot see the light of the gospel of Christ.

Only God the Creator can open eyes the devil has blinded. So Paul takes us back to the beginning of Genesis and reminds us that into the primeval darkness God's voice rang out, "Let there be light." Just as in creation God said, "Let there be light," so in the new creation God has shone in our hearts. Regeneration is just as much a divine creative act as was God's original creative fiat.

Here, then, are two so-called gods locked in a life-and-death struggle – on the one hand, "the god of this age" (v. 4) and on the other, "the God and Father of our Lord Jesus Christ" (1:3). Moreover, the characteristic action of each is plain. The devil blinds the minds of unbelievers, but God shines into darkened hearts (v. 6). In this supernatural conflict we wonder if we have anything to contribute. If the devil blinds and God shines, would it not be prudent for us to withdraw from the field of battle and leave them to fight it out? This is, in fact, the conclusion that some Christians draw. But it is not Paul's. See verse 5, which I have so far deliberately omitted. If we put the three verses together, we find that the devil blinds (v. 4), God shines (v. 6), and we preach Christ Jesus as Lord (v. 5). That is, evangelism (the proclamation of the gospel of Christ), far from being superfluous, is actually indispensable. If the light by which God rescues people from darkness is the gospel, we had better preach it! The faithful preaching of the gospel is the God-appointed means by which the prince of darkness is overthrown and God shines his light into human hearts.

For further reading: 2 Corinthians 4:1–6

FRIDAY

Good News of Reconciliation

ALL THIS IS FROM GOD, WHO RECONCILED US TO HIMSELF THROUGH
CHRIST AND GAVE US THE MINISTRY OF RECONCILIATION...

2 Corinthians 5:18

Of the four main New Testament models or metaphors of the atonement (propitiation, redemption, justification, and reconciliation), reconciliation is arguably the most popular, because it is the most personal. And of the four main New Testament passages about reconciliation, this one in 2 Corinthians 5 is the fullest and most striking. It depicts three actors in the drama.

Firstly, *God is the author of the reconciliation.* "All this is from God" (v. 18). There are eight main verbs in this paragraph, all of which have God as their subject. The whole initiative was his. So no account of the atonement is biblical that takes the initiative away from God and gives it to Christ or, indeed, to us.

Secondly, *Christ is the agent of the reconciliation.* "God the author, Christ the agent" is a satisfactory summary. Both verse 18 and verse 19 speak of God reconciling in or through Christ. As P. T. Forsyth put it, "'God was in Christ reconciling,' actually reconciling, finishing the work. It was not a tentative preliminary affair... Reconciliation was finished in Christ's death." How did this happen? Negatively, God refused to count our sins against us (v. 19); positively, he made the sinless Christ to be sin instead (v. 21) in order that in Christ we might become the righteousness of God. As Richard Hooker expressed it, "Let it be counted folly or frenzy or whatsoever. It is our wisdom and our comfort; we care for no knowledge in the world but this, that man has sinned and God has suffered; that God has made himself the sin of men and that men are made the righteousness of God."

Thirdly, *we are the ambassadors of the reconciliation.* Both the ministry and the message of reconciliation have now been committed to us. In consequence, as we implore people to be reconciled to God, it is God himself who is making his appeal through us. Our task is first to expound what God has done at the cross and then to issue the appeal. It is a safe rule that there must be no appeal without an exposition and no exposition without an appeal.

For further reading: 2 Corinthians 5:11–21

SATURDAY

Grace and Giving

YOU KNOW THE GRACE OF OUR LORD JESUS CHRIST, THAT THOUGH HE
WAS RICH, YET FOR YOUR SAKE HE BECAME POOR, SO THAT YOU THROUGH
HIS POVERTY MIGHT BECOME RICH.

2 Corinthians 8:9

Grace is a synonym for *generosity*, and the Lord Jesus Christ has given us in his birth
and death a superlative example of it. Consider these four stages. Firstly, he was rich,
existing eternally in his heavenly riches, sharing his Father's being and his rule over the
created universe, immune to sin, pain, and death.

Secondly, he became poor. He not only "made himself nothing" and "humbled
himself" (Phil. 2:7–8), but "we might even dare say that he beggared himself" (Handley
Moule). He laid aside his royal splendour and became a servant. He was obedient unto
death, even death on the cross.

Thirdly, he did it for poor sinners like us, whose poverty is seen in our having
forfeited paradise and lost our fellowship with God.

Fourthly, it was to make us rich that he impoverished himself – rich with "the
boundless riches of Christ" (Eph. 3:8), that is to say, with salvation in its fullness.

Thus the rich Christ became poor so that we in our poverty might become rich with
his riches. Christ impoverished himself in order to enrich us. It is a beautiful statement
of the gospel. But the most amazing thing about this text is its context. It is embedded
in 2 Corinthians 8 and 9, in which Paul is persuading the Greek churches to help
relieve the poverty of the Judean church. Although he deploys an array of arguments
in these two chapters, his trump card is the cross of Christ. It was because Christ gave
himself to the uttermost that they too must learn to give. Authentic Christian giving
is spontaneous, sacrificial, and symbolical. The latter was especially important to the
apostle. For the collection he was organizing was no mere transfer of cash from Greece
to Judea, and from the rich to the poor, but a gift from Gentile churches to the Jewish
church. Paul saw it as a wonderful opportunity to promote Gentile–Jewish solidarity
in the body of Christ. Our gifts also symbolize our support of the causes to which we
give them.

For further reading: 2 Corinthians 8:1–9

On his arrival in Rome the apostle Paul was kept under house arrest, manacled to a Roman soldier, for about two years (AD 60–62). He referred to himself as "a prisoner for the Lord" (Eph. 4:1) and "in chains for Christ" (Phil. 1:13).

We reflected about three weeks ago on the providence of God, which permitted Paul to be incarcerated. We wondered if it was that, delivered from the feverish activity of his missionary days and unable either to evangelize more cities or to visit the churches, he would have had more time to meditate. Hence the three prison letters (the little letter to Philemon makes the fourth), each of which has a sublime Christology. In Philippians Jesus is depicted as descending to the depths and being exalted to the heights. In Ephesians we see everything put under his feet, and in Colossians he is seen as the supreme head of both creations, of the universe and of the church.

Sunday: Living a Life Worthy of the Gospel

Monday: Christianity is Christ

Tuesday: Knowing God's Power

Wednesday: God's New Society

Thursday: A Meditation on Marriage

Friday: The Goal of Maturity

Saturday: We are United with Christ

SUNDAY

Living a Life Worthy of the Gospel

WHATEVER HAPPENS, CONDUCT YOURSELVES IN A MANNER WORTHY OF
THE GOSPEL OF CHRIST.

Philippians 1:27

Because he is a prisoner, Paul's future is wholly uncertain. He knows that he may be approaching death. But "whatever happens," whether he lives or dies, his main concern is not for himself but for the gospel and what will happen to it when he is gone. So he issues to the Philippians an eloquent fivefold summons (vv. 27–30).

Firstly, there is the call to *live a life worthy of the gospel*. Our conduct is to be in tune with our calling. There is to be no dichotomy between what we say and what we are, but rather a fundamental consistency.

Secondly, Paul calls us to *stand firm in the gospel*. Stability is important in every sphere. We talk about a stable government, economy, and building. Luke tells us that the apostles revisited the towns they had evangelized, establishing the converts. Yet stability in doctrine and ethics is in short supply today.

Thirdly, there is the call to *contend for the faith of the gospel*. This describes a combination of evangelism and apologetics, not only proclaiming the gospel, but also defending it and arguing for its truth.

Fourthly, we are to *work together for the gospel*. This is the call to unity that is much emphasized in Philippians. Paul urges the Christians in Philippi to "stand firm in one spirit, striving together as one for the faith of the gospel" (v. 27). The apostle does not, of course, advocate unity at any price, even compromising fundamental truths in order to attain it, but unity in the essentials of the gospel.

Fifthly, Paul issues a call to *suffer for the gospel*. "For it has been granted to you on behalf of Christ not only to believe in him, but also to suffer for him" (v. 29). It is very striking that faith and suffering are twin Christian privileges that are given to the people of God. The Philippians had seen Paul suffer physical persecution in their city, and they will suffer too. For "suffering is the badge of the true Christian," wrote Dietrich Bonhoeffer.

For further reading: Philippians 1:27–30

Christianity is Christ

BUT WHATEVER WERE GAINS TO ME I NOW CONSIDER LOSS FOR THE SAKE OF CHRIST. WHAT IS MORE, I CONSIDER EVERYTHING A LOSS BECAUSE OF THE SURPASSING WORTH OF KNOWING CHRIST JESUS MY LORD, FOR WHOSE SAKE I HAVE LOST ALL THINGS.

Philippians 3:7–8

It is extraordinary how many people think that the essence of Christianity is either believing the creed or living an upright life or going to church, all of which are important but miss the centrality of Christ. They need to read Paul's letter to the Philippians and especially note 1:21: "For to me, to live is Christ."

The apostle enlarges on this in chapter 3. He draws up a kind of profit-and-loss account. On one side of the ledger he puts everything he can think of that could be considered profitable – his ancestry, parentage, and education; his Hebrew culture; his religious zeal and legalistic righteousness. In the other column he writes one word only – *Christ*. Then he makes a careful calculation and concludes, "I count everything sheer loss, far outweighed by the gain of knowing Christ Jesus my Lord" (v. 8 REB). "Knowing Christ" is the claim to a personal relationship with Christ that occurs repeatedly in the New Testament.

Next, the apostle continues, "For whose sake I have lost all things. I consider them garbage, that I may gain Christ" (v. 8), where he is likened to a treasure one can "gain."

Paul also writes of being "found in him, not having a righteousness of my own that comes from the law, but that which is through faith in Christ – the righteousness that comes from God on the basis of faith" (v. 9). We need to unpack this involved sentence. God is righteous. It stands to reason, therefore, that if we are to enter his presence, we must be righteous too. There are only two possible ways of doing this. One is to establish our own righteousness by obedience to the law, which is impossible. The other is to receive righteousness as a gift from Christ who died for us, if we trust in him.

So for salvation we are those who glory in Christ Jesus and put no confidence in ourselves. Christianity is Christ – knowing him, gaining him, and trusting him.

For further reading: Philippians 3:3–11

TUESDAY

Knowing God's Power

I PRAY THAT THE EYES OF YOUR HEART MAY BE ENLIGHTENED IN ORDER
THAT YOU MAY KNOW... HIS INCOMPARABLY GREAT POWER FOR US WHO
BELIEVE. THAT POWER IS THE SAME AS THE MIGHTY STRENGTH HE
EXERTED WHEN HE RAISED CHRIST FROM THE DEAD...

Ephesians 1:18–20

Ephesians 1 is divided into two parts. In part one Paul blesses God for blessing us in Christ. In part two he prays that God will open our eyes to see the fullness of this blessing. It is very important to keep praise and prayer together. Some Christians do little but pray for fresh blessings, oblivious to the blessings they have already received. Others emphasize that all spiritual blessings are already theirs in Christ, and they have no appetite for any more. Both positions are unbalanced.

Paul's prayer is essentially that the Ephesians may know (both in understanding and in experience) the hope of God's call, the glory of his inheritance, and meanwhile the greatness of his power. It is on God's power that the apostle concentrates. So certain is he that God's power is sufficient that he accumulates words, writing of the energy of the might of his strength. And he prays that the Ephesians may know the immeasurable greatness of his power. How might they know it? Because he has given a public demonstration of it in the resurrection, enthronement, and coronation of Christ. This great power, which God exerted in Christ, is now available for us.

The whole thrust of Paul's prayer is that his readers might have a thorough knowledge of God's call, inheritance, and power, especially the latter. But how did he expect his prayer to be answered? Firstly, by the enlightenment of the Holy Spirit, who is "the Spirit of wisdom and revelation" (v. 17) in our knowledge of Christ. And secondly, by our reflection on the objective revelation of God's power in the resurrection and exaltation of Jesus. Once again we note Paul's healthy combination of the objective and the subjective, of revelation and illumination, of history and experience, of Christ and the Holy Spirit.

For further reading: Ephesians 1:15–23

God's New Society

HIS [GOD'S] PURPOSE WAS TO CREATE IN HIMSELF ONE NEW HUMANITY
OUT OF THE TWO, THUS MAKING PEACE...

Ephesians 2:15

Nobody can emerge from a study of Ephesians with a privatized gospel. For Ephesians might be called "the gospel of the church." It sets forth God's purpose to create through Jesus Christ a new society.

Firstly, however, in Ephesians 2 Paul depicts the Gentile world in its double alienation – from God ("dead in your transgressions and sins" [v. 1]) and from his people Israel ("alienated from the commonwealth of Israel" [v. 12 RSV]). In the second half of Ephesians 2 the apostle concentrates on the plight of the Gentiles. It is almost impossible for us to grasp, let alone feel, the contempt in which the Jews held the Gentiles. They called them "dogs"; they were "far off," alienated both from God and from the people of God.

Of this double alienation the "middle wall of partition" (v. 14 KJV) or "dividing wall of hostility" (RSV) was a standing symbol. It was a notable feature of the magnificent temple built in Jerusalem by Herod the Great. The temple was enclosed by three inner courts for the priests and the laypeople of Israel. Beyond these, and at a lower level, was the outer court or Court of the Gentiles. And between the inner and the outer courts was the dividing wall, a stone barricade one and a half meters high. Gentiles might look up and view the temple but not enter it. Warning notices at regular intervals on the wall forbade entry on pain of death.

The grand theme of Ephesians 2 is that Jesus Christ through his cross has abolished the dividing wall (even though physically it was not destroyed until forty years later) and has created a single, undivided humanity, whose characteristic is no longer alienation but reconciliation, no longer division and hostility but unity and peace.

It is a wonderful vision. But the contemporary reality tells a different story, namely of barriers of race, ethnicity, nationality, tribe, and gender. But how dare we erect walls of partition in the only community in which Christ has destroyed them?

For further reading: Ephesians 2:11–22

THURSDAY

A Meditation on Marriage

WIVES, SUBMIT YOURSELVES TO YOUR OWN HUSBANDS AS YOU DO TO
THE LORD… HUSBANDS, LOVE YOUR WIVES, JUST AS CHRIST LOVED THE
CHURCH…

Ephesians 5:22, 25

The apostle Paul is widely regarded as having been an incorrigible misogynist. But those who think this cannot have considered the implications of Ephesians 5:21–33. For here, centuries before its time, is sublime Christian teaching that urgently needs to be better known. Consider these five aspects of it.

Firstly, the requirement that the wife submits to her husband is a particular example of a general Christian duty. For the injunction "wives, submit" (v. 22) immediately follows the requirement that we "submit to one another" (v. 21). If therefore it is the bride's duty to submit to the bridegroom, it is also his duty as a member of God's new society to submit to her. Submissiveness is not to be unilateral. It is a universal Christian obligation, exemplified by our Lord Jesus himself. Secondly, the wife's submission is to be given to a lover, not to an ogre. The apostle's instruction is not "Wives, submit; husbands, boss." It is "Wives, submit… Husbands, love." And there is all the difference in the world between a lover and a tyrant.

Thirdly, husbands are to love like Christ (three times). Submission may sound hard, but love is harder. The highest pinnacle of demand is reached in verse 25, where husbands are to love their wives "as Christ loved the church and gave himself up for her." No nobler standard can be conceived than Calvary love. Fourthly, the husband's love, like Christ's, sacrifices in order to serve. That is, his love and self-sacrifice for the church were positive and purposive, namely to free her from all defects and so display her in her full glory. The husband's headship similarly is not to suppress or oppress his wife, but rather to liberate her into the fullness of her femininity.

Fifthly, submission is another aspect of love. Although *submit* and *love* are two different verbs, it is difficult to distinguish between them. For what is it to submit? It is to give oneself up to somebody. What is it to love? It is to give oneself up to somebody. Thus selfless self-giving by both husband and wife is the foundation of an enduring and growing marriage.

For further reading: Ephesians 5:21–33

FRIDAY

The Goal of Maturity

IT IS HE [CHRIST] WHOM WE PROCLAIM, WARNING EVERYONE AND
TEACHING EVERYONE IN ALL WISDOM, SO THAT WE MAY PRESENT
EVERYONE MATURE IN CHRIST.

Colossians 1:28 NRSV

We tend to think of Paul as a pioneer missionary who won converts, planted churches, and moved on. But the goal of his ministry, he tells us, was to go beyond conversion to discipleship, namely to "present everyone mature in Christ" (NRSV), enjoying a relationship with Christ in which we worship, love, trust, and obey him.

How, then, do Christians mature? Our text gives us a plain answer. It is through the proclamation of Christ. If Christian maturity is maturity in our relation to Christ, then the clearer our vision of Christ, the more convinced we are that he is worthy of our commitment. As Dr J. I. Packer has written in his classic book *Knowing God*, "We are pygmy Christians because we have a pygmy God," or indeed, "a pygmy Christ." The truth is that there are many Jesuses on offer in the world's religious supermarkets, caricatures of the authentic Jesus. There is Jesus the ascetic, Jesus the clown of *Godspell*, Jesus Christ Superstar, Jesus the capitalist and Jesus the socialist, Jesus the founder of modern business, and Jesus the urban guerrilla. All these images are defective; none of them is calculated to win our wholehearted allegiance.

Instead, we need to see Jesus as Paul presents him in verses 15–21. This is one of the most sublime Christological passages in the New Testament. It portrays Jesus as the visible image of the invisible God, the agent and heir of creation. He is also the firstborn from the dead so that in everything he might have the preeminence. Indeed, the fullness of the Godhead dwells in Christ and has reconciled all things through Christ. Thus Jesus Christ has a double supremacy as head of the universe and head of the church. He is the Lord of both creations. When we see him thus, our place is on our faces, prostrate before him. Away, then, with our petty, puny, pygmy Jesuses! Away with our Jesus clowns and Jesus pop stars, our political messiahs and revolutionaries. If this is how we think of Christ, no wonder our immaturities persist. If only the veil could be taken from our eyes and we could see Jesus as he is in the fullness of his divine–human person and saving work. Then we would give him the honour that is due to his name, and we would grow into a mature relationship with him.

For further reading: Colossians 1:15–29

SATURDAY

We are United with Christ

SINCE, THEN, YOU HAVE BEEN RAISED WITH CHRIST, SET YOUR HEARTS ON
THINGS ABOVE, WHERE CHRIST IS, SEATED AT THE RIGHT HAND OF GOD.

Colossians 3:1

Colossians 3 is a set passage for Easter Day. It illustrates the vital union between theology and ethics, and in particular that we must *know* who we are before we can *be* who we are. Paul's exhortation to Christian behaviour is based on his exposition of Christian identity. The exhortation is "set your hearts on things above," and the exposition is that we have died and risen with Christ.

So who are we? Paul refers in succession to the four major events in the saving career of Jesus, namely his death, resurrection, exaltation, and Parousia. At the same time, he writes of these events not only as happening to Christ but also as being shared by us. Four times he uses the little Greek word *sun*, meaning "together with." You died *with Christ* (2:20), you have been raised *with Christ* (3:1), your life is hidden *with Christ* (3:3), and you will appear *with Christ* (3:4). These great statements are not make-believe; they tell us what happens to us as a result of being united to *Christ* through faith inwardly and baptism outwardly. We are the same people with the same face, name, passport, nationality, and appearance. But we are new people, enjoying a hidden life with Christ. Indeed, Christ is our life (3:4).

We turn now from Paul's exposition of who we are if we are Christians to his exhortation regarding how we should behave. "Set your hearts on things above," he writes (v. 1). Again, "set your minds on things above, not on earthly things" (v. 2).

By "earthly things" Paul did not mean that we should neglect our earthly responsibilities at home and work, in church and community. For he goes on to lay down the duties of husbands and wives, children and parents, slaves and masters. No, the idea of earthly things is repeated in verse 5, where it refers to greed and immorality, slander, anger, malice, and other sins. These we are to put to death.

We need to keep talking to ourselves and reminding ourselves of who we are. Only then will we behave accordingly.

For further reading: Colossians 3:11–14

Timothy and Titus occupied a special place in the affection and ministry of the apostle Paul. His letters to them contain extremely valuable teaching in relation to the life of the local church.

The background of all three letters is the apostle's absence. It may be temporary (on account of his hope to visit them) or permanent (on account of his impending death). So his overriding preoccupation is not for himself but for the gospel, which he also calls "the faith," "the truth," "the teaching," or "the deposit." What would happen to it when he has gone? Ten times he exhorts Timothy and Titus to "teach these things" (1 Tim. 4:11), both guarding the truth and passing it on. Timothy and Titus were also instructed to select and appoint pastors (Timothy in Ephesus, Titus in Crete), whose main responsibility would be both to teach the truth and to refute error. Paul's strategy is outlined in 2 Timothy 2:2: "The things you have heard me say in the presence of many witnesses entrust to reliable people [the pastors] who will also be qualified to teach others." This is the true apostolic succession – a continuity of apostolic teaching from generation to generation, made possible by the New Testament.

Sunday: The Church's Global Perspective

Monday: Advice to a Young Leader

Tuesday: A Charge to a Man of God

Wednesday: Qualifications for the Presbyterate

Thursday: The Two Epiphanies of Christ

Friday: Resisting the Pressures of the World

Saturday: Paul's Last Imprisonment

The Church's Global Perspective

GOD OUR SAVIOUR... WANTS ALL PEOPLE TO BE SAVED AND TO COME TO A
KNOWLEDGE OF THE TRUTH.

1 Timothy 2:3–4

What is immediately noteworthy about the first seven verses of 1 Timothy 2 is the repetition (surely deliberate) of the expression "all people."

Firstly, *the church's prayers should concern everybody* – not only all people in general but in particular kings and other national leaders as preservers of the peace – even though at that time there were no Christian rulers anywhere in the world.

Secondly, *God's desire concerns everybody*. God wants everybody to be saved (v. 4). That is, the reason why the church is concerned for everybody is that God is. Further, the universality of the gospel offer rests on the unity of God: "For there is only one God" (v. 5 NJB). The first essential basis for world mission is monotheism.

Thirdly, *Christ's death concerns everybody*: "There is... one mediator between God and mankind, the man Christ Jesus, who gave himself as a ransom for all people" (vv. 5–6). It is not enough to affirm that there is only one God; we have to add that there is only one Mediator, one Saviour. The Son of God who first became "the man Christ Jesus" in his birth then in his death gave himself as a ransom for us. It is important for us to keep these three nouns together – *man, ransom,* and *mediator*; they allude to his birth, death, and resurrection. Because in no other person has God first become man and then become a ransom, there is no other mediator. Nobody else has his qualifications.

Fourthly, *the apostle's proclamation concerned everybody*, for he had been appointed an apostle, a herald, and a teacher to the Gentiles (that is, to all nations). Although there are no apostles today comparable to Paul, there is an urgent need for more heralds and teachers of the gospel.

To sum up, the church must pray for everybody (v. 1) and preach to everybody (v. 7). Why? Chrysostom gave the answer in the fourth century: "Imitate God!" It is because God's desire and Christ's death both concern everybody that the church's duty must concern everybody too. Each church is a local community, but it should have a global perspective.

For further reading: 1 Timothy 2:1–7

Advice to a Young Leader

COMMAND AND TEACH THESE THINGS. DON'T LET ANYONE LOOK DOWN
ON YOU BECAUSE YOU ARE YOUNG...
1 Timothy 4:11–12

I confess that I find Timothy a very congenial character. For he was one of us in all our human frailty. He was far from being a stained-glass saint, and a halo would not have fit comfortably on his head. On the contrary, he was an authentic human being, with all the vulnerability that implies. Firstly, he was comparatively young and inexperienced. Secondly, he was temperamentally diffident, so Paul had to ask the Corinthians to put him at ease among them. Thirdly, he was physically infirm. He had a recurrent gastric problem, for which the apostle prescribed a little medicinal alcohol. So that is Timothy – young, shy, and frail. The danger was that these things might undermine his ministry. It is a perennial problem for young people. What is the remedy? As J. B. Phillips wrote, Paul responds, "Do not let people look *down* on you because you are young; see that they look *up* to you because..." and he elaborates six reasons.

Firstly, Timothy must set an example (v. 12). People would not despise his youth if they admired his life and character. Secondly, Timothy must devote himself to the public reading of Scripture, drawing his teaching out of it, thus showing where his authority lay (v. 13).

Thirdly, Timothy must not neglect the gift that was given him at his ordination (v. 14). People would not despise God's gifts. Fourthly, Timothy must be diligent and wholehearted so that everybody could see his progress (v. 15). Fifthly, Timothy must watch his life and his teaching closely, making sure that they are consistent (v. 16). Sixthly, Timothy must be sensitive in his relationships, treating people in a way that is appropriate to their gender and generation. He must treat elders with respect, his own age with equality, the opposite sex with restraint, and all ages with that affection that binds the church family together (5:1–2).

We might express these six instructions as words of command: Watch your example! Identify your authority! Exercise your gift! Show your progress! Be consistent! Adjust your relationships! If young leaders follow these instructions, other people will gladly and gratefully receive their ministry.

For further reading: 1 Timothy 4:11–5:2

Tuesday

A Charge to a Man of God

BUT YOU, MAN OF GOD, FLEE FROM ALL THIS, AND PURSUE
RIGHTEOUSNESS, GODLINESS, FAITH, LOVE, ENDURANCE AND GENTLENESS.
FIGHT THE GOOD FIGHT OF THE FAITH. TAKE HOLD OF THE ETERNAL LIFE
TO WHICH YOU WERE CALLED...

1 Timothy 6:11–12

Paul begins his charge to Timothy with the words, "But you." It is a call to him not to drift with the stream but to be different from the prevailing culture. For Timothy was a man of God who derived his values and standards from God, not from the world. Paul now develops a threefold appeal.

Firstly, *the ethical appeal.* "Flee from all this" and "pursue righteousness, godliness, faith, love, endurance and gentleness." We human beings are great runners. We run from anything that threatens us, and we run after everything that attracts us. How about running from evil and running after righteousness instead? There is no passivity in the attainment of holiness, and no technique. We just have to run.

Secondly, *the doctrinal appeal.* Timothy was to "fight the good fight of the faith." Over against the postmodern fashion that truth is purely subjective and that each of us has our own truth, Paul keeps referring to what he calls "the faith," "the truth," "the teaching," and "the deposit" – a body of doctrine that Timothy had to fight for, that is, to guard and defend. Fighting is an unpleasant business, but it cannot be avoided, for it is a "good fight" for the glory of God and the welfare of the church.

Thirdly, *the experiential appeal.* "Take hold of the eternal life to which you were called." It may seem strange that a Christian leader of Timothy's maturity should need this appeal. Had he not been a Christian for a number of years? Yes. Had he not received eternal life? Yes. Then why did Paul tell him to lay hold of what he already had? The answer is that it is possible to possess something without enjoying it to the full.

In conclusion, we note the balance of Paul's threefold appeal, incorporating ethics, doctrine, and experience. Some Christians fight the good fight of the faith but do not pursue righteousness. Others are good and gentle but have no comparable concern for the truth. Yet others neglect both doctrine and ethics in their quest for religious experience. May God give us twenty-first century Timothys who go for all these three goals simultaneously!

For further reading: 1 Timothy 6:11–16

Qualifications for the Presbyterate

THE REASON I LEFT YOU IN CRETE WAS THAT YOU MIGHT... APPOINT
ELDERS IN EVERY TOWN, AS I DIRECTED YOU.

Titus 1:5

Paul explains that he had left Titus in Crete because certain matters had been unfinished, chief among them being the selection and ordination of pastors (presbyter-bishops) in every town. The apostle goes on to indicate the essential qualifications that candidates must have. The most striking of these is that they must be "blameless" (vv. 6–7). This cannot mean "unblemished," or no children of Adam could ever be eligible. The Greek word means not "without blemish" but "without blame," that is, with an unstained reputation. Since the pastorate is a public office, candidates must have a public record. Hence the need for references or testimonials.

Paul goes on to specify three spheres in which candidates for the presbyterate would need to have an untarnished reputation. Firstly, *elders must be blameless in their home life* (v. 6). Reference is made both to their spouse and to their children. "The husband of but one wife" (v. 6) has been variously interpreted, but it is perhaps best understood broadly as a man of unquestioned sexual morality. As for the children, they must be believers and well behaved. The logic is clear that candidates cannot care for God's family if they fail to care for their own.

Secondly, *elders must be blameless in their character and conduct* (vv. 7–8). Paul uses eleven terms – five negative (e.g., not overbearing, not quick-tempered) and six positive (e.g., hospitable, upright, devout). The leading thought throughout is that the elder must be "master of himself" (v. 8 RSV) or "self-controlled." Thus candidates must give visible evidence in their behaviour that they have been regenerated by the Holy Spirit, that their new birth has led to a new life, and that the ninefold fruit of the Spirit (whose ninth fruit is self-control) has at least begun to ripen in their lives.

Thirdly, *elders must be blameless in their doctrinal orthodoxy* (v. 9). They must "hold firmly to the trustworthy message as it has been taught" (v. 9) or (literally) according to the apostles' teaching. For only then will they be able to exercise their two complementary ministries, namely to teach the truth and to refute those who oppose it. Indeed, Paul reveals his strategy. It is that when false teachers abound (vv. 10–16), we must multiply the number of true teachers.

For further reading: Titus 1:1–11

The Two Epiphanies of Christ

THE GRACE OF GOD THAT HAS APPEARED THAT OFFERS SALVATION TO ALL
PEOPLE ... WHILE WE WAIT FOR THE BLESSED HOPE – THE APPEARING OF
THE GLORY OF OUR GREAT GOD AND SAVIOUR, JESUS CHRIST...

Titus 2:11, 13

The first and second comings of Christ are here called his "epiphanies." *Epiphaneia* is a visible appearing of something hitherto invisible. In classical Greek it was used of sunrise. It comes in Acts 27, in which the ship carrying Paul to Rome was struck by a terrific northeasterly gale and the sky was so overcast that for many days the sun and the stars made no epiphany. Otherwise, the word occurs ten times in the New Testament – four times in reference to Christ's first coming and six times in reference to his second.

Firstly, *there has been an epiphany of grace*, that is, of God's undeserved favour in Jesus Christ. Grace did not, of course, come into existence with him, but it appeared visibly in him. Paul now personifies grace, saying that it teaches or trains us to say no to self-indulgence and yes to self-control.

Secondly, *there is going to be an epiphany of glory*. This is our "blessed hope," namely that he who appeared briefly on the stage of history and disappeared will one day reappear. He appeared in grace; he will reappear in glory. It will be "the appearing of the glory of our great God and Saviour, Jesus Christ." There has been a long and lively debate as to whether this epiphany will be of two persons (our great God, the Father, and Jesus Christ) or only one person whose full title is "our great God and Saviour Jesus Christ." Since all other New Testament allusions to an epiphany refer to Christ, the presumption is that this does too, in which case this is the most unambiguous affirmation in the New Testament of the deity of Jesus.

Thus in one short paragraph Paul has united the two termini of the Christian era. But at this point the critics of Christianity are just about ready to explode. "You Christians are so hopelessly unpractical! All you do is preoccupy yourselves with the distant past and the remote future. Why can't you live in the present?" But that is exactly what Paul summons us to do. He spells out the duties of older men, older women, younger women, and younger men and calls on all of us to live a godly life *in this present age*. Why? The basis of Christian behaviour is the two epiphanies of Christ.

For further reading: Titus 2:1–15

FRIDAY

Resisting the Pressures of the World

EVILDOERS AND IMPOSTORS WILL GO FROM BAD TO WORSE, DECEIVING
AND BEING DECEIVED. BUT AS FOR YOU [TIMOTHY], CONTINUE IN WHAT
YOU HAVE LEARNED...

2 Timothy 3:13–14

Paul's second letter to Timothy was his last, written shortly before his martyrdom. His main concern is still what will happen to the gospel when he will no longer be there to guide and teach the church.

In 2 Timothy 3:1–5 Paul warns Timothy that the "last days" (which Jesus inaugurated) would include "terrible times" (v. 1), and he goes on to give a vivid sketch of them. He lists nineteen characteristics, the most striking of which is misdirected love. People will be lovers of self, lovers of money, or lovers of pleasure instead of lovers of God and of goodness. Indeed, society will be "without love" (v. 3). This absence of authentic love will sour people's relationships. Paul is afraid lest Timothy be swept away by a torrent of self-centredness, and he urges him instead to stand firm and resist the pressures of the prevailing culture.

In 2 Timothy 3:10 and 14 Paul twice addresses Timothy with the same two little Greek monosyllables *su de*, meaning "but as for you." In stark contrast to contemporary culture, Timothy is to be different and, if necessary, to stand alone.

Paul describes Timothy's position in terms of a "following" of Paul, especially of his teaching and his manner of life. Then he exhorts Timothy to continue in the same path: "Continue in what you have learned" (v. 14). Thus verses 10–13 describe Timothy's *past* loyalty to the apostle, and verses 14–17 urge him to remain loyal in the *future*. He has good reason to do so – partly because he knows from whom he has been learning (namely Paul, whose apostolic authority he has come to accept) and partly because he has known the Holy Scriptures from childhood and accepted them as *theopneustos* (literally, "God-breathed") and profitable.

The same two grounds apply today. The gospel Christians believe is the biblical gospel, vouched for by both the prophets of God and the apostles of Christ. We are thankful for this double authentication.

For further reading: 2 Timothy 3:1–17

Saturday

Paul's Last Imprisonment

I HAVE FOUGHT THE GOOD FIGHT, I HAVE FINISHED THE RACE, I HAVE
KEPT THE FAITH.

2 Timothy 4:7

Paul is now no longer enjoying the comparative freedom and comfort of house arrest, in which Luke left him at the end of Acts. Twice in this letter he refers to his chains, and once he describes himself as "chained like a criminal" (2:9). So we are to imagine him languishing in some dark, dank, underground dungeon (according to tradition the Mamertime Prison in Rome) with only a hole in the ceiling for light and air. From this dreadful incarceration there was to be no escape except through death. Already with his mind's eye he could see the gleaming steel of the executioner's sword, for tradition says he was beheaded (as Roman citizens were) some three miles outside Rome on the Ostian Way.

Second Timothy 4, which perhaps contains the last words Paul wrote, teaches an important lesson. It shows that, however profoundly Jesus Christ has changed us, we remain human beings with human needs. As Bishop Handley Moule (1841–1920) wrote, "We are never for one moment denaturalized by grace." We see this in Paul.

Firstly, he was lonely. He wrote to Timothy, "Do your best to come to me soon" (4:9 RSV). The same apostle who had set his love and hope on the coming of Christ (v. 8), nevertheless also longed for the coming of Timothy. "I long night and day to see you," he wrote (1:4 RSV). Super-spiritual Christians may claim that they never feel lonely and have no need of earthly friends, since the companionship of Christ is sufficient. But Paul would not have agreed with them.

Secondly, as winter approached, warm clothing was also necessary, so Paul urged Timothy to bring his cloak with him when he came (4:13). And Paul's third necessity was "the books, and above all the parchments" (v. 13 RSV). These were Paul's conscious needs. They are ours too. When our spirit is lonely, we need friends. When our body is cold, we need clothing. When our mind is bored, we need books. To admit this is not unspiritual; it is human.

For further reading: 2 Timothy 4:1–8

The letter to the Hebrews is anonymous. Neither its author nor its readership is known, so debate about them continues. What is known, however, is the author's purpose in writing. Owing partly to his readers' persecutions and partly to their theological confusion, they were in danger of backsliding, even apostatizing. So the aim of the author of Hebrews is so to establish the finality of Jesus Christ – his priesthood, sacrifice, and covenant – that it would be inconceivable for his readers to fall away from the faith. The letter is a marvellous exposition of the person and work of Jesus Christ, his exalted person, and his finished work.

Whoever the author was, he was obviously well qualified to develop his theme, for he was extremely familiar with the Old Testament story and with the story of Jesus; he was able to demonstrate that all the Old Testament expectations had been fulfilled in Jesus Christ.

Sunday: Jesus the Divine Son

Monday: Jesus the Human Being

Tuesday: The Priesthood of Jesus

Wednesday: Seated at the Right Hand of God

Thursday: A Threefold Exhortation

Friday: Faith Defined and Illustrated

Saturday: Running the Christian Race

Jesus the Divine Son

IN THE PAST GOD SPOKE TO OUR ANCESTORS THROUGH THE PROPHETS
AT MANY TIMES AND IN VARIOUS WAYS, BUT IN THESE LAST DAYS HE HAS
SPOKEN TO US BY HIS SON...

Hebrews 1:1–2

The first two chapters of Hebrews beautifully balance each other in that chapter 1 gives us a portrait of Jesus Christ the divine Son, while chapter 2 adds a portrait of him as the human being. Hebrews 1 speaks of his uniqueness. It tells us five major truths about Christ. Firstly, *Jesus Christ is the climax of God's revelation.* Of course, God had been revealing himself throughout history through the prophets, but it was in a way that was partial and progressive, whereas his self-revelation in Christ was final and complete. So Jesus Christ is God's last word to the world. It is inconceivable that there could be a higher or fuller revelation than he has given us in his incarnate Son. No, Jesus Christ is the climax of his revelation.

Secondly, *Jesus Christ is the Lord of creation.* God has appointed him "heir of all things" (v. 2), since through him he had made the universe. So he is its beginning and its end, its source and its heir, and in between he is "sustaining all things by his powerful word" (v. 3).

Thirdly, *Jesus Christ is the Son of the Father.* He is both "the radiance of God's glory" (light from light, one in being with the Father) and "the exact representation of his being" (distinct from the Father as an impress is distinct from the seal) (v. 3).

Fourthly, *Jesus Christ is the Saviour of sinners.* Having finished the work of purification for sins, he sat down at the Father's right hand.

Fifthly, *Jesus Christ is the object of the angels' worship.* Indeed, he has become "as much superior to the angels as the name he has inherited is superior to theirs" (v. 4). Angels are doubtless great and glorious beings, but they do not compare with Jesus Christ. The author now collects and quotes a chain of Old Testament texts that speak in different ways of his supremacy. For example, "Let all God's angels worship him" (v. 6). The author concludes this section with a solemn warning that we must pay careful attention to the message of the apostles, lest we drift away from it (2:1–4).

For further reading: Hebrews 1:1–2:4

Jesus the Human Being

SINCE THE CHILDREN HAVE FLESH AND BLOOD,
HE TOO SHARED IN THEIR HUMANITY...

Hebrews 2:14

Unique as Jesus Christ is in his divine glory, which we considered yesterday, this is only half the story. If we were to stop there, we would be guilty of serious heresy, affirming his deity but denying or neglecting his humanity. Hebrews 1 emphasizes that Jesus Christ is one with the Father (sharing his being); Hebrews 2 emphasizes that Jesus Christ became one with us (sharing our being). He who is in every way superior to the angels became for a while inferior to them. Indeed, there is a fundamental appropriateness in the Son of God becoming human: "In bringing many sons and daughters to glory, it was fitting that God... should make the pioneer of their salvation perfect" (v. 10). Four main truths are spelled out.

Firstly, *he entered into our humanity*. He took our "flesh and blood" to himself (v. 14). He experienced the frailty and vulnerability of a human being. For he had a real human body (eating, drinking, and getting tired) and real human emotions (joy and sorrow, compassion and anger).

Secondly, *he entered into our temptations*. "He himself suffered when he was tempted" (v. 18). Indeed, he was "tempted in every way, just as we are" (4:15). By his incarnation he laid aside his immunity to temptation and exposed himself to it. And his temptations were real, like ours, except that he never succumbed to them and so never sinned.

Thirdly, *he entered into our sufferings*. God made the pioneer of our salvation perfect through suffering (2:10). Not that he was ever imperfect in the sense of being sinful, but that his identification with us in our humanity would have been incomplete if he had not suffered as we suffer.

Fourthly, *he even entered into our death*. "We... see Jesus... now crowned with glory and honour because he suffered death, so that by the grace of God he might taste death for everyone" (v. 9). It is not that he needed to die, for he had no sin of his own. But he bore our sins, and it was for our sins that he died. As a result of the incarnation, Jesus Christ can represent us to the Father and can sympathize with our weaknesses.

For further reading: Hebrews 2:9–18

The Priesthood of Jesus

NOW THERE HAVE BEEN MANY OF THOSE PRIESTS, SINCE DEATH
PREVENTED THEM FROM CONTINUING IN OFFICE; BUT BECAUSE JESUS
LIVES FOR EVER, HE HAS A PERMANENT PRIESTHOOD.

Hebrews 7:23–24

One of the major themes of Hebrews is the stark contrast it draws between the Old Testament Levitical priests with all their inadequacies and the perfect adequacy of the priesthood of Christ. The author of Hebrews sees in the strange Old Testament figure of Melchizedek a foreshadowing of the priesthood of Jesus.

Firstly, Melchizedek was both a king and a priest, as Jesus was. Secondly, Melchizedek showed his superiority to Abraham (Levi's ancestor) by blessing him and receiving a tithe from him. Thirdly, Melchizedek appears in the Genesis story with neither parentage nor posterity, which is symbolic of the eternity of Jesus.

What, then, were the inadequacies of the Old Testament Aaronic priesthood?

Firstly, *their priesthood was mortal.* The Old Testament priests could not stay in office for ever, but "Jesus lives for ever" (v. 24). Again, "he always lives to intercede" for his people (v. 25). Nothing will ever interrupt or terminate his priesthood.

Secondly, *their character was sinful.* One of the obvious anomalies of the Old Testament system was that before the priests could offer sacrifices for the people, they had to offer sacrifices for themselves. Jesus, however, had no sins of his own for which atonement needed to be made. Verse 26 contains a wonderful statement of the sinlessness of Jesus: "holy, blameless, pure, set apart from sinners, exalted above the heavens."

Thirdly, *their sacrifices were repeated daily.* Everything they did was only a temporary expedient, for they kept repeating the same sacrifices. But Jesus offered himself as a sacrifice for sin once and for all.

Here, then, is the perfect adequacy of the priesthood of Christ. Firstly, his earthly life was sinless. Secondly, his sin-bearing death was complete. Thirdly, his heavenly intercession is eternal. "Such a high priest truly meets our need" (v. 26).

For further reading: Hebrews 7:11–28

Seated at the Right Hand of God

BUT WHEN THIS PRIEST HAD OFFERED FOR ALL TIME ONE SACRIFICE FOR
SINS, HE SAT DOWN AT THE RIGHT HAND OF GOD...

Hebrews 10:12

According to the Apostles' Creed, "He ascended into heaven and sat down at the right hand of God." How are we to understand his heavenly "session"?

Firstly, *Jesus Christ is resting.* The picture is taken from everyday experience that after a day's work in the office or the home, we sit down and put our feet up. So Jesus, "after he had provided purification for sins... sat down" (1:3). The Old Testament priests continued their ministry day after day, week after week, and month after month, but Jesus "offered for all time one sacrifice for sins" (10:12). They stood daily, for no seats were provided in the temple, but when he had offered his sacrifice, he sat down. The priests' standing posture symbolized that their ministry was incomplete, whereas Jesus sat down to indicate that his work was done.

Secondly, *Jesus Christ is reigning.* For he has been promoted to the right hand of God, to the supreme place of honour and power in the universe. From that position he sent the Holy Spirit on the day of Pentecost and sends his people out on their mission. Already all authority in heaven and earth has been given to him. Not yet, however, has the devil conceded defeat.

Thirdly, *Jesus Christ is waiting* "for his enemies to be made his footstool" (v. 13). The words come from Psalm 110:1, which Jesus applied to himself. In it Yahweh says to the Messiah, "Sit at my right hand until I make your enemies a footstool for your feet." The psalm combines the two perspectives. He reigns while he waits and waits while he reigns.

This rich theology is included in the ascension and session of Jesus Christ, namely that he is resting, reigning, and waiting. Resting, he looks back to the past and declares his atoning work to be finished. Reigning, he supervises the present and sends his people out on their mission. Waiting, he anticipates the future, when his enemies will be finally subdued and his kingdom will have come in its fullness.

For future reading: Hebrews 10:11–18

THURSDAY

A Threefold Exhortation

SINCE WE HAVE CONFIDENCE... LET US DRAW NEAR TO GOD... LET US
HOLD UNSWERVINGLY TO THE HOPE WE PROFESS... LET US CONSIDER HOW
WE MAY SPUR ONE ANOTHER ON TOWARDS LOVE AND GOOD DEEDS...

Hebrews 10:19, 22–24

Behind this threefold exhortation there lies the layout and ministry of the temple. The temple was built in two sections or rooms, the further and smaller of them being called the Holy of Holies or the Most Holy Place. In it the shekinah glory, the symbol of God's presence, was to be seen. A thick curtain (the "veil") hung between the two rooms and barred entrance into the Holy of Holies. Access was strictly forbidden except for only one person (the high priest) on one occasion (the Day of Atonement) on one condition (that he took with him the blood of a sacrifice).

Our author assumes that his readers know this and have understood his teaching that these things have been fulfilled in the high priesthood and sacrifice of Jesus. Access through the veil into the presence of God was now open to all believers.

Firstly, then, "*Let us draw near to God*" (v. 22) with a sincere heart in full assurance of faith, inwardly cleansed from a guilty conscience and outwardly in baptism having our bodies washed with pure water. This continuous access to God is a most marvellous privilege. Secondly, "*Let us hold unswervingly to the hope we profess*" (v. 23). The Christian hope (which is a sure expectation) focuses on the coming of Christ and the glory that will follow. But how can we hold fast to this hope when so many – even in the church – have given it up? There is only one answer, namely that "he who promised is faithful" (v. 23). The Lord Jesus promised that he would come in power and great glory, and he keeps his promises. Thirdly, "*Let us consider how we may spur one another on towards love and good deeds*" (v. 24). The author clearly considered that his readers had grown slack in meeting. For Christian one-anotherness (provoking one another and encouraging one another) depends on meeting one another.

Here, then, is the Christian life to which we are summoned: access to God by faith, waiting for Christ in hope, and stirring one another up to love. It is the familiar triad of faith, hope, and love.

For further reading: Hebrews 10:19–25

FRIDAY

Faith Defined and Illustrated

NOW FAITH IS CONFIDENCE IN WHAT WE HOPE FOR AND ASSURANCE
ABOUT WHAT WE DO NOT SEE.

Hebrews 11:1

There are two major spheres of uncertainty for all of us human beings. The first is the unknown future, and the second the unseen present. For we find our security in the present, not the future, and in the seen, not the unseen. As for the future, even the forecasts of the meteorological office are often unreliable. As for the unseen, our scientific upbringing has schooled us to be skeptical of everything that is not amenable to empirical investigation.

It comes therefore as a shock that these two spheres of human uncertainty (the future and the unseen) are precisely those in which faith specializes and even flourishes! It is the function of faith to apprehend both the unseen present and the unrealized future. Put simply, faith is the assurance that the future we anticipate will take place and that the present we cannot see is nevertheless real.

Of course, unbelievers scoff at Christian faith. According to H. L. Mencken, the so-called sage of Baltimore, "Faith may be defined briefly as an illogical belief in the occurrence of the improbable." It is witty but inaccurate. *Faith* is not a synonym for *credulity* or *superstition*. It is neither irrational nor illogical. No, faith and reason are never placed in antithesis to one another in Scripture. Faith and sight are contrasted, but not faith and reason. On the contrary, "Those who know your name put their trust in you" (Ps. 9:10 NRSV). They trust because they know. The reasonableness of trust arises from the trustworthiness of its object, and nobody is more trustworthy than God.

All this is clear in the examples of Hebrews 11. In each case faith is a response to what God has said. Noah built the ark because God had warned him of the flood. Abraham left his home and relatives because God had promised him an alternative home and a huge posterity. In both cases a word from God came first. It is the same with us. We are not spiritual giants like Enoch, Abraham, and Moses. God does not normally address us in direct speech. But he continues to speak through what he has spoken in Scripture. So faith is our response to his Word.

For further reading: Hebrews 11:1–10

Running the Christian Race

THEREFORE, SINCE WE ARE SURROUNDED BY SUCH A GREAT CLOUD OF
WITNESSES, LET US THROW OFF EVERYTHING THAT HINDERS AND THE SIN
THAT SO EASILY ENTANGLES. AND LET US RUN WITH PERSEVERANCE THE
RACE MARKED OUT FOR US, FIXING OUR EYES ON JESUS...

Hebrews 12:1–2

Everybody in the ancient world knew about the Greek games. As Greek culture permeated the Roman Empire, the games accompanied it. Every city had its amphitheater, in which athletes displayed their prowess before huge and appreciative crowds – running, boxing, wrestling, spear throwing, and chariot racing. Several times in the New Testament the Christian life is likened to an athletic race, not because we are competing with one another, but because it demands great self-discipline. Our author's concern is that we "run with perseverance the race marked out for us" (v. 1). He seems to lay down three requirements as means to endurance in the race.

Firstly, *remember the spectators!* "We are surrounded," he writes, "by such a great cloud of witnesses" (v. 1). These certainly include the Old Testament heroes of faith portrayed in chapter 11, and probably their equivalents in New Testament days. But in what sense are they "witnesses"? It surely means that they once bore witness on earth. But could it also include the Christian dead who are watching now from heaven? Tentatively, I think it does, because we are said to be "surrounded" by them, which suggests that we should envisage tier upon tier of excited spectators in the local amphitheater. To remember the spectators is to be inspired to greater exertion.

Secondly, *go into training!* All serious athletes accept a strenuous régime of food, drink, exercise, and sleep. And for the race itself they lay aside both surplus body weight and inappropriate clothing. In Christian terms this means turning away from sin and laying aside "weights," which may not be sinful in themselves but nevertheless hinder the race.

Thirdly, *keep looking to the finish line!* Christian athletes are to look away from all distractions and fix their eyes on Jesus, who seems to be standing at the finish line. "Consider him," the author writes (v. 3), and especially his endurance of the cross and of hostility against himself. Thus, surrounded by witnesses, profiting from strenuous training, and fixing our eyes on Jesus, we will run our race with perseverance; the very possibility of dropping out is unthinkable.

For further reading: Hebrews 12:1–3

Tucked away at the end of the New Testament, immediately before the book of Revelation, are the general letters by James, Peter, and John. They are so called because they are not addressed to any particular church. James' letter, for example, is addressed "to the twelve tribes scattered among the nations" (James 1:1), that is, to all Jewish Christians everywhere.

James was one of the Lord's brothers. During Jesus' ministry he was not a believer, but by the day of Pentecost he was. Indeed, he soon became the acknowledged leader of the church in Jerusalem and of Jewish Christians worldwide. His letter may have been written as early as AD 45, and in it he laid his emphasis on consistent Christian behaviour.

Two general letters are attributed in the New Testament to the apostle Peter, although the authorship of the second, with all its similarities to the letter of Jude, is disputed by many. Although Peter handles many topics, in his first letter his main emphasis is on how Christians should react to persecution. There is a reference to suffering in every chapter.

The three letters of John were evidently written by the beloved disciple, who was also the author of the fourth Gospel. If the purpose of John's Gospel was to lead its readers into faith and so into eternal life (John 20:31), the purpose of his letters was to lead believers into assurance that they had received eternal life (1 John 5:13).

Sunday: Responding to the Word of God

Monday: Faith and Works

Tuesday: The Necessity of the Cross

Wednesday: An Appeal to Pastors

Thursday: The Nature of Biblical Truth

Friday: True and False Assurance

Saturday: The Integrated Christian Life

Sunday

Responding to the Word of God

DO NOT MERELY LISTEN TO THE WORD, AND SO DECEIVE YOURSELVES. DO
WHAT IT SAYS.

James 1:22

On first reading the first chapter of James' letter, one is immediately struck by its threefold warning against deception (vv. 16, 22, 26). James' antidote to deception is the Word of God or "word of truth" (v. 18), namely the revelation that God has given us in Christ and in the biblical witness to Christ. It is by paying attention to God's Word that we will avoid the tragedy of being deceived. Our response to the Word needs to be in two stages.

Stage 1: an attentive hearing of God's Word. "Everyone should be quick to listen, slow to speak" (v. 19). Our natural tendency in every situation is to make premature responses. We rush in with our opinion, forgetting that "the mouth of the fool gushes folly" (Prov. 15:2). Often the last thing we do (which should be the first) is to hold our tongue and listen. Here is a general principle of wide application. It is better to listen than to speak. Respectful listening is a major secret of all harmonious relationships. But it is especially true of our relationship with God. For he has spoken and calls us to listen to his voice. Yet sometimes we hear from Scripture only what we want to hear – the soothing echoes of our own cultural prejudice – and then we miss the thunderclap of his Word as he challenges us to listen.

Stage 2: an obedient doing of God's Word. James' use of the mirror metaphor is especially telling (vv. 22–23). For a mirror gives us a double message. It tells us both what we are and therefore what we should be. The mirror says, "You've got a dirty smudge on your right cheek, so you'd better go and wipe it off." Whenever we look at ourselves in the mirror, we have to act on what we see. Just so, as we gaze intently into the mirror of God's Word, it tells us what we are and what we should be.

God's Word is to be heard, received, and obeyed. There can be no true discipleship without this.

For further reading: James 1:16–27

MONDAY

Faith and Works

WHAT GOOD IS IT, MY BROTHERS AND SISTERS, IF SOMEONE CLAIMS TO
HAVE FAITH BUT HAS NO DEEDS? CAN SUCH FAITH SAVE THEM?

James 2:14

It is well known that James and Paul are supposed to have disagreed with one another on the subject of justification, that is to say, on how sinners can become accepted and pronounced righteous in the sight of God. Further, on account of this apparent theological discord, Luther excluded James' letter from his New Testament canon, calling it a "letter of straw."

Certainly there is an apparent discrepancy between these two apostles. For Paul taught that "a person is justified by faith apart from the works of the law" (Rom. 3:28), whereas James wrote, "You see that a person is considered righteous by what they do and not by faith alone" (James 2:24). Moreover, both apostles claimed Abraham as their champion.

But the discrepancy is more imaginary than real. Paul and James had a different ministry but not a different message. They proclaimed the same gospel but with a different emphasis. The reason for this different emphasis is that they were opposing different false teachers. Paul's opponents were Jewish legalists, or Judaizers, who taught that justification is by works done in obedience to the law. James' opponents, however, were Jewish intellectualizers who taught that justification is by faith, meaning a barren orthodoxy.

To the Judaizers Paul insisted that justification is not by works but by faith; to the intellectualizers James insisted that justification is not by orthodox faith (which the demons also possess – and shudder!) but by a faith that works.

Both apostles clarified the nature of authentic faith, namely that it is a living faith that works. "I will show you my faith by my works," wrote James (2:18 NASB); "faith working through love," wrote Paul (Gal. 5:6 NASB). We cannot be saved by works, yet we cannot be saved without them. The place of works is not to earn salvation but to evidence it, not to procure salvation but to prove it. Thus both apostles taught that an authentic faith works. But Paul emphasized the faith that issues in works, whereas James emphasized the works that issue from faith. Both would agree that faith without works is dead.

For further reading: James 2:14–26

The Necessity of the Cross

HE HIMSELF BORE OUR SINS IN HIS BODY ON THE CROSS, SO THAT WE
MIGHT DIE TO SINS AND LIVE FOR RIGHTEOUSNESS...

1 Peter 2:24

When Jesus first told his disciples that the Son of Man must suffer many things and die, it was Peter who immediately and vehemently contradicted him. He could not come to terms with the concept of a suffering Messiah. Yet here is Peter now, some three decades later, in his first letter, contradicting his own contradiction! Each of his letter's five chapters contains a major passage on the Messiah's sufferings.

Peter makes two statements about the purpose of the cross. The first is that Christ left us an example (which we have already considered), and the second that he "bore our sins in his body on the cross" (v. 24). To "bear sin" is an Old Testament expression for "to bear the penalty of sin." Normally it is the offender who bears the penalty of his own sin. Sometimes, however, in God's great mercy, he provides a substitute to bear the penalty instead, such as the sin offering and especially the scapegoat on the Day of Atonement.

Godly Israelites knew, however, that this was only symbolical, for the blood of bulls and goats could not take away sins (Heb. 10:4). So they looked forward to the day when the suffering servant of Isaiah 53 would bear their sin, and Jesus applied this prophecy to himself.

There is a problem, however. If Christ took our place, bore our sin, paid our penalty, and died our death, and in consequence we have been forgiven, does this not mean (as some people ask) that we can now behave as we like and go on sinning? Paul's critics certainly developed this slander, and Peter's may have done too. But both apostles vigorously denied the charge. See how Peter continued: he bore our sins *in order that* we might die to sin and live for righteousness. So the purpose of the death of Christ is not just to secure our forgiveness but to secure our holiness as well.

There is no Christianity without the cross. A Christianity without the cross is a fraud.

For further reading: 1 Peter 2:18–25

An Appeal to Pastors

BE SHEPHERDS OF GOD'S FLOCK THAT IS UNDER YOUR CARE,
WATCHING OVER THEM...

1 Peter 5:2

Shepherding as a metaphor for leadership recurs on many occasions in the Bible. Yahweh is the shepherd of Israel. Political leaders inherited the same title but were condemned for allowing their sheep to be scattered (Ezek. 34). Jesus took over the role as the Good Shepherd, who knows, leads, calls, loves, and feeds his sheep and who lays down his life for them.

It is, however, particularly poignant that Peter should here appeal to the elders of the church as "shepherds of God's flock," for this was his ministry ("feed my sheep" [John 21:18]) when the risen Lord recommissioned him on the shore of the Sea of Galilee. It is very likely that Peter was remembering this episode when he issued his appeal to church elders to shepherd God's flock. His message is summed up in three antitheses.

Firstly, *their spirit must be voluntary*: serving "not because you must, but because you are willing, as God wants you to be" (1 Pet. 5:2). The very concept of being a conscript in the service of Christ is grotesque.

Secondly, *their motive must be free from anything mercenary*: "not pursuing dishonest gain, but eager to serve" (v. 2). Yet throughout history bad men have tried to make money out of ministry. In the ancient world there were many quacks who made a good living by posing as itinerant teachers. But Paul renounced his right to support and earned his own living in order to demonstrate the sincerity of his motives. In our day there are still some disreputable evangelists who make themselves wealthy by financial appeals.

Thirdly, *their manner must be humble*: "not lording it over those entrusted to you, but being examples to the flock" (v. 3). Jesus gave his disciples a clear warning about this very thing. Secular rulers, he said, "lord it over them," and "their high officials exercise authority over them. Not so with you" (Mark 10:42–43). Instead, Christian leaders must exercise a humble servant ministry. They must lead not by power but by example.

For further reading: 1 Peter 5:1–11

The Nature of Biblical Truth

Prophets, though human, spoke from God
as they were carried along by the Holy Spirit.

2 Peter 1:21

The second half of the first chapter of 2 Peter is a wonderful passage about the nature of biblical truth. Firstly, *biblical truth is written truth*. Peter is conscious of his mortality and is anticipating his death. While he is alive, he is still able to remind his readers of his teaching, but after his departure it will need to be written and so made accessible. Behind this human background there lay a divine providence. If God has said and done something unique in Christ, provision must be made for its preservation; it is inconceivable that God would allow it to be lost. Scripture is God's Word written.

Secondly, *biblical truth is eyewitness truth*. Peter alludes to the transfiguration when he saw God's glory and heard his voice: "We were eye-witnesses of his majesty" (v. 16). But the eyewitness principle lies behind all Scripture, for God raised up witnesses to record and interpret what he was doing in Israel. The meaning of his actions was not self-evident. For example, many tribal migrations were taking place in the ancient Near East, but nobody would have known that the exodus was unique unless God had raised up Moses. Again, thousands of crucifixions took place under Roman rule, but nobody would have known that the cross of Jesus was unique unless God had raised up the apostles.

Thirdly, *biblical truth is enlightening truth*. "You will do well to pay attention to it, as to a light shining in a dark place" (v. 19). The people of God are pictured as pilgrims travelling by night. They need a lamp, and Scripture is a plain book with a practical purpose.

Fourthly, *biblical truth is divine truth*. No prophecy, Peter writes, ever originated in the mind or will of men, but rather of God. "Prophets, though human, spoke from God as they were carried along by the Holy Spirit" (v. 21).

Thank God for his revealed Word! Without it we would grope in the darkness. Has he given us a lamp to illumine our path, and shall we not use it?

For further reading: 2 Peter 1:12–21

True and False Assurance

I WRITE THESE THINGS TO YOU WHO BELIEVE IN THE NAME OF
THE SON OF GOD SO THAT YOU MAY KNOW THAT YOU HAVE ETERNAL LIFE.

1 John 5:13

Is assurance a legitimate – even necessary – ingredient of Christian discipleship? Is it ever appropriate for followers of Jesus to say, "We know"? – not only in relation to the truth of the gospel but especially in relation to personal salvation? If our answer to these questions is yes, then how can we discern between true assurance and false, the authentic and the bogus? By what criteria may we judge which is which? It was Robert Law who entitled his 1885 commentary on 1 John *Tests of Life*. In it he set out the three cardinal tests, three criteria by which to discern between true and false teachers.

The *doctrinal* test was whether the teachers believed in the incarnation: "Every spirit that acknowledges that Jesus Christ has come in the flesh is from God" (4:2).

The *ethical* test was whether these teachers practised righteousness and obeyed God's commandments: "We know that we have come to know him if we obey his commands" (2:3).

The *social* test was whether they were bound to the Christian community in love: "We know that we have passed from death to life, because we love each other" (3:14).

It seems that the apostle John, living in Ephesus in his old age, was being opposed by an early Gnostic named Cerinthus. John calls him a liar and a deceiver because he denied the divine-human person of Jesus, he claimed to have fellowship with God while walking in darkness, and he made arrogant claims to spiritual superiority, claiming to love God while hating his brother. By applying the three tests, John both undermined the false assurance of counterfeit Christians and buttressed the right assurance of genuine Christians.

Unless we Christians are marked by right belief, godly obedience, and love, we are counterfeit. We cannot have been born again, for it is those who are born of God who believe, obey, and love.

For further reading: 1 John 1:1–10

SATURDAY

The Integrated Christian Life

I ASK THAT WE LOVE ONE ANOTHER.
AND THIS IS LOVE: THAT WE WALK IN OBEDIENCE TO HIS COMMANDS.

2 John 5–6

The anonymous "chosen lady and her children" (v. 1) to whom John's second letter is addressed was almost certainly the personification of a local church. And its main characteristic is its integration, that is, its integration of different elements, which we are often foolish enough to allow to be separated.

Firstly, *truth and love belong together*. Each is mentioned five times in the letter's first few verses. John writes of "the truth, which lives in us" (v. 2) and of the love that united them. John's words remind us of one of Paul's similar expressions. According to John, we are to love in truth. According to Paul, we are to speak the truth in love (Eph. 4:15). According to both, they should be integrated. The Holy Spirit is the source of both.

Secondly, *love and obedience belong together*. John reminds his readers of the old commandment, which is to love one another. The opposite is also true. If obedience issues in love, love issues in obedience. It was so in the Old Testament, in which God described his people as "those who love me and keep my commandments" (Exod. 20:6). It is amazing that Jesus applied this to himself: "He who has my commandments and keeps them, he it is who loves me" (John 14:21 RSV). Here is the second integration: to obey is to love, and to love is to obey *ad infinitum*.

Thirdly, *the Father and the Son belong together*. The false teachers "do not acknowledge Jesus Christ as coming in the flesh" (v. 7). They taught either that the Son of God only *seemed* to become human or that he was adopted into the Godhead for a brief period. In each case they denied the incarnation, and this was not a minor Christological deviation; it was Antichrist. John also describes these teachers as running ahead (v. 9). Perhaps they were claiming to be go-ahead or progressive thinkers. With a touch of sarcasm John comments that they have gone ahead so far that they have left the Father behind. Instead, John begs his readers to continue in the original teaching of the apostles. Nobody can deny the Son and retain the Father. May God lead us into a truly integrated Christian life in which truth, love, and obedience all flourish!

For further reading: 2 John 1–13

We come now to the last book of the Bible, the book of Revelation. It claims in its first verse to be "the revelation from Jesus Christ" (Rev. 1:1), and in its first chapter John is given a magnificent vision of him, once crucified, now glorified. He announces himself as "the First and the Last… the Living One" (vv. 17–18) and "the ruler of the kings of the earth" (v. 5), which is the very title which the Roman emperor assumed.

With Revelation 2 the scene changes. The resurrected and glorious Jesus is now patrolling and supervising his churches on earth. He tells John to write a letter to each of seven churches in the Roman province of Asia. The seven letters all have the same outline, beginning with Christ's claim that he knows their circumstances and concluding with a message of praise or blame appropriate to each church and a promise to those who overcome.

It seems legitimate to regard the seven individual churches as representing the universal church. Together they tell us the marks of an ideal church.

Sunday: The Letter to Ephesus – Love

Monday: The Letter to Smyrna – Suffering

Tuesday: The Letter to Pergamum – Truth

Wednesday: The Letter to Thyatira – Holiness

Thursday: The Letter to Sardis – Sincerity

Friday: The Letter to Philadelphia – Mission

Saturday: The Letter to Laodicea – Wholeheartedness

The Letter to Ephesus – Love

YET I HOLD THIS AGAINST YOU: YOU HAVE FORSAKEN THE LOVE YOU HAD
AT FIRST.

Revelation 2:4

Jesus' first letter was addressed to Ephesus. It was the capital of the Roman province of Asia, and its citizens liked to call it their metropolis. It was also a prosperous business centre and the proud guardian of the temple to Diana, which was one of the seven wonders of the world.

Moreover, the church in Ephesus had much to commend it. Jesus singled out three virtues for special mention, namely their hard work, their endurance of hardships, and their theological discernment, coupled with an unwillingness to tolerate evil or error. A few years later, at the beginning of the second century, Bishop Ignatius of Antioch, on his way to Rome to be executed as a Christian, wrote to the Ephesians in very complimentary terms: "You all live according to truth, and no heresy has a home among you; indeed you do not so much as listen to anyone if they speak of anything except concerning Jesus Christ and his truth."

Nevertheless, although the Ephesian church appeared to be a model church, Jesus had a complaint to register: "You have forsaken your first love." All the Ephesians' virtues did not compensate for this lack. It was no doubt at the time of their conversion that their love for him had been ardent and fresh, but now the fires had died down. One remembers Yahweh's complaint to Jeremiah about Jerusalem: "I remember the devotion of your youth, how as a bride you loved me" (Jer. 2:2). As with Jerusalem so with Ephesus, the heavenly bridegroom sought to woo his bride back to the first ecstasy of her love: "Consider how far you have fallen! Repent and do the things you did at first" (Rev. 2:5). Without love everything is nothing.

For further reading: Revelation 2:1–7

Monday

The Letter to Smyrna – Suffering

DO NOT BE AFRAID OF WHAT YOU ARE ABOUT TO SUFFER...
YOU WILL SUFFER PERSECUTION...

Revelation 2:10

If the first mark of a model church is love, the second is suffering. A willingness to suffer for Christ proves the genuineness of our love for him.

The town of Smyrna (now Izmir) is about thirty-five miles up the coast from Ephesus. It was the next town the postman would reach on his circular tour of the seven churches. It was well-known for its splendour and for its sensitivity to the rivalry of Ephesus.

The church of Smyrna was a suffering church. Jesus assures them that he knows their afflictions, their poverty, and the slander of their enemies. It seems probable that their sufferings were associated with the emperor cult. For Smyrna boasted of her temple in honour of Emperor Tiberius. From time to time citizens were required to sprinkle incense on the fire burning before the emperor's bust, simultaneously confessing that Caesar was lord. But how could Christians call Caesar lord when they had confessed Jesus as Lord?

This was the dilemma that in AD 156 confronted the venerable Polycarp, bishop of Smyrna. In the crowded amphitheater the proconsul urged him to swear by the genius of Caesar and revile Christ. But Polycarp refused, saying, "For eighty-six years I have served him, and he has done me no wrong; how then can I blaspheme my King who saved me?" The proconsul persisted, warning him of death by wild beasts or by fire if he would not change his mind. But Polycarp stood firm. So the fire was lit, and the saintly bishop thanked God for counting him worthy to share the cup of Christ and be numbered among his martyrs.

More than half a century before this, Christ had already warned the Smyrnaen church of prison and even death. "Be faithful, even to the point of death," he wrote to them, "and I will give you life as your victor's crown" (v. 10).

For further reading: Revelation 2:8–11

The Letter to Pergamum – Truth

YOU REMAIN TRUE TO MY NAME. YOU DID NOT RENOUNCE
YOUR FAITH IN ME...

Revelation 2:13

The church in Pergamum was dedicated to truth. This fact is all the more remarkable because of their religious and cultural environment. Twice Jesus writes that he knows where they live, namely "where Satan has his throne" and "in your city – where Satan lives" (v. 13). It is not certain what Jesus meant by these expressions. In general he was referring to the non-Christian society with which they were surrounded. In particular he may have meant either pagan idolatry or the imperial cult.

Pergamum has been described as a strong centre of paganism. Many temples and altars had been erected there. Near the summit of Pergamum's acropolis there was an immense altar to Zeus, and Pergamum was famous as the headquarters of the worship of Aesculapius, the god of health and healing.

But some scholars think it more likely that Satan's throne was associated with the imperial cult. Back in 29 BC permission had been granted to the citizens of Pergamum to erect a temple to Augustus. It was the first provincial temple to be built in honour of a living emperor, and some think that the imperial cult had its centre in Pergamum.

In spite of these Satanic influences, the church of Pergamum had not capitulated. On the contrary, Jesus was able to write to the church his words of congratulation: "Yet you remain true to my name. You did not renounce your faith in me, not even in the days of Antipas, my faithful witness, who was put to death in your city" (v. 13). It is moving that Jesus gives Antipas the very title "faithful witness," which has earlier been given to him (1:5).

Nevertheless, Jesus adds a word of complaint. It is that, although Pergamum as a whole remained loyal to him, it tolerated in its fellowship some false teachers who held to "the teaching of Balaam" and to "the teaching of the Nicolaitans" (vv. 14–15) – teaching that seems to have condoned both idolatry and immorality.

For further reading: Revelation 2:12–17

The Letter to Thyatira – Holiness

YOU ARE NOW DOING MORE THAN YOU DID AT FIRST.
Revelation 2:19

If Thyatira was noted for anything in the ancient world, it had a commercial rather than a political distinction. It was a prosperous trading centre. Inscriptions that archaeologists have discovered reveal that Thyatira boasted numerous trade guilds. There were, for example, associations for bakers and bronze workers, for clothiers and cobblers, for weavers, tanners, dyers, and potters. This is of particular interest to us because it was from Thyatira that Lydia, one of Philippi's notable converts, had come. She traded in material treated with Thyatira's purple dye and is described by Luke as "a dealer in purple cloth" (Acts 16:14). Is it possible that Lydia, newborn in Christ, on returning to Thyatira, had been the means of planting the Christian church there?

In his letter to Thyatira, Jesus emphasized holiness as the next essential mark of a model church. He begins his letter in terms of warmest commendation, for he knows their love and faith, their service and perseverance. These are four fine virtues and include the triad of faith, hope, and love. It is also noteworthy that, whereas Ephesus had declined from a good beginning, Thyatira was now doing more than she had done at first.

But unfortunately, this was not a complete picture of the church. In that fair garden a poisonous weed was growing. Alongside Thyatira's sterling qualities she was guilty of moral compromise. The church tolerated an evil self-styled prophetess. Symbolically named Jezebel after King Ahab's wicked queen, she was leading some of Thyatira's church members astray, persuading them that Christian freedom gave Christians license to engage in immorality.

Jesus had called on her to repent, but she had been unwilling. So his judgment would inevitably fall on her and also on her followers unless they repented of her ways.

The holiness of self-control and Christlikeness is another essential characteristic of a model church. Tolerance is not a virtue if it is evil that is being tolerated. God still says to his people, "Be holy, because I am holy" (1 Pet. 1:16; see Lev. 19:2).

For further reading: Revelation 2:18–29

THURSDAY

The Letter to Sardis – Sincerity

I KNOW YOUR DEEDS; YOU HAVE A REPUTATION OF BEING ALIVE,
BUT YOU ARE DEAD.

Revelation 3:1

The letter that the risen Jesus dictated to John for delivery to the church of Sardis is the only one that contains no commendation of any kind. Its criticism is almost unrelieved. Only a few simple words were needed by which to expose its spiritual bankruptcy: "You have a reputation of being alive, but you are dead." The church in Sardis had acquired a name. It was well known by the other six churches in the province for its vitality. No false doctrine was taking root in its fellowship. We hear of neither Balaam nor Nicolaitans nor Jezebel.

But outward appearances are notoriously deceptive, and this socially distinguished congregation was a spiritual graveyard. It had a name for vitality, but it had no right to the name. As the eyes of Christ looked beneath the surface, he said, "I have found your deeds unfinished in the sight of my God" (v. 2). The reputation that Sardis had acquired was a reputation with human beings but not with God. This distinction between reputation and reality, between what human beings see and what God sees, is of great importance everywhere. "The LORD does not look at the things people look at. People look at the outward appearance, but the LORD looks at the heart" (1 Sam. 16:7).

To be obsessed with appearance and reputation leads naturally to hypocrisy, which Jesus hated. Originally the *hupokritēs* was an actor who plays a part on the stage. But the word came to be applied to any charlatan or pretender who assumes a role. Hypocrisy can permeate the life of a church, especially its worship. It makes no difference whether the service is liturgical or nonliturgical, whether it is marked by Catholic ritual or Protestant austerity; the same unreality can be present. Hypocrisy is make-believe, whereas a true and living church is characterized by sincerity.

For further reading: Revelation 3:1–6

FRIDAY

The Letter to Philadelphia – Mission

SEE, I HAVE PLACED BEFORE YOU AN OPEN DOOR THAT NO ONE CAN SHUT.

Revelation 3:8

In writing to the church in Philadelphia, Jesus describes himself as holding the key of David, with which he is able both to open closed doors and to close open ones. In consequence, he could say to the Philadelphian church, "See, I have placed before you an open door that no can shut" (v. 8). The most likely meaning of this open door is that it is a door of opportunity, especially of opportunity for mission, since the apostle Paul several times resorted to this metaphor in his letters. For example, on his return from his first missionary journey Paul reported that God had "opened a door of faith to the Gentiles" (Acts 14:27), while on his third missionary journey he wrote that "a great door for effective work" had opened to him in Ephesus (1 Cor. 16:9).

In the case of Philadelphia, perhaps the open door was a reference to the city's strategic location. Situated in a broad and fertile valley, it commanded the trade routes in all directions. Sir William Ramsay, the early-twentieth-century archaeologist, wrote that it had been the founder's intention in the second century BC "to make it a centre of the Greco-Asiatic civilization and a means of spreading the Greek language and manners... Philadelphia was a missionary city from the beginning." So what the city had been for Greek culture it was now to be for the Christian gospel. It was built on one of the great Roman roads, which thrust its way like an arrow into the heart of the interior. No one could shut this door. Let the church of Philadelphia seize its opportunity and go out boldly with the good news.

Thank God there are many open doors for mission in the world today. But we must also face the reality of closed doors elsewhere. One is a legal door, the power of hostile governments that curtail religious liberty. Another is a cultural door, the power of alien ideas that prejudice people's minds. A third is an ethnic door, the power of national loyalties that confuse religion with patriotism. We need to keep our eyes on the great key in Christ's hand.

For further reading: Revelation 3:7–13

SATURDAY

The Letter to Laodicea – Wholeheartedness

I KNOW YOUR DEEDS, THAT YOU ARE NEITHER COLD NOR HOT.
I WISH YOU WERE EITHER ONE OR THE OTHER!
Revelation 3:15

Christ's message to the Laodicean church is plain. He wants them to be characterized by wholeheartedness. He is very outspoken. He prefers his professing disciples to be either hot in their devotion to him or icy cold in their hostility rather than tepid in their indifference. He finds apathy nauseating.

Directly opposite Laodicea, across the River Lycus, stood Hierapolis, whose hot springs sent lukewarm waters over the cliffs of Laodicea, leaving limestone deposits that are still very visible today. So the adjective *Laodicean* has entered our vocabulary to denote people who are lukewarm in religion, politics, or anything else. Laodicea represents a church that is outwardly respectable but inwardly uncommitted, one of the purely nominal churches with which we are familiar today.

When the metaphor changes to naked, blind beggars (v. 17), one wonders whether the members of the Laodicean church were genuine Christians at all. Then it changes again to that of an empty house (v. 20). Christ stands on the front doorstep, knocks, speaks, and waits. If any individual opens the door, as I did in February 1938, he enters according to his promise, not only to eat with us, but to take possession of the house. This is the essence of the wholeheartedness to which Christ calls us.

True, the church has always been scared of what it likes to call "enthusiasm." John Wesley and his friends knew all about this, for the bishops dismissed them as "enthusiasts." But enthusiasm is an essential characteristic of every authentic disciple of Jesus. This is not fanaticism, which is zeal without knowledge.

Looking back over this week's studies, we have seen the risen Lord patrolling, inspecting, and supervising his churches. As he does so, he pinpoints the seven marks he wants his church to display – love for him and willingness to suffer for him, truth of doctrine and holiness of life, commitment to mission, together with sincerity and wholeheartedness in everything.

For further reading: Revelation 3:14–22

With Revelation 4 we turn abruptly from the church on earth to the church in heaven, from Christ among the flickering lampstands to Christ at the very centre of the unchangeable throne of God. It is the same Christ but from an entirely different perspective.

John saw before him a door standing open in heaven, and a voice like a trumpet spoke to him: "Come up here, and I will show you what must take place after this" (Rev. 4:1). It was the open door of revelation, and as John looked through the door, what he saw developed in three stages: firstly, *a throne*, from which God rules over the universe; secondly, *a scroll*, the book of history, closed, sealed, and held in God's right hand; and, finally, *a Lamb*, as slain, who alone is found worthy to open the scroll, that is, to interpret and control history.

Sunday: The Central Throne

Monday: The Creation's Worship

Tuesday: John's Vision of a Scroll

Wednesday: John's Vision of the Lamb

Thursday: Six Seals are Broken

Friday: The Two Redeemed Communities

Saturday: The Great International Community

SUNDAY

The Central Throne

THERE BEFORE ME WAS A THRONE IN HEAVEN
WITH SOMEONE SITTING ON IT.

Revelation 4:2

It is immensely significant that, when John peeped through the open door, the very first thing he saw was a throne, symbol of the sovereignty, majesty, and kingly rule of God. The throne is mentioned seventeen times in Revelation 4 and 5.

The churches of Asia were small and struggling in comparison with the might of Rome. What could a few defenceless Christians do if an imperial edict were to banish them from the face of the earth? Yet they need have no fear, for at the centre of the universe stands a throne. From it the wheeling planets receive their orders. To it gigantic galaxies give their allegiance. In it the tiniest living organism finds its life.

Everything John saw in his vision was related to the throne. He uses seven prepositions to indicate its centrality. On it somebody was sitting. The occupant of the throne is not described, because God is indescribable. All John saw were brilliant colours like flashing jewels. Encircling the throne, a rainbow symbolized God's covenant mercy. Surrounding the throne were twenty-four other thrones occupied by twenty-four elders representing the church (twelve tribes and twelve apostles). From the throne issued thunder and lightning as from Mount Sinai. Before the throne seven lamps were blazing, standing for the Holy Spirit. In front of the throne there stretched an infinite expanse, speaking of God's transcendence. Then in the centre, around the throne, as a kind of inner circle, were four living creatures representing creation.

We pause and reflect whether this is our vision of ultimate reality. Our vision of the future tends to be too negative. We seize on the assurances of the Revelation that one day there will be no more hunger or thirst; no more pain or tears; no more sin, death, or curse, for all these things will have passed away. It would be better and more biblical, however, to focus not so much on these absences as on the cause of their absence, namely on the central dominating presence of God's throne.

For further reading: Revelation 4:1–6

MONDAY

The Creation's Worship

YOU ARE WORTHY, OUR LORD AND GOD, TO RECEIVE GLORY AND HONOUR
AND POWER, FOR YOU CREATED ALL THINGS, AND BY YOUR WILL
THEY WERE CREATED AND HAVE THEIR BEING.

Revelation 4:11

We revert today to the two circles, inner and outer, that surround the throne of God. The outer circle is said to consist of twenty-four elders. The number twelve in the book of Revelation always stands for the church, and twenty-four is therefore a recognizable cipher for the church of both Testaments – the twelve patriarchs or tribal heads of the Old Testament and the twelve apostles of Jesus Christ in the New. Their white clothing and golden crowns indicated their righteousness and their authority.

The inner circle, however, surrounding the throne of God, consisted of four "living creatures." They were "covered with eyes, in front and behind" (expressing their ceaseless vigilance), and they resembled a lion, an ox, a man, and an eagle (vv. 6–7), which represent, according to one commentator, "whatever is noblest, strongest, wisest and swiftest in animate nature."

Day and night, all nature never stops singing the praise of the Lord God Almighty, who was and is and is to come, and as they do so, the twenty-four elders join in. Thus nature and church, the old creation and the new, unite in proclaiming God as worthy of worship because by his will all things were created and continue to have their being.

It is instructive to bring together the worship of Revelation 4 and of Revelation 5. In both, the elders and the living creatures combine. But the emphasis in chapter 4 is on creation ("by your will [all things] were created" [v. 11]), while the emphasis in chapter 5 is on redemption ("because… with your blood you purchased people for God" [v. 9]). Our Creator and Redeemer is doubly worthy of our worship.

As we take our leave of the heavenly choirs, we need to remember their anthems. We are called to anticipate on earth the God-centred life of heaven. We are to live our lives now in conscious relationship to the throne of God, until every thought, word, and deed comes under his rule.

For further reading: Revelation 4:6–11

John's Vision of a Scroll

THEN I SAW IN THE RIGHT HAND OF HIM WHO SAT ON THE THRONE
A SCROLL WITH WRITING ON BOTH SIDES AND SEALED WITH SEVEN SEALS.

Revelation 5:1

Looking now more closely at the throne and its occupant, John notices in his right hand a scroll that is covered with writing and closed with seven seals. John does not tell us what it is, but from what follows when the seals are broken we see that it is the book of history, the sealed record of the unknown future, "what must take place after this" (4:1).

In John's vision a mighty angel appears and asks in a loud voice exactly what all of us would like to ask, namely, "Who is worthy to break the seals and open the scroll?" (5:2), that is, to disclose the future, let alone control it? There was no answer to this challenging question. So John says, "I wept and wept" (v. 4). He was overcome with emotion, with deep disappointment that nobody was fit to open the scroll or even look inside it. Nobody could supply a clue to the mystery of history.

Then one of the elders came forward and spoke up. He told John not to weep and added, "See, the Lion of the tribe of Judah, the Root of David [that is, the Messiah], has triumphed. He is able to open the scroll and its seven seals" (v. 5) and so to reveal the contents and the meaning of history.

It was a dramatic moment. John looked to see this triumphant Lion, but to his astonishment he saw instead a Lamb, looking as if it had been slaughtered and yet standing in the very centre of the throne, sharing it with God (see 3:21). In this central position he is surrounded by the four living creatures (nature) and by the elders (the church). He is also described as having seven horns and seven eyes, which are identified as "the seven spirits of God sent out into all the earth" (5:6), probably symbolizing the Holy Spirit in his sevenfold operation.

Thus our attention is redirected first from the throne to the scroll and now from the scroll to the Lamb.

For further reading: Revelation 5:1–6

WEDNESDAY

John's Vision of the Lamb

TO HIM WHO SITS ON THE THRONE AND TO THE LAMB BE PRAISE AND
HONOUR AND GLORY AND POWER, FOR EVER AND EVER!

Revelation 5:13

In John's vision the Lamb now took action. He came to the throne occupant and took the scroll from his right hand. This was the signal for the four living creatures and the twenty-four elders to fall prostrate before the Lamb and sing a new song, declaring his worthiness to take the scroll and open its seals, not now because of the creation, but because of the redemption.

> *Because you were slain,*
> *and with your blood you purchased for God*
> *persons from every tribe and language and people and nation.*
> *You have made them to be a kingdom and priests to serve our God,*
> *and they will reign on the earth.*

Revelation 5:9–10

Next, millions of angels joined in, proclaiming the worthiness of the Lamb, because he had been slain, to receive seven blessings, since all power and wisdom must be ascribed to him. And finally, John heard every creature throughout the whole universe ascribing praise and honour "to him who sits on the throne and to the Lamb" (v. 13). The four living creatures endorsed it with their amen, and the twenty-four elders fell down and worshipped.

It is a most magnificent vision of the whole creation on their faces before God and his Christ, and it is truly amazing that the Lamb is bracketed with the occupant of the throne as sharing it with him and receiving equal praise.

If it be asked why Jesus Christ alone is able to interpret history, we have to reply, "Because he was slain." By the cross he has conquered evil, redeemed us for God, suffered as we do, and is a conspicuous example of power through weakness, the Lamb on the throne.

For further reading: Revelation 5:7–14

Six Seals are Broken

I WATCHED AS THE LAMB OPENED THE FIRST OF THE SEVEN SEALS.
Revelation 6:1

Having celebrated the Lamb's unique authority to open the scroll, and having seen him take it from the throne occupant, John now watches as the Lamb breaks the seals one by one. After each of the first four seals is broken, one of the living creatures shouts in a voice like thunder, "Come!" And, behold, a horse and its rider appears. These are the famous four horsemen of the Apocalypse, well known to Christian artists.

Many commentators argue that the first horse (being white, its rider wearing a crown and riding out "as a conqueror bent on conquest" [v. 2]) symbolizes military conflict. But in the book of Revelation white stands for righteousness, crowns and conquests belong to Christ, and in chapter 19 the rider on a white horse is definitely Christ. So before the other horsemen spread the horrors of war, famine, and death, Christ rides out first at the head of the cavalcade, resolved to win the nations by the gospel. And he succeeds, judging by the countless multitude of the redeemed in chapter 7. The second horse is fiery red and symbolizes bloodshed, the third is black and symbolizes famine, and the fourth is pale green (6:8 NRSV) and symbolizes death.

The breaking of the fifth seal reveals the souls of Christian martyrs "under the altar" (the place of sacrifice) who are appealing for justice (v. 9). Then after the breaking of the sixth seal there is a great earthquake, followed by the most appalling cosmic convulsions in the sun, moon, stars, sky, and mountains, which are probably not to be interpreted literally but as social and political upheavals described in familiar apocalyptic imagery. Judgment follows as people of every rank (from kings to slaves) cry to be hidden from the face of God and the wrath of the Lamb.

This opening drama of the first six seals gives us a general overview of history between the first and second comings of Christ. It will be a time of violent disturbance and suffering. But the eye of faith will look beyond it to Christ, who is both the crowned and conquering rider on the white horse and the Lamb who breaks the seals, controlling the course of history.

For further reading: Revelation 6:1–16

FRIDAY

The Two Redeemed Communities

THEN I HEARD THE NUMBER OF THOSE WHO WERE SEALED: 144,000
FROM ALL THE TRIBES OF ISRAEL.

Revelation 7:4

We now have to wait until Revelation 8 for the seventh seal to be broken. Meanwhile, John treats us to an interlude that stresses the security of the people of God. Revelation 7 describes two human communities. The first (vv. 1–8) numbers 144,000 and is drawn from the twelve tribes of Israel; the second (vv. 9–17) is a huge unnumbered multitude drawn from all nations, languages, and tribes.

At first sight they seem to be two distinct groups (numbered and unnumbered, Israel and the Gentiles), and several ingenious attempts have been made to distinguish between them. But on closer inspection it becomes clear that both are pictures of the same redeemed community of God, although viewed from different perspectives. In the first, the people are assembled like soldiers in battle array – the church militant on earth; in the second, they are assembled before God, their conflicts passed – the church triumphant in heaven.

Take the first community today. They are called "the servants of our God" (v. 3) and are sealed or stamped on the forehead to indicate that they belong to him. The number 144,000 is an obvious symbol for the complete church (12 x 12 x 1,000); they are later identified in Revelation 14:3 as those "who had been redeemed from the earth." And the only reason why they are represented as the twelve tribes of Israel is that throughout the New Testament the church is seen as "the Israel of God" (Gal. 6:16), "the circumcision" (Phil. 3:3 NRSV), and "a chosen people... a holy nation, God's special possession" (1 Pet. 2:9), in whom God's covenant promises are being fulfilled.

We will postpone until tomorrow a consideration of the second community, which is described as "a great multitude that no one could count" (Rev. 7:9).

For further reading: Revelation 7:1–8

The Great International Community

AFTER THIS I LOOKED, AND THERE BEFORE ME WAS A GREAT MULTITUDE
THAT NO ONE COULD COUNT, FROM EVERY NATION, TRIBE, PEOPLE AND
LANGUAGE, STANDING BEFORE THE THRONE AND BEFORE THE LAMB.

Revelation 7:9

The second community, we are told, is international and countless. Just as Abraham was commanded by God to count the stars (which is impossible) and was then promised that his descendants would be equally numerous, so God's promise is being fulfilled in the huge multiplication of Abraham's spiritual children today (Gen. 12:1–3; 15:5).

Next, the unnumbered crowd is standing before God's throne, wearing white robes of righteousness and waving palm branches of victory. They are also singing loud songs of worship, ascribing their salvation to God and to the Lamb. The angels, elders, and living creatures also join in, falling on their faces and worshipping God. For the life of heaven is a continuous joyful celebration, and earthly choirs and orchestras are rehearsing for the eschatological concert.

How, then, can we make sure that we belong to this redeemed international throng? One of the elders expressed this very anxiety by asking the question, "These in white robes – who are they, and where did they come from?" (Rev. 7:13). He then proceeded to answer his own question. On the one hand, "They have washed their robes and made them white in the blood of the Lamb" (v. 14). We cannot possibly stand before God's dazzling throne in the soiled and tattered rags of our own morality, but only if we have sought cleansing from the Lamb who died for us. On the other hand, they "have come out of the great tribulation" (v. 14). Since all the redeemed are being described, this cannot refer to the specific period of tribulation between the appearance of Antichrist and that of Christ. It must rather be a description of the whole Christian life, which the New Testament repeatedly designates a time of tribulation (see John 16:33; Acts 14:22; Rev. 1:9). Therefore they are before the throne of God.

Revelation 7 ends with glorious assurances that God will shelter his people; that they will never again suffer from hunger, thirst, or scorching heat; that – in the boldest reversal of roles – the Lamb will be their shepherd; and that God will wipe away all their tears (vv. 15–17).

For further reading: Revelation 7:9–17

The book of Revelation or "Christian Apocalypse" is above all a celebration of the victory of God. It depicts the continuing conflict between God and Satan, the Lamb and the dragon, the church and the world, the holy city Jerusalem and the great city Babylon, the bride and the harlot, and those marked on their forehead with the name of Christ and those marked with the name of the beast.

The book of Revelation depicts more than conflict, however; it celebrates conquest. The book's perspective is that already Christ has conquered (Rev. 5:5) and that God intends his people to share in his victory. For Christ says, "To the one who is victorious, I will give the right to sit with me on my throne, just as I was victorious and sat down with my Father on his throne" (3:21). Thus H. B. Swete wrote at the beginning of the twentieth century that "the whole book is a *sursum corda*," a summons to John's readers to lift up their hearts and to see their tribulations in relation to the victorious, reigning, and returning Christ.

This is the essential background to our studies this week. We are about to be introduced to the great red dragon (Satan) and his three allies, namely two monsters and Babylon the prostitute (representing Rome as persecutor, idolater, and seducer). Their doom is certain.

Sunday: The Seven Trumpets

Monday: The Dragon and His Allies

Tuesday: The Lamb and the 144,000

Wednesday: The Seven Bowls of God's Wrath

Thursday: Babylon Identified and Destroyed

Friday: The Rider on the White Horse

Saturday: The Doom of Satan

The Seven Trumpets

I SAW THE SEVEN ANGELS WHO STAND BEFORE GOD,
AND SEVEN TRUMPETS WERE GIVEN TO THEM.

Revelation 8:2

It is important to remember (according to the method of interpretation I have adopted) that the breaking of the seven seals and the blowing of the seven trumpets denote the same period (stretching between the two comings of Jesus), although from different perspectives.

It seems that the purpose of the trumpets was to warn the world of the righteous judgment of God and to call people to repentance. Certainly trumpets were used in the Old Testament for warning. Thus Ezekiel wrote that if a watchman "sees the sword coming... and blows the trumpet to warn the people" (Ezek. 33:3), then the people will be held responsible for their reaction. Further, the calamities that follow seem to be warnings in the same sense that the collapse of the tower of Siloam was, which Jesus interpreted as a call to repentance (Luke 13:4).

Following the sounding of the trumpets, John saw a mighty angel coming down from heaven holding a little scroll. From John's description, this angel seems to have been none other than the Lord Jesus Christ himself bringing the gospel that John was to preach. So John was told to eat the little scroll, making its contents his own. It would taste sweet at first but later would turn his stomach sour. Recommissioned to take the gospel to the nations, John would find the sweetness of the gospel turn sour in the case of those who would reject it.

Suddenly two witnesses appear who seem to represent the witnessing and suffering church (Rev. 11:3). They are given power to prophesy; that is, to proclaim the gospel throughout the period between Christ's comings. But they will be persecuted and killed. Then later the martyred and silenced church will be resurrected (its testimony revived), to the great consternation of their enemies.

The ministry of the little scroll and of the two witnesses needs to be understood in relation to the warning trumpets. For the negative message of warning to the world is supplemented by the positive preaching of the gospel.

For further reading: Revelation 9:20–10:11

Monday

The Dragon and His Allies

THEY TRIUMPHED OVER HIM BY THE BLOOD OF THE LAMB
AND BY THE WORD OF THEIR TESTIMONY...

Revelation 12:11

In the opening vision of Revelation 12 there are three actors – a pregnant woman about to give birth, the male child she bears, and an enormous red dragon poised to devour the child at birth. The dragon is plainly the devil. The child is the Messiah, whose destiny is to rule the nations. And the woman is a symbol of the people of Israel from whose twelve patriarchs the human ancestry of the Christ is traced. But when the boy was born, he was snatched up to God, and the woman fled to the desert for protection. More visions follow, which celebrate the victory of the Messiah. Indeed, the dominant theme of Revelation 12 is the decisive overthrow of the devil. He was foiled in his malicious attempts to devour the Christ and destroy the church.

The devil's allies are now introduced to us one by one. They are called the beast out of the sea; the beast out of the earth; and Babylon, a gaudy prostitute. They seem to masquerade as a diabolical parody of the Trinity. All three also represent the city and empire of Rome, though from different points of view. Firstly, the beast out of the sea represented Rome as *a persecuting power*. The Jews were always afraid of the sea. So a monster emerging out of the sea would be a particular horror to them. Secondly, the beast out of the earth represented Rome as *an idolatrous system*, with special reference to the imperial cult. This beast had no independent role. Instead, his ministry related wholly to the first beast, to whom he was subservient. He made people worship the first beast.

Thirdly, Babylon the prostitute represented Rome as *a corrupting influence*: she "made all the nations drink the maddening wine of her adulteries" (14:8). The dragon's three allies, then, when John was writing, were Rome the persecutor (the first beast), Rome the idolater (the second beast or false prophet), and Rome the seductress (Babylon the harlot).

All over the world today the same threefold assault on the church is being mounted by the devil, as we saw in the early chapters of the Acts – physical (persecution), moral (compromise), and intellectual (false teaching). The devil's three allies are still very active.

For further reading: Revelation 12:1–12

The Lamb and the 144,000

THEN I LOOKED, AND THERE BEFORE ME WAS THE LAMB, STANDING ON
MOUNT ZION, AND WITH HIM 144,000 WHO HAD HIS NAME AND
HIS FATHER'S NAME WRITTEN ON THEIR FOREHEADS.

Revelation 14:1

It would be hard to conceive a sharper contrast than the one John paints between chapters 13 and 14 of Revelation. It is a relief to turn from the dragon and his first beast, whose habitat is the unruly sea, to the Lamb who stands on firm and holy ground; from persecution and the threat of martyrdom to security on Mount Zion; from the incompleteness of the number 666 to the completeness of 144,000; and from those who have received the mark of the beast on their forehead (13:16) to those who have the name of the Lamb and of his Father written on theirs.

John now hears some marvellous music, which he likens to a waterfall, a clap of thunder, and an orchestra of harpists. And a choir was singing a new song, which presumably celebrated the victory of the Lamb. As for the 144,000, they have been redeemed, have been faithful to Christ as his virgin bride, and follow the Lamb wherever he goes.

Thus assured of the safety of God's people, we are ready to hear the messages brought by three angels. Basic to their ministry is the conviction that "the hour of his [God's] judgment has come" (14:7). Moreover, John depicts it in terms of both a grain harvest and a vintage. Christ is the reaper, and his judgment will be radical, destroying every vestige of evil.

Before John describes the outpouring of the seven bowls of God's wrath, which will be reminiscent of the plagues in Egypt, he draws a striking analogy between Israel's exodus from Egypt and the redemption achieved by Christ. As the Israelites gathered by the Red Sea, victorious over Pharaoh, so John sees a multitude of people standing by what looks like a sea of glass and fire, victorious over the beast and his image. As Miriam took her tambourine to celebrate God's triumph, so the victorious people of God celebrate with harps. And as Moses and Miriam sang a song of praise to God, so the Song of Moses (the Old Testament victor) has become the song of the Lamb (the New Testament victor).

For further reading: Revelation 14:1–5

The Seven Bowls of God's Wrath

THEN I HEARD A LOUD VOICE FROM THE TEMPLE SAYING TO THE
SEVEN ANGELS, "GO, POUR OUT THE SEVEN BOWLS OF GOD'S WRATH
ON THE EARTH."

Revelation 16:1

A major clue to the understanding of Revelation 15 and 16 is to be found in two expressions. Firstly, "God's wrath is completed" (15:1). Secondly, "It is done!" (16:17). "Completed" and "done." In each case it is a single Greek word in the perfect tense, indicating that God's work of judgment has been accomplished once for all, and perhaps drawing a deliberate parallel to the "it is finished" (John 19:30) of the cross. The previous judgments (the seals and the trumpets) were partial; those of the bowls are final. It could be expressed thus: the eye of faith sees in the breaking of the seals the permissive will of God, in the blowing of the trumpets the reformative purpose of God, and in the pouring out of the bowls the retributive justice of God.

The first four bowls, like the first four trumpets, were targeted in the same sequence upon earth, sea, freshwater, and sun. Talk about earth, sea, water, and sun has a very modern sound in our era of environmental sensitivity. We are concerned about the earth's biodiversity, the plankton of the oceans, the availability of clean water, and the preservation of the ozone layer to protect us from radiation and its harmful effects. The pouring out of the fifth bowl plunged the kingdom of the beast into darkness and consequent anarchy, causing great suffering. But still the people "refused to repent" (Rev. 16:9, 11). Like Pharaoh they hardened their hearts.

The sixth bowl was poured out on the River Euphrates, a symbol of anti-God forces assembling for the final battle "on the great day of God Almighty" (v. 14). And lest the people of God should be unduly alarmed at this prospect, Jesus himself intervenes, crying out, "Look, I come like a thief!" (v. 15), warning us to be ready. The anticipated battle is surely not literal, however; it symbolizes the final battle between the Lamb and the dragon, between Christ and Antichrist.

As the sequences of the seals and trumpets ended in the climax of the Parousia, so does the sequence of the bowls. Christ comes in power and glory to rout and destroy the forces of evil.

For further reading: Revelation 16:17–22

Babylon Identified and Destroyed

**FALLEN! FALLEN IS BABYLON THE GREAT, WHICH MADE
ALL THE NATIONS DRINK THE MADDENING WINE OF HER ADULTERIES.**

Revelation 14:8

So far in Revelation "Babylon" has been mentioned very briefly only twice, but neither text tells us what it symbolizes. So now two whole chapters are devoted to the phenomenon "Babylon." Chapter 17 identifies it for us, while chapter 18 describes in graphic detail its destruction.

The identification of Babylon we owe to one of the seven angels who volunteered to instruct John. The angel both showed him a prostitute and then went on to explain to John what he had seen. The woman was sitting on a scarlet beast (readily recognizable as the beast from the sea). Thus, wrote Richard Bauckham, "Roman civilization, as a corrupting influence, rides on the back of Roman military power." John also saw that the woman was drunk with the blood of martyrs (17:6). In conclusion, the angel said to John, "The woman you saw is the great city that rules over the kings of the earth" (17:18).

Now that the identity of Babylon has been established, John goes on at once to describe her overthrow. The literal sack of Rome under Alaric the Goth would not take place for more than another 320 years. Yet John used the prophetic past tense, expressing the certainty of God's judgment as if it had already taken place. "Fallen! Fallen is Babylon the Great!" (14:8). Three groups of human beings are singled out for mention in chapter 18, namely the kings, the merchants, and the seafarers of the world. Each group is heard lamenting the destruction of Babylon: "Woe! Woe, great city" (18:10). The chapter concludes with a combination of celebration and lament – a celebration of the justice of God in judgment and a lament over the disappearance of all good aspects of culture – the sound of music, the skill of craftsmen, the preparing of food for the family, and the joyful laughter of bridegroom and bride.

In the first century, "Babylon" was Rome. But Babylon has flourished throughout history and throughout the world. Babylon is Vanity Fair. Its profile can easily be drawn from this chapter – idolatry, immorality, extravagance, sorcery, tyranny, and arrogance. The urgent call still summons God's people to come out of her in order to avoid contamination.

For further reading: Revelation 18:21–24

The Rider on the White Horse

THERE BEFORE ME WAS A WHITE HORSE, WHOSE RIDER IS CALLED
FAITHFUL AND TRUE. WITH JUSTICE HE JUDGES AND MAKES WAR.

Revelation 19:11

In contrast to the silence of burned-out Babylon, John now heard what sounded like the roar of a great multitude shouting "Hallelujah!" Four times the word was repeated at the beginning of Revelation 19 like a heavenly hallelujah chorus, and the reason for this summons to praise God was the justice of his judgment and the supremacy of his reign. Further, in antithesis to the destruction of the prostitute Babylon, the wedding of the Lamb had come, and his bride had made herself ready (v. 7).

Next, John saw heaven standing open, and there before him was a white horse whose rider was wearing many crowns, symbolizing his universal authority. His robe is bloodstained, indicating that he carries with him the achievement of his sacrificial death. And he was given the sensational title King of Kings and Lord of Lords. There can be no possible doubt that this rider was the Lord Jesus Christ himself in the fullness of his divine majesty, riding forth in judgment, with the armies of heaven following him.

One expects the final battle to come next, for the two armies – divine and demonic – now stand in confrontation. But instead, nothing happens, for Jesus has already won the victory over evil by his death and resurrection. Instead, the forces of evil are now destroyed in the opposite order to that in which they were introduced. First came Babylon, which has already been destroyed. Next came the beast from the sea (the persecuting power) and the beast from the earth, also called "the false prophet," the symbol of false religion, responsible for persuading people to worship the emperor or his statue (v. 20). Both were thrown into the lake of fire and so destroyed. This leaves the doom of the dragon until the next chapter, which we will consider tomorrow.

For further reading: Revelation 19:11–16

The Doom of Satan

AND THE DEVIL... WAS THROWN INTO THE LAKE OF BURNING SULPHUR,
WHERE THE BEAST AND THE FALSE PROPHET HAD BEEN THROWN.
Revelation 20:10

Revelation 20 divides itself naturally into three paragraphs – the thousand years (vv. 1–6), the final battle (vv. 7–10), and the last judgment (vv. 11–15).

Firstly, the millennium. It is mentioned six times, and each time with a different reference. During it, we are told, the devil will be chained, the nations will be undeceived, and the saints and martyrs will be risen and reigning with Christ. This surely indicates that the millennium is symbolic of the whole present period between the first and second comings of Christ. If it be objected that Satan does not appear to be chained, we respond that this is a problem throughout the New Testament, since everywhere it is affirmed that by his death and resurrection Jesus has disarmed and bound the devil (see, e.g., Mark 3:27). Moreover, John does not say that the devil was bound in relation to everything, but specifically in relation to the nations, which explains the enormous ingathering of converts (see Rev. 7:9).

Secondly, when the thousand-year period is over, John tells us, Satan will be released from his prison for a brief period and will deceive the nations again. That is, the church's missionary outreach will be opposed and curtailed. Satan will gather hostile peoples together for a last assault against the church. But Christ will forestall the conflict as the rider on the white horse. Then the dragon will be thrown into the lake of fire to meet the two beasts there in a fate with neither intermission nor end.

Thirdly, now that the dragon, the two beasts, and the prostitute have all been destroyed, the time has come for the judgment of individuals before the great white throne. John writes, "The dead were judged according to what they had done as recorded in the books" (20:12). Most emphatically he is not saying that sinners are justified by their good works. No, we sinners are *justified* by God's grace alone through faith in Christ crucified alone. At the same time we will be *judged* by our works, for judgment day will be a public occasion, and good works will be the only public and visible evidence that can be produced to attest the authenticity of our faith. "Faith without deeds is dead" (James 2:26). True believers have their names written in the Lamb's Book of Life (Rev. 13:8; 20:15).

For further reading: Revelation 20:1–15

Revelation 20 concluded with the fearful contrast between those who are registered in the Book of Life and those whose fate is the second death, and so between life and death as the alternative destinies awaiting humankind. Revelation 21 and 22 (the book's last two chapters) also mention the second death, but their whole focus is on life – the Book of Life, the water of life, and the tree of life.

Eternal life means the personal knowledge of God through Jesus Christ, as Jesus himself taught (John 17:3). John now illustrates this by three metaphors – security in the city of God, the New Jerusalem; restored access to the tree of life in the Garden of Eden; and the intimate relationship of bride and bridegroom in marriage. John jumps from one metaphor to another – the city, the garden, and the wedding – without any apparent sense of incongruity. For all three represent our close personal fellowship with God, which begins now (once we have been reconciled to him through Christ) and will be consummated when he returns.

Sunday: All Things New

Monday: The Holy City

Tuesday: The Garden

Wednesday: The Words of This Prophecy

Thursday: "I Am Coming Soon!"

Friday: The Wedding

Saturday: The Waiting Church

All Things New

HE WHO WAS SEATED ON THE THRONE SAID,
"I AM MAKING EVERYTHING NEW!"

Revelation 21:5

The first eight verses of Revelation 21 are variations on the theme of newness. For John saw a new heaven and a new earth, to which the New Jerusalem descended. As a result, "the old order of things had passed away" (v. 4), and God could declare, "I am making everything new!" (v. 5). This promise of a new universe was first made by God to Isaiah (Isa. 65:17; 66:22). Jesus himself spoke of it as "the renewal of all things" (Matt. 19:28, literally, "the new birth"), and Paul wrote of it as the liberation of creation from its bondage to decay (Rom. 8:18–25).

It is important, therefore, to affirm that our Christian hope looks forward not to an ethereal heaven but to a renewed universe that will be related to the present world by both continuity and discontinuity. Just as the individual Christian is a new creation in Christ, the same person but transformed, and just as the resurrection body will be the same body with its identity intact (remember the risen Jesus' scars) yet invested with new powers, so the new heaven and the new earth will be not a replacement universe (as if created *de novo*) but a regenerated universe, purged of all present imperfection. John adds the detail that "there was no longer any sea" (Rev. 21:1), for the sea symbolizes both restlessness and separation.

Next, John heard God's voice addressing him and explaining the meaning of the descent of the new Jerusalem: "God's dwelling-place is now among the people, and he will dwell with them. They will be his people, and God himself will be with them and be their God" (v. 3). This marvellous declaration is all the more impressive because it incorporates the covenant formula that occurs again and again throughout Scripture: "I will be your God, and you shall be my people."

The result of this living relationship between God and his people is that there will be no more pain, tears, mourning, or death. For these things belong to the old fallen world order that has now passed away. And only God can do this, since he is the Alpha and the Omega, the Beginning and the End (v. 6).

For further reading: Revelation 21:1–8

The Holy City

AND HE... SHOWED ME THE HOLY CITY, JERUSALEM,
COMING DOWN OUT OF HEAVEN FROM GOD.

Revelation 21:10

We have seen (p. 425) how easily John mixes his metaphors. When he first saw the Holy City, the New Jerusalem, it was "prepared as a bride beautifully dressed for her husband" (v. 2). And now, when invited to see the Lamb's bride, he is shown "the Holy City, Jerusalem" (v. 10). Most of chapter 21 is devoted to an elaborate description of the holy city, the New Jerusalem, which was shining with the glory of God. Its twelve gates were inscribed with the names of Israel's twelve tribes, while its foundations were inscribed with the names of the twelve apostles. The city was a cube, like the Holy of Holies in the temple. Although we must agree with Dr Bruce Metzger that the New Jerusalem is "architecturally preposterous" (about fifteen hundred miles cubed, stretching from London to Athens), the symbolism is clear. The holy city is a massive, impregnable fortress representing the completed church of both Old and New Testaments and symbolizing the security and peace of the people of God.

The city John saw was not only enormous and solid but also beautiful, each of its twelve foundations being decorated with a different jewel, each of its twelve gates being made from a single pearl, and the great street of the city being pure gold. Having grasped the vast dimensions and colourful magnificence of the New Jerusalem, John draws our attention to some consequent absences. Firstly, he did not see a temple in the city. But of course not! The Lord and the Lamb are its temple. Their presence permeates the city; they have no need of a special building. Secondly, it needs neither sun nor moon, since the glory of God illumines it, and his light will be enough even for the nations.

At this point we need to note verses 24 and 26: "The kings of the earth will bring their splendour into it," and "The glory and honour of the nations will be brought into it." We should not hesitate to affirm that the cultural treasures of the world will adorn the New Jerusalem. At the same time, nothing impure will ever enter the city, nor will anybody enter who is guilty of shameful or deceitful deeds, but only those registered in the Lamb's Book of Life (v. 27).

For further reading: Revelation 21:15–27

The Garden

THEN THE ANGEL SHOWED ME THE RIVER OF THE WATER OF LIFE,
AS CLEAR AS CRYSTAL, FLOWING FROM THE THRONE OF GOD...

Revelation 22:1

The city has now been transformed into a garden city, with emphasis on the river, the tree of life, and the throne. Firstly, the river. Its crystal-clear waters flowed out of the throne (symbol of God's sovereign grace) and down the middle of the city's main street. Thus the water is available at all times to the thirsty.

Secondly, the tree of life. John sees it growing on both banks of the river. Access to it had been forbidden after the fall, but now the prohibition has been lifted. Perhaps John sees only one tree on each side of the river. But I prefer the view of some commentators that, as already predicted in Ezekiel 47, many trees of life will be lining both riverbanks along its full length, making their fruit available to all. Thus the hungry may eat and the thirsty drink to their heart's content. Every month fresh fruit will be available, while the leaves will be for the healing of the nations, indicating the widespread positive benefits that the gospel will bring to the Gentile world. John adds that there will be no more curse, another clear allusion to the Garden of Eden.

Thirdly, John moves on from the river and the tree to the throne. Its centrality will be restored, as in Revelation 4 and 5, and the whole of life will be subservient to the rule of God. Moreover, his servants will worship him, and "they will see his face" (v. 4). God had told Moses plainly, "You cannot see my face, for no one may see me and live" (Exod. 33:20). So all that human beings have seen so far is the glory of God, which has been defined as the outward shining of his inward being. We have seen his glory in the person and work of his incarnate Son. But one day the veil will be lifted and we shall see him "as he is" (1 John 3:2), even "face to face" (1 Cor. 13:12). The beatific vision is an indispensable part of God's ultimate purpose for his people.

For further reading: Revelation 22:1–5

The Words of This Prophecy

BLESSED IS THE ONE WHO KEEPS
THE WORDS OF THE PROPHECY IN THIS SCROLL.
Revelation 22:7

The last sixteen verses of the book of Revelation form a kind of appendix or epilogue, containing an assortment of warnings and exhortations.

John is concerned to authenticate his book and demonstrate its authority. It was Jesus himself, he affirms, who through an angel had given him this message for the churches. In consequence, John both "heard and saw" what he went on to record, and his words were "trustworthy and true" (vv. 6–8). They were, in fact, a prophecy, that is, a revelation from God. To indicate this, John uses a particular expression (with slight variations) five times, namely "the words of the prophecy of this scroll" (vv. 7–19).

The duty of John's readers toward this revelation is made clear. They are to "keep" it (v. 9), that is, to believe and obey it. They are not to "seal" or conceal it (v. 10) but rather to make it known to others. And in doing so, they must on no account either add to it or subtract from it. For if anyone adds anything to the book, God will add to him the judgments described in it, and if anyone takes anything away from the book, God will take away from him his share in the tree and the city (vv. 18–19).

The background to John's appeals and warnings is the anticipation of judgment. For when Christ comes, the terrible separation will take place between those who have washed their robes and those who have not, between those who enjoy access to the New Jerusalem and those who are excluded.

Thus Jesus Christ, who originated all things as Creator, will consummate all things as Judge. For he is "the Alpha and the Omega, the First and the Last, the Beginning and the End" (v. 13). These very same titles were given both to God and to Christ in chapter 1 (vv. 8, 17) as they are now in its final chapter. It is with these tremendous claims of Christ that John opens and closes his book.

For further reading: Revelation 22:6–13

"I Am Coming Soon!"

LOOK, I AM COMING SOON! MY REWARD IS WITH ME, AND I WILL GIVE TO
EACH PERSON ACCORDING TO WHAT THEY HAVE DONE.

Revelation 22:12

One of the striking features of Revelation 22 is that it is punctuated three times by the cry of Jesus, "I am coming soon!" (vv. 7, 12, 20). How are we to interpret this? Does it mean that Jesus predicted that his return would take place almost immediately, and that he was mistaken? This is a widely held view, but it is not necessary to reach this conclusion for a number of reasons.

Firstly, Jesus said he did not know the day of his coming (Mark 13:32); only his Father knew it. It is therefore unlikely that he would now pronounce on what he knew he did not know. He was not ignorant of his ignorance. Secondly, Jesus and his apostles urged his followers in other places to marry and have children, to earn their own living, and to take the gospel to the ends of the earth. These instructions are not compatible with belief in an imminent Parousia.

Thirdly, Jesus did predict the destruction of Jerusalem within the lifetime of his contemporaries, and it is sometimes hard to discern whether he is referring to this or to the end. Fourthly, "apocalyptic" is a particular literary genre with its own literary conventions. For example, it expresses what will happen *suddenly* in terms of what will happen *soon*. This was so in Old Testament prophecies.

How then should we understand the adverb *soon*? We need to remember that, with the great events of Christ's birth, death, resurrection, and exaltation, the new age had already dawned and that there is now nothing on God's eschatological calendar before the Parousia. The Parousia is the very next event on his timetable. It was, and still is, true to say, wrote Charles Cranfield, "that the Parousia is at hand." Thus Christian disciples are characterized by faith, hope, and love. Faith apprehends the *already* of Christ's achievement. Hope looks forward to the *not yet* of his salvation. And love marks our life *now* in the meanwhile. So *soon* may be chronologically inexact, but at the same time it is theologically correct.

For further reading: Mark 13:28–37

FRIDAY

The Wedding

I SAW THE HOLY CITY, THE NEW JERUSALEM, COMING DOWN OUT OF
HEAVEN FROM GOD, PREPARED AS A BRIDE BEAUTIFULLY DRESSED FOR
HER HUSBAND.

Revelation 21:2

According to Jewish custom, a marriage took place in two stages, the betrothal and the wedding. The betrothal included an exchange of promises and gifts and was regarded as being almost as binding as a marriage. The betrothed couple could be called husband and wife, and if a separation took place, it would have to be a divorce. The wedding followed some time after the betrothal and was essentially a public social occasion. It began with a festive procession, accompanied by music and dancing, in which the bridegroom and his friends went out to fetch his bride, who would have made herself ready. He would then bring her and friends and relatives back to his home for the wedding feast, which might last as long as a week. During it the bride and bridegroom would receive a public blessing from their parents and be escorted to the nuptial chamber, where they would consummate their marriage in the intimacy of physical union.

The Bible betrays no embarrassment about sex and marriage. It is uninhibited in its use of the marriage metaphor to depict the covenant between God and Israel. Yahweh's love for Israel is portrayed, especially by Isaiah, Jeremiah, Ezekiel, and Hosea, in bluntly physical terms.

Jesus himself implied, in a daring statement, that he was his followers' bridegroom, so that while he was still with them it would be inappropriate for them to fast. Then Paul, though much maligned as a misogynist, developed the metaphor further. He pictured Christ as the bridegroom who had loved his bride the church and sacrificed himself for her in order that he might present her to himself unblemished and radiant (Eph. 5:25–27). When Paul added that "this is a profound mystery" (Eph. 5:32), he seems to have meant that the one flesh experience in marriage symbolizes the union of Christ with his church.

For further reading: Ezekiel 16:7–8

The Waiting Church

HE WHO TESTIFIES TO THESE THINGS SAYS, "YES, I AM COMING SOON."
AMEN. COME, LORD JESUS.

Revelation 22:20

It is the same vivid imagery of betrothal and marriage that John picks up at the end of Revelation. Already he has made allusion to the coming wedding. He tells us he has heard the redeemed multitude singing their hallelujah because "the wedding of the Lamb has come, and his bride has made herself ready" (19:7). Indeed, "fine linen, bright and clean" has been given her to wear (19:8). Already, too, the interpreting angel has said to John, "Blessed are those who are invited to the wedding supper of the Lamb" (19:9). And John has also described the New Jerusalem as "coming down out of heaven from God, prepared as a bride beautifully dressed for her husband" (21:2; see v. 9).

But where is he? He is nowhere to be seen! It is not for the bride to fetch her bridegroom; it is for the bridegroom to go and fetch his bride. She has made herself ready. She is dressed and bejewelled. Now she can do no more than wait for him to appear – except that she takes the liberty of expressing her longing for him: "The Spirit and the bride say, 'Come!'" (22:17). For the supreme ministry of the Holy Spirit is to bear witness to Christ, and the supreme desire of the bride is to welcome her bridegroom.

It is thus that the book of Revelation ends. It leaves the church waiting, hoping, expecting, longing – the bride eagerly looking for her bridegroom, crying out for him, clinging to his threefold promise that he is coming soon, and encouraged by others who echo her call: "Amen. Come, Lord Jesus."

Meanwhile, she is confident that his grace will be sufficient for her (v. 21) until the eternal wedding feast begins and she is united to her bridegroom forever.

For further reading: Revelation 22:14–21